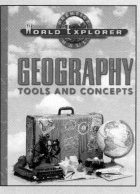
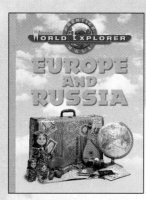
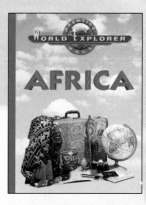

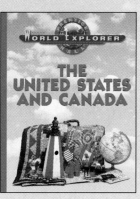
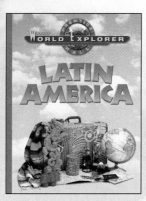
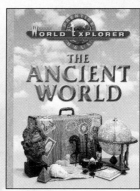

The world studies program
that lets you choose.

PRENTICE HALL
Simon & Schuster Education Group
A VIACOM COMPANY

Upper Saddle River, New Jersey
Needham, Massachusetts

ISBN 0-13-433705-0

2 3 4 5 6 7 8 9 10   01 00 99 98 97

The only middle grades world
that can truly provide
the right materials to fit your

Prentice Hall World Explorer lets you choose the right balance of history, geography, and cultures for the regions of the world that you cover in your middle grades curriculum. No more being confined to the contents of a single text. No more having to spend valuable time locating additional resources. All this with hands-on activities and skills; interdisciplinary connections; integrated technology; and manageable resources to support your teaching style.

YOU CHOOSE what's right

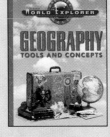

**A few of
the most popular
COURSE
CONFIGURATIONS:**

	GEOGRAPHY TOOLS AND CONCEPTS	EUROPE AND RUSSIA	AFRICA
Eastern Hemisphere*	GEOGRAPHY TOOLS AND CONCEPTS	EUROPE AND RUSSIA	AFRICA
Western Hemisphere*	GEOGRAPHY TOOLS AND CONCEPTS		
World History			
Western Civilization		EUROPE AND RUSSIA	
Pacific Rim	GEOGRAPHY TOOLS AND CONCEPTS		
World Cultures		EUROPE AND RUSSIA	AFRICA

studies program curriculum.

for your course of study.

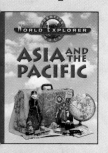
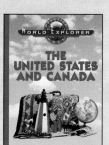

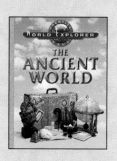

ASIA AND THE PACIFIC				
	THE UNITED STATES AND CANADA	LATIN AMERICA		
			THE ANCIENT WORLD	MEDIEVAL TIMES TO TODAY
	THE UNITED STATES AND CANADA		THE ANCIENT WORLD	
ASIA AND THE PACIFIC	THE UNITED STATES AND CANADA	LATIN AMERICA		
ASIA AND THE PACIFIC	THE UNITED STATES AND CANADA	LATIN AMERICA		

* Available in single, hard-bound volume

Only World Explorer provides this many management resources— built right into the program.

Designed from the start to have more time-saving resources for middle grades teachers, the World Explorer program has brand-new ways to help you coordinate your program, scheduling, assessment, team teaching, interdisciplinary connections, and other valuable resources.

- **Managing Time and Instruction**
- **Block Scheduling**
- **Assessment Opportunities**
- **Activities and Projects**
- **Resource Pro CD-ROM**
- **FYI**
- **Technology Options**
- **Flexible Planning Guide**

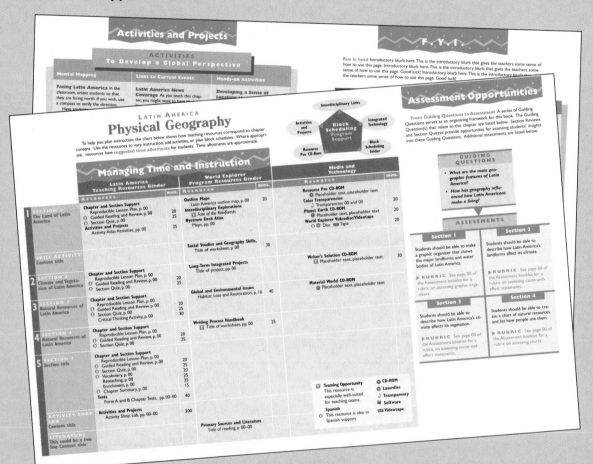

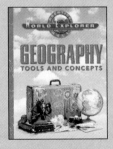

TECHNOLOGY OPTIONS

- **Teacher's Edition wraparound with barcodes**
- **Point-of-use technology references**
- **Integrated video presentations**

Guided Reading Audiotapes *
Computer Test Bank
 (MAC/Windows)
 World Video Explorer
  Videodiscs *
  Videotapes
Resource Pro™ CD-ROM
Material World CD-ROM
Planet Earth CD-ROM
Writer's Solution CD-ROM
available in Spanish

FLEXIBLE PLANNING GUIDE

This key supplement makes it easy to plan, schedule, and coordinate World Explorer's multi-book program.

- **Course configurations**
- **Pacing charts**
- **Scope and sequence of skills**
- **Correlations to national standards**

RESOURCE PRO CD-ROM

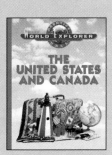

- **Teaching Resources**
- **Planning Express™**
- **Computer Test Bank**

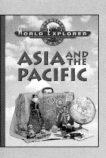 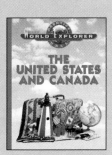  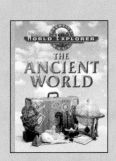 

Coverage of all World Explorer program skills is provided in the Student Edition and Teacher's Edition.

LATIN AMERICA
SKILLS SCOPE AND SEQUENCE

SKILL	BOOK	PAGE
MAP AND GLOBE SKILLS		
Using Parts of a Map	STUDENT	172
Comparing Maps of Different Scale	STUDENT	173
Understanding Distortions in Map Projections	STUDENT	170–171
Using Political and Physical Maps	STUDENT	174,175
Using Regional Maps	STUDENT	20–21
Using Isolines to Show Elevation	STUDENT	140–141
Using Distribution Maps	TEACHER	85
Using Route Maps	TEACHER	45
CRITICAL THINKING SKILLS		
Expressing Problems Clearly	TEACHER	101
Identifying Central Issues	TEACHER	123
Distinguishing Facts from Opinons	STUDENT	78–79
Recognizing Bias	TEACHER	47
Recognizing Cause and Effect	TEACHER	67
Drawing Conclusions	TEACHER	17
CHART, GRAPH, AND ILLUSTRATION SKILLS		
Interpreting Graphs	TEACHER	149
Interpreting Diagrams	TEACHER	37
Using a Time Line	STUDENT	48–49
Reading Tables and Analyzing Statistics	TEACHER	109
Understanding Special Geography Graphs	TEACHER	133
READING AND WRITING SKILLS		
Previewing a Reading Selection	STUDENT	94–95
Reading Actively	TEACHER	25
Assessing Your Understanding	TEACHER	75
Using the Writing Process	TEACHER	71
Writing for a Purpose	TEACHER	87
STUDY AND RESEARCH SKILLS		
Locating Information	STUDENT	118–119
Organizing Information	TEACHER	19
Organizing Your Time	TEACHER	153

Skills Activity
Students learn, practice, and apply core social studies skills through the use of hands-on activities.

Skills Mini-lessons
These lessons supplement and reinforce core social studies skills that are not formally presented in the student book.

Map and Globe Handbook
Students practice and review basic geography skills that focus on understanding maps and charts.

Use this daily pacing chart to help plan a nine-week course or a twelve-week course for Latin America.

	9-WEEK COURSE	12-WEEK COURSE
ACTIVITY ATLAS	2 DAYS	3 DAYS
CHAPTER 1 **LATIN AMERICA: PHYSICAL GEOGRAPHY**		
Section 1 Land and Water	1	1.5
Section 2 Climate and Vegetation	1	1.5
SKILLS ACTIVITY Using Regional Maps to Show Climate	1.5	1.5
Section 3 Natural Resources	1	1
CHAPTER 1 REVIEW, ACTIVITIES, AND ASSESSMENT	1.5	1.5
LITERATURE	1	1
CHAPTER 2 **LATIN AMERICA: SHAPED BY ITS HISTORY**		
Section 1 Early Civilizations of Middle America	1.5	2
Section 2 The Incas: People of the Sun	1	1.5
Section 3 European Conquest	1	1.5
SKILLS ACTIVITY Using a Time Line	1	1.5
Section 4 Independence	1	1.5
Section 5 Issues in Latin America Today	1	1.5
CHAPTER 2 REVIEW, ACTIVITIES, AND ASSESSMENT	1.5	1.5
CHAPTER 3 **CULTURES OF LATIN AMERICA**		
Section 1 The Cultures of Mexico and Central America	1	1.5
Section 2 The Cultures of the Caribbean	1	1.5
Section 3 The Cultures of South America	1.5	2
SKILLS ACTIVITY Distinguishing Facts from Opinions	1	1.5
CHAPTER 3 REVIEW, ACTIVITIES, AND ASSESSMENT	1.5	1.5

	9-WEEK COURSE	12-WEEK COURSE
CHAPTER 4 **EXPLORING MEXICO AND CENTRAL AMERICA**		
Section 1 Mexico: One Family's Move to the City	1	2
Section 2 Guatemala: Descendants of an Ancient People	1	1.5
SKILLS ACTIVITY Previewing a Reading Selection	1	1.5
Section 3 Panama: Where Two Oceans Meet	1	1.5
CHAPTER 4 REVIEW, ACTIVITIES AND ASSESSMENT	1.5	1.5
ACTIVITY SHOP LAB	1.5	2
CHAPTER 5 **EXPLORING THE CARIBBEAN**		
Section 1 Cuba: Clinging to Communism	1	1.5
Section 2 Haiti: The Road to Democracy	1	1.5
SKILLS ACTIVITY Locating Information	1	1.5
Section 3 Puerto Rico: Cultural Identity of a People	1.5	2
CHAPTER 5 REVIEW, ACTIVITIES, AND ASSESSMENT	1.5	1.5
CHAPTER 6 **EXPLORING SOUTH AMERICA**		
Section 1 Brazil: Resources of the Rain Forest	1	1.5
Section 2 Peru: Life in the Altiplano	1	1.5
SKILLS ACTIVITY Using Isolines to Show Elevation	1	1.5
Section 3 Chile: A Growing Economy Based on Agriculture	1	1.5
Section 4 Venezuela: Oil Powers the Economy	1	1.5
CHAPTER 6 REVIEW, ACTIVITIES AND ASSESSMENT	1.5	1.5
ACTIVITY SHOP INTERDISCIPLINARY	1.5	2
LITERATURE	1	1
TOTAL NUMBER OF DAYS	**45**	**60**

WORLD EXPLORER

Choose from this wide variety of resources for management, extensions, and assessment.

Components

- Student Editions
- Teacher's Editions

Teaching Resources Binders
    Chapter and
    Section Support
    Spanish Support
    Activities and Projects
    Tests
    Social Studies and
    Geography Skills

Program Teaching
Resources Binder
    Primary Sources and
    Literature Readings
    Long-term Integrated
    Projects
    Outline Maps
    Environmental and
    Global Issues
    Writing Process Handbook
    Assessment Handbook

Technology in the
Classroom
Social Studies Educator's
Handbooks
Nystrom Desk Atlas
Posters

- Teacher's Flexible
  Planning Guide
- Color Transparencies
  with Overlays

- Guided Reading Audiotapes *
- Computer Test Bank
  (MAC/Windows)
- World Video Explorer
    Videodiscs *
    Videotapes
- Resource Pro™ CD-ROM
- Material World CD-ROM
- Planet Earth CD-ROM
- Writer's Solution CD-ROM
- Interdisciplinary Explorations

* Available in Spanish

See us on the Internet http://www.phschool.com

Contact your local representative or call **1-800-848-9500.**

LATIN AMERICA

Program Authors

Heidi Hayes Jacobs

Heidi Hayes Jacobs has served as an educational consultant to more than 500 schools across the nation. Dr. Jacobs is an adjunct professor in the Department of Curriculum on Teaching at Teachers College, Columbia University. She completed her undergraduate studies at the University of Utah in her hometown of Salt Lake City. She received an M.A. from the University of Massachusetts, Amherst, and completed her doctoral work at Columbia University's Teachers College in 1981.

The backbone of Dr. Jacobs's experience comes from her years as a teacher of high school, middle school, and elementary school students. As an educational consultant, she works with K–12 schools and districts on curriculum reform and strategic planning.

Brenda Randolph

Brenda Randolph is the former Director of the Outreach Resource Center at the African Studies Program at Howard University, Washington, D.C. She is the Founder and Director of Africa Access, a bibliographic service on Africa for schools. She received her B.A. in history with high honors from North Carolina Central University, Durham, and her M.A. in African studies with honors from Howard University. She completed further graduate studies at the University of Maryland, College Park, where she was awarded a Graduate Fellowship.

Brenda Randolph has published numerous articles in professional journals and bulletins. She currently serves as library media specialist in Montgomery County Public Schools, Maryland.

Michal L. LeVasseur

Michal LeVasseur is an educational consultant in the field of geography. She is an adjunct professor of geography at the University of Alabama, Birmingham, and serves with the Alabama Geographic Alliance. Her undergraduate and graduate work is in the fields of anthropology (B.A.), geography (M.A.), and science education (Ph.D.).

Dr. LeVasseur's specialization has moved increasingly into the area of geography education. In 1996, she served as Director of the National Geographic Society's Summer Geography Workshop. As an educational consultant, she has worked with the National Geographic Society as well as with schools to develop programs and curricula for geography.

Special Program Consultant

Yvonne S. Gentzler, Ph.D.
School of Education
University of Idaho, Moscow, Idaho

Content Consultant on Latin America

Daniel Mugan
Center for Latin American Studies
University of Florida
Gainesville, Florida

PRENTICE HALL
Simon & Schuster Education Group
A VIACOM COMPANY

Upper Saddle River, New Jersey
Needham, Massachusetts

Student Edition ISBN: 0-13-433704-2
Teacher's Edition ISBN: 0-13-433705-0

3 4 5 6 7 8 9 10   01 00 99 98 97

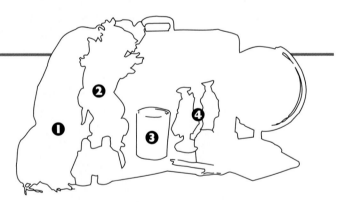

On the Cover
❶ Woven blanket from Mexico
❷ Mexican wood carving of an ancient Mayan snake god
❸ Reproduction of Mayan pottery
❹ Family of dolls from Peru dressed in traditional clothing

Content Consultants for the World Explorer Program

Teacher Advisory Board

The World Explorer Team

The editors, designers, marketer, market researcher, manager, production buyer, and manufacturing buyer who made up the World Explorer team are listed below.

Jackie Bedoya, Bruce Bond, Ellen Brown, David Lippman, Catherine Martin-Hetmansky,
Nancy Rogier, Olena Serbyn, Carol Signorino, John Springer, Susan Swan

TABLE OF CONTENTS

LATIN AMERICA

1

Readable, accessible content to motivate your students (see pp. 8-9)

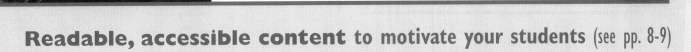

OF SPECIAL INTEREST

A hands-on, active approach to practicing and applying key social studies skills

Engaging, step-by-step activities for exploring important topics in Latin America

High-interest selections written by Latin American authors that shed light on the region's varied cultures

Active learning approaches to involve and engage students (see pp. 2–7)

Engage

Activate Prior Knowledge

Three sets of reading strategies are introduced on pages viii and ix. Before students read the strategies, use questions like these to prompt a discussion about reading:

- Before you read, what do you do to help you read better?

- How do you figure out the meaning of what you read?

- Do you take a different approach to different kinds of reading, such as a paperback novel or your math textbook?

Discussion of their answers will help students become aware of their own reading processes.

Introduce the Strategies

Point out to students that reading is a process. If students are conscious of their process, they can improve their reading. Point out that there are three sets of reading strategies: **Before You Read, While You Read,** and **After You Read.** Explain that these are the behaviors that good readers exhibit. As students practice these strategies, they too will increase their reading fluency and comprehension.

Be sure to reinforce the idea that students might use several of these strategies at the same time, or they might go back and forth among them. There is no set order for applying them.

READ ACTIVELY

How can I get the most out of my social studies book?

How does my reading relate to my world? Answering questions like these means that you are an active reader, an involved reader. As an active reader, you are in charge of the reading situation!

The following strategies tell how to think and read as an active reader. You don't need to use all of these strategies all the time. Feel free to choose the ones that work best in each reading situation. You might use several at a time, or you might go back and forth among them. They can be used in any order.

BEFORE YOU READ

Give yourself a purpose

The sections in this book begin with a list called "Questions to Explore." These questions focus on key ideas presented in the section. They give you a purpose for reading. You can create your own purpose by asking questions like these: How does the topic relate to your life? How might you use what you learn at school or at home?

Preview

To preview a reading selection, first read its title. Then look at the pictures and read the captions. Also read any headings in the selection. Then ask yourself: What is the reading selection about? What do the pictures and headings tell about the selection?

Reach into your background

What do you already know about the topic of the selection? How can you use what you know to help you understand what you are going to read?

Ask questions

Suppose you are reading about the continent of South America. Some questions you might ask are: Where is South America? What countries are found there? Why are some of the countries large and others small? Asking questions like these can help you gather evidence and gain knowledge.

Predict

As you read, make a prediction about what will happen and why. Or predict how one fact might affect another fact. Suppose you are reading about South America's climate. You might make a prediction about how the climate affects where people live. You can change your mind as you gain new information.

Connect

Connect your reading to your own life. Are the people discussed in the selection like you or someone you know? What would you do in similar situations? Connect your reading to something you have already read. Suppose you have already read about the ancient Greeks. Now you are reading about the ancient Romans. How are they alike? How are they different?

Visualize

What would places, people, and events look like in a movie or a picture? As you read about India, you could visualize the country's heavy rains. What do they look like? How do they sound? As you read about geography, you could visualize a volcanic eruption.

Respond

Talk about what you have read. What did you think? Share your ideas with your classmates.

Assess yourself

What did you find out? Were your predictions on target? Did you find answers to your questions?

Follow up

Show what you know. Use what you have learned to do a project. When you do projects, you continue to learn.

Develop Student Reading

Point out to students that the sections in this book have a Before You Read feature. Each one is enclosed in a yellow box (see page 9 for an example). It includes Reach Into Your Background, which helps students think about what they already know so that they can apply their prior knowledge to what they're reading. Before You Read also includes Questions to Explore, which focus on the main ideas in the section. Each Question to Explore relates to one of the Guiding Questions for the book. See the list of Guiding Questions on the following page.

Students will also find Read Actively margin notes in every section. Encourage them to respond to these prompts to reinforce their active reading process.

Support English Language Learners

Preview and predict Suggest that students look at the title, headings, maps, charts, and photos to guess what the section is about.

Ask questions Tell students that every fact an author puts in a section has a purpose. Have them question the purpose of details as they read them. As they find answers and discover meaning, they can formulate new, deeper questions.

Visualize You might have students think about how the places they are learning about would affect their senses. What would it smell like there? What would they see and hear and feel? What would things taste like?

Assess Have students review their predictions and see how well they did. What helped them make good predictions?

This book was developed around five Guiding Questions about Latin America. They appear on the reduced Student Edition page to the right. The Guiding Questions are intended as an organizational focus for the book. All of the chapter content, activities, questions, and assessments relate to the Guiding Questions, which act as a kind of umbrella under which all of the material falls. You may wish to add your own Guiding Questions to the list in order to tailor them to your particular course. Or, as a group activity, you may want to ask your class to develop its own Guiding Question.

Ask a volunteer to read the Guiding Questions out loud to the class. These questions will guide students as they learn about Latin America's geography, history, and culture.

The projects for this book are designed to provide students with hands-on involvement in the content area. On the reduced Student Edition page to the right, students are introduced to the projects. Complete information about them appears on pages 160–161. You may assign projects as cooperative activities, whole-class projects, or individual projects. Each project relates to one of the Guiding Questions.

LATIN AMERICA

The ancient peoples of Latin America built great civilizations from the riches of their land. Today, their descendants have mixed with newcomers from around the world to create a modern society with new traditions. Cities of steel and glass rise alongside ancient ruins. From villages in the rain forests, mountains, and countryside, people move to the thriving cities. Every day more families arrive, hoping to make a new life.

Guiding Questions

The readings and activities in this book will help you discover answers to these Guiding Questions.

- What are the main physical features of Latin America?

- What factors have affected cultures in Latin America?

- Why have many Latin Americans been moving to cities in recent years?

- What is the relationship of the nations of Latin America with the United States and the world?

- How has geography influenced the ways in which Latin Americans make a living?

Project Preview

You can also discover answers to the Guiding Questions by working on projects. Preview the following projects and choose one that you might want to do. For more details, see page 160.

A Latin American Concert Research Latin American music and find some examples on tape to play for your class.

Visions of Latin America Create a diorama and write a short report to show how Latin America's geography affects the way people live.

Latin America in the News Collect articles on Latin America from magazines and newspapers for a bulletin board display.

Explorer's Dictionary Create an illustrated dictionary of important terms translated from Latin American languages.

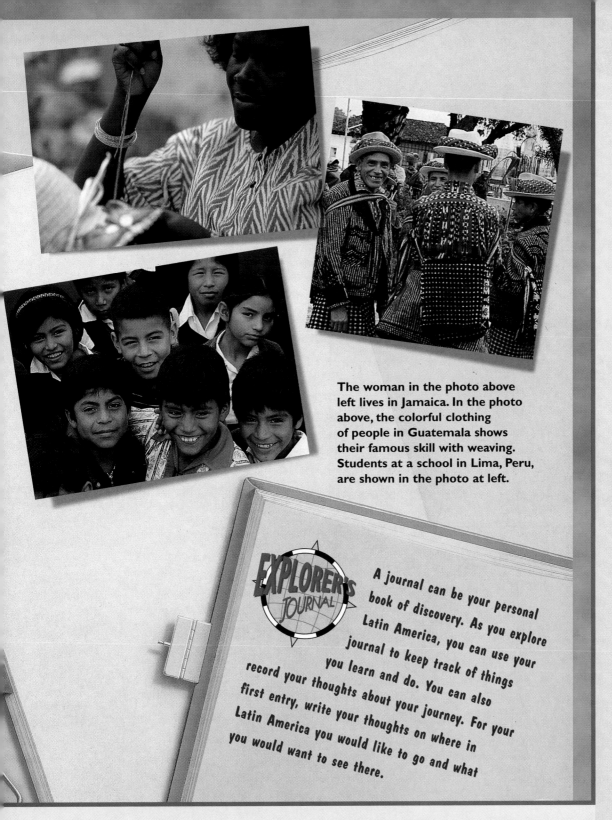

The woman in the photo above left lives in Jamaica. In the photo above, the colorful clothing of people in Guatemala shows their famous skill with weaving. Students at a school in Lima, Peru, are shown in the photo at left.

EXPLORER'S JOURNAL

A journal can be your personal book of discovery. As you explore Latin America, you can use your journal to keep track of things you learn and do. You can also record your thoughts about your journey. For your first entry, write your thoughts on where in Latin America you would like to go and what you would want to see there.

📁 **Teacher's Flexible Planning Guide** includes a guide to the Prentice Hall World Explorer Program, a skills correlation, and a variety of pacing charts for different course configurations. You may wish to refer to the guide as you plan your instruction.

📁 **Resource Pro™ CD-Rom** allows you to create customized lesson plans and print all Teaching Resources and Program Resources, plus the Computer Test Bank, directly from the CD-Rom.

Using the Pictures

Invite students to discuss the three photographs. Use them as a prompt for discussion of what students know about Latin America. You may want to begin a K-W-L chart on the board with the headings What We **K**now About Latin America, What We **W**ant to Know About Latin America, and What We **L**earned About Latin America. Have students fill in the first column with several things they agree they already know. Then ask them to brainstorm what they would like to know about Latin America to add to the second column. Students can fill in the third column as they work through the text.

Using the Explorer's Journal

Have students begin their Explorer's Journal as the paragraph on the student book page suggests. If at all possible, encourage students to use a separate small notebook for their Explorer's Journal entries. They can add to this Journal as they learn more about Latin America.

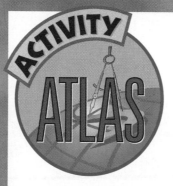

Latin America

Learning about Latin America means being an explorer and a geographer. No explorer would start out without first checking some facts. Begin by exploring the maps of Latin America on the following pages.

Relative Location

LOCATION

1. **Explore Latin America's Location** Notice where the United States and Latin America are located relative to the Equator. On the other side of the Equator, seasons come at the opposite time of year. For example, when it's summer here, it's winter there. Think about the season your birthday falls in. In what season would it fall if you lived in Argentina? What if you lived in Panama? How about in Bogotá, the capital city of Colombia? Or in Brasília, the capital of Brazil?

REGIONS

2. **Estimate Latin America's Size** How long is Latin America's west coast? To get an idea, curve a piece of string along the edge of the United States' west coast on the map above. Cut the string the same length as the coast. Now see how many string-lengths fit along the west coast of Latin America. Begin at the edge of the Pacific Ocean where Mexico borders California. Finish at the southern tip of South America. About how many times longer is Latin America's Pacific Coast than that of the United States?

Relative Size

LOCATION

3. Compare the Size of Countries The map below shows the countries that make up Latin America. Which two countries are the biggest in land area? Study the map to make your estimates. Check your answers in the World View section at the back of your textbook.

MOVEMENT

4. Investigate the Languages of Latin America The languages people speak give us clues about their history. Long ago, settlers from other countries took control of Latin America. Where were they from? Here are your clues: Portuguese is the official language of Brazil, and Spanish is spoken in most other Latin American countries.

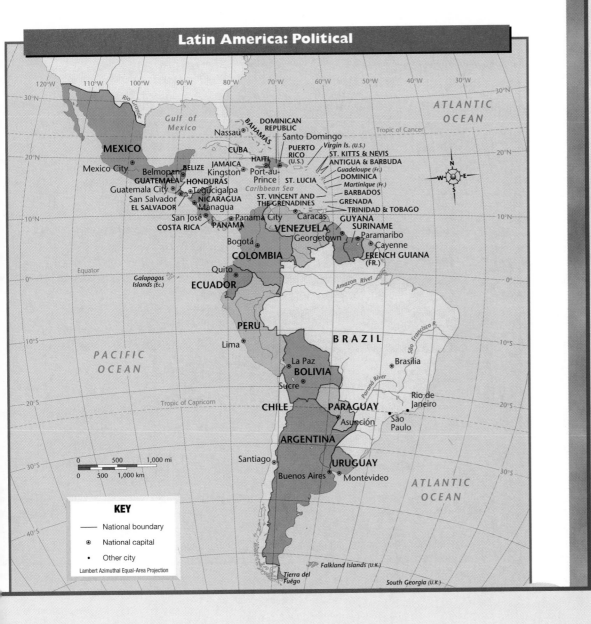

Latin America: Political

KEY

—— National boundary

⊛ National capital

• Other city

Lambert Azimuthal Equal-Area Projection

2 Explore

Direct students to read the six pages of the Activity Atlas. Then, ask students to work in pairs to study the maps and illustrations in the Activity Atlas and to think of one or two questions about the countries of Latin America. Have students write the questions and hold them. They can see if they can answer all the questions at the end of their study of Latin America.

3 Teach

Ask students to create a semantic, or cluster, map of Latin America. Write *Latin America* on the chalkboard, draw a circle around it, and ask volunteers to add secondary circles with additional information.

4 Assess

Semantic maps should locate Latin America relative to the United States and to the Equator. They should identify Latin America as an enormous area, with rain forests, deserts, high mountains, and many rivers, some of which are harnessed for hydroelectric power. Maps should note that most people speak either Spanish or Portuguese.

Answers to...

LOCATION

Largest—Brazil and Argentina; smallest—French Guiana and Suriname.

MOVEMENT

People from Portugal and Spain took control of most of Latin America.

Interdisciplinary Connections

Mathematics Ask students to use an atlas or an almanac to find the heights of the six highest mountains in South America (Aconcagua, Argentina, 22,831 ft. [6,959 m]; Ojos del Salado, Argentina-Chile, 22,572 ft. [6,880 m]; Bonete, Argentina, 22,546 ft. [6,872 m]; Tupungato, Argentina-Chile, 22,310 ft. [6,800 m]; Pissis, Argentina, 22,242 ft. [6,779 m]; Mercedario, Argentina, 22,211 ft. [6,769 m]. Ask students to create a bar graph comparing the heights of these mountains to the height of Mt. McKinley, the highest peak in the United States at 20,320 ft. (6,194 m).

PLACE

5. Examine the Physical Features of Latin America Volcanoes created many of Latin America's dramatic features. Long ago, volcanoes erupting along the west coast of South America formed the Andes Mountains. Volcanoes that exploded under the Caribbean Sea became a chain of islands called th Lesser Antilles. Central America has volcan mountains, too. Some are still active! Trac the Andes Mountains, the Lesser Antilles, an the mountains in Central America with yo finger. Which of these areas has the highe altitude?

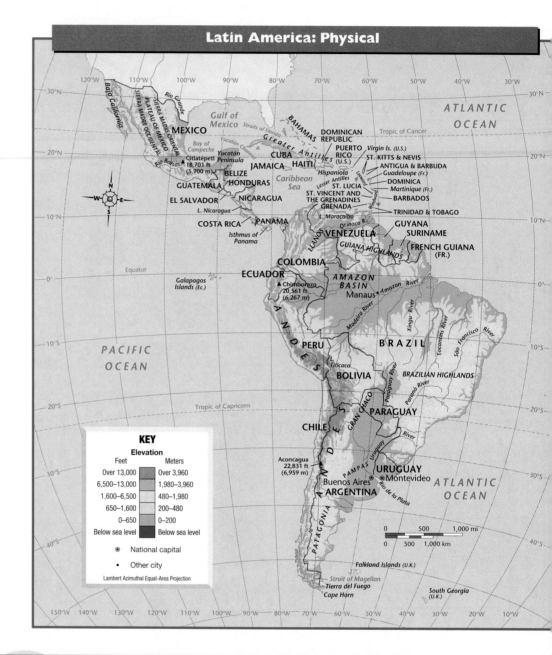

Latin America: Physical

Answers to ...

PLACE

The Andes Mountains have the highest altitudes.

6. Guide Geo Leo Geo Leo is exploring Latin America by boat, and he's taking you along to navigate. Read the passages below. To answer Geo Leo's questions, use the map below and the map on the opposite page.

A. We board our ship on the south side of the island of Hispaniola. A dense rain forest covers the island's mountain slopes. Which way to the Panama Canal?

B. We are sailing south past one of the Earth's driest deserts. It is in a long, skinny South American country that extends north and south along the continent's west coast. Steep mountains rise to the east. Where are we?

C. From the Falkland Islands, we travel north. For days we sail past desert. Finally, we see tropical rain forest along the coast. What two major cities will we come to next?

D. We continue sailing north, past grassland. We reach more rain forest and sail down a river through a low-lying area. Just ahead the Madeira River joins the one we are traveling on. Which way to the city of Manaus, our final destination?

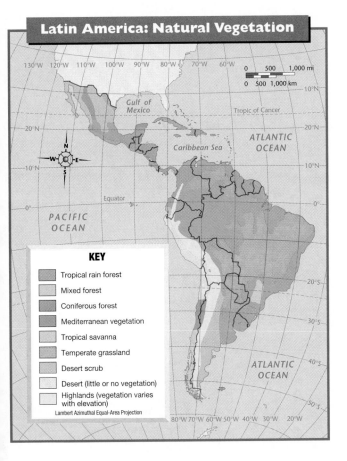

Latin America: Natural Vegetation

KEY
- Tropical rain forest
- Mixed forest
- Coniferous forest
- Mediterranean vegetation
- Tropical savanna
- Temperate grassland
- Desert scrub
- Desert (little or no vegetation)
- Highlands (vegetation varies with elevation)

Lambert Azimuthal Equal-Area Projection

GEO LEO

BONUS
List each body of water you and Geo Leo traveled over.

Background

Links Across Place

Elevation is an important factor in everyday life in Latin America because elevation helps govern climate. Assuming that air is not moving, air is 3.5°F (1.9°C) cooler for every 1,000 feet (305 meters) one climbs. Thus, while the city of Guayaquil on the coast of Ecuador may be very hot and sticky, at the same time in the city of Quito it is almost cold. That is because Quito is located high in the Andes Mountains.

Answers to...

REGIONS

a. You are in the Dominican Republic. The Panama Canal is southwest.
b. You are passing Chile.
c. Buenos Aires and Montevideo
d. Continue west on the Amazon River.
Bonus. Caribbean Sea, Pacific Ocean, Atlantic Ocean, Amazon River

Practice in the Themes of Geography

Place Ask students to use the Latin America physical map to find the Amazon Basin and the Brazilian Highlands. In which country are they located? (Brazil)

Regions Ask students what region is along the north border of Latin America. (North America)

Movement Ask students which of the following cities they could reach by boat: Manaus, Brazil; Buenos Aires, Argentina; La Paz, Bolivia; Santiago, Chile. (Manaus, Buenos Aires) Which map did they use? (Latin America political map)

Interaction Ask students where in Latin America they think most people live—along the coasts or in the interior? (along the coasts)

LOCATION

7. Investigate Latin America's Use of Hydroelectricity Hydroelectricity is electric power that is made by harnessing the power of water. One way to build a hydroelectric power plant is to build a dam across a river. The dam creates a large lake of water. To make electricity, the plant releases water from the lake into the river. As the water moves into the river, it turns a wheel. In some places, hydroelectric plants harness the power of ocean tides. Some of the largest hydroelectric plants are in Latin America. The world's largest is located on the border of Brazil and Paraguay. Look at the map below. What places in Latin America do you think would be good spots to build new hydroelectric power plants?

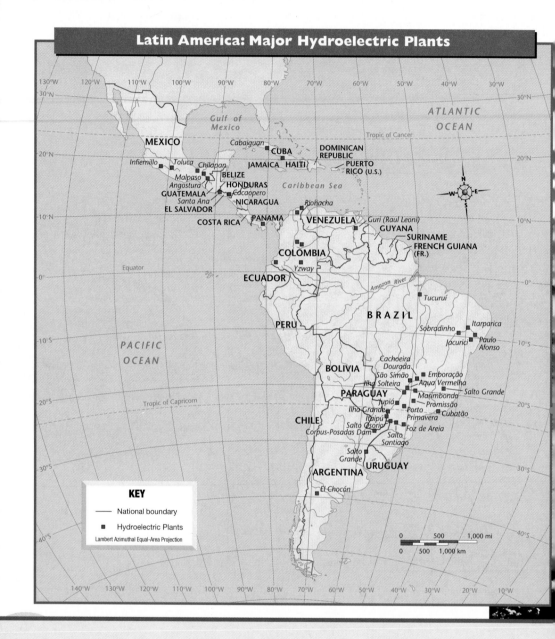

Latin America: Major Hydroelectric Plants

KEY

—— National boundary

■ Hydroelectric Plants

Lambert Azimuthal Equal-Area Projection

0   500   1,000 mi
0   500   1,000 km

Biggest Hydroelectric Dams

Name of Dam	Location
1. Itaipú	Brazil/Paraguay
2. Grand Coulee	United States
3. Guri (Raul Leoni)	Venezuela
4. Tucuruíi	Brazil
5. Sayano-Shushensk	Russia
6. Krasnoyarsk	Russia
7. Corpus-Posadas	Argentina/Paraguay
8. LaGrande 2	Canada
9. Churchill Falls	Canada
10. Bratsk	Russia

INTERACTION

8. **Explore the Effects of a River Dam** Unlike coal and petroleum, water power cannot be used up. It also does not cause air pollution. But building a dam does affect the environment of a river. It creates a large, artificial lake. It also reduces the amount of water that is in the river below the dam. What do you think are some advantages of building a dam across a river? What are some disadvantages?

◄▼ What percentage of its energy does Latin America get from hydroelectricity? How does this compare to energy use around the world?

Sources of Energy

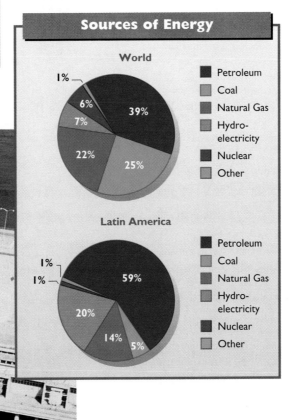

World

1%
6%
7%
39%
22%
25%

- Petroleum
- Coal
- Natural Gas
- Hydro-electricity
- Nuclear
- Other

Latin America

1%
1%
59%
20%
14%
5%

- Petroleum
- Coal
- Natural Gas
- Hydro-electricity
- Nuclear
- Other

◄ **Guri Dam** Only two other hydroelectric dams produce more electricity than Venezuela's Guri Dam, on the Caroni River.

Physical Geography

To help you plan instruction, the chart below shows how teaching resources correspond to chapter content. Use the resources to vary instruction, add activities, or plan block schedules. Where appropriate, resources have **suggested time allotments** for students. Time allotments are approximate.

Managing Time and Instruction

	Latin America Teaching Resources Binder		World Explorer Program Resources Binder	
	Resource	**mins.**	**Resource**	**mins.**
1 SECTION 1 **Land and Water**	**Chapter and Section Support** Reproducible Lesson Plan, p. 3 Ⓢ Guided Reading and Review, p. 4 Ⓢ Section Quiz, p. 5 **Activities and Projects** Activity Atlas Activities, pp. 3–5 **Social Studies and Geography Skills,** Using the Map Key, p. 3	20 25 25 30	**Outline Maps** Latin America physical map **Nystrom Desk Atlas** Ⓣ **Primary Sources and Literature Readings**	20 20 40
SKILL ACTIVITY **Using Regional Maps to Show Climate**	**Social Studies and Geography Skills,** Reading a Climate Map, p. 26	30		
2 SECTION 2 **Climate and Vegetation**	**Chapter and Section Support** Reproducible Lesson Plan, p. 6 Ⓢ Guided Reading and Review, p. 7 Ⓢ Section Quiz, p. 8 Critical Thinking Activity, p. 16	20 25 30	**Interdisciplinary Explorations** Ⓣ *Fate of the Rain Forest*	
3 SECTION 3 **Natural Resources**	**Chapter and Section Support** Reproducible Lesson Plan, p. 9 Ⓢ Guided Reading and Review, p. 10 Ⓢ Section Quiz, p. 11 Ⓢ Vocabulary, p. 13 Reteaching, p. 14 Enrichment, p. 15 Ⓢ Chapter Summary, p. 12 **Tests** Form A and B Chapter Tests, pp. 2–7	20 25 20 25 25 15 40	**Writing Process Handbook** Writing Effective Paragraphs, pp. 27–28	25
LITERATURE *The Surveyor* by Alma Flor Ada			Ⓣ **Primary Souces and Literature Readings**	40

Block Scheduling Folder
PROGRAM TEACHING RESOURCES

Activities and Projects

Interdisciplinary Links

Block Scheduling
Program Support

Resource Pro™ CD-ROM

Media and Technology

Assessment Opportunities

From Guiding Questions to Assessment A series of Guiding Questions serves as an organizing framework for this book. The Guiding Questions that relate to this chapter are listed below. Section Reviews and Section Quizzes provide opportunities for assessing students' insights into these Guiding Questions. Additional assessments are listed below.

Media and Technology

Resource	mins.
◖● ◉ ⑤ World Video Explorer	20
◉ Planet Earth CD-ROM	20
⬛ Color Transparencies 4, 34	20
◉ Planet Earth CD-ROM	20
⬛ Color Transparencies 6, 7	20
⬛ Color Transparencies 4, 34, 90, 91	20
◯ ⑤ Guided Reading Audiotapes	20
⬛ Color Transparency 174 (Graphic organizer table template)	20
◉ The Writer's Solution CD-ROM	30
🖫 Computer Test Bank	30

Ⓣ Teaming Opportunity
This resource is especially well-suited for teaching teams.

Ⓢ Spanish
This resource is also in Spanish Support.

◉ CD-ROM
◉ Laserdisc
⬛ Transparency
🖫 Software
◖● Videotape
◯ Audiotape

GUIDING QUESTIONS

- *What are the main physical features of Latin America?*
- *What factors have affected cultures in Latin America?*
- *How has geography influenced the ways in which Latin Americans make a living?*

ASSESSMENTS

Section 1

Students should be able to make a graphic organizer that shows the major landforms and water bodies of Latin America.

▶ **RUBRIC** See the Assessment booklet for a rubric on assessing graphic organizers.

Section 2

Students should be able to describe how Latin America's landforms affect its climate.

▶ **RUBRIC** See the Assessment booklet for a rubric on assessing cause-and-effect statements.

Section 3

Students should be able to create a chart of natural resources and list how people use them.

▶ **RUBRIC** See the Assessment booklet for a rubric on assessing charts.

Activities and Projects

Mental Mapping

Facing Latin America In the classroom, orient students so that they are facing north. If you wish, use a compass to verify the direction.

Have students extend their right arms and point. Tell them that they are pointing east to the Atlantic Ocean. Next have students extend their left arms and point. They are now pointing west to the Pacific Ocean. Have students point straight ahead. Now they are pointing north to Canada.

Have students carefully turn and face the opposite direction. Ask students what directions they are facing. (south). Tell students they are facing toward Mexico, one of the countries in Latin America. Now have students turn one small step to the left. Tell students they are facing southeast, in the general direction of South America.

Links to Current Events

Latin America News Coverage As you teach this chapter, you might want to have students keep a log of Latin American countries covered in the news media. Establish a period of time for students to keep the log. For example, you might want to choose the same number of days as for teaching the chapter. When students see coverage of a Latin American country, they write the name of that country in their logs.

Encourage students to look for Latin American coverage on television, radio, newspapers, and magazines. At the end of the time period, have students bring in their logs. As a class activity, review with students which countries appeared in their logs most often. Have students speculate on why some Latin American countries appeared in news coverage more than others.

Hands-On Activities

Developing a Sense of Location Have students use a globe to locate Latin America. Point out that Latin America is made up of Mexico, Central America, South America, and the Caribbean islands.

Have students find the Tropic of Cancer and the Tropic of Capricorn. Help students see that most of Latin America lies in the tropical latitudes, while northern Mexico and southern South America are within the middle latitudes. (Refer to the Map and Globe handbook at the back of the textbook if you need to review low and middle latitudes.)

Ask students to note how far east South America extends. Have them determine whether Latin America is closer to Africa or Asia. This activity will help students develop a sense of Latin America's location.

Cut-Out Map Hang a large sheet of poster board on the wall. Use an overhead projector to project an outline map of Latin America on the poster board. Have students trace the outline of Latin America and make a cut-out map. The cut-out can serve as the base for an illustrated map of the physical geography of Latin America. Students can illustrate the map with original drawings. *English Language Learners*

Position Paper The building of Tenochtitlán, the Aztec capital, and the growth of the Incan empire are examples of the ways ancient people changed the physical environment to meet human needs. Have students write a position paper explaining how the theme of human-environment interaction applies to these topics. *Challenging*

Fantastic Food Fair Have the class hold a Fantastic Food Fair about corn and potatoes, both domesticated in Latin America thousands of years ago. Ask students to use encyclopedias and other library resources to trace the origin of these two important foods. Students' research findings can be presented as captions for an exhibit of corn, potatoes, and products made from these foods such as tortillas, corn flakes, corn oil, corn syrup, corn meal, mashed potatoes, and French fries. *Average*

Geography Chart Work with students to develop a large Geography chart for the bulletin board. Make three columns: Physical Geography, Latin America, and Where We Live. As students read through the chapter, have volunteers insert into the first column elements of physical geography they read about such as examples of landforms, climate, or natural resources. Then they can fill in the other two columns with examples that exist in Latin America and comparable features of your area. *Basic*

F.Y.I.

This page can help you extend your own and students' understanding of the concepts in this chapter. You may want to browse through some of the suggestions in the **Bibliography**. **Interdisciplinary Links** can connect social studies understandings to areas elsewhere in the curriculum through the use of other Prentice Hall products. **National Geography Standards** reflected specifically in this chapter are listed for your convenience. Some hints about appropriate **Internet Access** are also provided. **School to Careers** provides insights into the practical uses of some of the concepts in this chapter as they might pertain to various careers.

BIBLIOGRAPHY

FOR THE TEACHER

The Eyewitness Atlas of the World. Dorling, 1994.

National Geographic Picture Atlas of Our World. National Geographic, 1993.

Schlessinger, Andrew. *The Rainforest.* Schlessinger, 1993. Video

South America. National Geographic 51441, 1991. Video

FOR THE STUDENT

Easy
Zak, Monica. *Save My Rainforest.* Volcano, 1992.

Average
Brusca, Maria Cristina. *On the Pampas.* Holt, 1991.

Blue, Rose and Corinne Naden. *Andes Mountains.* Raintree, 1995.

Challenging
Bernhard, Brendan. *Pizarro, Orellana, and the Exploration of the Amazon.* Chelsea, 1991.

LITERATURE CONNECTION

Cherry, Lynne. *The Great Kapok Tree: A Tale of the Amazon Rain Forest.* Harcourt, 1990.

Clark, Ann Nolan. *Secret of the Andes.* Viking, 1952.

George, Jean Craighead. *Shark Beneath the Reef.* HarperCollins, 1989.

INTERDISCIPLINARY LINKS

Subject	Theme: Discovery
MATH	Middle Grades Math: Tools for Success *Course 1*, Lesson 11–6, **Graphing on the Coordinate Plane** *Course 2*, Lesson 4–4, **Math and Weather: Subtracting Integers**
SCIENCE	Prentice Hall Science *The Nature of Science*, Lesson 1–3, **Science and Discovery** *Cells: Building Blocks of Life*, Lesson 1–1, **The Origin of Life**
LANGUAGE ARTS	Choices in Literature *The World of "What If . . . ?"*, **El Enano** *The Adventure of Me*, **Morning Girl** Prentice Hall Literature *Bronze*, **Circle of the Seasons** *Copper*, **Space Stations of the Mind**

NATIONAL GEOGRAPHY STANDARDS

Students explore the 18 National Geography Standards throughout Latin America. Chapter 1, however, concentrates on investigating the following: standards 1, 3, 4, 5, 7, 8, 15, 16, 18. For a complete list of the standards, see the *Teacher's Flexible Planning Guide.*

SCHOOL TO CAREERS

In Chapter 1 Latin America: Physical Geography, students learn about the land, water, climate, vegetation, and natural resources of Latin America. Additionally, they address the skill of using regional maps. Understanding physical geography can help students prepare for careers in many fields such as economics, politics, architecture, geology, mining, and so on. Map reading skills are particularly useful for travel agents, weather forecasters, salespeople, and others. The curriculum presented in this book, as in all eight titles of Prentice Hall's *World Explorer* program, is designed to prepare students not only for careers but also for good citizenship—of the world as well as of this country.

INTERNET ACCESS

Many social studies teachers and students use Internet browsers, or search engines, to investigate particular topics. For the best results, use narrow rather than broad topics. Try these for Chapter 1: Andes Mountains, Amazon River, Mexico City, Caribbean islands. Finding age-appropriate sites is an important consideration when using the Internet. For links to age-appropriate sites in world studies and geography, visit the Prentice Hall Home Page at: http://www.phschool.com

Connecting to the Guiding Questions

As students complete this chapter, they will focus on the regions that make up Latin America, examining physical features, climate and vegetation, and natural resources. Content in this chapter thus relates to these Guiding Questions:

● What are the main physical features of Latin America?

● How has geography influenced the ways in which Latin Americans make a living?

Using the Picture Activities

Lead a class discussion of the picture, focusing on significant details.

• Encourage students to consider how mountains might affect travel, clothing, farming, and settlement patterns.

• Students should respond that the climate is colder near the peaks of the Andes and warmer at the foot of the mountains.

Heterogeneous Groups

The following Teacher's Edition strategies are suitable for heterogeneous groups.

Cooperative Learning
Making a Puzzle Map   p. 12

Critical Thinking
Expressing Problems Clearly   p. 26

Interdisciplinary Connections
Science   p. 17

CHAPTER 1

LATIN AMERICA
Physical Geography

SECTION 1
Land and Water

SECTION 2
Climate and Vegetation

SECTION 3
Natural Resources

PICTURE ACTIVITIES

These rugged mountains are the Andes (AN deez). *They run the length of South America. To help you get to know this part of Latin America, do the following.*

Study the picture
What do you think it would be like to live in or near the Andes? Based on what you see in the photograph, where would be the best area to live?

Think about the climate
Have you ever climbed in the mountains? How did the temperature change as you climbed higher? Based on your experience, do you think the climate is the same at the top of the Andes as at the bottom? Where would it be colder? Where would it be warmer?

Resource Directory

Media and Technology

Opener: Journey Over Latin America, from the World Video Explorer, introduces students to the varied landforms of the regions.

Geography: The Gauchos of Argentina, from the World Video Explorer, enhances students' understanding of how the physical geography of the Pampas of Argentina contributes to the region's economy and way of life.

Chapter 2

Chapter 3

Land and Water

Reach Into Your Background

No two places in the world are exactly the same. Think about the state in which you live. What features set it apart from other states? List some features that make your state special.

Questions to Explore

1. What are the main geographic regions of Latin America?
2. How do Latin America's geographic features affect the lives of the people?

Key Terms

plateau
isthmus
coral
pampas
tributary

Key Places

Mexico
Central America
Caribbean
South America

High in the Andes Mountains, planes take off and land at El Alto airport. *El Alto* (ehl AHL toh) is Spanish for "the high one." It is an accurate name, for El Alto is the highest airport in the world. El Alto is the airport for La Paz, Bolivia.

Shortly after leaving the plane, tourists may get mountain sickness. The "thin" air of the Andes contains less oxygen than most people are used to. Oxygen starvation makes visitors' hearts beat faster and leaves them short of breath. Later on in the day, they may get terrible headaches. It takes a few days for visitors' bodies to get used to the mountain air. But the people who live in the Andes do not have these problems. Their bodies are used to the mountain environment.

The Andes mountain range is one of Latin America's major landforms. In this section, you will learn about Latin America's other landforms and about the people who live there.

Where Is Latin America?

Latin America is located in the Western Hemisphere south of the United States. Look at the map in the Activity Atlas. You will see that Latin America includes all the nations from Mexico to the tip of South America. It also includes the islands that dot the Caribbean (ka ruh BEE un) Sea.

Geographic features divide Latin America into three smaller regions. They are (1) Mexico and Central America, (2) the Caribbean, and (3) South America. South America is so large that geographers classify it as a continent. Look at the physical map in the Activity Atlas. Can you identify the geographic features that separate these three areas?

Teaching Resources

📁 **Reproducible Lesson Plan** in the Chapter and Section Resources booklet, p. 3, provides a summary of the section lesson.

📁 **Guided Reading and Review** in the Chapter and Section Resources booklet, p. 4, provides a structure for mastering key concepts and reviewing key terms in the section. Available in Spanish in the Spanish Chapter and Section Resources booklet, p. 3.

Program Resources

Material in the *Primary Sources and Literature Readings* booklet extends content with a selection from the region under study.

Outline Maps Latin America physical map

Lesson Objectives

1. Identify Latin America's main geographic regions.

2. Describe how the physical features of Latin America affect people's lives.

Lesson Plan

1 Engage

Warm-Up Activity

Ask students to describe the physical features of the area in which they live. Prompt students by asking whether the land is flat or hilly. Are there lakes or wooded areas? Are there open areas of land, such as parks, or do buildings and roads take up nearly all the space? List features on the chalkboard. Then discuss with students how these features affect their lives and the lives of other people living in the area.

Activating Prior Knowledge

Have students read Reach Into Your Background in the Before You Read box. Point out that every place in the world has unique features. In addition, explain that people adjust to the physical features around them in various ways. For example, people living near a river may build a bridge across it; people living near a lake may use boats to travel from one place to another. Ask for other examples of how people interact with their surroundings.

2 Explore

Direct students to read the section. Have them locate on a world map and then briefly describe the three regions that make up Latin America: the Caribbean, Mexico and Central America, and South America. Ask how mountains and rivers in Latin America affect travel in the area. Have students find South America's Pampas and the U.S. Great Plains on physical maps. Ask how the two regions are alike.

3 Teach

Have students draw three boxes. Label the boxes *The Caribbean, Mexico and Central America,* and *South America.* Tell students to list one or more physical features of the area in each box. Then ask them to describe ways in which the feature or features affect people's lives. Use students' work as the basis for a discussion of Latin America's regions and features. This activity should take about 20 minutes.

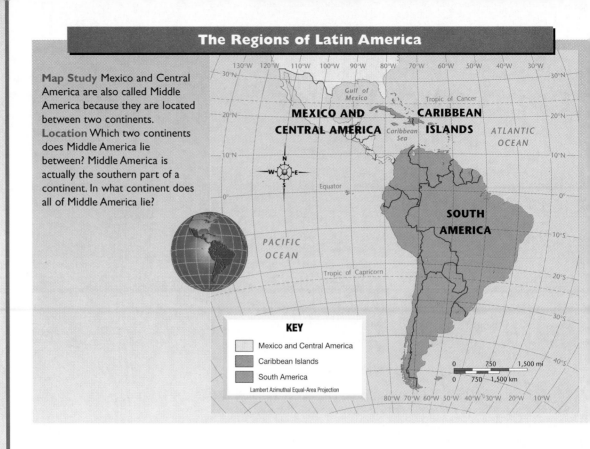

The Regions of Latin America

Map Study Mexico and Central America are also called Middle America because they are located between two continents. **Location** Which two continents does Middle America lie between? Middle America is actually the southern part of a continent. In what continent does all of Middle America lie?

KEY

Mexico and Central America

Caribbean Islands

South America

Lambert Azimuthal Equal-Area Projection

READ ACTIVELY

Predict How do you think the physical features of Latin America might be like those of the United States?

Perhaps you are wondering how Latin America got its name. About 500 years ago, Europeans sailed to Latin America. Most came from Spain and Portugal. European colonists brought their own languages and ways of life with them. Today, most Latin Americans speak Spanish, Portuguese, or French. These languages have their roots in the ancient language of Latin. As a result, the region is known as Latin America.

Landforms of Latin America

Imagine mountains that pierce the clouds and grassy plains that never seem to end. Picture wet rain forests and sunbaked deserts. This is Latin America, a region of variety and contrast.

Mexico and Central America   Mexico and Central America stretch 2,500 miles (4,023 km) from the U.S. border to South America. It is a distance that is almost equal to the width of the mainland United States. Mountains dominate this region. These mountains are part of a long system of mountain ranges. This huge system extends from Canada through the United States all the way to the tip of South America.

Resource Directory

Media and Technology

 Planet Earth CD-ROM includes physical maps of North America and South America that allow students to view the countries that make up the region of Latin America.

Color Transparencies 4, 34

Teaching Resources

Using the Map Key in the *Social Studies and Geography Skills* booklet, p. 3, provides additional skill practice.
Nystrom Desk Atlas

Answers to...

MAP STUDY

• North America and South America; North America

Between the mountains in Mexico lies Mexico's Central Plateau. A **plateau** (pla TOH) is a large raised area of mostly level land. Mexico's Central Plateau makes up more than half of the country's area. Most of Mexico's people live here. However, the surrounding mountains make it hard for people to travel to and from the Central Plateau. Another major landform in Mexico is the narrow coastal plains.

Central America, located south of Mexico, is an isthmus. An **isthmus** is a narrow strip of land that has water on both sides and joins two larger bodies of land. Find Central America on the map in the Activity Atlas. What two large bodies of land does the isthmus of Central America connect? As in Mexico, narrow plains run along Central America's coasts. Between these coastal plains are rugged, steep mountains. More than a dozen of these mountains are active volcanoes. Volcanic ash has made the soil fertile. As a result, many people tend farms in the region.

The Caribbean   Imagine islands made of skeletons. Imagine other islands that are the tops of underwater mountains. The Caribbean is made up of these two types of islands. The smaller islands are made up of the skeletons of tiny sea animals. Over hundreds of years, the skeletons meld together to form a rocklike substance called **coral.**

The larger islands of the Caribbean are the tops of huge underwater mountains. These include Cuba, Jamaica (juh MAY kuh), Hispaniola (his pun YOH luh), and Puerto Rico. Most people on the islands make a living farming.

LINKS TO LANGUAGE ARTS

The Tlaloques According to Aztec religion, a group of rain gods lived on the tops of mountains. They were called the Tlaloques. Tlaloc, the leader of the Tlaloques, was responsible for rain and lightning. The Aztecs were right, in a way—mountains affect rainfall. Clouds cool off and drop rain when they rise over the mountains.

Harvesting Alfalfa in Mexico

In Mexico, farming is an important way of making a living, even in the drier areas of the country. Raising crops requires fertile soil, a source of fresh water, and a long growing season. As in Central America, much of Mexico's fertile soil is the result of volcanic activity.

4 Assess

See answers to the Section Review. You may also use the students' completed boxes of physical features for assessment purposes.

Acceptable responses include three factually correct entries in each box.

Commendable responses include statements of cause and effect, relating geography and people's lives.

Outstanding responses show an understanding of how the effect of one cause can, in turn, be the cause of other effects.

Background

Global Perspectives

Asia's Mighty Himalaya Mountains   Only the Himalaya Mountains, a mountain system in Asia, stand taller than the Andes. The Himalaya Mountains make up the tallest range in the world. They extend along the India-Tibet border and through Pakistan, Nepal, China, and Bhutan. Have students find the Himalaya Mountains on a relief map. The tallest peak of this range is the well known—and often climbed—Mount Everest. At 29,028 feet (8,848 m) above sea level, Everest stands more than a mile higher than the tallest peak in the Andes.

Cooperative Learning

Making a Puzzle Map
Students can work in groups of four to create a puzzle map of one or more regions of Latin America. Remind students to include and label important places and physical features mentioned in the text.

One student can be responsible for researching the information, another for drawing the map on construction paper. You may wish to refer students to the physical map of Latin America in the Activity Atlas. Students may trace this map. A third student can mount the map onto cardboard, and the fourth can cut the map into jigsaw pieces. Have groups exchange puzzles and try to reassemble one another's puzzles.
Kinesthetic

South America South America contains many types of land forms. Perhaps the most impressive landform is the Andes Mountains. The Andes run some 4,500 miles (7,250 km) along the western coast of South America. In some places, the Andes rise to heights of more than 20,000 feet (6,100 m). That's about the same height as twenty 100-story buildings stacked one on top of another. Except for the Himalaya Mountains in Asia, the Andes are the highest mountains in the world.

The Andes are steep and difficult to cross. But their rich soil has drawn farmers to the region. East of the Andes are rolling highlands. These highlands spread across parts of Brazil, Venezuela (ven uh ZWAY luh), Guyana (gy AN uh), and other South American countries. Farther south are the Pampas (PAHM puz), a large plains area that stretches through Argentina (ar jun TEE nuh) and Uruguay (YOOR uh gway). **Pampas** are flat grassland regions that are very similar to the Great Plains in the United States.

The Pampas and other plains areas, the eastern highlands, and the Andes frame the Amazon River Basin. The Amazon River Basin contains the largest tropical rain forest in the world. This dense forest covers more than a third of the continent.

The Rivers of Latin America

Latin America is famous for its rivers and lakes. They are some of the longest and largest bodies of water in the world. Latin America's waters are important to the people of the region. Rivers serve as natural

Herding Cattle on the Pampas

Grasslands known as the Pampas can also be found in Brazil. These grasslands are perfect for raising cattle. **Critical Thinking** How are these grasslands similar to the Great Plains in the United States?

highways in places where it is hard to build roads. The fish that swim the waters of Latin America provide food. Rushing water from large rivers provides electric power.

Amazon: The Ocean River

Latin America's Amazon (AM uh zahn) River is the second-longest river in the world. Only the Nile in Africa is longer. The Amazon flows 4,000 miles (6,437 km) from Peru across Brazil into the Atlantic Ocean.

How large is the Amazon? The Amazon River carries more water than any other river in the world. It contains about 20 percent of all the fresh river water on Earth. The Amazon River gathers power from the more than 1,000 tributaries (TRIB yoo tehr eez) that spill into it. Tributaries are the rivers and streams that flow into a larger river. With its tributaries, the Amazon drains an area of more than two million square miles. No wonder people call the Amazon the "Ocean River."

Other Rivers and Lakes

Latin America has many other bodies of water besides the Amazon. The Paraná (pah rah NAH), Paraguay, and Uruguay rivers form the Río de la Plata system. The Río de la Plata separates Argentina and Uruguay. In Venezuela, people travel on the Orinoco River and Lake Maracaibo (mar uh KY boh). Lake Titicaca is the highest lake in the world on which ships can travel. It lies high in the Andes Mountains.

An Amazon Scene

The people who live near the Amazon River in Brazil rely on it for transportation, fish, and water. Families also wash their laundry right at the river bank.

READ ACTIVELY

Visualize How could a ship sail on a lake? What would the lake have to be like?

SECTION 1 REVIEW

1. **Define** (a) plateau, (b) isthmus, (c) coral, (d) pampas, (e) tributary.

2. **Identify** (a) Mexico, (b) Central America, (c) Caribbean, (d) South America.

3. Describe the main landforms of the three regions that make up Latin America.

4. Give one example of how the physical features of Latin America affect the people who live there.

Critical Thinking

5. **Making Comparisons** Explain two ways in which the three regions of Latin America are alike. Explain two differences.

Activity

6. **Writing to Learn** Suppose your family was planning to move to Latin America. If you had your choice, in which of the three regions of Latin America would you live? Explain why.

Resource Directory

Teaching Resources

Section Quiz in the Chapter and Section Resources booklet, p. 5, covers the main ideas and key terms in the section. Available in Spanish in the Spanish Chapter and Section Resources booklet, p. 4.

SECTION 2

Climate and Vegetation

BEFORE YOU READ

Reach Into Your Background

Suppose the temperature outside is 90°F (32°C). Would you feel more comfortable lying on a sandy beach or sitting under a tree in the woods? In what type of climate would you want to vacation someday?

Questions to Explore

1. What kinds of climate and vegetation does Latin America have?

2. In what ways do climate and vegetation affect how Latin Americans live?

Key Terms
El Niño
elevation

Key Places
Andes
Atacama Desert
Patagonia
Amazonian rain forest

Every few years, a warm ocean current flows along the western coast of South America. This warm current drives away fish that thrive in the cold waters of the Pacific Ocean. The current brings other changes to Latin America, too. Instead of dry weather, heavy rains pour down and low-lying regions are flooded. In other places, drought plagues the land and the people.

Just what is this strange ocean current that brings disaster? It is **El Niño** (el NEEN yoh). Because it usually strikes near Christmas time, Latin Americans named the phenomena El Niño, Spanish for "the Christ child." El Niño is one of many factors that affect climate in Latin America.

▼ Mexico's Sonoran Desert shows that even a hot, dry desert can be full of plant life.

Climate: Hot, Cold, and Mild

What's the climate like where you live? Is it hot? Cold? Rainy? If you lived in Latin America, the climate might be any of these. Climate in Latin America can vary greatly even within the same country.

In parts of the Andes, below-zero temperatures would set your teeth chattering. Travel down to the Amazon Basin, and you may be sweating in 80°F (27°C) heat. Don't forget your umbrella: This part of Latin America receives more than 80 inches (203 cm) of rain each year. If you prefer dry weather, visit the Atacama (ah tah KAH mah) Desert in Chile or the Sonoran Desert in Mexico. These are two of the driest places on Earth.

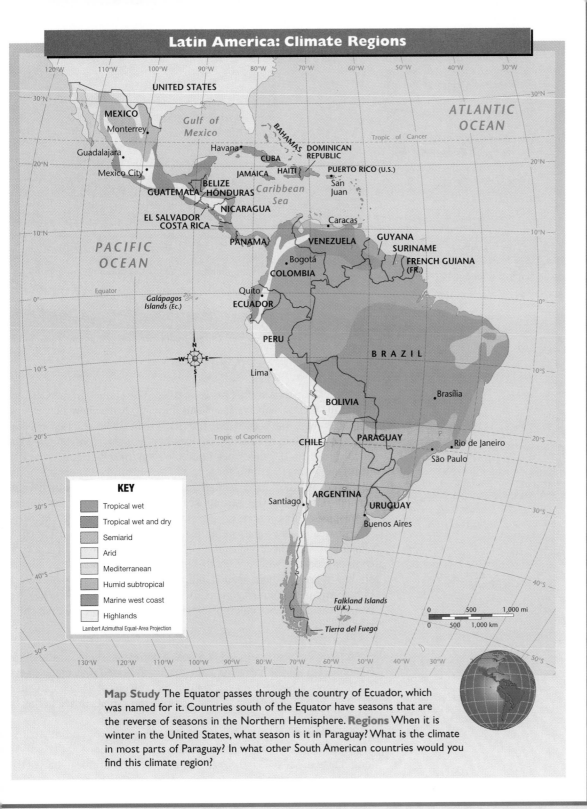

Latin America: Climate Regions

UNITED STATES

MEXICO
Monterrey
Guadalajara
Mexico City

Gulf of Mexico

BAHAMAS
Havana
CUBA
JAMAICA HAITI
DOMINICAN REPUBLIC
PUERTO RICO (U.S.)
San Juan

BELIZE
GUATEMALA HONDURAS
EL SALVADOR
COSTA RICA
NICARAGUA

Caribbean Sea

PANAMA

ATLANTIC OCEAN

Tropic of Cancer

PACIFIC OCEAN

Equator

Galápagos Islands (Ec.)

Caracas

VENEZUELA
GUYANA
SURINAME
FRENCH GUIANA (FR.)

Bogotá
COLOMBIA
Quito
ECUADOR

PERU
Lima

BRAZIL

Brasília

BOLIVIA

Tropic of Capricorn

CHILE
PARAGUAY
Rio de Janeiro
São Paulo

Santiago
ARGENTINA
URUGUAY
Buenos Aires

KEY
- Tropical wet
- Tropical wet and dry
- Semiarid
- Arid
- Mediterranean
- Humid subtropical
- Marine west coast
- Highlands

Lambert Azimuthal Equal-Area Projection

Falkland Islands (U.K.)

0   500   1,000 mi
0   500   1,000 km

Tierra del Fuego

Map Study The Equator passes through the country of Ecuador, which was named for it. Countries south of the Equator have seasons that are the reverse of seasons in the Northern Hemisphere. **Regions** When it is winter in the United States, what season is it in Paraguay? What is the climate in most parts of Paraguay? In what other South American countries would you find this climate region?

4 Assess

See answers to the Section Review. You may also use students' classroom discussion to gauge their understanding.

Acceptable responses include two factually correct descriptions of climate and vegetation, their relationship, and their effects on people's lives and livelihood.

Commendable responses include three factually correct descriptions of climate and vegetation, their relationship, and their effects on people's lives and livelihood.

Outstanding responses compare and contrast climate, vegetation, and livelihood in at least three areas of Latin America.

Activity

Journal Writing

Island Living Ask students to imagine life on a Caribbean island. Discuss possible pros and cons of the climate. For example, the island trees and flowers are beautiful, but job opportunities may be limited to farming, tourism, and small industry.

Ask students to write two paragraphs expressing some of the feelings of island residents toward the climate. One paragraph should express advantages of island living; the second should express disadvantages.

Answers to...

SUGAR CANE FARMING

* Responses may vary. Possible answer: Warm weather and adequate rainfall are good for crops while hurricanes and tropical storms can be dangerous for farms and farming.

Sugar Cane Farming

People in the Dominican Republic grow much of their own food, but they also grow sugar cane to export. **Regions** How does the climate in the Caribbean make the area good for farming? How is the climate in the Caribbean dangerous for farms?

The Climate and the People   The climate in the Caribbean is usually sunny and warm. From June to November, however, the region is often hit with fierce hurricanes. In 1988, Hurricane Gilbert shattered the sunny Caribbean weather like an atom bomb. Winds howled at over 180 miles per hour (300 km/hr). Waves nearly 20 feet (6 m) high smashed into the coast. The storm tore roofs off houses, shattered windows, and yanked huge trees from the ground. Gilbert turned out to be the strongest hurricane to strike the Western Hemisphere this century.

Hurricanes are a part of life for people living in the Caribbean. But climate affects the people of Latin America in other ways, too. For example, people who live in the mountains need warm clothing and shelter to protect them against falling temperatures. That's because the higher up the mountains you go, the cooler it gets. Those who live in the sunny, warm tropics think more about cooling sea breezes than chilling winter winds.

Climate Regions of Latin America   Look at the climate regions map on the previous page. You will notice that many parts of Latin America have a tropical wet climate. A tropical wet climate means hot, humid, rainy weather all year round. Rain forests thrive in this type of climate.

Other parts of Latin America have a tropical wet and dry climate. These areas are equally hot, but the rainy season does not last all year long. Parts of Mexico and Brazil and most of the Caribbean have a tropical wet and dry climate.

Resource Directory

Teaching Resources

Critical Thinking Activity in the Chapter and Section Resources booklet, p. 16, helps students apply the skill of drawing conclusions.

Much of Argentina, Uruguay, and Paraguay has a humid subtropical climate, similar to that of parts of the southern United States. People living in this climate usually have hot, wet summers and cool winters. Farmers in these areas can raise such crops as wheat and apples, which need a cold season to grow well. Farther south, the climate turns arid. Farmers raise sheep on the plains of this colder, drier area, called Patagonia (pat uh GOH nee uh).

What Factors Affect Climate? Have you ever hiked in the mountains? If you have, you probably noticed that as you climbed higher the temperature dropped. At some point during your hike, you may have stopped to put on a sweatshirt or jacket.

Elevation, the height of land above sea level, is a key factor in the climate of mountainous Latin America. Look at the diagram below. It shows how elevation affects climate. The higher the elevation, the colder the temperature. Suppose it is a warm 80°F (27°C) at sea level. At 3,000 feet (914 m), the temperature may be 72°F (25°C). Continue up to 6,000 feet (1,829 m), and the temperature may now be only about 65°F (13°C). Above 10,000 feet (3,048 m), the temperature may remain below freezing—too cold for people to live. Temperature also affects what crops people can grow in each region.

Other factors also affect Latin America's climate. Regions close to the Equator are generally warmer than those farther away. Look at the Latin America: Climate Regions map. Find the Equator. Which parts of Latin America are closest to the Equator? Which are farthest away?

Visualize Suppose that you were climbing a mountain. How would the vegetation you see change as you climb higher?

Vertical Climate Zones

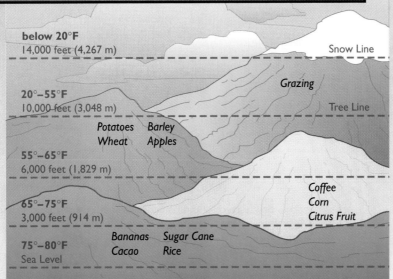

Diagram Study If you climb high enough on a mountain, you will reach a place where the temperature never warms up. This chart shows how the temperature near the Equator can vary with elevation. **Critical Thinking** Based on this chart, above what elevation will snow not melt?

below 20°F
14,000 feet (4,267 m)

Snow Line

Grazing

Tree Line

20°–55°F
10,000 feet (3,048 m)

Potatoes   Barley
Wheat   Apples

55°–65°F
6,000 feet (1,829 m)

Coffee
Corn
Citrus Fruit

65°–75°F
3,000 feet (914 m)

75°–80°F
Sea Level

Bananas   Sugar Cane
Cacao   Rice

SKILLS MINI LESSON

Drawing Conclusions
You may want to **introduce** the skill by telling students that they can combine what they already know with new knowledge to draw conclusions. To help students **practice** drawing conclusions, pose the following question: *The tropical rain forest is large and beautiful. Yet few people live there. Why?* (Vegetation is dense, and farming is difficult in both cleared and uncleared areas. The climate is hot and very humid.) Help students choose sound reasons to support their conclusions. Students can **apply** the skill to explain why desert plant growth is widely scattered. (There is not enough water to support many plants in one place.)

Global Perspectives

Vegetation Affects Climate
For hundreds of years, humans have understood that climate affects how crops and other plants grow. Early farmers chose crops that grew best in the local conditions, cool and dry or warm and wet. Now we understand that plants themselves can affect the climate, not just locally but worldwide. Trees, specifically the great numbers of trees in the tropical rain forest, are capable of removing huge amounts of carbon dioxide from the air and replacing it with oxygen. As a result, trees help keep the climatic temperature relatively constant. If huge stands of rain forest are removed from the Earth, it is likely that temperatures will rise over time.

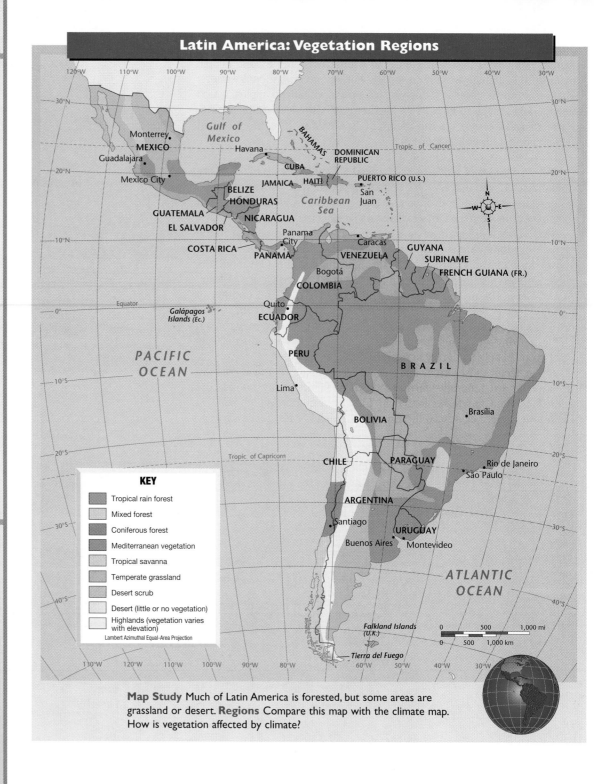

Latin America: Vegetation Regions

KEY
- Tropical rain forest
- Mixed forest
- Coniferous forest
- Mediterranean vegetation
- Tropical savanna
- Temperate grassland
- Desert scrub
- Desert (little or no vegetation)
- Highlands (vegetation varies with elevation)

Lambert Azimuthal Equal-Area Projection

Map Study Much of Latin America is forested, but some areas are grassland or desert. **Regions** Compare this map with the climate map. How is vegetation affected by climate?

Answers to...

MAP STUDY

- Responses should indicate that there is generally more vegetation in areas with warm, wet climates and less vegetation in areas with cold, dry climates.

Resource Directory

Teaching Resources

Section Quiz in the Chapter and Section Resources booklet, p. 8, covers the main ideas and key terms in the section. Available in Spanish in the Spanish Chapter and Section Resources booklet, p. 6.

Media and Technology

Planet Earth CD-ROM includes Natural Landscapes: Tropical Zones/Rain forest: The Amazon, which enhances students' understanding of this vegetation region.

Wind patterns affect the climate too. Winds move cold air from the North and South Poles toward the Equator. They also move warm air from the Equator toward the Poles. In the Caribbean, sea breezes blowing toward shore help to keep temperatures moderate. Winds also affect rainfall in the Caribbean. More rain falls on the sides of islands facing the wind than on sides facing away.

Natural Vegetation and Climate

Imagine a forest so dense and lush that almost no sunlight reaches the ground. Broad green leaves, tangled vines, and thousands of species of trees and plants surround you. The air is hot and heavy with moisture. Welcome to the Amazonian rain forest.

Now, suppose you have traveled to the coast of northern Chile. You're in the Atacama Desert. Winds carry no moisture to this barren land, and there is little sign of life. The Andes shield this parched region from rain. Parts of the desert have never felt a single raindrop.

Latin America's varied climate and physical features make such extremes possible. Look at the natural vegetation map on the previous page. How many different kinds of vegetation does the map show? Note which countries in Latin America have areas of tropical rain forest. Now, find these countries on the climate map. How do the tropical climate and heavy rainfall in these countries contribute to the vegetation that grows there?

Find Uruguay on the vegetation map and on the climate map. Uruguay's climate and vegetation have helped make sheep and cattle raising a key part of the country's economy.

Elevation also affects vegetation. For example, palm trees and fruit trees that grow well in the coastal plains of Mexico and Central America would not survive high in the Andes. To grow at higher elevations, plants must be able to withstand cooler temperatures, chill winds, and irregular rainfall.

Ask Questions What would you like to know about living in the rain forest?

▲ Tree sloths live in the rain forest trees. They rarely descend from the trees.

SECTION 2 REVIEW

1. **Define** (a) El Niño, (b) elevation.

2. **Identify** (a) Andes, (b) Atacama Desert, (c) Patagonia, (d) Amazonian rain forest.

3. Describe two climates in Latin America. Then explain how climate affects the vegetation that grows in those regions.

4. How do Latin America's climate and vegetation affect how and where the people live?

Critical Thinking

5. **Drawing Conclusions** In what ways would the life of a family living on a Caribbean island be different from a family living high in the Andes?

Activity

6. **Writing to Learn** Latin America has been called a land of extremes. Do you agree or disagree? Write a paragraph or more telling why. Begin with the following sentences: "Many people have called Latin America a land of extremes. I believe that . . ." Support your opinion with examples.

Section 2 Review

1. (a) warm ocean current that flows along the western coast of South America and affects weather patterns (b) the height of land above sea level

2. (a) mountain system extending along the western coast of South America (b) desert in Chile (c) plains region in southern South America (d) tropical rain forest in South America

3. Answers may vary. Sample answers: Tropical wet climates have tropical rain forest vegetation. Arid climates tend to have desert or desert scrub vegetation.

4. Accept reasonable responses. Possibilities may include the following: people living in cool mountain areas need warm clothes and shelter; climate and vegetation help determine whether an area is suitable for farming or ranching. Climate helps determine what types of crops can be raised.

5. Answers will vary. Responses should focus on how location, climate, and vegetation would affect the way families in two different locations live.

6. Answers will vary, but most students will agree. Students may contrast the barren desert with the lush rain forest, or the warm and steamy coastal lowlands with the cold and dry high mountains. Be sure students use specific examples.

SKILLS MINI LESSON

Organizing Information

To **introduce** the skill, suggest that students organize information by summarizing what they read. Point out that headings, pictures, maps, and charts can help them focus on important ideas and facts. To **practice** the skill, have students work in pairs to develop written summaries of Section 2. Indicate to students that (1) the summaries should incorporate the headings—rewritten using the students' own words—to present the most important ideas of each part of the text, and that (2) students should support these ideas with facts, details, and examples. Encourage students to **apply** the skill of organizing information as they read the next section.

Lesson Objectives

① Describe the four general climate categories found in Latin America.

② Use a regional map to identify and locate different climate zones.

Lesson Plan

1 Engage
Warm-Up Activity

To **introduce** the skill, ask a volunteer to read the opening paragraphs of the activity. Ask students to explain the difference between climate and weather.

Activating Prior Knowledge

Ask students why some people who live in the northern part of the United States go to Florida or southern California for vacation. Ask students what kinds of activities are popular with vacationers and why. Guide students in understanding that the mild climates of the two places are an important part of their appeal.

Using Regional Maps to Show Climate

f you could follow the Earth's weather for many years, no two years would look exactly alike. Think how the weather in your own location varies. Some years are colder, warmer, wetter, or drier than others. The same is true for every place on the planet.

Still, you could notice patterns in the weather. For example, one place may tend to have hot, rainy summers and cold, dry winters. Another place might be hot and dry all year round. The typical weather patterns in a location are called its climate.

Traveling across the Earth, you would find that no two places have exactly the same climate. Even the next town might be a degree cooler than your own. Still, you would find some similarities. Places in a large area that have similar weather make up a climate region.

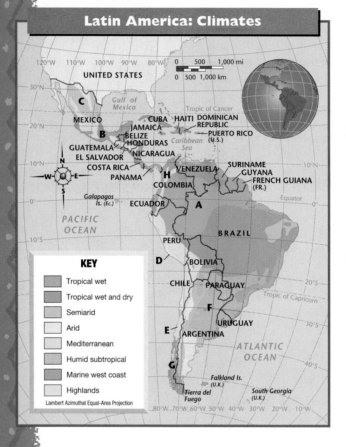

Latin America: Climates

KEY

- Tropical wet
- Tropical wet and dry
- Semiarid
- Arid
- Mediterranean
- Humid subtropical
- Marine west coast
- Highlands

Lambert Azimuthal Equal-Area Projection

Get Ready

A region's climate affects how its inhabitants live. Learning to read a climate map can help you understand what life is like in different regions of the world.

Try It Out

Climates in Latin America fall into four general categories: *tropical, dry, mild,* and *highland.* Read about the climates described below. Use the map to answer each question.

A. Find a tropical climate zone. Tropical climates are hot year round. There are two types. Tropical wet zones have rain nearly every day. Tropical wet and dry zones have a wet season and a dry season. Where are tropical wet and

Resource Directory

Teaching Resources

Social Studies and Geography Skills
Reading a Climate Map, p. 26

dry zones usually located in relation to tropical wet zones?

B. Find a dry climate. Dry climates have little rain. There are two types. Arid zones may go years without rain. Semiarid zones receive enough rain for short grasses to grow. Where are semiarid zones usually located in relation to arid zones?

C. Find a mild climate. Mild climates are more comfortable than tropical or dry climates. There are three types. Marine climates are wet and have only moderate changes in temperature during the year. Humid subtropical areas are also wet but warmer than marine climates. Mediterranean climates are warm, too, but only rainy in the winter. Where are mild climate regions usually located in relation to large bodies of water?

D. Find a highland climate. Highland climates are found in mountainous regions. In a highland climate, temperatures vary. The higher you climb up a mountain, the colder it gets. Where is South America's highland climate located?

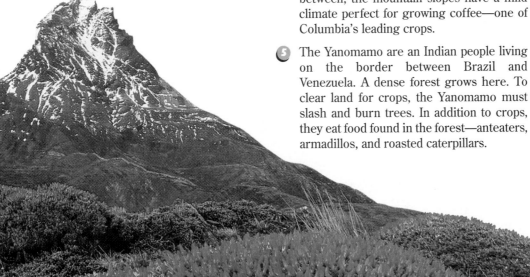

Apply the Skill

A region's climate can affect the kind of homes people build, the jobs they do, and the food they eat. Read the descriptions that follow. Then match each description with a letter on the map.

1. Few trees grow in Mexico's dry central region. Instead of building homes from wood, farmers often use sun-dried brick called adobe. Flat roofs are sometimes made of tile, straw, or sheet metal.

2. In the south of Mexico, more rain falls. The rain would eventually wash away an adobe home. So instead, some farmers build with wooden poles coated with a lime and clay mixture that keeps out the rain. Roofs are slanted so that rain water runs off.

3. Peru's west coast has one of the Earth's driest climates. To raise crops, farmers channel mountain streams to bring water to their fields.

4. Near the base of the Andes Mountains in Colombia, the weather is hot. High in the mountain peaks the climate is cold. In between, the mountain slopes have a mild climate perfect for growing coffee—one of Columbia's leading crops.

5. The Yanomamo are an Indian people living on the border between Brazil and Venezuela. A dense forest grows here. To clear land for crops, the Yanomamo must slash and burn trees. In addition to crops, they eat food found in the forest—anteaters, armadillos, and roasted caterpillars.

2 Explore

Ask students to read the paragraph under the Get Ready heading. Discuss with students how your region's climate affects the jobs people have, the sports that are popular, and even the clothes people wear.

3 Teach

Help students **practice** the skill by working with them to find answers to each of the questions in the Try It Out section.

A. Tropical wet and dry zones usually border or surround tropical wet zones.
B. Semiarid zones usually border or surround arid zones.
C. along coasts, in the southern part of South America
D. close to the west coast

For additional reinforcement, ask students to use the map to identify the climate types found in the following countries: Guyana (tropical wet); Uruguay (humid subtropical); Peru (arid, highlands, tropical wet, tropical wet and dry); Mexico (arid, semiarid, highlands, tropical wet and dry, tropical wet).

4 Assess

Have students **apply** the skill by completing the final part of the activity. To **assess,** evaluate students' accuracy in answering the questions.

SECTION ③

Natural Resources

BEFORE YOU READ

Reach Into Your Background

Do you know what natural resources are? They are things found in nature that people can use to meet their needs. For example, trees are a natural resource. List two other natural resources. Describe how people use each one.

Questions to Explore

1. What are Latin America's important natural resources?

2. Why is it important for Latin American nations to have more than one source of income?

Key Terms

hydroelectricity
diversify

Key Places

Jamaica
Venezuela
Brazil
Colombia
Chile

Bolivia has always depended on mineral resources for wealth. At first, silver helped to bring money into Bolivia's treasury. Soon, however, another metal became even more important than silver. That metal was tin.

For many years, Bolivia enjoyed the good times that wealth from tin brought. Then, in the 1920s and 1930s, a world-wide economic crisis hit. Industries stopped buying tin, as well as other natural resources. Bolivia suffered as its main resource failed to bring money into the economy. This economic crisis hit all of Latin America hard. It brought home a problem many Latin American nations have: They rely too much on one resource.

▼ Latin America has about 12 percent of the world's petroleum.

Latin America's Resources

What do the following items have in common? Fish, petroleum, water, silver, and bananas. You have probably guessed that all these items are natural resources of Latin America. Latin America's resources are as varied as its physical features and climate.

Mexico and Central America: Riches of Land and Sea

Mexico is a treasure chest of minerals. The country has deposits of silver, gold, copper, coal, iron ore, and just about any other mineral you can name. How many of these mineral resources can you find on the map on the next page? Mexico also has huge amounts of oil and natural gas. In addition, trees cover nearly a quarter of Mexico's land. Wood from these trees is turned into lumber and paper products.

Central America's climate and rich soil are good for farming. The people grow coffee, cotton, sugar cane, and bananas. They also plant cacao trees. Cacao seeds are made into chocolate and cocoa.

Not all of Central America's resources are on land. People catch fish and shellfish in the region's waters. Central Americans use the power of rushing water to produce electricity. This type of power is called **hydroelectricity** (hy droh ee lek TRIS ih tee). Countries build huge dams to harness and control the energy that rushing water produces.

The Caribbean: Sugar, Coffee, and More

Caribbean countries also have rich soil and a good climate for farming. Farmers grow sugar cane, coffee, bananas, cacao, citrus fruits, and other crops on the islands.

The Caribbean has other resources as well. For example, Jamaica is one of the world's main producers of bauxite—a mineral used to make aluminum. Cuba and the Dominican Republic have nickel deposits. Trinidad is rich in oil.

Drilling for Oil

Some of Mexico's petroleum reserves can only be reached through offshore drilling, or drilling into the ocean floor. **Interaction** What special precautions do you think that offshore drillers might have to take to avoid harming the environment?

Biography

Juan Domingo Perón One of South America's most famous leaders was Juan Domingo Perón (1895–1974). Perón served as president of Argentina from 1946 to 1955 and again from 1973 to 1974. Perón's goal was for Argentina to capitalize on its mineral resources, develop its industry, and increase its agricultural output. He also hoped to spread wealth more evenly among the people. Perón instituted reforms that benefited many workers. However, many of Perón's drastic reforms hurt Argentina economically.

Latin America: Natural Resources

KEY

Hydroelectric power		Coal	
Iron		Petroleum	
Copper		Uranium	
Bauxite		Tin	
Gold		Lead	
Silver		Nickel	

Lambert Azimuthal Equal-Area Projection

Map Study Natural resources are important to a country's economy because they can be sold to other countries or used to make products that can be sold. **Movement** Which countries have natural resources that are located close to waterways? How would this location make the resources more useful?

Answers to...

MAP STUDY

- Brazil, Cuba, Jamaica, Mexico, Peru, Chile, Paraguay, Uruguay, Venezuela, Colombia, Ecuador; Location close to waterways makes transporting resources easier. It is also easier to bring workers and equipment to the resources.

Resource Directory

Teaching Resources

Section Quiz in the Chapter and Section Resources booklet, p. 11, covers the main ideas and key terms in the section. Available in Spanish in the Spanish Chapter and Section Resources booklet, p. 8.

Vocabulary in the Chapter and Section Resources booklet, p. 13, provides a review of key terms in the chapter. Available in Spanish in the Spanish Chapter and Section Resources booklet, p. 10.

Reteaching in the Chapter and Section Resources booklet, p. 14, provides a structure for students who may need additional help in mastering chapter content.

Enrichment in the Chapter and Section Resources booklet, p. 15, extends chapter content and enriches students' understanding.

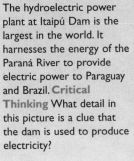

The hydroelectric power plant at Itaipú Dam is the largest in the world. It harnesses the energy of the Paraná River to provide electric power to Paraguay and Brazil. **Critical Thinking** What detail in this picture is a clue that the dam is used to produce electricity?

Daily Life

Living With Few Resources Although most of South America is rich in resources, little of the resource wealth reaches farmers in the Andes. Farmers sell some crops in city markets, but their main concern is to produce food for their families for the whole year. In many villages, people must hike to mountain streams to get drinking water. Houses are made entirely by hand of adobe or stone. They have thatched roofs. Families own few pieces of furniture and few possessions other than farming tools, cooking and eating utensils, and perhaps a single "luxury"—a battery-operated radio.

South America: A Wealth of Resources Like Mexico, South America is rich in minerals. It contains gold, copper, tin, bauxite, and iron ore. Businesses drill for oil in many South American countries. Much of South America's oil is found in Venezuela.

South America's plants and fish are natural resources, too. Forests cover about half the continent. Trees from these forests provide everything from wood for building to coconuts for eating. People harvest many rain forest plants to make medicines. Tuna, anchovies, and other fish are plentiful in the waters off the Pacific Coast.

Like other parts of Latin America, South America has rich soil. Farmers grow many different crops there. For example, coffee is a key crop in Brazil and Colombia. Wheat is important in Argentina. Many South American economies rely on the production of sugar cane, cotton, and rice.

Natural Resources and Latin America's Economy

Not every country shares in the wealth of Latin America's resources. Some Latin American countries have many resources, while others have few. Some countries do not have the money they need to develop all of their resources. Other countries rely too much on one resource or crop.

Sailors of the Seventh Century South Americans have been trading with the people of Mexico since at least A.D. 600. They sailed north from Ecuador, Colombia, and Peru on rafts. These adventurers traded not only goods, such as tweezers and bells, but also skills and ideas. For example, they taught people of Mexico how to make metal objects such as needles.

Reading Actively
You may **introduce** the skill by informing students that they can be active readers by asking themselves questions as they read. Looking for answers to the questions will help them focus on important points. Help students **practice** the skill by suggesting questions that they might ask themselves as they read: *What are the natural resources of the* *Caribbean? Why are these resources important? What role do people play in developing these resources?* Help students **apply** this skill by directing them to choose two pages of text and then write questions they might ask themselves while reading the information.

Answers to...

HARNESSING WATER POWER

- Power lines are visible.

Many Latin American economies are based on agriculture. Half of Colombia's exports are coffee, and one third of Honduras' exports are bananas. **Critical Thinking** What problems do you think one-crop economies face?

Expressing Problems Clearly *Suitable as an individual activity.* Encourage students to imagine that they are running for office in a Latin American nation. As a candidate, each must warn the nation of the possible dangers of depending on a single resource for money. Direct students to write a campaign speech on this topic. The speech should describe briefly and clearly the importance of having more than one source of income. Encourage students to use specific examples to make their point. *English Language Learner*

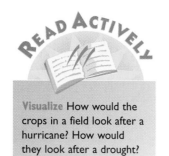

Visualize How would the crops in a field look after a hurricane? How would they look after a drought?

Prices, Weather, and Other Factors Depending on one resource or crop can lead to problems. For example, when world copper prices are high, the copper mining industry is very successful. But suppose copper prices drop sharply. Then copper exports are not worth as much. When this happens, the mining industry loses money. Mining workers may lose their jobs. Chile is the leading producer of copper in the world. When prices plunge, Chile's economy suffers.

Many people in Latin America make their living by farming. Some Latin American countries depend on one or two crops, such as coffee, bananas, or sugar. When the price of a crop goes down, exports of that crop bring less money into the country. As a result, workers' wages may drop, and some workers may lose their jobs.

Weather and disease also cause people and businesses to lose money. Hurricanes, droughts, and plant disease can damage crops. Weather sometimes hurts the fishing industry. The warm ocean current El Niño affects the fish that live in South America's coastal waters. Usually, the cold water of the Pacific supports a large number of small water plants on which the fish feed. When El Niño strikes, the warm water kills the plants and the fish die or move to other areas. Peru is among the countries affected by El Niño. Peruvian fishers have suffered great economic losses due to El Niño effects.

Answers to...

CASH CROP FARMING

- Responses should indicate that dependence on one crop makes the economies vulnerable to disasters such as drought or hurricanes. If the crop is an export crop, it is vulnerable to falling prices.

Resource Directory

Teaching Resources

Spanish Glossary in the Spanish Chapter and Section Resources, pp. 62–66, provides key terms translated from English to Spanish as well as definitions in Spanish.

Chapter Summary in the Chapter and Section Resources booklet, p. 12, provides a summary of chapter content. Available in Spanish in the Spanish Chapter and Section Resources booklet, p. 9.

Cooperative Learning Activity in the Activities and Projects booklet, pp. 20–23, provides two student handouts, one page of teacher's directions, and a scoring rubric for a cooperative learning activity on making a relief map.

Media and Technology

Guided Reading Audiotapes (English and Spanish)

Depending on Oil   Oil is one of Latin America's most valuable resources. But it is risky to depend on oil. Oil prices increase and decrease. Sometimes they change suddenly. Mexico, like Venezuela, is a major oil producer. In the mid-1980s, oil companies produced more oil than the world needed. As a result, prices dropped. Mexico earned much less income than it had expected. The same thing happened to Trinidad.

There are other problems as well. In the 1960s, people discovered oil in Ecuador. Soon, oil became the country's main export. But in 1987, earthquakes destroyed Ecuador's major oil pipeline. The country's income was slashed.

Avoiding the Problems of a One-Resource Country

Latin American nations know the risks of depending on one resource or crop. They are trying to diversify their economies. To **diversify** is to add variety. When Latin American nations try to diversify their economies, it means that they are looking for other ways to make money. Many are building factories. Factories make products that can be sold to bring more money into the economy. Factories also provide jobs for people.

Venezuela has been trying to set up more factories and farms. Venezuela is also improving its bauxite and iron mines. Ecuador passed a law to encourage industry. Businesses there built factories to make cloth, electrical appliances, and other products.

Brazil has also been building up its industries. That way Brazil does not have to depend on agriculture. Brazil now exports machinery, steel, and chemicals. Brazil has also encouraged cotton farming. As a result, cotton weaving has become a successful industry.

El Salvador used to depend too heavily on its coffee crop. Now, cotton, sugar, corn, and other crops play an important role in the nation's economy. Trinidad has also encouraged its farmers to raise more kinds of crops. The government realizes that the country depends too much on oil and sugar.

SECTION 3 REVIEW

1. **Define**   (a) hydroelectricity, (b) diversify.

2. **Identify**   (a) Jamaica, (b) Venezuela, (c) Brazil, (d) Colombia, (e) Chile.

3. **Describe** the important natural resources of Latin America.

4. Why is it important for Latin American nations to diversify their economies?

Critical Thinking

5. **Recognizing Cause and Effect**   Suppose a disease destroyed Colombia's coffee crop. How would this loss affect coffee-plantation workers and their families? How would it affect Colombia's economy?

Activity

6. **Writing to Learn**   Imagine that you are the president of a Latin American country. Your nation depends on bananas for nearly all of its income. What arguments would you use to persuade people to diversify?

Section 3 Review

1. (a) electricity generated by moving water (b) to add variety

2. (a) island country in the Caribbean (b) country in northern South America (c) largest country in South America (d) country in northwestern South America (e) country on the southwestern coast of South America

3. Important natural resources include oil and natural gas; fertile soil; fish; forests; and minerals such as copper, gold, bauxite, nickel, and iron.

4. Answers may vary but should reflect students' understanding of the danger of depending on only one resource. Sample answer: If that one resource is damaged or decreases in value, the country's economy would be severely hurt.

5. Answers may vary. Students may respond that workers would be unemployed and their families might not have enough money to live on. The coffee industry workers could no longer buy goods. Coffee shippers would have no coffee to ship, and the country would not have coffee to sell to other nations.

6. Answers will vary. Students' arguments should include mention of the danger of losing the banana crop to bad weather or disease or of the fact that another country might produce so many bananas that the price would drop.

Reviewing Main Ideas

1. The Caribbean, Mexico and Central America, and South America. Sample answers: The Caribbean is mostly islands; Mexico and Central America are mostly mountains and plateaus; South America is mostly mountains, plains, and forests.

2. Accept reasonable answers. For example, students may mention that mountains make travel difficult or that many islanders in the Caribbean rely on fishing for a living.

3. Climates are colder at higher elevations.

4. Accept reasonable answers. (a) Possibilities include: the warm, rainy weather near the equator helps create the lush vegetation of the rain forest. The dry, hot climate is responsible for the dry and barren deserts of Chile. (b) People within the rain forests can hunt or gather their food. Few people live in the desert regions of Latin America.

5. Resources provide a source of income for the nation and its people. The income allows both the nation and its people to purchase items they may need or want.

6. If the one source of income is reduced or lost, the country's economy would be severely hurt. Examples will vary.

7. Latin American nations are expanding their numbers of export crops and exploring and mining several sources of mineral wealth.

Reviewing Key Terms

1. e	**4.** d	**6.** c
2. b	**5.** g	**7.** a
3. f		

Critical Thinking

1. Accept reasonable answers. Students may mention that ample sun and rain help farmers grow crops, but hurricanes cause great destruction.

2. Most students will agree. Students' answers should reflect sound reasoning. For example, by encouraging cotton farming, Brazil has helped make cotton-weaving a successful industry. This means more jobs and more income for the nation.

CHAPTER 1

Review and Activities

Reviewing Main Ideas

1. List the three main regions of Latin America. Then choose two and describe their features.

2. In what ways do the physical features of Latin America affect the people and their way of life?

3. How does elevation affect climate?

4. (a) Give an example of how climate in one region of Latin America affects the vegetation that grows there.
(b) How does this affect the way in which people live?

5. How are a country's natural resources tied to its economy?

6. What problems arise when a country depends too heavily on a single source of income? Support your answer with one or two examples.

7. How are the nations of Latin America trying to avoid the problems of relying on a single source of income?

Reviewing Key Terms

Match the definitions in Column I with the key terms in Column II

Column I

1. height of land above sea level

2. plains in Argentina and Uruguay

3. to add variety

4. river or stream that flows into a larger body of water

5. electricity generated by the power of moving water

6. large raised area of mostly level land

7. narrow strip of land that has water on both sides and joins two larger bodies of land

Column II

a. isthmus

b. pampas

c. plateau

d. tributary

e. elevation

f. diversify

g. hydro-electricity

Critical Thinking

1. Identifying Central Issues Explain the meaning of this statement, and give examples: "The weather in Latin America is a great friend to the people, but also a terrible enemy."

2. Drawing Conclusions "How a country uses its natural resources affects the well-being of its people." Do you agree or disagree with this statement? Explain your answer.

Graphic Organizer

Copy the chart to the right onto a separate sheet of paper. Then fill in the empty boxes to complete the chart. Use the maps in this chapter to help you.

	Physical Features	Climate	Vegetation	Natural Resources
Mexico and Central America				
The Caribbean				
South America				

Graphic Organizer

Answers will vary. Some possible answers:

	Physical Features	Climate	Vegetation	Natural Resources
Mexico and Central America	mountains, lowlands, volcanoes	tropical wet and dry, semiarid	mixed forest, rain forest, Mediterranean	minerals, oil, trees
The Caribbean	mountains, volcanoes	tropical wet and dry	rain forest, temperate grassland	rich soil, bauxite
South America	Andes, Amazon River, pampas	tropical wet, tropical wet and dry, humid subtropical, highland, arid	rain forest, temperate grassland, arid, Mediterranean	minerals, oil, fish

Map Activity

For each place listed below, write the letter from the map that shows its location.

- Colombia
- Brazil
- Jamaica
- Mexico
- Venezuela

Latin America: Place Location

Writing Activity

Writing a Letter

Imagine that you are a visitor to Latin America. You are touring the whole region: Mexico, Central America, the Caribbean, and South America. Write a letter home, describing your trip. Write about such items as these: impressive sights, the weather, interesting facts you've learned, places you liked or didn't like.

Internet Activity

Use a search engine to find **The Green Arrow Guide to Central America.** Click on **El Salvador.** Click on **An Introduction to El Salvador** and read about El Salvador's geography and climate. Use the information to make a physical map of El Salvador.

Skills Review

Turn to the Skill Activity. Review the steps for reading a regional map. Then complete the following: (a) In your own words, describe two factors that vary from climate to climate. (b) What types of climates can be found in Latin America?

How Am I Doing?

Answer these questions to help you check your progress.

1. Can I identify and describe the main regions of Latin America?
2. Do I understand how Latin America's physical features, climate, and vegetation affect the people who live in the region?
3. Can I identify important natural resources of Latin America?
4. Can I explain why Latin American countries want to diversify their economies?
5. What information from this chapter can I use in my book project?

Map Activity

1. D   3. A   5. C
2. E   4. B

Writing Activity

Students should write about various places visited during their imaginary tour of Latin America. Letters should contain specific, descriptive details about the region. Students should support their opinions with reasons.

Skills Review

Answers will vary. Sample answer: Places at different distances from the equator and at different elevations have different climates. These include tropical wet, tropical wet and dry, semiarid, arid, Mediterranean, humid subtropical, marine west coast, and highlands.

Internet Link

If students are having difficulty finding this site, you may wish to have them use the following URL, which was accurate at the time this textbook was published:

http://www.greenarrow.com

You might also guide students to a search engine. Four of the most useful are AltaVista, Lycos, Infoseek, and Yahoo. For additional suggestions on using the Internet, refer to the Prentice Hall Social Studies' Educator's Handbook "Using the Internet," in the *Prentice Hall World Explorer Program Resources.*

For additional links to world geography and culture topics, visit the Prentice Hall Home Page at:

http://www.phschool.com.

How Am I Doing?

Point out to students that this checklist is a quick reminder for them of what they learned in the chapter. If their answer to any of the questions is *no* or if they are unsure, they may need to review the topic.

Resource Directory

Teaching Resources

Chapter Tests Forms A and B are in the Tests booklet, pp. 2–7.

Program Resources

Writing Process Handbook includes Writing Effective Paragraphs, pp. 27–28, to help students with the Writing Activity.

Media and Technology

Color Transparencies
Color Transparency 174
(Graphic organizer table template)

Prentice Hall Writer's Solution
Writing Lab CD-ROM

Computer Test Bank
Resource Pro™ CD-Rom

LITERATURE

The Surveyor

BY ALMA FLOR ADA

Lesson Objectives

1 Summarize a short story.

2 Relate a literary work to information about the country of its origin.

Lesson Plan

1 Engage

Building Vocabulary

Point out that notes in the margin can help students understand certain words and can give helpful hints as students read. Vocabulary defined in the margin include *surveyor* and *recruit*.

Ask students to read the title of the story and the definition of *surveyor* in the margin. Invite them to predict what the story will be about and where it might take place.

Activating Prior Knowledge

Read the paragraphs under the heading Before You Read with students. Discuss the value of family stories.

BEFORE YOU READ

Reach Into Your Background

Do people in your family tell you stories about interesting or exciting events that have happened to them? What stories do you remember the best? What do you learn from these stories?

The stories that family members tell each other become part of the family history. Family stories are important because they teach people about their cultural heritage. Alma Flor Ada grew up in Cuba. The following story shows what Ada learned from one of the stories her father used to tell her.

Questions to Explore

1. What can you learn from this story about family life in Cuba?

2. What does this story tell you about how geography affects people's lives in Cuba?

surveyor (sir VAY ur) *n.*: a person who measures land and geographic features

My father, named Modesto after my grandfather, was a surveyor. Some of the happiest times of my childhood were spent on horseback, on trips where he would allow me to accompany him as he plotted the boundaries of small farms in the Cuban countryside. Sometimes we slept out under the stars, stringing our hammocks between the trees, and drank fresh water from springs. We always stopped for a warm greeting at the simple huts of the neighboring peasants, and my eyes would drink in the lush green forest crowned by the swaying leaves of the palm trees.

Since many surveying jobs called for dividing up land that a family had inherited from a deceased parent or relative, my father's greatest concern was that justice be achieved. It was not enough just to divide the land into equal portions. He also had to ensure that all parties would have access to roads, to water sources, to the most fertile soil. While I was able to join him in some trips, other surveying work involved large areas of land. On these jobs, my father was part of a team, and I would stay home, eagerly awaiting to hear the stories from his trip on his return.

◀ The equipment that surveyors use must be strong and lightweight.

Latin American families tend not to limit their family boundaries to those who are born or have married into it. Any good friend who spends time with the family and shares in its daily experiences is welcomed as a member. The following story from one of my father's surveying trips is not about a member of my blood family, but instead concerns a member of our extended family.

Félix Caballero, a man my father always liked to recruit whenever he needed a team, was rather different from the other surveyors. He was somewhat older, unmarried, and he kept his thoughts to himself. He came to visit our house daily. Once there, he would sit silently in one of the living room's four rocking chairs, listening to the lively conversations all around him. An occasional nod or a single word were his only contributions to those conversations. My mother and her sisters sometimes made fun of him behind his back. Even though they never said so, I had the impression that they questioned why my father held him in such high regard.

Then one day my father shared this story.

"We had been working on foot in mountainous country for most of the day. Night was approaching. We still had a long way to go to return to where we had left the horses, so we decided to cut across to the other side of the mountain, and soon found ourselves facing a deep gorge. The gorge was spanned by a railroad bridge, long and narrow, built for the sugarcane trains. There were no side rails or walkways, only a set of tracks resting on thick, heavy crossties suspended high in the air.

"We were all upset about having to climb down the steep gorge and up the other side, but

READ ACTIVELY

Predict Why do you think that Ada's father admires Félix so much?

recruit (ree KROOT) v.: to enlist or hire to join a group
gorge (gorj) n.: a narrow canyon with steep walls
span (span) v.: to extend across a space

2 Develop Student Reading

Have volunteers read the Questions to Explore to the class. Then have students read the story.

After students have read the selection, have them discuss answers to the Questions to Explore.

1. Students may note the family's hospitality.
2. Students should note that the story is set in high mountains.

Background

About the Author

Alma Flor Ada was born in Camaguey, Cuba, where she had many relatives, including a grandmother who was the principal of both a school for children and a school for women. Dr. Ada lived in Spain and in Peru before moving to the United States. She now lives in California.

About the Selection

"Surveyor," appears in a collection of short stories, *Where the Flame Trees Bloom,* by Alma Flor Ada, Atheneum, 1994.

3 Assess

Work through the Exploring
Your Reading with students.

1. The author learns to
admire Felix for his courage
and calmness.

2. Land is very valuable.

3. He came to the house
daily; the father valued him.

4. A person's actions reveal
character.

5. He survived because he
was brave and thought calmly.

6. Acceptable stories will
have an introduction and a
conclusion explaining the
story's importance.
Outstanding stories will
describe events vividly.

▶ Walking across a rail-
road bridge is dangerous,
because most are just
wide enough for a train
to pass.

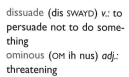

dissuade (dis SWAYD) *v.:* to
persuade not to do some-
thing
ominous (OM ih nus) *adj.:*
threatening

the simpler solution, walking
across the bridge, seemed too
dangerous. What if a cane train
should appear? There would be
nowhere to go. So we all began
the long descent . . . all except
for Félix. He decided to risk
walking across the railroad
bridge. We all tried to dissuade
him, but to no avail. Using an old
method, he put one ear to the
tracks to listen for vibrations.
Since he heard none, he decided
that no train was approaching.
So he began to cross the long
bridge, stepping from crosstie to
crosstie between the rails, balanc-
ing his long red-and-white surveyor's poles on his shoulder.

"He was about halfway across
the bridge when we heard the
ominous sound of a steam

engine. All eyes rose to Félix.
Unquestionably he had heard it,
too, because he had stopped in
the middle of the bridge and was
looking back.

"As the train drew closer, and
thinking there was no other solution, we all shouted, 'Jump!
Jump!', not even sure our voices
would carry to where he stood,
so high above us. Félix did look
down at the rocky riverbed,
which, as it was the dry season,
held little water. We tried to
encourage him with gestures and
more shouts, but he had stopped
looking down. We could not
imagine what he was doing next,
squatting down on the tracks,
with the engine of the train
already visible. And then, we
understood. . . .

"Knowing that he could not manage to hold onto the thick wooden crossties, Félix laid his thin but resilient surveyor's poles across the ties, parallel to the rails. Then he let his body slip down between two of the ties, as he held onto the poles. And there he hung, below the bridge, suspended over the gorge but safely out of the train's path.

"The cane train was, as they frequently are, a very long train. To us, it seemed interminable. . . . One of the younger men said he counted two hundred and twenty cars. With the approaching darkness, and the smoke and shadows of the train, it was often difficult to see our friend. We had heard no human sounds, no screams, but could we have heard anything at all, with the racket of the train crossing overhead?

"When the last car began to curve around the mountain, we could just make out Félix's lonely figure still hanging beneath the bridge. We all watched in relief and amazement as he pulled himself up and at last finished walking, slowly and calmly, along the tracks to the other side of the gorge."

After I heard that story, I saw Félix Caballero in a whole new light. He still remained as quiet as ever, prompting a smile from my mother and her sisters as he sat silently in his rocking chair. But in my mind's eye, I saw him crossing that treacherous bridge, stopping to think calmly of what to do to save his life, emerging all covered with soot and smoke but triumphantly alive—a lonely man, hanging under a railroad bridge at dusk, suspended from his surveyor's poles over a rocky gorge.

If there was so much courage, such an ability to calmly confront danger in the quiet, aging man who sat rocking in our living room, what other wonders might lie hidden in every human soul?

resilient (rih ZIL yunt) *adj.:* able to withstand shock and bounce back from changes

treacherous (TRECH ur us) *adj.:* dangerous

READ ACTIVELY

Visualize Visualize the team of surveyors as they watch the train go by. How do you think they looked? How might they have acted?

EXPLORING YOUR READING

Look Back

- How does this story change the way the author feels about Félix Caballero?

Think It Over

- Why is surveying land important in Cuba?

3. Why do you think that the author's family accepts Félix Caballero as a member of their extended family?

4. What lesson does the author of this story hope to teach?

Go Beyond

5. What does this story tell you about the character traits that help a person to act in an emergency?

Ideas for Writing: A Short Story

6. Choose a story that has been told to you by a family member or friend. Or, choose a story that you have told others about an event that happened to you. Write the story. Include an introduction and conclusion that explain why the story is important to you.

Shaped by Its History

To help you plan instruction, the chart below shows how teaching resources correspond to chapter content. Use the resources to vary instruction, add activities, or plan block schedules. Where appropriate, resources have **suggested time allotments** for students. Time allotments are approximate.

Managing Time and Instruction

		Latin America Teaching Resources Binder		World Explorer Program Resources Binder	
		Resource	**mins.**	**Resource**	**mins.**
1	**SECTION 1** **Early Civilizations of Middle America**	**Chapter and Section Support** Reproducible Lesson Plan, p. 18 Ⓢ Guided Reading and Review, p. 19 Ⓢ Section Quiz, p. 20	 20 25	**Outline Maps** Latin America physical map **Nystrom Desk Atlas** Ⓣ **Primary Sources and Literature Readings**	 20 20 40
	SKILL ACTIVITY **Using a Time Line**	**Social Studies and Geography Skills,** Reading a Time Line, p. 61	 30		
2	**SECTION 2** **The Incas People of the Sun**	**Chapter and Section Support** Reproducible Lesson Plan, p. 21 Ⓢ Guided Reading and Review, p. 22 Ⓢ Section Quiz, p. 23	 20 25	**Outline Maps** Latin America physical map	 20
3	**SECTION 3** **European Conquest**	**Chapter and Section Support** Reproducible Lesson Plan, p. 24 Ⓢ Guided Reading and Review, p. 25 Ⓢ Section Quiz, p. 26 **Social Studies and Geography Skills,** Reading a Historical Map, p. 28	 20 25 30		
4	**SECTION 4** **Independence**	**Chapter and Section Support** Reproducible Lesson Plan, p. 27 Ⓢ Guided Reading and Review, p. 28 Ⓢ Section Quiz, p. 29	 20 25		

5	**SECTION 5**
	Issues in Latin America Today
		Chapter and Section Support
		Reproducible Lesson Plan, p. 30
		Ⓢ Guided Reading and Review, p. 31
		Ⓢ Section Quiz, p. 32
		Critical Thinking Activity, p. 37
		Ⓢ Vocabulary, p. 34
		Reteaching, p. 35
		Enrichment, p. 36
		Ⓢ Chapter Summary, p. 33
		Tests
		Forms A and B Chapter Tests, pp. 8–13
			
			20
			25
			30
			20
			25
			25
			15
			
			40
				Outline Maps
				  Latin America political map
				Interdisciplinary Explorations
				Ⓣ *Fate of the Rain Forest*
				Writing Process Handbook
				  Writing Effective Paragraphs, pp. 27–28
					
					20
					
					25

Block Scheduling Folder
PROGRAM TEACHING RESOURCES

Activities and Projects

Block Scheduling
Program Support

Interdisciplinary Links

Resource Pro™ CD-ROM

Media and Technology

Media and Technology

Resource	mins.
⚫ 🖉 Ⓢ World Video Explorer	20
🖉 Planet Earth CD-ROM	20
⬛ Color Transparency 66	20
🖉 Planet Earth CD-ROM	20
⬛ Color Transparencies, Historical Map Set 4	20
⬛ Color Transparency 34	20
🎧 Ⓢ Guided Reading Audiotapes	20
⬛ Color Transparency 172	20
(Graphic organizer tree map template)	
🖉 The Writer's Solution CD-ROM	30
🖫 Computer Test Bank	30

T **Teaming Opportunity**
This resource is especially well-suited for teaching teams.

Ⓢ **Spanish**
This resource is also in Spanish Support.

🖉 **CD-ROM**

🖉 **Laserdisc**

⬛ **Transparency**

🖫 **Software**

⚫ **Videotape**

🎧 **Audiotape**

Assessment Opportunities

From Guiding Questions to Assessment   A series of Guiding Questions serves as an organizing framework for this book. The Guiding Questions that relate to this chapter are listed below. Section Reviews and Section Quizzes provide opportunities for assessing students' insights into these Guiding Questions. Additional assessments are listed below.

GUIDING QUESTIONS

- *What factors have affected cultures in Latin America?*
- *Why have many Latin Americans been moving to cities in recent years?*

ASSESSMENTS

Section 1

Students should be able to make a time line showing the development of the Mayan and Aztec civilizations in Middle America.

▶ **RUBRIC**   See the Assessment booklet for a rubric on assessing a time line.

Section 2

Students should be able to give an oral presentation on an Incan accomplishment of their choice.

▶ **RUBRIC**   See the Assessment booklet for a rubric on assessing an oral presentation.

Section 3

Students should be able to write an explanation of the effects of European rule on Native Americans in Latin America.

▶ **RUBRIC**   See the Assessment booklet for a rubric on assessing cause-and-effect statements.

Section 4

Students should be able to make a web that describes the people who led independence movements in Latin America.

▶ **RUBRIC**   See the Assessment booklet for a rubric on assessing graphic organizers.

Section 5

Students should be able to write a glossary of the key terms in the section.

▶ **RUBRIC**   See the Assessment booklet for a rubric on assessing a glossary.

Activities and Projects

Mental Mapping

What's Up? We are used to seeing maps that show North at the top of the map and South at the bottom. Early Arab maps, however, such as those used by Marco Polo to cross Asia, placed North at the bottom of the map. North is not really up, and South is not really down. "Up" is the top of a mountain or a high building.

Ask students to draw a map of the Americas on a sheet of notebook paper. Then ask them to turn their sketch upside down. Encourage discussion of how this map looks. Then ask them to draw the map again, this time placing South at the top of the page as they draw. How does their sense of South America, Central America, and Mexico change as they create this map and look at it? Invite them to speculate on the possible impact of portraying some parts of the world on the top and others on the bottom.

Links to Current Events

Issues in the News Provide one or more issues of major newspapers (such as *The New York Times, The Wall Street Journal, The Washington Post, Los Angeles Times,* or *Chicago Tribune*) and news magazines such as *Time, Newsweek,* and *U.S. News and World Report.* Periodicals need not be the current issue, but should be less than a year old. Ask students to look through periodicals to see what kinds of issues are discussed in United States news coverage of Latin America.

Have students create a chart listing the kinds of issues. Ask students whether they think these are the issues that people in Latin America are most likely to read or hear about in their own newspapers and TV news programs. Encourage students to discuss why or why not.

Hands-On Activities

History Speaks The countries of this region are called "Latin America" because most people in this region speak languages that come from Latin, such as Spanish, Portuguese, or French.

Using a large bulletin-board sized map of Latin America, have students use colored pins or tags to mark the countries where each language is spoken. Encourage students to check their knowledge by referring to almanacs, encyclopedias, or other sources. Have students note other languages they find in this region (such as Dutch and English).

Invite students to suggest the reasons for these language differences. You might extend this activity by having students locate European countries or countries in other parts of the world where these languages are spoken.

Illustrated Time Line Hang a long, narrow piece of paper marked with dates from A.D. 100 to 2000 marked at 100 year intervals. Invite students to place illustrations of events or people on the line as they learn about them in this chapter. Students should add and correctly position a specific date or range of dates to the line. Students may make their own illustrations or use illustrations clipped or photocopied from other sources. *Basic*

Pot Luck Have students find recipes that incorporate foods from both sides of the Columbian Exchange (possibilities include wheat, barley, beef, honey from Europe; tomatoes, potatoes, corn, choco-late, oranges from the Americas). Have them prepare a recipe and bring it to class. Invite them to identify the country the recipe came from. *English Language Learners*

Wish You Were Here Each country of Latin America has its own culture and history. Have students create a bulletin board of postcards from as many countries in the region as they can. They may use actual postcards, if they are available. They may also create postcards with their own drawings or clippings. Each postcard should illustrate an historic landmark or physical feature of a country in Latin America. *Average*

Technology Past and Present The peoples of Central and South America did not have the wheel, yet they overcame major physical barriers to build great cities. Suggest that students visit a construction site (from a safe distance) and note the many uses of wheels they observe. Have them do research to find out how the Aztecs, Incas, and other urban peoples of pre-Columbian America constructed cities without the wheel. Students may present their findings in the form of an illustrated report or by building models of some of the technology used. *Challenging*

F.Y.I.

This page can help you extend your own and students' understanding of the concepts in this chapter. You may want to browse through some of the suggestions in the **Bibliography**. **Interdisciplinary Links** can connect social studies understanding to areas elsewhere in the curriculum through the use of other Prentice Hall products. **National Geography Standards** reflected specifically in this chapter are listed for your convenience. Some hints about appropriate **Internet Access** are also provided. **School to Careers** provides insights into the practical uses of some of the concepts in this chapter as they might pertain to various careers.

BIBLIOGRAPHY

FOR THE TEACHER

Arnold, Caroline. *City of the Gods: Mexico's Ancient City of Teotihuacán.* Clarion, 1994.

Baquedano, Elizabeth. *Aztec, Inca, and Maya.* Dorling, 1993. Eyewitness Series.

Fritz, Jean et al. *The World in 1492.* Holt, 1992.

Stein, R. Conrad. *The Mexican Revolution: 1910–1920.* New Discovery, 1994.

FOR THE STUDENT

Easy
Defrates, Joanna. *What Do We Know About the Aztecs?* Bedrick, 1995.

Average
Garcia, Guy. *Spirit of the Maya: A Boy Explores His People's Mysterious Past.* Walker, 1995.

Wood, Marion. *Growing Up in Aztec Times.* Troll, 1993.

Wood, Tim. *The Aztecs.* Viking, 1992.

Challenging
Meyer, Carolyn and Charles Gallenkamp. *The Mystery of the Ancient Maya.* McElderry, 1995. (New ed.)

LITERATURE CONNECTION

Dorris, Michael. *Morning Girl.* Hyperion, 1992.

DeTreviño, Elizabeth Borton. *El Güero: A True Adventure Story.* Farrar, 1989.

INTERDISCIPLINARY LINKS

Subject	Theme: History
MATH	Middle Grades Math: Tools for Success Course 2, Lesson 10–4, **Independent and Dependent Events** Course 3, Lesson 1–1, **Graphing Integers on the Number Line**
SCIENCE	Prentice Hall Science *Evolution: Change Over Time*, Lesson 1–1, **Fossils: Clues to the Past** *Ecology: Earth's Living Resources*, Lesson 2–3, **Cycles of Change: Ecological Succession**
LANGUAGE ARTS	Choices in Literature *You Are the Solution*, **Popocatepetl and Ixtlaccihuatl** *Where Paths Meet*, **Achieving the American Dream**

NATIONAL GEOGRAPHY STANDARDS

Students explore the 18 National Geography Standards throughout Latin America. Chapter 2, however, concentrates on investigating the following: standards 1, 9, 10, 11, 12, 13, 14, 16, 17. For a complete list of the standards, see the *Teacher's Flexible Planning Guide*.

SCHOOL TO CAREERS

In Chapter 2 Latin America: Shaped by Its History, students learn about the early civilizations of Middle America and the European conquest and colonization. Additionally, they address the skill of using a time line. Understanding history can help students prepare for careers in education, publishing, journalism, and so on. Time line reading skills are particularly helpful for teachers, writers, editors, reporters, and others. The curriculum presented in this book, as in all eight titles of Prentice Hall's *World Explorer* program, is designed to prepare students not only for careers but also for good citizenship—of the world as well as of this country.

INTERNET ACCESS

Many social studies teachers and students use Internet browsers, or search engines, to investigate particular topics. For the best results, use narrow rather than broad topics. Try these for Chapter 2: Incan civilization, Tenochtitlán, Mexican revolution, Christopher Columbus. Finding age-appropriate sites is an important consideration when using the Internet. For links to age-appropriate sites in world studies and geography, visit the Prentice Hall Home Page at: http://www.phschool.com

CHAPTER 2

LATIN AMERICA

Shaped by Its History

Connecting to the Guiding Questions

As students complete this chapter, they will focus on the history of Latin America, tracing highlights of ancient cultures and European conquests. Content in this chapter thus corresponds to the following Guiding Questions:

● What factors have affected culture in Latin America?

● Why have many Latin Americans been moving to the city in recent years?

Using the Map Activities

As students complete the map activities, point out that great civilizations have existed in Latin America.

- (a) Incan, Mayan, and Aztec. (b) Mayan.

- Possible response: Mayan, because it could be attacked by land from two directions and from both seacoasts.

Heterogeneous Groups

The following Teacher's Edition strategies are suitable for heterogeneous groups.

Cooperative Learning
Talking With Liberators   p. 53

Interdisciplinary Connections
Science   p. 58

Critical Thinking
Recognizing Cause
and Effect   p. 45
Distinguishing Fact
From Opinion   p. 57

KEY

Aztec Empire
A.D. 1200s–A.D. 1521

Mayan Empire
A.D. 300–A.D. 900

Incan Empire
A.D. 1400s–A.D. 1535

Lambert Azimuthal Equal-Area Projection

0   600   1,200 mi
0   600   1,200 km

MAP ACTIVITIES

This map shows the location of three civilizations in Latin America that existed before Europeans arrived in the region.

Study the map
(a) What are the names of the civilizations shown on the map?
(b) Which civilization is the oldest?

Consider the geography
Which civilization do you think was the most difficult to defend from invaders? Explain your answer.

Resource Directory

Media and Technology

 **A Trip to: Ruins of the Maya,** from the World Video Explorer, enhances students' understanding of ancient Mayan culture and its contributions to Latin America culture today.

Chapter 4

Early Civilizations of Middle America

BEFORE YOU READ

Reach Into Your Background

What does the word *pyramid* bring to mind? Write down three things you know about pyramids. Then, compare what you know about pyramids with the pyramids you will read about in this section.

Questions to Explore

1. What were the chief characteristics and accomplishments of Mayan and Aztec civilizations?

2. How have Latin America's early civilizations affected present-day cultures in Latin America?

Key Terms

maize
hieroglyphics

Key Places

Copán
Tikal
Valley of Mexico
Tenochtitlán

Lesson Objectives

1. Describe the chief characteristics and accomplishments of Mayan and Aztec civilizations.

2. Explain how Latin America's early civilizations have affected present-day cultures in Latin America.

Lesson Plan

1 Engage

Warm-Up Activity

Write the word *civilization* on the board. Ask students to list all the things that they think of when they hear this word. When students have finished their lists, call on volunteers to write their responses on the chalkboard. Invite discussion.

Activating Prior Knowledge

Have students read Reach Into Your Background in the Before You Read box. Tell students that, generally, a civilization is a culture that has built cities and has developed a writing system, the arts, the sciences, and a system of education. The culture also generally has a government, public buildings, and thriving commerce. Ask students to name some features of American civilization. (Sample responses: airplane, Washington D.C.)

Fans cheered as the players brought the ball down the court. Suddenly, the ball flew into the air and sailed through the hoop. Fans and players shouted and screamed. Although this may sound like a championship basketball game, it is actually a moment of a game played over 1,000 years ago. The game was called pok-a-tok.

Pok-a-tok was a game played by the ancient Mayas. Using only their leather-padded hips and elbows, players tried to hit a five-pound (1.9 kg), six-inch (15.2 cm) rubber ball through a stone hoop mounted 30 feet (9.1 m) above the ground.

▼ This pok-a-tok court is in Copán, Honduras. How is it similar to a basketball court?

Mayan Civilization

How do we know about this ancient game? Crumbling ruins of pok-a-tok courts and ancient clay statues of players have been found at sites in Central America and southern Mexico. In these areas, Mayan civilization thrived from about A.D. 300 to A.D. 900. By studying ruins, scientists have learned much about Mayan civilization.

Answers to...

POK-A-TOK COURT

• Both courts are rectangular and open, each has a space for an audience.

Teaching Resources

📁 **Reproducible Lesson Plan** in the Chapter and Section Resources booklet, p. 18, provides a summary of the section lesson.

📁 **Guided Reading and Review** in the Chapter and Section Resources booklet, p. 19, provides a structure for mastering key concepts and reviewing key terms in the section. Available in Spanish in the Spanish Chapter and Section Resources booklet, p. 12.

Media and Technology

Planet Earth CD-ROM includes World Wonders, Cultural: Chichen Itza, which enhances students' understanding of the Mayan people.

Program Resources

Material in the *Primary Sources and Literature Readings* booklet extends content with a selection from the region under study.

2 Explore

Have students read the section and use the illustrations to investigate the Mayan and Aztec civilizations. Students should find supporting details for the following headings: Major Achievements, Reasons for Decline, Influences on Today.

3 Teach

Have students create two concept maps, one entitled *Mayas,* and the other, *Aztecs.* The maps should include facts for subtopics such as Cities, Achievements, Decline, Influence on Latin American Empire, and Religion. Discuss how the achievements of the two civilizations have influenced students' lives. Activity should take about 30 minutes.

4 Assess

See answers to the Section Review. You may also use students' completed concept maps as an assessment, evaluating the maps on the basis of number of facts and overall organization.

Background

Global Perspectives

Hieroglyphics The term *hieroglyph,* meaning "sacred carving," was used by the Greeks to describe the characters on Egyptian monuments. Eventually, *hieroglyphic* was applied to the picture-writing of other cultures, such as the Mayas. The Mayan writing system is pictorial, but bears no other relation to Egyptian hieroglyphics.

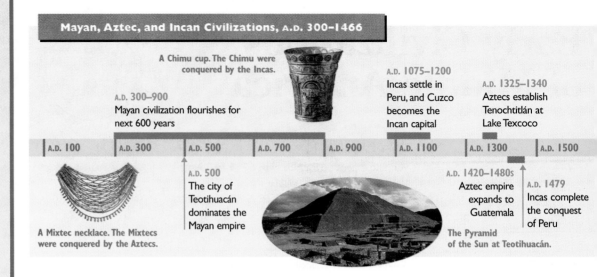

Mayan, Aztec, and Incan Civilizations, A.D. 300–1466

A Chimu cup. The Chimu were conquered by the Incas.

A.D. 300–900
Mayan civilization flourishes for next 600 years

A.D. 1075–1200
Incas settle in Peru, and Cuzco becomes the Incan capital

A.D. 1325–1340
Aztecs establish Tenochtitlán at Lake Texcoco

A.D. 100 · A.D. 300 · A.D. 500 · A.D. 700 · A.D. 900 · A.D. 1100 · A.D. 1300 · A.D. 1500

A Mixtec necklace. The Mixtecs were conquered by the Aztecs.

A.D. 500
The city of Teotihuacán dominates the Mayan empire

A.D. 1420–1480s
Aztec empire expands to Guatemala

A.D. 1479
Incas complete the conquest of Peru

The Pyramid of the Sun at Teotihuacán.

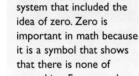

The Concept of Zero The Mayas created a numbering system that included the idea of zero. Zero is important in math because it is a symbol that shows that there is none of something. For example, to write the number 308, you need a symbol to show that there are no tens. Mathematicians consider the idea of zero to be one of the world's greatest inventions.

The Mayas built great cities. One such city was Copán (ko PAHN) in the present-day country of Honduras. Another was Tikal (tee KAHL) in present-day Guatemala. Mayan cities were religious centers. A large pyramid-shaped temple stood in the center of the city. The Mayas worshipped their gods there. Farmers worked in fields surrounding the cities. Past the fields lay the dense tropical rain forest.

Mayan Farming and Science The Mayan farmers' most important crop was **maize,** or corn. Maize was the main food of the Mayas. They also grew beans, squash, peppers, avocados, and papayas. Mayan priests studied the stars and planets. They designed an accurate calendar, which they used to decide when to hold religious ceremonies. The Mayan calendar was more accurate than any used in Europe until the 1700s. The Mayas developed a system of writing using signs and symbols called **hieroglyphics** (hy ur oh GLIF iks). They also developed a number system that is similar to the present-day decimal system.

The Great Mystery of the Mayas About A.D. 900, the Mayas suddenly left their cities. No one knows why. Crop failures, war, disease, drought, or famine may have killed many Mayas. Or perhaps people rebelled against the control of the priests and nobles. The Mayas left their cities, but stayed in the region. Millions of Mayas still live in the countries of Mexico, Belize, Guatemala, Honduras, and El Salvador.

Aztec Civilization

Another ancient civilization of Middle America is that of the Aztecs. They arrived in the Valley of Mexico in the 1100s. The Valley of Mexico is in Central Mexico and includes the site of present-day Mexico City.

Resource Directory

Media and Technology

 Color Transparency 66

Program Resources

Nystrom Desk Atlas

Outline Maps Latin America physical map

The Aztecs wandered about the valley looking for a permanent home until 1325. They finally settled on an island in Lake Texcoco. They changed the swampy lake into a magnificent city, which they called Tenochtitlán (tay nawch tee TLAHN). Tenochtitlán stood on the site of present-day Mexico City.

Tenochtitlán

Tenochtitlán, the Aztec capital, was built in the center of a lake. The Aztecs built floating islands by piling rich earth from the bottom of the lake onto rafts made of wood. After a while, the roots of plants and trees grew down to the lake bottom, anchoring the rafts. Some islands were the size of football fields. What do you think it would be like to live on a lake?

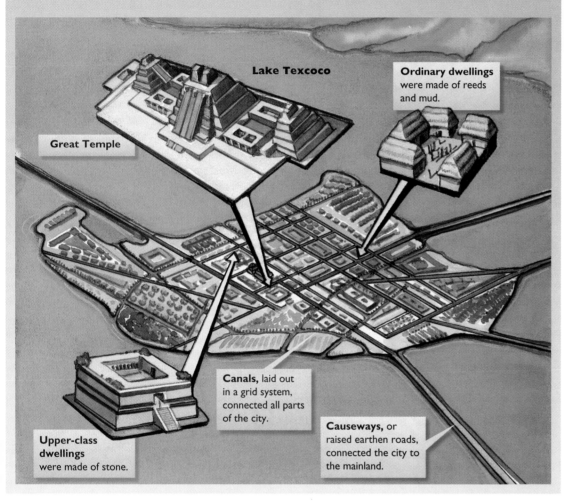

Lake Texcoco

Ordinary dwellings were made of reeds and mud.

Great Temple

Canals, laid out in a grid system, connected all parts of the city.

Causeways, or raised earthen roads, connected the city to the mainland.

Upper-class dwellings were made of stone.

SKILLS MINI LESSON

Interpreting Diagrams As a way to **introduce** the skill, tell students that a picture or diagram can help explain a complex idea or process or how something is organized. Direct students' attention to the diagram of Tenochtitlán. Suggest that students **practice** the skill by finger-tracing the wall that defined the heart of the city or locating causeways that connected the islands. Encourage students to **apply** the skill by using the diagram to find out how all parts of the city were connected.

Aztec Astronomy

The Aztecs observed the stars and planets carefully. They named them after their gods, like Quetzalcoatl, shown at right. The Aztecs used their knowledge of astronomy to make calendars like the one below.

The Aztecs Expand Their Empire In the 1400s, Aztec warriors began conquering the other people in the region. They forced the people they conquered to pay tribute, or taxes. Tribute could be paid in food, cotton, gold, or slaves. The Aztecs grew rich from the tribute.

The Aztecs had an emperor who ruled over all Aztec lands. The rest of Aztec society had several classes. Nobles and priests helped the emperor. Warriors fought battles. Traders carried goods throughout the empire and beyond. Craftworkers created jewelry, garments, pottery, sculptures, and other goods. Most people, however, were farmers.

Other Aztec Accomplishments Tenochtitlán was a center of trade and learning. Aztec doctors made more than 1,000 medicines from plants. They used the medicines to lower fevers, cure stomachaches, and heal wounds. Like the Mayas, Aztec astronomers predicted eclipses and the movements of planets. Aztec priests kept records using hieroglyphics similar to those used by the Mayas.

SECTION 1 REVIEW

1. Define (a) maize, (b) hieroglyphics.

2. Identify (a) Copán, (b) Tikal, (c) Valley of Mexico, (d) Tenochtitlán.

3. What were the main features of Mayan civilization?

4. How was Aztec society organized?

Critical Thinking

5. Distinguishing Fact From Opinion Tell if the following statements are facts or opinions. Explain why. (a) Mayan calendars were very accurate. (b) Aztec civilization was more advanced than Mayan civilization.

Activity

6. Writing to Learn What are some reasons for the decline of Mayan and Aztec civilizations? Does every society decline sooner or later?

The Incas

PEOPLE OF THE SUN

Section 2

BEFORE YOU READ

Reach Into Your Background

The United States has roads that run from state to state. These roads are called inter-state highways. Think about some ways that interstate highways are useful. Then, compare what you know about interstate highways with the roads you will read about in this section.

Questions to Explore

1. What was Incan civilization like?

2. How did the Incas interact with and change their environment to increase farmland and farm production?

Key Terms

aqueduct   quipu

Key People and Places

Pachacuti   Cuzco
Topa Inca

The runner sped along the mountain road. He lifted a horn made from a shell to his lips and blew. A second runner appeared and began running beside him. Without stopping, the first runner relayed to the second runner the message he carried. The second runner took off like the wind. He would not stop until he reached the next runner.

The Incas used runners to spread news from one place in their empire to another. Incan messengers carried news at a rate of 250 miles (402 km) a day. Without these runners, controlling the vast empire would have been very difficult.

The Rise of the Incas

This great and powerful empire had small beginnings. In about 1200, the Incas settled in Cuzco (KOOS koh), a village in the Andes that is now a city in the country of Peru. Most Incas were farmers. They grew maize and other crops. Through wars and conquest, the Incas won control of the entire Cuzco valley, one of many valleys that extend from the Andes to the Pacific Ocean.

In 1438, Pachacuti (PAHTCH an koo tee) became ruler of the Incas. The name Pachacuti means "he who shakes the earth." Pachacuti conquered the people who lived near the Pacific Ocean, from Lake Titicaca north to the city of Quito.

▼ The Incas shaped their stones so well that they did not need cement to hold a wall together.

Teaching Resources

📁 **Reproducible Lesson Plan** in the Chapter and Section Resources booklet, p. 21, provides a summary of the section lesson.

📁 **Guided Reading and Review** in the Chapter and Section Resources booklet, p. 22, provides a structure for mastering key concepts and reviewing key terms in the section. Available in Spanish in the Spanish Chapter and Section Resources booklet, p. 14.

Section 2

Lesson Objectives

1. Identify three main features of Incan civilization.

2. Explain how the Incas altered their environment to increase farm production.

Lesson Plan

1 Engage

Warm-Up Activity

Ask students to complete the following: *Americans, People of _____.* Tell them to fill in the blank with a term that they think best tells what is important to people in the United States today. Call on volunteers to share their statements.

Activating Prior Knowledge

Have students read Reach Into Your Background in the Before You Read box. Lead students to the conclusion that interstate highways make travel easier between cities. Bring out the point that goods, information, and people all use the highways.

2 Explore

Have students read the section to learn about the achievements of the Incas. Ask students why they think the Incas might have been referred to as "People of the Sun." Some students might indicate that the sun was important to the Incas because farming was their main way of making a living. Others might indicate that the sun was important to them as a god.

3 Teach

Provide students with the following topic sentence: *The Incas used their environment wisely.* Have students use the information in the section to write a paragraph that supports the topic sentence. Use volunteers' paragraphs as discussion springboards. This activity should take about 20 minutes.

4 Assess

See answers to the Section Review. You may also use students' paragraphs as an assessment.

Acceptable paragraphs list three achievements of the Incas.

Commendable paragraphs describe four or more achievements, including those in farming.

Outstanding paragraphs show an understanding of how the Incas altered their environment, both to increase farm productivity and to maintain a widespread empire.

Connect How do your family and community depend on roads?

▼Pachacuti built many cities. The most famous one is the "lost city" of Machu Picchu. It lies high in the Andes Mountains, 54 miles (87 km) northwest of Cuzco.
Interaction Look closely at the picture. How did the Incas adapt their city to the mountains?

Pachacuti demanded loyalty from the people he conquered. If they proved disloyal, he forced them off their land. He replaced them with people loyal to the Incas.

Pachacuti's son, Topa Inca, expanded the empire. In time, it stretched some 2,500 miles (4,023 km) from what is now Ecuador south along the Pacific coast through Peru, Bolivia, Chile, and Argentina. The 12 million people ruled by the Incas lived mostly in small villages.

Incan Accomplishments

The Incas were excellent farmers, builders, and managers. Their capital, Cuzco, was the center of government, trade, learning, and religion. In the 1500s, one of the first Spaniards to visit Cuzco described it as "large enough and handsome enough to compare to any Spanish city."

The emperor, and the nobles who helped him run the empire, lived in the city near the central plaza. They wore special headbands and earrings that showed their high rank. Most of the farmers and workers outside Cuzco lived in mud huts.

Roads and Aqueducts The Incas built more than 19,000 miles (30,577 km) of roads. The roads went over some of the most mountainous land in the world. The road system helped the Incas to govern their vast empire. Not only did runners use the roads to deliver messages, but Incan armies and trade caravans also used the roads for speedy travel.

Answers to...

MACHU PICCHU, LOST CITY OF THE INCAS

• Students should recognize that like Incan farm land, the city is terraced.

The Incas used quipus to record information about births, deaths, trade, and taxes. **Critical Thinking** Think of some other ways to communicate information without using spoken or written words.

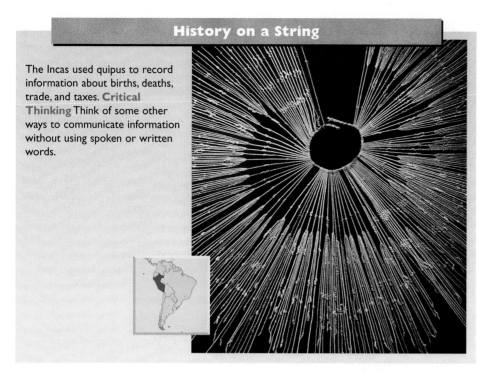

The Incas also built canals and aqueducts to carry water to dry areas. An **aqueduct** is a pipe or channel designed to carry water from a distant source. One stone aqueduct carried water from a mountain lake almost 500 miles (805 km) to its destination. The system of canals and aqueducts allowed the Incas to irrigate land that was otherwise too dry to grow crops.

Government and Records The Incas organized their government carefully. The emperor chose nobles to govern each province. Each noble conducted a census to count people so they could be taxed. Local officials collected some of each village's crops as a tax. The villagers also had to work on government building projects. However, the government took care of the poor, the sick, and the elderly.

The Incas did not have a written language. Incan government officials and traders recorded information on knotted strings called **quipus** (KEE poos). Every quipu had a main cord with several colored strings attached to it. Each color represented a different item, and knots of different sizes at certain intervals stood for numbers.

Religion Like the Mayas and the Aztecs, the Incas worshipped many gods. The sun god, Inti, was an important god of the Incas. They believed Inti was their parent. They referred to themselves as "children of the sun." Another important Incan god was Viracocha (vee ra KOCH ah), the creator of all the people of the Andes.

LINKS ACROSS TIME

Earthquake-proof Buildings Incan stone walls were so firmly constructed that even violent earthquakes could not knock them down. The walls swayed but did not crumble the way some modern buildings do. Engineers today are learning to make buildings that can resist an earthquake.

Section 2 Review

1. (a) a pipe or channel designed to carry water from a distant source (b) knotted strings used by the Incas to keep records

2. (a) Incan ruler who demanded loyalty from the people he conquered (b) ruler who expanded the Incan empire (c) Incan capital

3. Roads connected all parts of the empire. This made travel easier for the army, traders, and especially the message runners.

4. Sample answer: The Incas worshipped many gods. The main god, Inti, was the sun god.

5. Sample response: Being in the valley would make it difficult to defend the empire. The mountains would help keep enemies from attacking the empire.

6. Students' lists might include building aqueducts to carry water to dry areas to make farming possible and building terraces in hilly areas. Students might indicate that Incas used their environment wisely.

Answers to...

FARMING IN THE MOUNTAINS

- Responses will vary. Sample answers: plowing terraces might be difficult; there may be less direct sunlight because mountain peaks cast shadows; cold weather may last longer than in non-mountain regions.

The Incas increased the amount of farmland in hilly areas by building terraces into the sides of steep slopes. The terraces helped keep soil from washing down the mountain. These terraces are at Pasaq, an ancient Incan fortress in Peru. **Interaction** Think of some other reasons why farming in the mountains might be hard.

Quechua Descendants of the Incas The Spanish conquered the Incan empire in the 1500s. However, descendants of the Incas still live in present-day Peru, Ecuador, Bolivia, Chile, and Colombia. They speak Quechua (KECH wah), the Incan language.

They use farming methods that are like those of the ancient Incas. The Incan culture also survives in the poncho and in other clothing styles, as well as in cloth woven into brightly colored complex patterns.

SECTION 2 REVIEW

1. **Define** (a) aqueduct, (b) quipu.

2. **Identify** (a) Pachacuti, (b) Topa Inca, (c) Cuzco.

3. Why was a good network of roads important to the Incan empire?

4. Describe a few features of the Incan religion.

Critical Thinking

5. **Drawing Conclusions** Look at the shape of the Incan empire on the map on the opening page of this chapter. In an attack, what features would make the empire difficult to defend? What features would help defend the empire?

Activity

6. **Writing to Learn** Make a list of some of the ways the Incas used land for farming. Do you think the Incas made good use of farmland? Why or why not?

Resource Directory

Teaching Resources

Section Quiz in the Chapter and Section Resources booklet, p. 23, covers the main ideas and key terms in the section. Available in Spanish in the Spanish Chapter and Section Resources booklet, p. 15.

European Conquest

to do. As you read this section, notice how the people made decisions. Think about whether or not you agree with the decisions they made.

Reach Into Your Background

How do you decide what is right and what is wrong? Think of a time when you were not sure what was the right thing

Questions to Explore

1. Why did Europeans sail to the Americas?
2. What were the effects of European rule on Native Americans in the region?

Key Terms

Treaty of Tordesillas
treaty
Line of Demarcation
conquistador
mestizo
hacienda
encomienda

Key People

Hernan Cortés
Malinche
Christopher Columbus
Moctezuma
Francisco Pizarro

Hernan Cortés was the Spanish soldier who conquered the Aztecs. He landed in Mexico in 1519 and soon met Malinche (mah LIHN chay). She was the daughter of a Mayan leader. Malinche, whom Cortés called Doña Marina, spoke several languages in addition to Mayan. She quickly learned Spanish. Malinche became Cortés's main translator. She also kept an eye on Aztec spies. Without Malinche, Cortés could not have conquered the Aztecs. Why did European explorers, like Cortés, want to conquer Native Americans? Why did some Native Americans, like Malinche, help the conquerers?

Europeans Arrive in the Americas

In the 1400s, Spain and Portugal searched for new trade routes to Asia. They knew that in Asia they would find expensive goods such as spices and silks. These goods could be traded for a profit.

Columbus Reaches America Christopher Columbus thought he could reach Asia by sailing west across the Atlantic Ocean. Columbus knew the world was round, as did most educated

▼ Sailors in the 1400s guided their ships using only the stars, a compass, and an astrolabe. Below is a drawing of an astrolabe.

3 Teach

Have students write an essay that answers the question: How did European rule affect both the Europeans and the Native Americans in the Americas? Encourage students to include specific examples from this section in their essays. This activity should take about 25 minutes.

4 Assess

See answers to the Section Review. You may also use students' completed essays as an assessment.

Acceptable essays include the facts that Europeans gained land and wealth and that the Native Americans lost their empires.

Commendable essays include details about the conquistadors and how they conquered the Native American civilizations.

Outstanding essays provide information about the organization of the Portuguese and Spanish empires and show an understanding of the effects of the cultural interaction between the Native Americans and the Europeans.

44 CHAPTER 2

Spanish Conquest and Colonization of the Americas

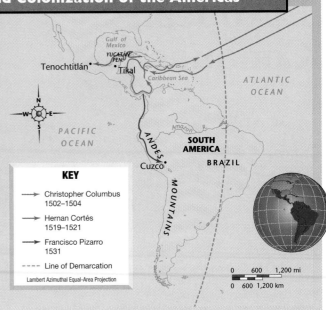

Map Study Columbus sailed to the Americas in 1492, 1493, 1498, and 1502. His 1502 voyage is shown here. Cortés sailed to the Americas in 1504 and conquered the Aztecs in 1519. Pizarro sailed in 1502 and conquered the Incas in 1533. **Movement** Once they reached the Caribbean, what factors do you think helped the Spanish to find the Aztec and Incan empires so quickly? **Regions** South America has two major language regions: Spanish and Portuguese. How did the Line of Demarcation create these regions?

KEY

→ Christopher Columbus 1502–1504

→ Hernan Cortés 1519–1521

→ Francisco Pizarro 1531

---- Line of Demarcation

Lambert Azimuthal Equal-Area Projection

0   600   1,200 mi

0   600 1,200 km

Navigating Without Modern Instruments Explorers like Columbus did not have radar, satellites, and computers to guide their ships. They used the stars as a reference. Sailors imagined a triangle with a straight line from the ship to the horizon, and a line from the horizon to a star. Measuring the angle between the line to the star and the horizon helped them figure out their location.

Europeans. But Columbus believed the distance around the world was shorter than it was. First Columbus asked Portugal to sponsor his voyage. Then he asked Spain. Queen Isabella of Spain finally agreed.

Columbus set sail in early August, 1492. Some 10 weeks later, on October 12, he spotted land. Columbus thought he had reached the East Indies in Asia, so he described the people there as Indians.

Dividing the World Spain and Portugal soon became fierce rivals. Each country tried to stop the other from claiming land in the Americas. In 1494, Spain and Portugal signed the **Treaty of Tordesillas** (tor day SEE yas). A **treaty** is an agreement in writing made between two or more countries. The treaty set an imaginary line from North Pole to South Pole at about 50° longitude, called the **Line of Demarcation.** It gave Spain the right to settle and trade west of the line. Portugal could do the same east of the line. The only part of South America that is east of the line is roughly the eastern half of present-day Brazil. Because of the Treaty of Tordesillas, the language and background of Brazil are Portuguese.

A Clash of Cultures

Spanish explorers heard stories of wealthy kingdoms in the Americas. They hoped to find gold and other treasures. Spanish rulers did not pay for the trips of the explorers. Instead, they gave the **conquistadors** (kon KEES ta dors), or conquerors, the right to hunt for treasure. The conquistadors could also settle in America. In exchange, conquistadors agreed to give Spain one fifth of any treasures they found. If a conquistador failed, he lost his own fortune. If he succeeded, both he and Spain gained fame, wealth, and glory.

Cortés Conquers the Aztecs In 1519, Hernan Cortés sailed to the coast of Mexico in search of treasure. He brought a small army with him. The Aztec ruler Moctezuma (mahk the ZOOM uh) heard that a strange ship was offshore. He sent spies to find out about it. The spies reported back to Moctezuma:

> "We must tell you that we saw a house in the water, out of which came white men, with white hands and faces, and very long, bushy beards, and clothes of every color: white, yellow, red, green, blue, and purple, and on their heads they wore round hats."

The Aztecs demanded heavy tribute from the peoples who lived near them, so these groups disliked the Aztecs. Cortés made agreements with these groups. Then he headed for Tenochtitlán with 500 soldiers and 16 horses. Aztec spies told Moctezuma that the Spanish were coming. The Aztecs had never seen horses before. Moctezuma's spies described the Spanish as "supernatural creatures riding on hornless deer, armed in iron, fearless as gods." Moctezuma thought Cortés might be the god Quetzalcoatl (ket sahl koh AHTL). According to Aztec legend, Quetzalcoatl had promised to return to rule the Aztecs.

With a heavy heart, Moctezuma welcomed Cortés and his soldiers. Cortés tried to convince Moctezuma to surrender to Spain. After several months, Moctezuma agreed. But the peace did not last long. Spanish soldiers killed some Aztecs. Then the Aztecs began to fight against the Spanish. The battle was fierce and bloody. Moctezuma was killed, and Cortés and his army barely escaped.

With the help of the Aztecs' enemies, Cortés surrounded and attacked Tenochtitlán. In 1521, the Aztecs finally surrendered. By then, about 240,000 Aztecs had died and 30,000 of Cortés's allies had been killed. Tenochtitlán and the Aztec empire lay in ruins.

Pizarro Conquers the Incas Francisco Pizarro (fran SIS koh pih ZAR oh), like Cortés, was a Spanish conquistador. He heard stories about the rich Incan kingdom. Pizarro planned to attack the Pacific coast of South America. In 1531, Pizarro set sail with a small force of 180 Spanish soldiers. Pizarro captured and killed the Incan

READ ACTIVELY

Connect How would you feel if you saw people riding on a large animal that you had never seen before?

emperor. He also killed many other Incan leaders. By 1535, Pizarro had conquered most of the Incan empire, including the capital, Cuzco.

The conquistadors defeated the two most powerful empires in the Americas. It took them only 15 years. How did they do it? The Spanish had guns and cannons that the Native Americans had never seen. They also rode horses. At first, horses terrified Native Americans. The Europeans also carried diseases such as smallpox, measles, and chicken pox. These diseases wiped out entire villages. And, because of local rivalry, some Native Americans like Malinche helped the Spanish conquistadors.

Colonization

By the 1540s, Spain claimed land throughout much of the Americas. Spain's lands stretched from what today is Kansas all the way south to the tip of South America. Brazil was claimed by Portugal.

Spain Organizes Its Empire   Spain divided its territory into provinces. Spain also set up a strong government. The two most important provinces were New Spain and Peru. The capital of New Spain was Mexico City. Lima became the capital city of Peru.

Lima's geographic layout was based on the Spanish social classes. The most powerful citizens lived in the center of Lima. They either came from Spain or had Spanish parents. **Mestizos,** people of mixed Spanish and Native American descent, lived on the outskirts of the city. Many

READ ACTIVELY

Ask Questions Suppose that you were a doctor living in South America at the time of the Conquest. What questions would you ask to discover why so many Native Americans were dying of European diseases?

Spanish and Portuguese Empires in the Americas

Map Study Portuguese sailor Pedro Cabral landed on the coast of Brazil by accident. He was trying to sail around Africa to India and was blown off course. Since Cabral landed east of the Line of Demarcation, Portugal built an empire there. **Location** Where was Portugal's empire relative to Africa? How far did Spain's empire reach into North America?

NORTH AMERICA
ATLANTIC OCEAN
Gulf of Mexico
CENTRAL AMERICA
Caribbean Sea
SOUTH AMERICA
PACIFIC OCEAN

KEY
Spanish Empire
Portuguese Empire
Lambert Azimuthal Equal-Area Projection

0   600   1,200 mi
0   600 1,200 km

mestizos were poor. But some were middle class or quite wealthy. Native Americans were the least powerful class. Most Native Americans continued to live in the countryside. The Spanish forced them to work on haciendas. A **hacienda** (hah see EN duh) was a plantation owned by Spaniards or the Catholic Church.

The Effect of European Rule Spain gave its settlers **encomiendas** (en KOH mee en dus), which were rights to demand taxes or labor from Native Americans. Native Americans were allowed to stay on their own land, so the Spanish claimed that encomiendas protected Native Americans. In fact, encomiendas forced Native Americans to work for the settlers. At first, the Native Americans worked only on the haciendas. But when silver was discovered in Mexico and Peru, the Spanish forced Native Americans to also work in the mines. Some died from overwork and malnutrition. Many died from European diseases. In 1519, New Spain had a Native American population of 25 million. Only 3 million survived the first 50 years of Spanish rule. In 1532, 12 million Native Americans lived in Peru. Fifty years later, there were fewer than 2 million.

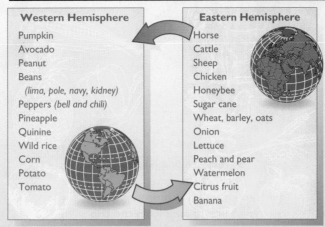

The Columbian Exchange

Western Hemisphere	Eastern Hemisphere
Pumpkin	Horse
Avocado	Cattle
Peanut	Sheep
Beans	Chicken
(lima, pole, navy, kidney)	Honeybee
Peppers (bell and chili)	Sugar cane
Pineapple	Wheat, barley, oats
Quinine	Onion
Wild rice	Lettuce
Corn	Peach and pear
Potato	Watermelon
Tomato	Citrus fruit
	Banana

Chart Study Goods, as well as people, crossed the Atlantic in the years after the conquest. . Do you think that the Eastern and Western hemispheres benefitted equally from the Columbian Exchange? Why or why not?

SECTION 3 REVIEW

1. **Define** (a) Treaty of Tordesillas, (b) treaty, (c) Line of Demarcation, (d) conquistador, (e) mestizo, (f) hacienda, (g) encomienda.

2. **Identify** (a) Hernan Cortés, (b) Malinche, (c) Christopher Columbus, (d) Moctezuma, (e) Francisco Pizarro.

3. What was the effect of the Treaty of Tordesillas on the European settlement of the Americas?

4. How did the Spanish conquest affect Native Americans?

Critical Thinking

5. **Recognizing Bias** The Treaty of Tordesillas affected the lives of millions of Native Americans. However, Native Americans were not asked about the treaty. What do you think this says about European attitudes toward Native Americans?

Activity

6. **Writing to Learn** Write two paragraphs: one by a Native American who has just seen a European for the first time and another by a European who has just seen a Native American for the first time.

Section 3 Review

1. (a) treaty between Spain and Portugal that gave Spain the right to settle and trade west of the line. Portugal could do the same east of the line. (b) an agreement in writing between two or more countries (c) imaginary line from the North Pole to the South Pole at about 50° longitude (d) conqueror (e) people of Spanish and Native American descent (f) plantation owned by Spaniards or the Catholic Church (g) rights to demand taxes or labor from Native Americans

2. (a) Spanish soldier who conquered the Aztecs (b) Cortés's main translator (c) explorer who reached the Americas in 1492 (d) Aztec ruler (e) Spanish conquistador who conquered the Incas

3. Sample answer: Lands in the western Americas were settled by Spain; eastern lands were settled by the Portuguese.

4. Native Americans were forced to farm for the settlers and to work in dangerous mines. Native Americans also died from diseases brought by the Europeans.

5. Sample answer: Europeans believed that Native Americans were inferior to them.

6. Answers may vary. Paragraphs should reflect the two perspectives.

Answers to...

CHART STUDY

• Responses will vary. Students should support their responses with details from the chart.

Using a Time Line

Lesson Objectives

1 Identify the purpose of a time line.

2 Construct and use a time line to relate events to each other.

Lesson Plan

1 Engage

Warm-Up Activity

To **introduce** the skill, have students read the opening paragraphs. Ask students to describe the mistake Biff made. Did he go too far back in time or did he not go back far enough? (He didn't go back far enough.) Discuss with students how a time line that placed dates and events in sequence might have helped Biff land in the right place at the right time.

Activating Prior Knowledge

Ask students to think of time lines they have seen. Have they encountered time lines in other textbooks? In magazines or on television? Discuss with students why time lines are useful in a variety of contexts.

The year is A.D. 2098. Biff Bucko, a star geography student, jumps into his shiny new time machine. He's off on a weekend trip to ancient Mayan civilization.

The centuries whiz by. As our hero approaches the year A.D. 1000, he slows to a stop. "When was Mayan culture at its height?" he wonders. Biff looks to the left and right. "Hmm . . . I think it's this way." Biff should have checked the time line in his glove compartment. If he had, he would have known that Mayan civilization declined after A.D. 900. Instead, he's landed in the 1400s where the Aztecs are busy conquering Middle America. "Oops," thinks Biff as a band of Aztec warriors descends upon him.

Studying the past makes you a kind of time traveler, too. Still, it's always best to know where you're going. Creating a time line can help.

Get Ready

A time line is like a map of the past. It keeps important dates in order so you don't get lost in time. Keep yours handy while you study for a test, research a report, or read for fun.

To make a time line you'll need:
- two sheets of paper
- thirteen paper clips

Try It Out

A. Make a paper ruler. Fold one sheet of paper in half the long way. Now fold it over again. You'll use this paper as a ruler to measure your time line.

B. Mark the divisions of time periods. Attach three paper clips along the top edge of your paper ruler. Slide one to the left corner, one to the right corner, and one to the exact center.

Resource Directory

Teaching Resources

Social Studies and Geography Skills
Reading a Time Line, p. 61

C. Look at dates for your time line. Your time line will cover a span of about 1,200 years. Label the left paper clip on your ruler with the year 300. Label the right paper clip 1500 and the middle one 900.

D. Figure out time intervals. Space your other paper clips evenly across the top of the ruler. The space between each will stand for 100 years. Label your clips with the years 400, 500, and so on.

E. Locate the dates on your time line. Turn your other paper so the long side is on top. Draw a straight line across it. Using your ruler, mark the 100-year intervals. Then mark where each of the four time line dates belongs on the line. (Estimate for the dates 1345 and 1438.) Label each mark with its date and event.

Dates for Your Time Line			
300	**900**	**1385**	**1438**
Mayan civilization rises	Mayas leave their cities	Aztecs found the city of Tenochtitlán	Pachacuti founds the Incan Empire

Apply the Skill

Now choose some other dates in Latin American history that you want to remember. Follow the steps below to create a time line.

① Design a time line ruler. First look at the dates you've selected. What time span will your time line cover? For a long span, each paper clip could mark 100 years. For a shorter span, you could mark every 50 years, 10 years, or 1 year. Choose a measurement that makes sense.

② Find a date to start your ruler. Take the earliest date you chose for your time line. Round it to a lower number. For example, if you are measuring every 50 years, round the date 1492 down to 1450.

③ Find a date to end your ruler. Take your last date. Round it up.

④ Count the paper clips you'll need. Say your ruler starts at 1450, ends at 1650, and marks every 50 years. Count: 1450, 1500, 1550, 1600, 1650. That's five clips.

⑤ Put a clip at each end of the ruler. Space the others evenly. Label each with its year. Now use the ruler to mark points on your time line. Label each point with its date and event.

2 Explore

Have students read the text under the heading Get Ready. Provide materials for students and call attention to the boxed dates and events they will use to make their time lines. Then ask them to read the rest of the skills activity.

3 Teach

Students may **practice** making a time line by carrying out the instructions listed under the heading Try It Out. Before students begin, point out the photograph so students can see how the time line should look. You might monitor students' progress and allow students who finish early to assist any students who are having difficulties.

For additional reinforcement, have students calculate how many years passed between successive events on their time lines.

4 Assess

Have students **apply** the skill by completing the rest of the activity. Suggest that students review Chapter 2 to select dates and events they would like to include on their time lines. To **assess,** evaluate students' time lines on the basis of accuracy and the suitability of the time scale.

SECTION **4**

Independence

Lesson Objectives

1 Describe how Latin American nations won independence from their European rulers.

2 Analyze the ways in which the American and French Revolutions influenced events in Latin America.

Lesson Plan

1 Engage

Warm-Up Activity

Write *Fourth of July* on the board. Ask students what they think of when they see these words. Students might indicate fireworks, parades, and picnics. Then ask students what the Fourth of July commemorates. Ask them why they think Americans continue to celebrate this day.

Activating Prior Knowledge

Have students read Reach Into Your Background in the Before You Read box. Students' responses might include bravery, courage, perseverance.

BEFORE YOU READ

Reach Into Your Background

What qualities do you think make a hero? What about bravery, or doing the right thing no matter what the personal cost? Jot down at least three qualities that you think a hero should have.

Questions to Explore

1. How did Latin American nations win independence from their European rulers?
2. How did the American and French revolutions influence events in Latin America?

Key Terms

revolution
criollo
caudillo

Key People

Miguel Hidalgo
Agustín de Iturbide
Simón Bolívar
José de San Martín
Dom Pedro

▼ Toussaint L'Ouverture was captured by the French, but his followers won Haiti's independence.

O n August 24, 1791, the night sky over Saint-Domingue (san duh MANG) glowed red and gold. The French Caribbean colony was on fire. The slaves were sick of being mistreated by their white masters. They finally had rebelled. Now they were burning every piece of white-owned property they could find. This Night of Fire was the beginning of the first great fight for freedom in Latin America. Toussaint L'Ouverture (too SAN loo vur TOOR), a former slave, led the people of Saint-Domingue in this fight for more than 10 years. Eventually they won. They founded the independent country of Haiti (HAY tee) in 1804.

The flame of liberty lit in Haiti soon spread across Latin America. By 1825, most of the region was independent. Latin Americans would no longer be ruled by Europe.

Independence in Mexico

Haiti's leaders drew encouragement from two famous revolutions. A **revolution** is a political movement in which the people overthrow the government and set up another. During the 1770s and early 1780s, the 13 British colonies in North America fought a war to free themselves from Britain's rule. In 1789, the ordinary people of France staged a violent uprising against their royal rulers. These actions inspired not only the people of Haiti, but also people across Latin America.

Criollos (kree OH yohz) paid particular attention to these events. A **criollo** had Spanish parents, but had been born in Latin America.

Resource Directory

Teaching Resources

📁 **Reproducible Lesson Plan** in the Chapter and Section Resources booklet, p. 27, provides a summary of the section lesson.

📁 **Guided Reading and Review** in the Chapter and Section Resources booklet, p. 28, provides a structure for mastering key concepts and reviewing key terms in the section. Available in Spanish in the Spanish Chapter and Section Resources booklet, p. 18.

Media and Technology

 Color Transparency 34

Criollos often were the wealthiest and best-educated people in the Spanish colonies. Few criollos had any political power, however. Only people born in Spain could hold government office. Many criollos attended school in Europe. There, they learned about the ideas that inspired revolution in France and the United States. The criollos especially liked the idea that people had the right to govern themselves.

The "Cry of Dolores"   Mexico began its struggle for self-government in 1810. Miguel Hidalgo (mee GEHL ee DAHL goh) led the way. He was a criollo priest in the town of Dolores. With other criollos in Dolores, he planned to begin a revolution.

In September 1810, the Spanish government discovered Hidalgo's plot. But before the authorities could arrest him, Hidalgo took action. He wildly rang the church bells. A huge crowd gathered. "Recover from the hated Spaniards the land stolen from your forefathers," he shouted. "Long live America, and death to the bad government!"

Hidalgo's call for revolution became known as the "Cry of Dolores." It attracted some 80,000 fighters in a matter of weeks. This army consisted mostly of mestizos and Native Americans. They were angry. They wanted revenge against anybody connected with the Spanish government. The rebels won some victories. Their luck, however, soon changed. By the beginning of 1811, they were in full retreat. Hidalgo tried to flee the country. However, government soldiers soon captured him. He was put on trial and convicted of treason. Hidalgo was executed by firing squad in July 1811.

READ ACTIVELY

Ask Questions What would you like to know about the attitudes of Mexican criollos toward the revolution?

The Cry of Dolores

Hidalgo made the "Cry of Dolores" on September 16. Mexico celebrates its independence every year on that day. **Critical Thinking** Why do you think that the painter of this mural included so many people in the background behind Hidalgo?

Have students read the section and examine the pictures, maps, charts, and diagrams. Ask students to focus on the significance of the following people to the independence movement in Latin America: Toussaint L'Ouverture, Miguel Hidalgo, Simón Bolívar, and José de San Martín.

3 Teach

Ask students to create an illustrated poster entitled *Independence in Latin America* using the information in this section. Suggest that students work with a partner. Encourage them to include information about the people who worked for independence, the locations of battles, the countries that gained their independence as a result of the movement, and the years in which they became independent. Display and discuss completed posters. This activity should take about 90 minutes.

Answers to...

THE CRY OF DOLORES

• Accept any reasonable answer. Sample answer: The artist is trying to show that Hidalgo had the support of the people.

4 Assess

See answers to the Section Review. You might also use students' completed posters as an assessment.

Acceptable posters include basic information about three of the major figures involved.

Commendable posters include basic information concerning the people involved and illustrate the locations of battles.

Outstanding posters present the basic information as well as information about the influences of the American and French Revolutions on the Latin American revolutions.

Answers to...
MAP STUDY

• Antonio José de Sucre, 1825

African Independence
Although Africa is closer to Europe than to Latin America, Europeans began to colonize Africa later. Europeans began claiming parts of Africa in the 1880s. Like the people of Latin America, many people in Africa later were inspired by the ideas of self-government and independence. African countries began to achieve independence in the 1950s and 1960s.

Independence Finally Comes The Spanish could execute the revolution's leaders, but they could not kill its spirit. Small rebel groups kept fighting. Then Agustín de Iturbide (ee toor BEE day) joined the rebels. He was a high-ranking officer in the Spanish army. Many people who had opposed the rebellion changed their minds. They had viewed Hidalgo as a dangerous hothead. But Iturbide was different. He was a criollo and an army officer. They could trust Iturbide to protect their interests. They decided to support the rebellion. In 1821, Iturbide declared Mexico independent.

South American Independence

Simón Bolívar (see MOHN boh LEE vahr) was not the first Latin American revolutionary leader. Almost certainly, however, he was the greatest. He was born in the country of Venezuela in 1783. His family was one of the richest and most important families in Latin America. Like most wealthy Latin Americans, he went to school in Spain. There, he met Prince Ferdinand, the heir to the Spanish throne. They decided to play a game similar to present-day badminton. Custom required that Bolívar show respect for the prince by losing. Instead, Bolívar played hard and tried to win. He even knocked the prince's hat off with his racquet! The angry prince demanded an apology. Bolívar refused. He claimed it was an accident. Furious, the prince insisted that they fight a duel. He soon calmed down, however.

South America: Independence

Map Study The dates on this map show when each of the Spanish colonies achieved independence. **Movement** Which revolutionary leader traveled from Lima to La Paz? When was the area now known as Bolivia liberated?

Caribbean Sea
Cartagena · Caracas
BRITISH GUIANA
DUTCH GUIANA
FRENCH GUIANA
Bogotá · VENEZUELA 1830
COLOMBIA 1819
ECUADOR 1822 · Quito
Guayaquil
PERU 1824
BRAZIL 1822
Lima
La Paz
BOLIVIA 1825
PARAGUAY 1811
· Asunción
PACIFIC OCEAN
ATLANTIC OCEAN
URUGUAY 1828
Santiago · Montevideo
CHILE 1818
Buenos Aires
ARGENTINA 1816
Islas Malvinas (Argentine until 1833)

0   400   800 mi
0 400 800 km

KEY
→ Simón Bolívar
→ José de San Martín
→ Antonio José de Sucre
Modified Chamberlain Projection

Many years later, these two faced off again. This time, Bolívar knocked Spanish America from under Ferdinand's feet.

Bolívar and San Martín: The Liberators Bolívar joined the fight for Venezuelan independence in 1804. Six years later he became its leader. Bolívar was completely certain that he would win. His confidence, courage, and daring inspired his soldiers. They enjoyed victory after victory. By 1822, Bolívar's troops had freed a large area from Spanish rule (the future countries of Colombia, Venezuela, Ecuador, and Panama). This newly liberated region formed Gran Colombia. Bolívar became its president. Even though his country was free, Bolívar did not give up the cause of independence. "The Liberator," as he was now known, turned south toward Peru.

José de San Martín (san mahr TEEN), an Argentine, had lived in Spain and served in the Spanish army. When Argentina began its fight for freedom, he quickly offered to help. San Martín took good care of his troops. He shared each hardship they had to suffer. They loved him for it. Many said they would follow San Martín anywhere—even over the snow-capped Andes Mountains. In 1817, his soldiers had to do just that. He led them through high passes in the Andes into Chile. This bold action took the Spanish completely by surprise. In a matter of months, Spain was defeated. San Martín declared Chile's independence. Then he turned his attention to Peru.

Again, San Martín took an unexpected action. This time, he attacked from the sea. The Spanish were not prepared for San Martín's tactics. Spanish defenses quickly collapsed. In July 1821, San Martín pushed inland and seized Lima, the capital of Peru.

▶ Nearly every town or city in South America has a central square with a statue of Bolívar or San Martín. These high school girls are visiting the statue of Bolívar in Meridá, Venezuela.

Activity

Cooperative Learning

Talking With Liberators
Organize students into groups of six or seven. Have each group prepare a talk show featuring the heroes of the Latin American independence movement as guests. Individual group members should work on the following tasks: preparing questions to ask the heroes, creating props, writing the script, assigning roles for heroes and talk-show host, rehearsing the show. Call on groups to present their shows to the class. Activity should take about 40 minutes. *Auditory*

Activity

Journal Writing

Ask students to imagine that they are soldiers in San Martín's army. Have students write a journal entry describing their experiences and their feelings about fighting for independence. Invite volunteers to share their journal entries with the class.

A year later, San Martín met with Bolívar to discuss the fight for independence. Historians do not know what happened in that meeting. But afterward, San Martín suddenly gave up his command. He left Bolívar to continue the fight alone. This Bolívar did. Eventually, he drove the remaining Spanish forces out of South America altogether. By 1825, only Cuba and Puerto Rico were still ruled by Spain.

Brazil Takes a Different Route to Freedom   Portugal's colony, Brazil, became independent without fighting a war. In the early 1800s, French armies invaded Spain and Portugal. Portugal's royal family fled to Brazil for safety. The king returned to Portugal in 1821. However, he left his son, Dom Pedro, to rule the colony. Dom Pedro used more power than the king expected. He declared Brazil independent in 1822. Three years later, Portugal quietly admitted that Brazil was independent.

Challenges of Independence

After winning independence, Latin American leaders faced hard challenges. They had to decide how to govern their nations. Also, after years of fighting, Latin American nations were very poor.

Simón Bolívar dreamed of uniting South America as one country. Gran Colombia was the first step. Bolívar hoped it would become the "United States of South America." In trying to govern Gran Colombia, however, Bolívar found that his dream was impossible. Latin America was a huge area, divided by the Andes and dense rain forests. Also, the leaders of the countries in Gran Columbia wanted little to do with Bolívar. In poor health, he retired from politics.

Even though he did not last long in office, Bolívar set the standard for Latin American leaders. Most were **caudillos** (kow DEE yohs), military officers who ruled very strictly. Bolívar cared about the people he governed. Many other caudillos did not. These others just wanted to stay in power and get rich.

Ask Questions What questions would you ask Simón Bolívar about his dream of a "United States of South America"?

SECTION 4 REVIEW

1. Define   (a) revolution, (b) criollo, (c) caudillo.

2. Identify   (a) Miguel Hidalgo, (b) Agustín de Iturbide, (c) Simón Bolívar, (d) José de San Martín, (e) Dom Pedro.

3. What world events influenced the independence movement in Latin America?

4. How was Brazil's path to independence different from that of the rest of South America?

Critical Thinking

5. Identifying Central Issues   What do you think Simón Bolívar had in mind when he wanted South America to become the "United States of South America"?

Activity

6. Writing to Learn   Imagine you are a journalist with Bolívar's or San Martín's army. Describe the army's main actions.

Issues in Latin America Today

BEFORE YOU READ

Reach Into Your Background

Most people like the feeling of being able to take care of themselves. What could you do now to prepare for your own independence?

Questions to Explore

1. How are Latin American nations trying to improve their economies?
2. What issues has the move to the cities created in Latin America?

Key Terms

invest
economy
campesino
rural
urban

Key Places

Brazil

Samuel Zemurray came from Russia to the United States in 1892. He worked for his aunt and uncle, who owned a store in Alabama. As part of his job, Zemurray sometimes traveled to the port city of Mobile. He noticed that fruit and vegetable traders there often threw away ripe bananas. They knew the bananas would spoil before reaching stores. Zemurray bought the ripe bananas and delivered them to stores overnight. The quick delivery meant that the fruit was still fit to be sold. Zemurray's business was so successful that he decided to expand. He did this by buying land in the country of Honduras, where bananas were grown. Zemurray soon became a leading banana grower.

Foreign Investment

In the 1900s, many companies like Zemurray's invested in Latin America. To **invest** means to spend money to earn more money. Some companies owned farms and grew crops such as sugar and bananas. Other foreign companies ran mines. By the mid-1900s, most businesses in Latin America were owned by or did work for foreign companies. As a result, foreign companies became powerful in Latin American economies. A country's **economy** is made up of the ways that goods and services are produced and made available to people. When money from the sale of goods and services comes into or goes out of a country, it affects the country's economy.

▼ Many large-scale farming operations in Latin America are still foreign-owned.

Teaching Resources

📁 **Reproducible Lesson Plan** in the Chapter and Section Resources booklet, p. 30, provides a summary of the section lesson.

📁 **Guided Reading and Review** in the Chapter and Section Resources booklet, p. 31, provides a structure for mastering key concepts and reviewing key terms in the section. Available in Spanish in the Spanish Chapter and Section Resources booklet, p. 20.

Program Resources

Outline Maps Latin America political map

Section 5

Lesson Objectives

1. Describe how Latin American nations are trying to achieve economic independence.

2. Identify the issues that land use and the move to the cities have created in Latin America.

Lesson Plan

1 Engage

Warm-Up Activity

Write the following statement on the chalkboard for students to complete: *After independence, the biggest problems facing Latin American nations were _____.* When students have completed the statement, call on volunteers to read their versions. Have students explain their responses.

Activating Prior Knowledge

Have students read Reach Into Your Background in the Before You Read box. Students' answers will vary. Allow students to express their plans and how they might prepare to carry out those plans.

2 Explore

Write the four main headings of Section 5 on the board. At the same time, have students write the headings on a sheet of paper, leaving space after each for notes. As students read the section, have them jot down the main ideas in the space following each heading. Record some of their ideas on the chalkboard.

3 Teach

Ask students to construct a diorama that illustrates some of the issues facing Latin America today. Issues might include the problem of foreign investment, improving the Latin American economy, distributing and conserving land, and urbanization. Have students use the completed dioramas to explore possible ways that Latin America might deal with the issues.

Predict What steps do you think Latin American countries took to balance their economies?

Foreign companies made huge profits from their businesses in Latin America. However, these companies did little to help Latin American countries build their economies. Many Latin Americans realized that it was important to improve their economies. They needed to build factories so that they could make their own manufactured goods. They also needed to grow many different kinds of crops and to develop a wide range of resources.

Some Latin American countries soon took steps to carry out these economic building plans. And they proved successful. During the 1960s and early 1970s, the economies of many Latin American countries grew. However, in the early 1980s, oil prices went up. Latin American countries needed oil to run their factories—and they had to pay higher and higher prices for it. At the same time, the prices of Latin American products fell. Latin American countries had to spend more money, but they were making less and less. To make up the difference, they borrowed money from wealthy countries such as the United States. By the 1980s, many Latin American countries had huge foreign debts.

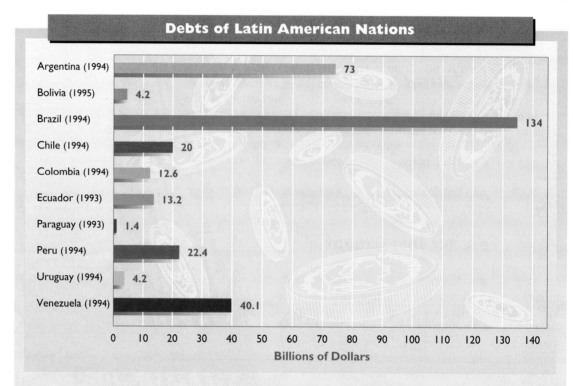

Debts of Latin American Nations

Country	Billions of Dollars
Argentina (1994)	73
Bolivia (1995)	4.2
Brazil (1994)	134
Chile (1994)	20
Colombia (1994)	12.6
Ecuador (1993)	13.2
Paraguay (1993)	1.4
Peru (1994)	22.4
Uruguay (1994)	4.2
Venezuela (1994)	40.1

Chart Study Argentina and Brazil are the two Latin American countries with the most industry. They also have the most foreign debt. **Critical Thinking** Why do you think that Argentina and Brazil have more debt than other countries?

Answers to...

CHART STUDY

• Responses will vary but may indicate that the greater debt is a result of borrowing money to build factories.

Facing Economic Challenges

People in Latin American countries have expanded their economies by building more factories and growing different kinds of crops. And they have taken other steps to improve their economies.

Foreign companies still invest in Latin America. But most Latin American countries limit how investments can be made. They want to prevent foreign countries from having too much control over important parts of their economies. Some countries, for instance, have tried to stop foreign companies from acquiring too much land.

Latin American countries have tried to improve their economies by cooperating with one another. For a long time, most Latin American countries did not trade with one another. They did not need to because, for the most part, they all produced the same kinds of goods. Recently, however, some countries have developed new industries. The products these countries make can be traded to other countries in the region. This kind of trade has increased in the last few years. Latin American countries also have formed several organizations that encourage cooperation in the region.

Land Distribution

The issue of how land is used greatly affects the future of Latin America's economies. Land is one of Latin America's most important resources. Some people and companies own great amounts of land in

ACROSS THE WORLD

African Economies Many African countries are also trying to improve their economies with less foreign investment. Africans are trying to earn more money by growing more types of cash crops. They are also working to build their own industries and mine their own resources without help from foreign companies.

Building Televisions on an Assembly Line

In the last 50 years, Latin American countries have begun to produce many more products in factories like this one in Brazil. **Critical Thinking** What skills do you think these factory workers need?

Interdisciplinary Connections

Science Tell students that there is much concern about conserving the Amazon Rain Forest. One reason for the concern is the great number of species that live in the forest. It contains several million species of plants, fish, birds, insects, and other forms of life.

Ask students to find out about the Amazon Rain Forest and report on 10 kinds of plants or animals found there. Indicate to students that their reports should include some information about the animals' habits and food. Information about plants might include the possible economic benefits of protecting the plants. Have students present their findings in the form of a two-minute newscast. Encourage students to accompany their newscasts with photos or drawings of some of the plants and animals found in the Amazon Rain Forest. Activity should take about 60 minutes.

In El Salvador, many farmers do not have modern farming equipment. They use traditional wooden plows and oxen. **Critical Thinking** What would it cost a farmer to own oxen? How would this cost compare to the cost of owning a tractor?

Latin America but most people in the region do not own any land. In Brazil, for example, 45 percent of the land is owned by only 1 percent of the population.

Dividing the Land Much of the farmland in Latin America is owned by a few wealthy families. This land is occupied by haciendas where crops are grown to sell abroad. In contrast, many poor farmers—known as **campesinos** (kahm peh SEE nohs)—own only small tracts of land. They often grow enough only to meet their own needs.

Starting in the 1930s, many Latin American countries tried to help the campesinos by dividing the land more equally. These programs have met with mixed success. In some cases, the land given to the campesinos was of poor quality. No matter how hard they tried, they could not make a living from it. In other cases, the campesinos struggled because they had neither the money to buy seeds and equipment nor the skills necessary for success. Many Latin American countries have begun to see that taking land from one person and giving it to another does not necessarily improve people's lives or the economy.

Using and Protecting the Land Dividing up the land has raised other issues. Brazil gave land to landless peasants by moving them to the Amazonian rain forest. The peasants burned down trees to clear the land for farming. After a few years, however, the soil in the rain forest became unfit for farming.

Answers to...

A FARM IN EL SALVADOR

- Responses should indicate that farmers would have to provide food and water for the oxen, but would have to spend money for fuel for a tractor.

Many people around the world expressed worries about the clearing of the rain forest. Some believed that this would hurt the environment. Others said that it would change the way of life of the Native Americans who live there. Some people, however, have challenged this view. Economic progress, they say, will come only if Brazil uses all its resources. Brazilian leaders are looking for a balance. They want to find ways to help the economy and the campesinos without destroying the rain forest.

The Move to the City

Many campesinos have decided that making a living from the land is just too difficult. They have left the land and gone to the cities in search of different economic opportunities. This move has resulted in the rapid growth of the populations of large cities. Since the 1950s, many Latin American countries have had a population explosion. The population has increased dramatically in both the **rural,** or countryside, and the **urban,** or city, areas of Latin America. The population of urban areas, however, has gone up the most.

Many Latin Americans who move to the cities are looking for better jobs. They also want to improve the quality of their lives. They hope to find comfortable homes, better medical care, and good schools for their children. However, they do not always realize their hopes. As Latin American countries strive to build their economies, there will be greater opportunities for people to have a better life.

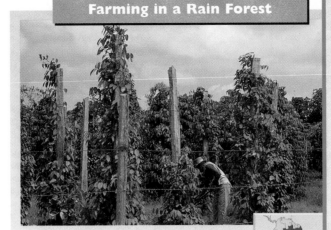

Farming in a Rain Forest

This pepper farmer has cleared land on an island in the Amazon River, in northern Brazil. **Critical Thinking** How does pepper farming contribute to Brazil's economy?

SECTION 5 REVIEW

1. **Define** (a) invest, (b) economy, (c) campesino, (d) rural, (e) urban.

2. **Identify** Brazil.

3. What steps have Latin American countries taken to improve their economies?

4. How have Latin American countries tried to change the landowning system in the region?

Critical Thinking

5. **Recognizing Cause and Effect** How has the increase in population contributed to the growth of cities in Latin America?

Activity

6. **Writing to Learn** You have read that many people oppose Brazil's plans to move poor farmers to the rain forest. Write a paper that explores both the pro and the con sides of the following statement: "A country has the right to use its resources as it sees fit."

Chapter Summary in the Chapter and Section Resources booklet, p. 33, provides a summary of chapter content. Available in Spanish in the Spanish Chapter and Section Resources booklet, p. 22.

Cooperative Learning Activity in the Activities and Projects booklet, pp. 24–27, provides two student handouts, one page of teacher's directions, and a scoring rubric for a cooperative learning activity on Mayan Math Bowl.

Critical Thinking Activity in the Chapter and Section Resources booklet, p. 37, helps students apply the skill of drawing conclusions.

Media and Technology

Guided Reading Audiotapes (English and Spanish)

Section 5 Review

1. (a) to spend money to earn money (b) the ways in which goods and services are produced and made available to people (c) poor farmers (d) countryside (e) city

2. South American country with land distribution problems

3. Students should provide any or all of the following: by building factories, growing more crops, developing a range of resources, limiting foreign investment, and cooperating with one another.

4. by buying or taking land from the rich and distributing it to the poor

5. Because many people in rural areas did not own enough land to make a living, they moved to the urban areas in search of a better life.

6. Students' papers should include reasons that support the pro and con positions of the statement.

Answers to...

FARMING IN A RAIN FOREST

• Responses will vary but should indicate that pepper is a crop that can be sold and/or exported.

Review and Activities

Reviewing Main Ideas

1. They needed it to decide when to hold ceremonies.

2. by conquering other people in the region, forcing them to pay taxes, and ruling them

3. They built canals and aqueducts to water their crops.

4. Answers will vary, but might include the facts that many people in Mexico today eat foods similar to those eaten by the Aztecs and that Mayan and Incan languages are still spoken.

5. These Native Americans disliked the Aztecs because they had to pay the Aztecs tribute.

6. (a) and (b) the Line of Demarcation divided the land such a way that Spain received most of Latin America and Portugal received Brazil.

7. They supported the fight for independence. A criollo priest named Miguel Hidalgo began the fight for independence by assembling an army made up of 80,000 fighters.

8. In Chile, San Martín invaded from the high passes in the Andes. In Peru, he attacked from the sea.

9. They have built more factories, diversified their crops, not allowed foreign companies to own too much land, and cooperated among each other.

Reviewing Main Ideas

1. Why was an accurate calendar important to Mayan priests?
2. How did the Aztecs expand their empire?
3. How were the Incas able to change their environment in order to grow more food?
4. Give two examples of how the Mayan, Aztec, or Incan empires affect culture in Latin America today.
5. Why was Hernan Cortés able to persuade many Native Americans in the region to fight the Aztecs?
6. (a) Why did Spain gain control over most of Latin America?
   (b) How did Portugal come to control Brazil?
7. What role did the criollos play in the fight for Latin American independence?
8. How did José de San Martín surprise the Spanish in Chile and Peru?
9. How have many Latin American countries been trying to improve their economies in recent years?

Reviewing Key Terms

Use each key term below in a sentence that shows the meaning of the term.

1. maize
2. hieroglyphics
3. aqueduct
4. quipu
5. Line of Demarcation
6. conquistador
7. mestizo
8. hacienda
9. encomienda
10. criollo
11. caudillo
12. invest
13. economy
14. campesino
15. rural
16. urban

Critical Thinking

1. **Recognizing Cause and Effect** What were two causes of the fall of the Aztec and Incan empires? What were two effects on the Native American people of the region?

2. **Making Comparisons** Compare the way in which Mexico gained its independence with the way in which the countries of South America gained theirs.

Graphic Organizer

Copy this tree map onto a separate sheet of paper. Then use the empty boxes to outline Latin American history from Mayan civilization through the Spanish conquest.

Latin American History

Reviewing Key Terms

Students' sentences will vary but should show the correct meanings of words through context.

Critical Thinking

1. Possible causes: killing the leader and taking over the capital. Possible effects: The Native Americans were forced to work for the Spanish settlers; they died from European diseases.

2. Mexico's bid for independence was led, at first, by two priests. Other South American countries were freed by the actions of military men.

Graphic Organizer

Students' graphic organizers should contain information similar to that shown in this sample.

Latin American History			
Maya	**Aztec**	**Inca**	**European Conquest**
• great cities like Copán, Tikal • present-day Honduras, Guatemala • priest and nobles controlled the cities • most people were farmers or artisans • achievements: calendar, corn	• built city on a lake • present-day Mexico • expanded empire • one ruler over all • rellgion central to life • medicine and astronomy	• empire started in Peru • built cities and roads • constructed aqueducts to irrigate crops • farmers, builders • religion important in everyday life	• Spain and Portugal decide to divide up Latin America • Cortes conquers Aztecs, looking for gold • Pizzaro conquers Incas, looking for gold • Spain and Portugal force Native Americans to work on haciendas

Map Activity

For each place listed below, write the letter from the map that shows its location.

- Brazil
- Guatemala
- Mexico
- Chile
- Peru
- Andes
- Mexico City

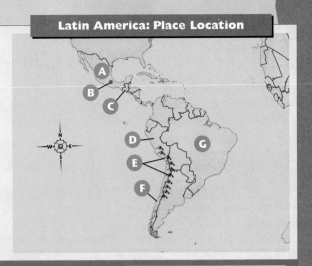

Latin America: Place Location

Writing Activity

Writing a Story
The Mayas, Aztecs, and Incas had spoken histories. Information was passed from generation to generation in stories and songs. Suppose that you lived at the time of the Spanish conquest. Write a story or a song that tells about the conquest.

Internet Activity

Use a search engine to find the site **Rabbit in the Moon: Mayan Glyphs and Architecture.** Explore and learn about the ancient Mayan civilization. Then, click on **How to Write Your Name in Mayan Glyphs.** Write your name in Mayan hieroglyphics, or play Bul, the on-line Mayan Game of Chance.

Skills Review

Turn to the Skill Activity. Review the steps for using a time line. Then: (a) Explain in your own words how using a time line can help you to understand history. (b) What kinds of events should you list on a time line?

How Am I Doing?

Answer these questions to help you check your progress.

1. Can I identify and describe characteristics of the Mayan, Aztec, and Incan civilizations?
2. Can I explain how European rule affected Native Americans?
3. Can I explain how Latin American countries achieved independence?
4. Can I explain how foreign investment has affected Latin America?
5. What information from this chapter can I use in my book project?

Map Activity

1. G   4. F   6. E
2. C   5. D   7. B
3. A

Skills Review

Student responses will vary but should indicate (a) that a time line is a useful way of keeping events in the correct sequence, and (b) that important events that change the course of a culture or nation should be listed.

Writing Activity

Students' stories or songs should include the names of the conquistadors and the time of the conquest. Songs or stories should contain specific descriptive details about the conquest. Encourage volunteers to perform their songs or tell their stories to the class.

Internet Link

If students are having difficulty finding this site, you may wish to have them use the following URL, which was accurate at the time this textbook was published:

http://www.he.net/~nmcnelly/

You might also guide students to a search engine. Four of the most useful are AltaVista, Lycos, Infoseek, and Yahoo. For additional suggestions on using the Internet, refer to the Prentice Hall Social Studies Educator's Handbook "Using the Internet," in the *Prentice*

Hall World Explorer Program Resources.

For additional links to world geography and culture topics, visit the Prentice Hall Home Page at:

http://www.phschool.com.

How Am I Doing?

Point out to students that this checklist is just a quick reminder for them of what they learned in the chapter. If their answer to any of the questions is *no* or if they are unsure, they may need to review the topic.

Resource Directory

Teaching Resources
Chapter Tests Forms A and B are in the Tests booklet, pp. 8–13.

Media and Technology
Computer Test Bank
Resource Pro™ CD-Rom

Cultures of Latin America

To help you plan instruction, the chart below shows how teaching resources correspond to chapter content. Use the resources to vary instruction, add activities, or plan block schedules. Where appropriate, resources have **suggested time allotments** for students. Time allotments are approximate.

Managing Time and Instruction

	Latin America Teaching Resources Binder		World Explorer Program Resources Binder	
	Resource	mins.	Resource	mins.
SECTION 1 **The Cultures of Mexico and Central America**	**Chapter and Section Support** Reproducible Lesson Plan, p. 39 Ⓢ Guided Reading and Review, p. 40 Ⓢ Section Quiz, p. 41	20 25	**Outline Maps** Mexico political map Central America and the Caribbean political map **Nystrom Desk Atlas** Ⓣ Primary Sources and Literature Readings	20 20 20 40
SKILL ACTIVITY **Distinguishing Facts From Opinions**	**Social Studies and Geography Skills,** Distinguishing Facts From Opinions, p. 43	30		
2 **SECTION 2** **The Cultures of the Caribbean**	**Chapter and Section Support** Reproducible Lesson Plan, p. 42 Ⓢ Guided Reading and Review, p. 43 Ⓢ Section Quiz, p. 44	20 25	**Outline Maps** Central America and the Caribbean political map	20
3 **SECTION 3** **The Cultures of South America**	**Chapter and Section Support** Reproducible Lesson Plan, p. 45 Ⓢ Guided Reading and Review, p. 46 Ⓢ Section Quiz, p. 47 Critical Thinking Activity, p. 52 Ⓢ Vocabulary, p. 49 Reteaching, p. 50 Enrichment, p. 51 Ⓢ Chapter Summary, p. 48 **Social Studies and Geography Skills,** Analyzing a Photograph, p. 58 **Tests** Forms A and B Chapter Tests, pp. 14–19	20 25 30 20 25 25 15 30 40	**Outline Maps** South America political map **Writing Process Handbook** Outlining Your Material, p. 25	20 25

Block Scheduling Program Support

Block Scheduling Folder
PROGRAM TEACHING RESOURCES

- Activities and Projects
- Interdisciplinary Links
- Resource Pro™ CD-ROM
- Media and Technology

Block Scheduling Program Support

Media and Technology

Resource	mins.
💿 🎞 World Video Explorer	20
🗂 Color Transparencies 63, 64, 65	20
🗂 Color Transparency 64	20
🗂 Color Transparency 69	20
🎧 Ⓢ Guided Reading Audiotapes	20
🗂 Color Transparency 174 (Graphic organizer table template)	20
🎞 The Writer's Solution CD-ROM	30
💾 Computer Test Bank	30

Legend

T Teaming Opportunity This resource is especially well-suited for teaching teams.	🎞 **CD-ROM**
	🎞 **Laserdisc**
	🗂 **Transparency**
Ⓢ **Spanish** This resource is also in Spanish Support.	💾 **Software**
	💿 **Videotape**
	🎧 **Audiotape**

Assessment Opportunities

From Guiding Questions to Assessment A series of Guiding Questions serves as an organizing framework for this book. The Guiding Question that relates to this chapter is listed below. Section Reviews and Section Quizzes provide opportunities for assessing students' insights into this Guiding Question. Additional assessments are listed below.

GUIDING QUESTION

- *What factors have affected cultures in Latin America?*

ASSESSMENTS

Section 1

Students should be able to make a web that describes the causes of Mexican and Central American immigration to the United States.

▶ **RUBRIC** See the Assessment booklet for a rubric on assessing graphic organizers.

Section 2

Students should be able to give an oral presentation outlining the key characteristics of Caribbean cultures.

▶ **RUBRIC** See the Assessment booklet for a rubric on assessing an oral presentation.

Section 3

Students should be able to describe how geography has created cultural diversity in South America.

▶ **RUBRIC** See the Assessment booklet for a rubric on assessing cause-and-effect statements.

Activities and Projects

ACTIVITIES
To Develop a Global Perspective

Mental Mapping

Everything in Its Place List the names of some Central American, South American, and Caribbean countries on the chalkboard. Include Mexico, Panama, Haiti, Brazil, Puerto Rico, Peru, Guatemala, Cuba, Chile, and Venezuela.

Have students draw three columns on a sheet of notebook paper. The columns should have the following heads: "North and Central America," "The Caribbean," and "South America." Ask students to sort the countries into the appropriate columns.

Distribute outline maps of Latin America and ask students to locate as many countries on the maps as they can. Tell them to write the names of the countries they cannot locate on the water area of the map near the correct landmass. Ask them to keep their lists and outline maps. They may add, correct, or update information as they work through these chapters.

Links to Current Events

Many Cultures, Many Songs Provide recent recordings of music from Brazil, Peru, Cuba, and Mexico. If you have Internet access, you can obtain information on recordings and listen to selections from recordings at www.brazilonlin.com/mhl.html. You can also look, in a library with a good music collection, for recordings by artists such as Willy Chirino (Cuba), Elis Regina (Brazil), Beth Carvalho (Brazil), Trina Medina (Venezuela), and Willy Rosario (Puerto Rico). Play selections, giving students a chance to compare and contrast the tempos and rhythms, instrumentation, and vocal arrangements. Ask students whether they think the Latin American recordings influenced U.S. recording artists.

Hands-On Activities

What's For Dinner? Provide phone book yellow pages (or photocopies of pages) that show listings of restaurants in your own city or a large city with a diverse population. Have students go through listings and find restaurants that offer food from Latin America. Ask them to make a chart showing the countries and cultures for which they find restaurants. If possible, have them find out the names of dishes or characteristic ingredients of that culture's cuisine. They may do this by examining display ads for restaurants, by calling restaurants in the local area, or by researching library cookbooks.

If practical, invite students to extend this activity by visiting local restaurants to examine menus.

PROJECTS
To Develop a Global Perspective

A Tropical Christmas Christmas is a very important holiday in Latin America because of the importance of the Roman Catholic religion. Contrast the evergreen and yule logs used to celebrate Christmas in the northern United States with the ripe fruit and fresh flowers used in Latin America's Christmas. Invite students to find pictures of Christmas ornaments in Mexico, Brazil, or another part of Latin America by looking through travel magazines, *National Geographic,* or illustrated books about different countries. Have them make versions of these ornaments with construction paper, clay, or other materials. *English Language Learners*

Culture Map Tell students that Latin American traditions are practiced in many parts of the United States. Just as the different countries of Latin America have their own cultures and traditions, however, parts of the United States that have been settled by people from different parts of Latin America have distinctive traditions. For example, there are many people of Mexican ancestry in Texas, New Mexico, and California. Many people from Cuba live in Florida, while there are many people from Puerto Rico in New York City. Have students locate these parts of the United States and Latin America on a map. Ask students of Cuban, Mexican, or Puerto Rican ancestry to offer some examples of

traditions unique to their culture. Alternatively, have volunteers research to find some examples. *Basic*

Natural Resources Have students refer back to Chapter 1, where they learned about the climate, vegetation, and natural resources of Latin America. Remind them that the geography of a country influences its culture. As students explore the cultures of Latin America, have them make a poster showing how some aspect of culture is linked to the geography of different countries. Suggest they create a poster showing two countries from each region of Latin America (two from Mexico and Central America, two from the Caribbean, and two from South America). *Challenging*

F.Y.I.

This page can help you extend your own and students' understanding of the concepts in this chapter. You may want to browse through some of the suggestions in the **Bibliography**. **Interdisciplinary Links** can connect social studies understandings to areas elsewhere in the curriculum through the use of other Prentice Hall products. **National Geography Standards** reflected specifically in this chapter are listed for your convenience. Some hints about appropriate **Internet Access** are also provided. **School to Careers** provides insights into the practical uses of some of the concepts in this chapter as they might pertain to various careers.

BIBLIOGRAPHY

FOR THE TEACHER

Moss, Joyce. *People of the World: The Culture, Geographical Setting, and Historical Background of 42 Latin American Peoples.* Gale Research, 1989.

Machado, Ana Maria. *Exploration into Latin America.* New Discovery, 1995.

Ortiz Cofer, Judith. *Silent Dancing: A Partial Remembrance of a Puerto Rican Childhood.* Arte Publicao, 1990.

FOR THE STUDENT

Easy

Dorros, Arthur. *Tonight Is Carnaval.* Dutton, 1992.

Average

Lehtinen, Ritva and Kari E. Nurmi. *The Grandchildren of the Incas.* Carolrhoda, 1991.

Challenging

Peterson, Marge. *Argentina: A Wild West Heritage.* Dillon, 1990.

LITERATURE CONNECTION

Joseph, Lynn. *Coconut Kind of Day: Island Poems.* Lothrop, 1990.

O'Dell, Scott. *The Black Pearl.* Houghton, 1967.

Wisniewski, David. *Rain Player.* Clarion, 1991.

INTERDISCIPLINARY LINKS

Subject	Theme: Customs
MATH	Middle Grades Math: Tools for Success *Course 1*, Lesson 1–3, **Three Kinds of Averages** *Course 1*, Lesson 10–4: **Probability**
SCIENCE	Prentice Hall Science *Heredity: The Code of Life*, Lesson 3–1, **Inheritance in Humans** *Parade of Life: Monerans, Protists, Fungi, and Plants*, Lesson 1-1, **History of Classification**
LANGUAGE ARTS	Choices in Literature *Where Paths Meet*, **Foul Shots** and **Color-Blind** *Deciding What's Right*, **The Judgment of the Wind**

NATIONAL GEOGRAPHY STANDARDS

Students explore the 18 National Geography Standards throughout Latin America. Chapter 3, however, concentrates on investigating the following: standards 6, 9, 10, 11, 12, 15, 17, 18. For a complete list of the standards, see the *Teacher's Flexible Planning Guide.*

SCHOOL TO CAREERS

In Chapter 3 Cultures of Latin America, students learn about the cultures of Mexico and Central America, the Caribbean, and South America. They also learn the skill of distinguishing fact from opinion. These understandings can help prepare students for careers in economics, politics, education, and the arts. Distinguishing fact from opinion is useful for attorneys, customer service representatives, journalists, and police officers. The curriculum presented in this book, as in all eight titles of Prentice Hall's *World Explorer* program, is designed to prepare students not only for careers but also for good citizenship—of the world as well as of this country.

INTERNET ACCESS

Many social studies teachers and students use Internet browsers, or search engines, to investigate particular topics. For the best results, use narrow rather than broad topics. Try these for Chapter 3: maquiladora, Carnival, Caribs, Brasília. Finding age-appropriate sites is an important consideration when using the Internet. For links to age-appropriate sites in world studies and geography, visit the Prentice Hall Home Page at:

http://www.phschool.com

Connecting to the Guiding Questions

As students complete this chapter, they will focus on the cultures of Latin America. By linking history and culture, students will compare and contrast the unique cultural influences found throughout Latin America. Content in this chapter thus corresponds to the following Guiding Question:

● What factors have affected culture in Latin America?

Using the Picture Activities

Invite members of the class to describe several cultural characteristics of their own town or city. List the characteristics on the chalkboard. In a positive manner, help students compare these characteristics with those represented in the picture.

• Answers will vary.

• Student responses should indicate that successive waves of people coming to Latin America helped make the diversity shown.

Heterogeneous Groups

The following Teacher's Edition strategies are suitable for heterogeneous groups:

Cooperative Learning
Creating a Culture
Mural   p. 71

Interdisciplinary Connections
Language Arts   p. 66

Critical Thinking
Distinguishing Fact
From Opinion   p. 71

CHAPTER 3
Cultures of Latin America

SECTION 1
The Cultures of Mexico and Central America

SECTION 2
The Cultures of the Caribbean

SECTION 3
The Cultures of South America

PICTURE ACTIVITIES

These people are attending a festival in Peru. Get to know more about the people of Latin America by completing the following.

Link culture and history
Look at the people in this scene. Based on what you know about the history of Latin America, what do you think is the ethnic background of the people in the picture.

Compare regions
The cultures of Latin America are a unique blend of Native American, African, and European influences. How do you think the variety of peoples found in Latin America compares with that in the United States?

Resource Directory

Media and Technology

 Cultures of Latin America, from the World Video Explorer, provides students with a visual overview of the region's many cultures.

The Cultures of Mexico and Central America

Section 1

BEFORE YOU READ

Reach Into Your Background

What are your hopes and dreams for the future? Do you hope to work in a particular profession? Do you plan to go to college? Many Mexicans and Central Americans have the same kinds of dreams.

Questions to Explore

1. What is the ethnic heritage of the people of Mexico and Central America?
2. Why have many people in this region been moving from the country to the city?
3. What are the causes of Mexican and Central American immigration to the United States?

Key Terms

diversity
indigenous
injustice
maquiladora
emigrate
immigrant

Key Places

Mexico City

E lvia Alvarado (el VEE ah ahl vah RAH doh) walks the back roads of rural Honduras. She helps poor campesinos make a living. Honduran campesinos are like rural people in all of Central America. Many have little land of their own. It is hard for them to make enough money to support their families.

Alvarado is a mother and grandmother. She works for an organization of campesinos. She helps people get loans to buy seeds and farm machinery. Alvarado also helps them get more land. She works with community groups.

Alvarado's work is not easy. "The communities we work in are hard to get to," she says. "Sometimes I don't eat all day, and in the summertime the streams dry up and there's often no water to drink." Sometimes Alvarado does not get paid. "But I couldn't be happy if my belly was full while my neighbors didn't have a plate of beans and tortillas to put on the table," she says. "My struggle is for a better life for all Hondurans."

Cultural Heritage

Alvarado lives and works in Honduras, in Central America. It is one of seven nations in this area. Together they form a crooked, skinny isthmus. The isthmus links Mexico and South America.

Teaching Resources

📁 **Reproducible Lesson Plan** in the Chapter and Section Resources booklet, p. 39, provides a summary of the section lesson.

📁 **Guided Reading and Review** in the Chapter and Section Resources booklet, p. 40, provides a structure for mastering key concepts and reviewing key terms in the section. Available in Spanish in the Spanish Chapter and Section Resources booklet, p. 25.

Program Resources

Material in the *Primary Sources and Literature Readings* booklet extends content with a selection from the region under study.

Lesson Objectives

1. Describe the heritage of the people of Mexico and Central America.
2. Explain why people in this region have been moving from the country to the city.
3. Identify the causes of Mexican and Central American immigration to the United States.

Lesson Plan

1 Engage

Warm-Up Activity

Ask students to list three things that come to mind when they think of Mexico and Central America. Ask students to share their ideas. Then extract key words or terms to make a list of geographical features, clothing, food items, and so on. Allow students to create a master list on a colorful piece of poster board. Add to the master list as students progress through the chapter.

Activating Prior Knowledge

Have students read Reach Into Your Background in the Before You Read box. Student responses may vary. Allow students to express their hopes and dreams without judgment.

2 Explore

Have students read the section. Then have them identify some of the major characteristics of Central American and Mexican culture. The following questions may provide prompts: *What groups of people live in these countries? What is the main language in most Central American countries? Which religion is common in all the countries?*

3 Teach

Work with students as they create a chart similar to the "Increased Urbanization and Emigration" chart below:

Increased Urbanization and Emigration	
Conditions/ Problems in Mexico	Results/ Solutions

Work with the class to put one or two items in each column. Then suggest that students complete the chart with facts from the section. Indicate to students that case histories can help support their entries. Use the completed chart as the basis for discussion about the future of Central America and Mexico. This activity should take about 20 minutes.

Answers to...

SALVADORAN PAINTING

• the Plaza and the style of the church

64   CHAPTER 3

Huipiles Huipiles, or Mayan blouses, are works of art as well as clothing. The beautiful designs in a huipile have existed for thousands of years. Diamond-shaped designs stand for the universe. Other designs identify the weaver.

 The people of El Salvador are mostly mestizo, and their mixed heritage is reflected in their paintings. **Critical Thinking** What in this painting illustrates the Salvadorans' Spanish heritage?

One Region, Many Faces There is much **diversity,** or variety, among the people of Central America. Hondurans, like Alvarado, are mostly mestizo. They have both Spanish and indigenous ancestors. **Indigenous** (in DIJ uh nus) people are descendants of the people who first lived in a region. In Latin America, indigenous people are also called Native Americans or Indians. About half of Guatemala's people are mestizo. The other half are indigenous. Many Costa Ricans are direct descendants of Spaniards. And more than half the people of Belize are of African or mixed African and European descent.

These countries have many languages, too. Guatemala is home to more than 20 languages. Spanish is the language of government and business. But the indigenous people in Guatemala speak their own languages. So do indigenous people in Panama, El Salvador, and Nicaragua. Spanish is the main language in six of the seven countries. People in Belize speak English.

Mexico's Heritage Mexico blends Native American and Spanish influences. Spanish is the first language for most Mexicans, and Mexico is the largest Spanish-speaking country. Some Mexicans speak Native American languages. About 30 percent of the people of Mexico are indigenous, and some Mexicans are mestizos.

The Church Religion is important to the people of Mexico and Central America. In the 1500s and 1600s, Spanish missionaries converted many Native Americans to Christianity. The Roman Catholic Church has been important to this region ever since. Most of the people are Catholic. Native Americans have blended many elements of their religions with Christianity.

Resource Directory

Media and Technology

Color Tranparencies 63, 64, 65

Program Resources

Nystrom Desk Atlas

Outline Maps Mexico political map, and Central America and Caribbean political map

A Growing Population

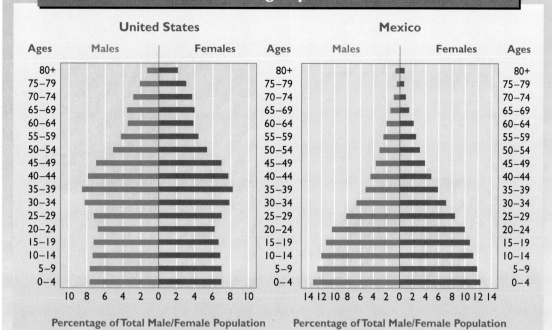

United States

Ages	Males	Females	Ages
80+			80+
75–79			75–79
70–74			70–74
65–69			65–69
60–64			60–64
55–59			55–59
50–54			50–54
45–49			45–49
40–44			40–44
35–39			35–39
30–34			30–34
25–29			25–29
20–24			20–24
15–19			15–19
10–14			10–14
5–9			5–9
0–4			0–4

10 8 6 4 2 0 2 4 6 8 10

Percentage of Total Male/Female Population

Mexico

Ages	Males	Females	Ages
80+			80+
75–79			75–79
70–74			70–74
65–69			65–69
60–64			60–64
55–59			55–59
50–54			50–54
45–49			45–49
40–44			40–44
35–39			35–39
30–34			30–34
25–29			25–29
20–24			20–24
15–19			15–19
10–14			10–14
5–9			5–9
0–4			0–4

14 12 10 8 6 4 2 0 2 4 6 8 10 12 14

Percentage of Total Male/Female Population

Chart Study Unlike the United States, Mexico is a nation of young people. **Critical Thinking** Think about what different skills and needs people have at different ages. What challenges do you think Mexico faces because so many of its people are very young?

Often, the Roman Catholic Church has fought injustice. **Injustice** is the unfair treatment of people. There are many examples of injustice. Injustice occurs when people have their property taken from them unfairly. It also occurs when people are imprisoned without first having a trial. Injustice often happens in countries that have undemocratic governments. Priests and bishops have called for all people to be treated fairly.

Following the Church's lead, many citizens have taken their own steps to end poverty and injustice. People have started their own health clinics, farms, and organizations. Like Elvia Alvarado and her campesino families, they hope that by working together they will be able to create a better way of life.

Looking for Work

The population of Mexico and Central America is growing rapidly. If it continues at the current rate, it will double in 20 to 30 years. Rapid population growth has made it hard for young people in rural areas to

HEROES

A Voice of Protest In the late 1600s, Mexican nun Sor Juana Inez de la Cruz was punished by her bishop for writing a letter defending women's right to learn. Sor Juana was a published poet, but the bishop took away her books and writing materials. However, Sor Juana's essay inspired later generations of women to stand up for their rights.

Interdisciplinary Connections

Language Arts Have students reread the stories of Elvia Alvarado and Fermin Carrillo. Organize students into two groups and assign one of the stories to each. Have students write their own dialogue for a short play about either Alvarado or Carrillo. Be sure students identify the main characters in the story, as well as the supporting roles. Students may wish to present their playlets to other classes. *English Language Learners, Kinesthetic*

Daily Life

Learning English as a Second Language Many immigrants who come to the United States from Mexico and Central America have limited knowledge of the English language. While some may speak English adequately, they may need to learn how to read and write the language. Immigrants who migrate to large cities such as New York, Los Angeles, and Chicago can usually find free adult-education classes at a local community college. Often these people work long hours and then fit English classes into their evening or Saturday hours. They continue their studies, spurred on by the hope of gaining a better-paying job, adapting to their new home in the United States, and helping their family.

Many Mexican and Central American immigrants to the United States find jobs on farms, picking crops. The farm workers on the right are picking strawberries near Salinas, California. The worker below is harvesting broccoli in Texas' Rio Grande Valley.

Ask Questions What questions about maquiladoras would you like answered?

find jobs. Many have left their homes to look for work in the city. Today most people in Mexico and Central America live in cities.

In Mexico, some people move to towns along the border with the United States. There, they can work in factories owned by American companies. These companies place their factories in Mexico because wages are lower there. Border factories are called **maquiladoras** (ma kee la DOR as).

Life in the City In many cities in the region, there are big contrasts between the lives of the wealthy and the lives of the poor. Wealthy people live in big houses on wide streets. They go to good schools and can afford to pay for medical care. Many of them have a lifestyle similar to that of wealthy people in the United States.

For the poor, however, life in the city can be hard. There is a shortage of housing. It is not easy to find work. Sometimes, the only job available is selling fruit or soda on street corners. It is hard to feed a family

Teaching Resources

Section Quiz in the Chapter and Section Resources booklet, p. 41, covers the main ideas and key terms in the section. Available in Spanish in the Spanish Chapter and Section Resources booklet, p. 26.

on the wages such work commands. Yet people are willing to live with hardships they find in the city. Cecilia Cruz can explain why. She moved with her husband and their two sons to Mexico City from the southern state of Oaxaca (wah HAH kah). They live in a two-room house made of cinder blocks. It is on the outermost boundary of the city. "We came here for the schools," says Cruz. "There are more choices here. The level of education is much higher." Most newcomers to the city would agree.

Moving to the United States   Most people in Mexico and Central America move somewhere else within their own country if they cannot find work. Some move to cities or border towns. In addition, however, thousands of people emigrate. To **emigrate** means to move out of one country into another. Most leave because they cannot find work at home. Also, rising prices have made living more expensive. Many people emigrate to the United States.

Fermin Carrillo (fair MEEN kah REE yoh) is one worker who did just that. He left his home town of Huaynamota, Mexico. There were no more jobs at home, and his parents needed food and medical care. Carrillo moved to a town in Oregon. Now he works in a fish processing plant. He sends most of the money he earns home to his parents. Carrillo hopes one day to become a U.S. citizen. Other immigrants are different. They want to return home after earning some money to help their families. An **immigrant** is a person who has moved into one country from another.

Many Mexicans and Central Americans, like Fermin Carrillo, have left the region in search of a better life. Many more have followed Elvia Alvarado's example. They have stayed and begun to build a better life for themselves at home.

Visualize What would a house made of cinder blocks look like? What problems might you notice if you went inside a cinder block house?

SECTION 1 REVIEW

1. Define   (a) diversity, (b) indigenous, (c) injustice, (d) maquiladora, (e) emigrate, (f) immigrant.

2. Identify   Mexico City.

3. (a) What is the main language and religion of the people of Mexico and Central America? (b) How do the languages and religions of the region reflect its history?

4. What is one reason that rural people in Mexico and Central America are moving to the cities?

Critical Thinking
5. Recognizing Cause and Effect   Explain several reasons for Mexican and Central American immigration to the United States.

Activity
6. Writing to Learn   Write a journal entry from the point of view of one of the people mentioned in this section. Write about that person's hopes and dreams. How are they like your own? How are they different?

The Cultures of the Caribbean

BEFORE YOU READ

Reach Into Your Background

Have you ever been on an island? Have you ever read a story about someone who lived on an island? What was the island like? What do you remember most about life there?

Questions to Explore

1. How did European, African, and Native American cultures blend to create unique Caribbean cultures?

2. What are the key characteristics of Caribbean cultures?

Key Terms
ethnic group
Carnival

Key Places
Jamaica
Cuba
Hispaniola
Trinidad and Tobago

▼ Many Jamaican women carry goods on their heads. This practice came to the Caribbean from Africa.

D orothy Samuels is a ten-year-old from Jamaica, a tropical island in the Caribbean Sea. She lives in a village near the ocean and goes to a village school. Dorothy is a good student. She hopes one day to go to college in Kingston, Jamaica's capital city. Jamaican laws require that women have as much opportunity to educate themselves as men do. Equality of women is important to Jamaican culture because many Jamaican women are independent farmers and business owners.

Dorothy's family are farmers. They plant yams and other vegetables and fruits. They also plant cocoa beans. Every Saturday, Dorothy's mother and grandmother take their fruits and vegetables to the market to sell. All the traders at the market are women.

The People of the Caribbean

People in the Caribbean can make a living farming because most Caribbean islands have very fertile soil. These islands stretch over 2,000 miles (3,219 km) from Florida to the northeast coast of South America. As you might expect, a variety of peoples and cultures live within this large area.

The First People of the Caribbean The Caribbean islands are also called the West Indies because when Christopher Columbus arrived there, he thought he had reached the Indies in Asia.

The first people to live in the Caribbean were Native Americans, the Ciboney (SEE boh nay). The Ciboney lived on the islands for thousands of years. In about 300 B.C., they were joined by another indigenous group, the Arawaks (AR ah wahks), who came from South America. In about 1000, the Caribs (KA ribz), another South American group, arrived.

The Caribs gave the region its name. They lived there for more than 400 years before the first Europeans came to the area. Christopher Columbus and other Spaniards enslaved the Native Americans. Almost all of the Caribs, Arawaks, and other groups died of overwork and of diseases the Spanish brought with them. Today, just a few hundred Caribs still live on the island of Dominica.

Other Europeans followed the Spanish. They hoped to make money from the region's wealth of natural resources. Dutch, French, and English colonists began claiming territory in the 1600s. They built large sugar plantations and brought many enslaved Africans to work on them.

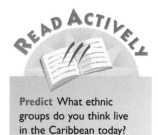

READ ACTIVELY

Predict What ethnic groups do you think live in the Caribbean today?

Caribbean Customs

	Jamaica	Puerto Rico	Dominican Republic
Greetings	A handshake; "Good morning/afternoon/evening"; use Mr., Mrs., Miss.	A handshake. Women kiss each other on the cheek.	Shake hands. Greet everyone when you enter a room. Ask about people's families.
Gestures	Show approval of an idea by touching fists. Suck air through your teeth to mean "Give me a break."	Wiggle your nose to mean, "What's going on?" Point with puckered lips.	Point with puckered lips. Clap hands to request your check in a restaurant.
Table Manners	Keep the fork in the left hand. If you buy food from a street cart, eat it on the spot.	Keep both hands above the table. Stay at the table after the meal to relax and chat.	Guests are served first and sometimes separately. They often are given more elaborate food than the hosts.
Clothing	Women wear colorful skirts and matching headdresses. Many people have tailors make their clothes. Jewelry is common.	Casual clothing is worn for everyday occasions. Parties and social events require formal clothing.	Dressing well is considered important. Clothing is always clean and well-pressed. Men have a traditional suit called a chacabana, which is a white shirt over dark trousers.

Chart Study When you visit another culture, knowing the local customs can help you understand what you see. **Critical Thinking** Name some customs that are unique to the United States.

Program Resources

Outline Maps Central America and the Caribbean political map

2 Explore

Have students read the section. Then ask them to describe the unique blend of cultures on the Caribbean islands. Lead the discussion so that students address the following characteristics: many islands; first inhabitants were Native Americans called the Ciboney; most natives died from overwork and disease once Spain established rule over the islands; Caribbean culture today is a blend of Native American, African, European, Asian, and Middle Eastern cultures.

3 Teach

Provide the following topic sentence for a paragraph: *Caribbean culture is known for its liveliness.* Direct students to write a paragraph that supports the sentence using details from the section to identify the rich traditions in food, music, art, and entertainment from the Caribbean region. This activity should take from 20 to 30 minutes.

Answers to...

CHART STUDY

- Accept any reasonable answer such as saying "hello" or waving good-bye.

4 Assess

See answers to the Section Review. You may also use students' completed paragraphs as an assessment.

Acceptable paragraphs include at least four factually correct supporting details, one for each cultural element listed.

Commendable paragraphs include some specific examples from countries mentioned in the text.

Outstanding paragraphs mention the origins of some of these cultural traditions.

Background

Global Perspectives

Cultural Comparison
Also known for its Caribbean culture is the northern part of South America, including Colombia, Venezuela, Guyana, and parts of Brazil. Largely Roman Catholic, the people here also celebrate Carnival in the days before the beginning of Lent. Brazil's diverse African, Native American, and European cultures result in its cities' lively celebrations, featuring people in dramatic costumes playing traditional rhythms and improvising dances. The many cultures are represented in different forms of celebration.

Most of the Caribbean people today are descended from these Africans. Immigrants from China, India, and the Middle East also came to the area to work.

People in the Caribbean Today   Since slavery was legally ended in the Caribbean, its population has grown to about 36 million. Nearly one third of these people live on the region's largest island, Cuba.

Because so many people came to the Caribbean as colonists, slaves, or immigrants, the area has great ethnic variety. An **ethnic group** is a group of people who share race, language, religion, or cultural traditions. The ethnic groups of the Caribbean are Native American, African, European, Asian, and Middle Eastern.

Depending on their island's history, the people of a Caribbean island may speak one of several European languages. Their language may also be a mixture of European and African languages. For example, two countries and two cultures exist on the island of Hispaniola. On the eastern half is one country, the Dominican Republic. Its population is Spanish-speaking and mostly mestizo. West of the Dominican Republic is the country of Haiti. Nearly all of Haiti's people are descended from Africans. They speak French and Creole, which is a blend of French and African languages.

Most West Indians are Christians, but there are also small groups of Hindus, Muslims, and Jews. Some people practice traditional African religions.

A Caribbean Family

Family life is very important to people in the Caribbean. This family, from Montserrat, British West Indies, is made up of parents and their children. Many people in the Caribbean live in family groups that also include grandparents, uncles, aunts, and cousins.

Haiti was one of the first places where the work of folk artists was recognized as real art. Large, colorful murals comment on religious and political themes. Bus drivers gain prestige by painting public buses, called taptaps.

Food, Music, Art, and Fun

Caribbean culture is known for its liveliness. People play music, dance, and tell stories. People also play many sports. Baseball, soccer, and track and field are popular. On some islands, people also play cricket, which is a British game similar to baseball. Dominoes is a popular game throughout the region.

Food Caribbean food is a mixture from all the cultures of the islands. Caribbean people can enjoy many types of seafood that are not found in U.S. waters. For instance, the people of Barbados love to eat flying fish and sea urchin eggs. Bammy—a bread made from the cassava plant—is still made the way the Arawaks made it. People also cook spicy curries from India, sausages from England, and Chinese dishes. Many tropical fruits grow on the islands. West Indians use the fruit to make many juices and other drinks that are not readily available in the United States.

Music Caribbean music is famous around the world. Calypso is a form of song that uses humor in its lyrics. You may have heard reggae (REG ay) music. It is from Jamaica. Steel drums are Caribbean musical instruments. They are made from recycled oil drums. A steel drum can be "tuned" so that different parts of it play different notes. Players strike the instruments with rubberized drumsticks. The rubber hitting the drum makes an almost liquid sound.

LINKS TO MUSIC

Soca—Calypso with Soul
In the 1970s, a new form of Caribbean music evolved. It blended calypso with two other styles— funk and ska. Funk is an earthy, blues music. Ska is similar to reggae. The first song to use this music was Lord Shorty's "Soul Calypso." The name of the new musical form comes from the title "Soul Calypso." It is called *soca*.

SKILLS MINI LESSON

Using the Writing Process
You may **introduce** the skill by reviewing the basic steps of the writing process: prewriting, writing, editing, and presenting. Have students **practice** by following the steps to write a paragraph about Caribbean culture. Help students **apply** the skill by following the writing process as they develop writing assignments throughout this book.

Section 2 Review

1. (a) groups of people distinguished by race, language, religion, or cultural traditions (b) a celebration held throughout the Caribbean just before the beginning of Lent

2. (a) large tropical island in the Caribbean (b) the largest island in the Caribbean region (c) Caribbean island that is home to the Dominican Republic and Haiti (d) where the largest Carnival celebration takes place

3. the Ciboney

4. Native American, African, European, Asian, and Middle Eastern cultural traditions

5. Answers may vary, but should include elements such as these: All the region's islands have fertile soil. The native populations of the islands were enslaved by the Spanish. Enslaved Africans were brought from Africa to work in the islands. The Caribbean culture is known for its liveliness.

6. Responses will vary, but students should compare and contrast an aspect of Caribbean culture with their own.

Many people in Caribbean countries dress in lavish, colorful costumes to celebrate before Lent. **Critical Thinking** What similar celebrations take place in the United States?

Carnival Many islanders observe the Roman Catholic tradition of Lent, which is the period of 40 days before Easter Sunday. People consider Lent to be a very solemn time, so just before Lent they throw a huge party. The party is called **Carnival.**

Different countries celebrate Carnival in different ways. The biggest Carnival takes place in Trinidad and Tobago. People spend all year making costumes and floats. Lent always starts on a Wednesday. At 5 A.M. the Monday before, people go into the streets in their costumes. Calypso bands play. Thousands of fans follow the bands through the streets, dancing and celebrating. At the stroke of midnight Tuesday, the party stops. Lent has begun.

SECTION 2 REVIEW

1. Define (a) ethnic group, (b) Carnival.

2. Identify (a) Jamaica, (b) Cuba, (c) Hispaniola, (d) Trinidad and Tobago.

3. Who were the first inhabitants of the Caribbean islands?

4. Which traditions does modern Caribbean culture blend?

Critical Thinking

5. Making Comparisons What common elements in their histories have shaped the cultures of the various Caribbean islands?

Activity

6. Writing to Learn Select one aspect of Caribbean culture (food, music, celebrations, and so on) and jot down what you have learned about it in this section. Then, write ways in which it is similar to and different from your own culture.

Resource Directory

Teaching Resources

Section Quiz in the Chapter and Section Resources booklet, p. 44, covers the main ideas and key terms in the section. Available in Spanish in the Spanish Chapter and Section Resources booklet, p. 28.

Answers to...

CARNIVAL AT PORT OF SPAIN, TRINIDAD

• Mardi Gras

The Cultures of South America

Lesson Objectives

❶ Identify the major cultural groups living in South America.

❷ Explain how geography has created diversity in this region.

Lesson Plan

1 Engage
Warm-Up Activity

Ask students to recall the major ethnic groups that live in the Latin American regions of Mexico, Central America, and the Caribbean. Then have students compare the picture of the reed boat and its builder to the picture of Peru in the chapter opener. Ask students to predict which photo best shows the present-day cultures of South America.

Activating Prior Knowledge

Have students read Reach Into Your Background in the Before You Read box. Students may mention that their culture is a result of their families or the part of the country they are from. Some students might mention that different kinds of music are favored in different regions.

Reach Into Your Background

Think about the books you read, the music you like to listen to, and the clothes you wear. These things are all part of your culture. How is your culture related to the history of your family and your region? How does the geography in your region affect your culture?

Questions to Explore

1. What major cultural groups live in South America?
2. How has geography created diversity in this region?

Key Terms

subsistence farming
import

Key Places

Andes
Chile
Argentina
Brazil

B etween Peru and Bolivia is the deep lake called Lake Titicaca. It lies high in the Andes Mountains. This area is bitterly cold. There are few trees. Native Americans here make their living from totora reeds, a kind of thick, hollow grass that grows on the lakeshore. They use these reeds to make houses, mats, hats, ropes, sails, toys, roofs, and floors. They eat the reeds, feed them to livestock, and brew them into tea. Totora reeds can even be made into medicine. Long ago, some Native American groups built floating islands with tortora reeds. They used the islands to hide from the Incas. Today, some Native Americans live on floating islands.

▼ The Native Americans who live on Lake Titicaca in Peru use tortora reeds to make boats.

The People of South America

Most South Americans today are descended from Native Americans, Africans, or Europeans. In this way, they are like the people of Mexico and Central America. South America's history is also like that of its neighbors to the north. It was colonized mainly by Spain. Most South Americans speak Spanish and are Catholic. Each nation has its own unique culture, however.

Teaching Resources

📁 **Reproducible Lesson Plan** in the Chapter and Section Resources booklet, p. 45, provides a summary of the section lesson.

📁 **Guided Reading and Review** in the Chapter and Section Resources booklet, p. 46, provides a structure for mastering key concepts and reviewing key terms in the section. Available in Spanish in the Spanish Chapter and Section Resources booklet, p. 29.

2 Explore

Have students read the section. Then ask them to identify the major cultural groups living in South America. Lead the discussion to elicit the following information from students: Many Native Americans live high in the Andes. People have lived in South America since prehistoric times. Most South Americans are descended from Native Americans, Africans, Europeans, or a blend of these.

3 Teach

Compose a chart on the chalkboard. Allow one column for each of the four regions discussed in the section. Place two categories along the side of the chart: *Geographic Characteristics* and *Cultural Characteristics.* Work with students to fill in the first cell on the chart. Suggest that students complete their own charts by using the information from the section. Use the charts to discuss the features of each region. This activity will take about 20 minutes.

Regions Within South America There are four cultural regions in South America. The first region includes Colombia, Venezuela, Guyana, Suriname, and French Guiana, which are in the northern part of South America. They each border the Caribbean Sea. The cultures of these countries are like those of the Caribbean islands.

To the south and west, the culture is very different. Peru, Ecuador, and Bolivia are Andean countries. Many Native Americans live high in the Andes. In Bolivia, there are more indigenous people than mestizos. The Quechua and Aymara (eye muh RAH) people each speak their own languages.

The third cultural region consists of Chile, Argentina, and Uruguay. The long, thin country of Chile has mountains, beaches, deserts, forests, and polar regions. Although its geography is diverse, its people are not. Most people in Chile are mestizos. The big cities of Argentina and Uruguay, however, are very diverse. Many different ethnic groups live there. Another culture exists on Argentina's Pampas, or plains. On the Pampas, gauchos (GOW chohz), or cowhands, herd cattle.

Brazil is South America's largest country. Brazil was a colony of Portugal. Its people speak Portuguese. However, Brazil is culturally diverse. Many Native Americans live in Brazil. So do people of African and European descent. Some Brazilians are of mixed descent. Many people have moved to Brazil from other countries. Brazil's largest city, São Paulo (sow PAW loh), is home to more Japanese than any other place in the world except Japan!

READ ACTIVELY

Connect How are the Pampas of Argentina like the plains of the United States?

Herding Llamas in Peru

Some of the indigenous people of the Andes raise llamas, a relative of the camel. **Interaction** How do you think the people of the Andes use llamas?

Resource Directory

Teaching Resources

Analyzing a photograph in the *Social Studies and Geography Skills* booklet, p. 58, provides additional skill practice.

Media Technology

Color Transparency 64

Program Resources

Outline Maps South America political map

Answers to...

HERDING LLAMAS IN PERU

Students' responses may vary. Sample response: for their wool, to carry loads.

Yhaninc Puelles Enriquez
age 12
Cuzco, Peru

The scene shown by this student artist is similar to the photograph on the previous page. **Critical Thinking** How are the scenes in the art and the photograph alike and different?

Art and Literature in South America   South America has produced many famous artists, novelists, filmmakers, and poets. Chilean poets Pablo Neruda (PAH bloh nay ROO duh) and Gabriela Mistral (gah bree AY lah mees TRAHL) both were awarded the Nobel Prize for their work. Neruda wrote about everyday objects, including rain, tomatoes, and socks. Mistral wrote for and about children. Colombian Gabriel García Márquez (gah bree EL gar SEE uh MAR kays) and Chilean Isabel Allende (EES uh bel ah YEN day) both are famous for writing novels telling about several generations of life in one family. García Márquez was awarded the Nobel Prize.

Country and City Life

South America contains cities with millions of people, but it also has vast areas with hardly any people at all. Many people still live in the countryside. Others are leaving farms and moving to cities.

Farming in South America   Outside of Chile, Argentina, and Uruguay, most rural people with land of their own do **subsistence farming.** That means they grow only enough food for their families to eat. They only have small plots of land. Farmers plant corn, beans, potatoes, and rice.

LINKS TO LANGUAGE ARTS

Gabriela Mistral Chilean poet Gabriela Mistral was awarded the Nobel Prize for Literature in 1945. But Mistral considered herself to be more a teacher than a writer. Mistral taught school in rural Chile in the early 1900s, but she was frustrated by the low quality of the textbooks that were available. In response, Mistral began to write poetry and prose for children.

Assessing Your Understanding
To **introduce** the skill to students, point out that building knowledge of a subject is much like building a house. What students learn today forms the foundation for what they learn next week or next year. Point out that one way to ensure that their foundation is strong is to check their learning as they go. Help students **practice** assessing their understanding by asking them to read each of the paragraphs following "Regions Within South America." Tell students to read one paragraph and then stop and restate the ideas from the paragraph in their own words. After reading another paragraph, students might list the paragraph's important points. Tell students that if they have trouble restating or summarizing a paragraph they should reread it and try again.

4 Assess

See answers to the Section Review. You may also use students' completed charts as an assessment.

Acceptable charts include at least one characteristic for each country and category.

Commendable charts include two or three facts for each.

Outstanding charts include some cause and effect relationships linking culture and unique features.

Activity

Journal Writing

Travel Diary   Ask students to write a travel diary or journal entry about one of the regions mentioned in the section. Explain that they should describe physical and human characteristics. Students might include illustrations from travel magazines to illustrate their entries.

Answers to...
A PERUVIAN SCENE

• Responses should indicate that each shows an aspect of life in the Andes.

Brasília Point out that this capital city is in the interior of the country, far from the crowded, noisy cities of the Atlantic Coast.

Read the following quotation from Oscar Neimeyer, the chief architect of the city:

"[Those who live there] can enjoy tree-lined avenues. The light from the sky seems to bring with it kindlier ways of living. . . ."

Tell students that as early as 1789, Brazilians thought of building a new capital city in the interior of the country. The idea came up again when Brazil won its independence from Portugal. Have students speculate on why the people might have wanted to build a new capital. (crowded settlements along the ocean, desire to build a capital that had no influence of European conquerors) Ask students to point out features of the capital that indicate that the country is no longer under European rule. (Presidential Palace, the Plaza of the Three Powers)

Have students use the diagram to explain why the Presidential Palace is called the Palace of the Dawn. (It faces east, the direction of the sunrise.)

Very large farms grow crops to export to other countries. The main export crops of South America are coffee, sugar, cocoa, and bananas. Export farming uses so much land for cash crops that South America has to import food to eat. To **import** means to buy from another country.

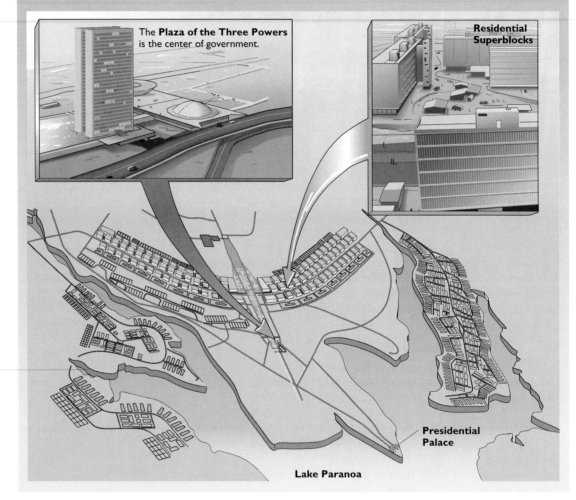

Brasília

Brasília is a planned city. Some people think it looks like a bow and arrow. Others think it looks like a jet plane. Government offices and shopping areas are located in the middle of the city, where the two "wings" meet. The wings contain superblocks, or residential neighborhoods. Each includes 10 to 16 apartment buildings, a school, and shops. What would you like about living in a completely new city? What would you dislike?

The **Plaza of the Three Powers** is the center of government.

Residential Superblocks

Presidential Palace

Lake Paranoa

Resource Directory

Teaching Resources

Section Quiz in the Chapter and Section Resources booklet, p. 47, covers the main ideas and key terms in the section. Available in Spanish in the Spanish Chapter and Section Resources booklet, p. 30.

Vocabulary in the Chapter and Section Resources booklet, p. 49, provides a review of key terms in the chapter. Available in Spanish in the Spanish Chapter and Section Resources booklet, p. 32.

Reteaching in the Chapter and Section Resources booklet, p. 50, provides a structure for students who may need additional help in mastering chapter content.

Enrichment in the Chapter and Section Resources booklet, p. 51, extends chapter content and enriches students' understanding.

Spanish Glossary in the Spanish Chapter and Section Resources, pp. 62–66, provides key terms translated from

The population of South America is booming. Latin America is the fastest-growing region in the world. Like Mexicans and Central Americans, South Americans cannot find enough jobs in rural areas. Every day, thousands of rural South Americans move to the cities looking for work.

South America's Cities The cities of South America illustrate the region's mix of cultures. Many major cities—Lima, Peru, and Buenos Aires, Argentina, for example—were built by Spanish colonists more than 400 years ago. Some of the buildings in these older cities follow Native American designs. In contrast, modern office blocks and apartment buildings of concrete, steel, and glass tower above the downtown areas. One or two cities were built quite recently. Brasília, the Brazilian capital, was constructed in the 1950s. It was a completely planned city, designed to draw people to the country's interior.

By contrast, one of the unplanned things about many South American cities is the slums. They are called *favelas* (fuh VEH luz) in Brazil and *barrios* (BAR ee ohs) in Venezuela. More and more people have migrated into the cities in recent years. Usually they have ended up in poor neighborhoods. City governments try to provide electricity and running water to everyone. But people move into cities so quickly that it is hard for city governments to keep up.

The Role of Women In some ways, women do not yet play a role equal to that of men in South America. Women in South America are more likely than men to be poor. They also do not attend school for as many years as men do.

More and more women in South America today are fighting to make a living for themselves and their children. They are demanding equal rights. Women are struggling for the rights to go to school, to get into different types of jobs, to have good health care, and to have a voice in government. Some women are getting bank loans to start small businesses. These businesses are sometimes based on traditional skills such as sewing, weaving, or preparing food.

HEROES

Working Together From 1976 to 1983, Argentina had a military government. The government took thousands of people prisoner. Many were never seen again. The mothers and grandmothers of the "disappeared" marched in protest every day for six years in Buenos Aires. Their actions forced the government to explain what happened to the missing people.

SECTION 3 REVIEW

1. **Define** (a) subsistence farming, (b) import.

2. **Identify** (a) Andes, (b) Chile, (c) Argentina, (d) Brazil.

3. What pressures does rapid population growth place on the countries of South America?

4. Name two ways in which the geography of South America has shaped how people live.

Critical Thinking

5. **Recognizing Cause and Effect** What is one cause of rapid population growth in the cities? What is one effect?

Activity

6. **Writing to Learn** Choose one region of South America you'd like to visit, and write a paragraph explaining why.

English to Spanish as well as definitions in Spanish.

📁 **Chapter Summary** in the Chapter and Section Resources booklet, p. 48, provides a summary of chapter content. Available in Spanish in the Spanish Chapter and Section Resources booklet, p. 31.

📁 **Cooperative Learning Activity** in the Activities and Projects booklet, pp. 28–31, provides two student handouts, one page of teacher's directions, and a scoring rubric for a cooperative learning activity on sharing the music.

📁 **Critical Thinking Activity** in the Chapter and Section Resources booklet, p. 52, helps students apply the skill of identifying central issues.

Media and Technology

🎧 **Guided Reading Audiotapes** (English and Spanish)

Distinguishing Facts From Opinions

Lesson Objectives

1 Define the terms *fact* and *opinion*.

2 Identify facts and opinions in context.

Lesson Plan

1 Engage

Warm-Up Activity

To **introduce** the skill, invite a volunteer to read the introduction to the class. Write the terms *fact* and *opinion* on the chalkboard.

Activating Prior Knowledge

Ask students if they can define the terms *fact* and *opinion*. Have them write their definitions on a piece of paper.

Kate was nervous, but excited. This was her first trip out of the United States. For two weeks, she had seen more fantastic things in Mexico than she could have dreamed of: beautiful countryside, ancient ruins ... the list was endless. Now, she was about to start a new adventure.

Today, she would travel from Mexico City to Paplanta, a small town near the coast to the east. A fellow traveler had discouraged her. "The train trip is very long," she had said.

> The train trip is very long and boring!

> The train ride to Paplanta is three hours long.

"And boring. There's nothing to look at out the windows. The town is not interesting, either. You should skip that trip altogether."

"Hmmm," Kate thought as she pulled out her guidebook and train schedule. The guidebook said that the ruins of an old Spanish mission were located at Paplanta. The El Tajin ruins were also there. On Sundays, the town hosted an open-air market. The train schedule said it was only a three-hour train ride away, through mountainous country. "A long trip? Nothing to look at? Ha!" More determined than ever, Kate headed to the train station.

Get Ready

Kate decided to go to Paplanta because she relied on facts instead of opinions. Facts are statements that can be proved true. Opinions are beliefs. That the train ride was three hours long is a fact. The traveler's statement that the train ride "is very long" is an opinion. Distinguishing facts from opinions, as Kate found out, is a valuable skill.

Distinguishing facts from opinions is something you will need to do almost every day of your life. You will do it as you watch television, read books and magazines, and—like Kate—as you reach your own decisions.

Resource Directory

Teaching Resources

Social Studies and Geography Skills
Distinguishing Facts From Opinions, p. 43

How can you distinguish, or tell the difference between, facts and opinions? It's as simple as A-B-C:

A. Facts can be proved true.

B. Opinions cannot be proved true.

C. Opinions are often indicated by words and phrases like "I think," "I believe," "should," and "ought to," and by adjectives like "beautiful" or "ugly."

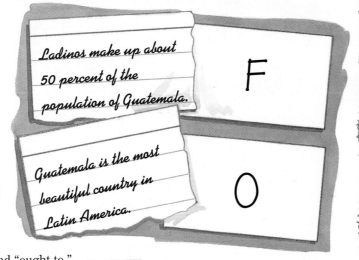

Try It Out

Learn to distinguish facts from opinions by playing a simple game. All you need are some note cards, a couple of pens, and a partner.

A. Deal the cards. Deal ten note cards to your partner and ten to yourself. Each of you should then write one fact or one opinion about Latin America on each of your note cards. You can get the facts from your textbook. The opinions should be your own beliefs. On the back of each note card, write an F if you wrote a fact and an O if you wrote an opinion. Don't let your partner see these!

B. Shuffle the cards. Shuffle your cards, and give them to your partner. Challenge him or her to identify each sentence as a fact or an opinion. Award one point for each correct answer. Give a bonus point if your partner can explain how the statement could be proved true if it is a fact or how your partner knew it was an opinion. Total your partner's score, and write it down.

C. Switch cards. Now try your hand at your partner's note cards. Compare scores. Which of you won? The winner should help the loser learn more about distinguishing fact from opinion.

Apply the Skill

Now distinguish facts from opinions in a real case.

① **Read for understanding.** Read the paragraph in the box below once or twice, until you are sure you understand its meaning.

② **Read for facts and opinions.** Now reread *one sentence at a time.* For each sentence, apply the A-B-C method of distinguishing facts from opinions. Ask yourself: A) Is this a fact that *can* be proved true? B) Is this an opinion that *cannot* be proved true? C) Are there words in the sentence that identify it as an opinion? Which sentences are facts and which are opinions? How could you prove the facts true? How do you know the other sentences express opinions?

> Urbanization takes place when people move from rural areas to urban areas. I believe that urbanization in Mexico is a bad thing. First, the cities are already too crowded. There are thousands of homeless people in urban areas. Lots of people can't find jobs. Second, the city streets were not designed for so many cars. Traffic jams are a huge headache. Finally, the water and electric systems do not have the capacity to serve more people. I think the time has come for the government to try to stop urbanization.

2 Explore

Read the material under the heading Get Ready with students. Ask volunteers to write the definitions for fact (a statement that can be proved true) and opinion (a belief) on the board under the terms. Tell students to compare these definitions with the ones they wrote down earlier. Then have them read the rest of the skills activity.

3 Teach

Pair students and allow them to **practice** by playing the game described in Try It Out. Monitor their discussions and share interesting examples of facts and opinions with the entire class.

For additional reinforcement, ask students to write three facts and three opinions on a topic of their own choice.

4 Assess

Have students **apply** the skill by completing the final part of the activity. To **assess,** evaluate students' contributions to a sentence-by-sentence judgment of the facts and opinions in the paragraph. You might want to display the paragraph on an overhead projector and identify each sentence as a class. Highlight opinion words such as "believe" and "think."

Reviewing Main Ideas

1. (a) Mexican border factories that are owned by United States companies (b) they provide jobs

2. the United States

3. (a) Native Americans called the Ciboney (b) They were joined by another indigenous group from South America. Once the Europeans enslaved them, nearly all native groups died of overwork and disease.

4. Sample answer: Calypso is a form of song that features humor in its lyrics. Reggae music is from Jamaica.

5. Communities of Native Americans make their living harvesting reeds used for housing, mats, ropes, sails, toys, roofs, and floors. Totora reeds can also be eaten or made into medicine.

6. (a) Chile has mountains, beaches, deserts, forests, and polar regions. (b) The people include members of many Native American groups, as well as descendants of Africans, Europeans, and people of mixed descent. Immigrants to Brazil include large numbers of Japanese.

Reviewing Key Terms

1. F	4. F	6. F
2. T	5. T	7. F
3. T		

Critical Thinking

1. Answers may differ, but possibilities may include the facts that the cultures and history of Latin America were influenced by Native Americans, Africans, and Europeans, especially Spaniards. Geographically, these regions are quite diverse, and their living conditions may vary accordingly.

2. Thousands of Latin Americans emigrate each year because they cannot find work in their own countries.

---

3 Review and Activities

Reviewing Main Ideas

1. (a) What are maquiladoras? (b) Why are they important to the economy of Mexico?

2. To which country are some Mexicans and Central Americans emigrating to find jobs?

3. (a) Who were the first people on the Caribbean islands? (b) What happened to those people?

4. What are some of the musical styles that began in the Caribbean?

5. How do some of the people of the Andes make a living?

6. (a) How is the country of Chile geographically diverse? (b) How is Brazil culturally diverse?

Reviewing Key Terms

Decide whether each statement is true or false. If it is true, write "true." If it is false, change the underlined term to make the statement true.

1. Border factories are called mestizos.

2. Indigenous people are descendants of a region's first inhabitants.

3. To emigrate is to move from one's home country to another country.

4. Many Mexicans become pampas in the United States because they cannot find jobs in their home countries.

5. Ethnic diversity refers to people with a variety of cultures, customs, religions, or languages.

6. Imports occur when a government does not respect people's human rights.

7. To immigrate means to buy from another country.

Critical Thinking

1. Making Comparisons Consider these three regions: Mexico and Central America; the Caribbean; South America. What do the cultures of these regions have in common? How are they different?

2. Recognizing Cause and Effect What is the main reason that many Latin Americans move from one region or one country to another?

Graphic Organizer

Copy the chart to the right onto a separate sheet of paper. Then fill in the empty boxes to complete the chart.

	Mexico and Central America	The Caribbean	South America
Languages			
Religions			
Ethnic Background			
Special Features			

Graphic Organizer

	Mexico and Central America	The Caribbean	South America
Languages	many indigenous, Spanish, English	European, Creole	mostly Spanish
Religions	Roman Catholic and blend of Christianity and traditional religions	Christian and small groups of Hindu, Muslim, and Jewish	mostly Catholic and traditional
Ethnic Background	mestizo, indigenous, Spanish, African, and European	African, indigenous, and European	indigenous, African, and European
Special Features	Central Plateau Panama Canal	rich soil, musical traditions	Andes Mountains, Amazon River, rain forest

Map Activity

For each place listed below, write the letter from the map that shows its location.

1. Andes
2. Argentina
3. Brazil
4. Honduras
5. Jamaica
6. Mexico City
7. Trinidad and Tobago

Latin America: Place Location

Writing Activity

Writing a Magazine Article

In this chapter, you've taken a guided tour of the cultures of Latin America. Write an article

for a travel magazine describing the "high points" of your tour. As you write, consider how historical events and geography influenced the region's culture.

Internet Activity

Use a search engine to find the site **amigo! Mexican Art & Culture.** Explore several links to learn about various aspects of Mexican culture. Make a travel brochure highlighting some of your favorite findings, create a portfolio of Mexican culture, or give a class presentation on the aspect that interested you the most.

Skills Review

Turn to the Skill Activity. Review the steps for distinguishing facts from opinions. Then, write a brief paragraph about the cultures of Latin America that includes both facts and opinions.

How Am I Doing?

Answer these questions to help you check your progress.

1. Can I explain how the cultures in a region reflect its history?
2. Can I explain how most people make a living in the countryside?
3. Can I identify the reasons why many people in Latin America are moving from rural to urban areas?
4. What information from this chapter can I use in my book project?

Exploring Mexico and Central America

To help you plan instruction, the chart below shows how teaching resources correspond to chapter content. Use the resources to vary instruction, add activities, or plan block schedules. Where appropriate, resources have suggested time allotments for students. Time allotments are approximate.

Managing Time and Instruction

		Latin America Teaching Resources Binder		World Explorer Program Resources Binder	
		Resource	mins.	Resource	mins.
1	**SECTION 1** Mexico One Family's Move to the City	**Chapter and Section Support** Reproducible Lesson Plan, p. 54 Ⓢ Guided Reading and Review, p. 55 Ⓢ Section Quiz, p. 56	20 25	**Outline Maps** Mexico political map **Nystrom Desk Atlas** Ⓣ Primary Sources and Literature Readings	20 40
	SKILL ACTIVITY Previewing a Reading Selection	**Social Studies and Geography Skills,** Previewing the Headings and the Pictures, p. 68	30		
2	**SECTION 2** Guatemala Descendants of an Ancient People	**Chapter and Section Support** Reproducible Lesson Plan, p. 57 Ⓢ Guided Reading and Review, p. 58 Ⓢ Section Quiz, p. 59 Critical Thinking Activity, p. 67 **Social Studies and Geography Skills,** Reading a Circle Graph, p. 55	20 25 30 30	**Outline Maps** Central America and the Caribbean political map	20
3	**SECTION 3** Panama Where Two Oceans Meet	**Chapter and Section Support** Reproducible Lesson Plan, p. 60 Ⓢ Guided Reading and Review, p. 61 Ⓢ Section Quiz, p. 62 Ⓢ Vocabulary, p. 64 Reteaching, p. 65 Enrichment, p. 66 Ⓢ Chapter Summary, p. 63 **Tests** Forms A and B Chapter Tests, pp. 20–25	20 25 20 25 25 15 40	**Outline Maps** Central America and the Caribbean political map **Writing Process Handbook** Limiting a Topic, p. 15	20 25
	ACTIVITY SHOP Lab Making A Model Canal	**Activities and Projects** Activity Shop: Lab, p. 6	30		

Activities and Projects

Block Scheduling Program Support

Interdisciplinary Links

Resource Pro™ CD-ROM

Media and Technology

Assessment Opportunities

From Guiding Questions to Assessment A series of Guiding Questions serves as an organizing framework for this book. The Guiding Questions that relate to this chapter are listed below. Section Reviews and Section Quizzes provide opportunities for assessing students' insights into these Guiding Questions. Additional assessments are listed below.

Media and Technology

Resource	mins.
◖▸ ◿ Ⓢ World Video Explorer	20
◿ Planet Earth CD-ROM	20
◿ Material World CD-ROM	20
⌐ Color Transparencies 19, 24, 65	20
◖▸ Ⓢ World Video Explorer	20
◿ Planet Earth CD-ROM	20
◿ Material World CD-ROM	20
⌐ Color Transparency 66	20
◿ Planet Earth CD-ROM	20
⌐ Color Transparency 66	20
◠ Ⓢ Guided Reading Audiotapes	20
⌐ Color Transparency 172	20
(Graphic organizer tree map template)	
◿ The Writer's Solution CD-ROM	30
⊟ Computer Test Bank	30

T **Teaming Opportunity**
This resource is especially well-suited for teaching teams.

Ⓢ **Spanish**
This resource is also in Spanish Support.

◿ **CD-ROM**

◿ **Laserdisc**

⌐ **Transparency**

⊟ **Software**

◖▸ **Videotape**

◠ **Audiotape**

GUIDING QUESTIONS

- *Why have many Latin Americans been moving to cities in recent years?*
- *How has geography influenced the ways in which Latin Americans make a living?*

ASSESSMENTS

Section 1

Students should be able to write a report outlining the challenges Mexicans from the country face when they move to cities.

▶ **RUBRIC** See the Assessment booklet for a rubric on assessing a report.

Section 2

Students should be able to describe how Rigoberta Menchú became a leader of the people of Guatemala.

▶ **RUBRIC** See the Assessment booklet for a rubric on assessing cause-and-effect statements.

Section 3

Students should be able to create a map of Panama showing the location of the Panama Canal.

▶ **RUBRIC** See the Assessment booklet for a rubric on assessing a map produced by a student.

Activities and Projects

Mental Mapping

Centrally Located Display a map of Latin America. Ask students a series of location questions about Mexico and Central America, such as:

- What U.S. states share a border with Mexico? [Texas, New Mexico, Arizona, California]
- Which bodies of water lie on either side of Central America? [Pacific Ocean; Gulf of Mexico or Atlantic Ocean]
- Traveling from the border of Mexico, in what direction does Central America extend? [southeast]
- What Central American country lies closest to South America? [Panama]
- If you took a bus or train in a direct route from the border of Mexico to the border of South America, approximately how far would you travel? [1,500 miles]

Links to Current Events

Prepare for an Interview If possible, invite a first- or second-generation immigrant from Mexico or Central America to come to the class to speak and be interviewed. Tell the visitor that students will be interested in hearing about both the achievements and appealing aspects of that country as well as about some of the challenges faced by people there.

Before the visitor arrives, ask students to prepare questions they would like to have answered. Have students review Chapters 1, 2, and 3 to prepare one question about geography, one question about history, and one question about the culture of the visitor's country of origin.

If it is not possible to invite someone from this region to visit the class, have students prepare questions and then try to research the answers themselves.

Hands-On Activities

Short Cut Using a wall map, let students compare the length of sea journeys from San Francisco to New York; from Los Angeles to São Paulo, Brazil; and from Philadelphia to Santiago, Chile, with and without the Panama Canal.

Suggest that they do this by making model ships out of construction paper or lightweight cardboard. These ships need not be to scale, but the same ship should be used to measure the distance for each journey with and without the canal. Have students count the number of ship lengths for each journey using both routes.

Encourage students to discuss some of the reasons why people would want to decrease the length of time required for such voyages.

Mexico City Sights Have students look at newspaper or magazine travel articles or at travel books about Mexico City. Ask them to identify three "sights" they would want to visit on a trip to Mexico City. Each student may describe the three things they would want to see in writing or in an oral presentation. *Basic*

Labels Tell students that trade with Mexico and Central America is very important to the United States. Ask students to look at labels of clothing, toys, and other objects at home, as well as at the labels on produce in a supermarket or grocery store. Have them list the things they find that come from Mexico or Central America. *Average*

Make a Map Give students an outline map of Mexico and Central America. As they work through this chapter, have them locate and label countries, cities, and natural features of this region on their maps. They may also create icons to show natural resources or principal products of the countries on the map. Direct students to provide a key to information shown on the map. *English Language Learners*

Canal Diary Have students write several diary entries that might have been written by someone involved in the building of the Panama Canal. Diary entries might be written by a worker, by a director of the project, by a politician involved with the project, or by someone living in Panama at the time. Students should do additional research into the building of the canal and the controversies surrounding it so that they can include historically accurate concerns and details in their diary entries. *Challenging*

F.Y.I.

This page can help you extend your own and students' understanding of the concepts in this chapter. You may want to browse through some of the suggestions in the **Bibliography**. **Interdisciplinary Links** can connect social studies understandings to areas elsewhere in the curriculum through the use of other Prentice Hall products. **National Geography Standards** reflected specifically in this chapter are listed for your convenience. Some hints about appropriate **Internet Access** are also provided. **School to Careers** provides insights into the practical uses of some of the concepts in this chapter as they might pertain to various careers.

BIBLIOGRAPHY

FOR THE TEACHER

Ancona, George. *The Piñata Maker: El Piñatero.* Harcourt, 1994.

Nye, Naomi Shihab, ed. *The Tree Is Older Than You Are: A Bilingual Gathering of Poems and Stories from Mexico with Paintings by Mexican Artists.* Simon, 1995.

St. George Judith. *Panama Canal: Gateway to the World.* Putnam, 1989.

Silverthorne, Elizabeth. *Fiesta!: Mexico's Great Celebrations.* Millbrook, 1992.

FOR THE STUDENT

Easy
Herrera, Juan Felipe. *Calling the Doves/El canto de las palomas.* Children's Book Press, 1995.

Average
Lazo, Caroline. *Rigoberta Menchú.* Dillon, 1994.

Challenging
Dolan, Edward F. *Panama and the United States: Their Canal, Their Stormy Years.* Watts, 1990.

Rummel, Jack. *Mexico.* Chelsea, 1990.

LITERATURE CONNECTION

Casteñada, Omar S. *Among the Volcanoes.* Lodestar, 1992.

Moeri, Louise. *The Forty-Third War.* Houghton, 1989.

Strasser, Todd. *The Diving Bell.* Scholastic, 1992.

INTERDISCIPLINARY LINKS

Subject	Theme: Transitions
MATH	Middle Grades Math: Tools for Success *Course 3*, Lesson 11–6, **Technology: Changing Dimensions**
SCIENCE	Prentice Hall Science *Evolution: Change Over Time*, Lesson 2–3, **The Development of a New Species**
LANGUAGE ARTS	Choices in Literature *You Are the Solution*, **Tenochtitlán: Inside the Aztec Capital** Prentice Hall Literature *Bronze*, **Barrio Boy** *Copper*, **Change**

NATIONAL GEOGRAPHY STANDARDS

Students explore the 18 National Geography Standards throughout Latin America. Chapter 4, however, concentrates on investigating the following: standards 1, 2, 3, 4, 5, 6, 8, 9, 10, 11, 12, 13, 14, 18. For a complete list of the standards, see the *Teacher's Flexible Planning Guide.*

SCHOOL TO CAREERS

In Chapter 4 Exploring Mexico and Central America, students learn about issues important to the peoples of Mexico, Guatemala, and Panama. Additionally, they address the skill of previewing. Understanding issues of other countries can help students prepare for careers in economics, politics, education, and business.

Previewing is particularly useful for actors, human resource workers, researchers, secretaries, and others. The curriculum presented in this book, as in all eight titles of Prentice Hall's *World Explorer* program, is designed to prepare students not only for careers but also for good citizenship—of the world as well as of this country.

INTERNET ACCESS

Many social studies teachers and students use Internet browsers, or search engines, to investigate particular topics. For the best results, use narrow rather than broad topics. Try these for Chapter 4: ladinos, Rigoberta Menchú, Panama Canal, Quiché Maya. Finding age-appropriate sites is an important consideration when using the Internet. For links to age-appropriate sites in world studies and geography, visit the Prentice Hall Home Page at: http://www.phschool.com

Connecting to the Guiding Questions

As students complete this chapter, they will focus on the countries of Mexico, Guatemala, and Panama. A compelling issue—migration to cities, the status of the indigenous people, or the operation of the Panama Canal—provides a starting point for study. Content in this chapter corresponds to two Guiding Questions:

- Why have many Latin Americans been moving to the city in recent years?

- How has geography influenced the ways in which Latin Americans make a living?

Using the Map Activities

Point out to students the shape of Mexico and Central America. Encourage students to trace the outline of the region, while describing its funnel shape.

- seven; the Pacific Ocean and the Caribbean Sea

- Mountain ranges and rivers helped divide Central America.

Heterogeneous Groups

The following Teacher's Edition strategies are suitable for heterogeneous groups.

Critical Thinking
Recognizing Cause and Effect   p. 87

Cooperative Learning
Scenes From a Life of Purpose   p. 92

Interdisciplinary Connections
Math   p. 100

CHAPTER 4

Exploring Mexico and Central America

SECTION 1
Mexico
ONE FAMILY'S MOVE TO THE CITY

SECTION 2
Guatemala
DESCENDANTS OF AN ANCIENT PEOPLE

SECTION 3
Panama
WHERE TWO OCEANS MEET

KEY
— National boundary
⊛ National capital
• Other city

0   200   400 mi
0 200 400 km
Lambert Conformal Conic Projection

MAP ACTIVITIES

Look at the map above. Notice that the shape of Mexico and Central America is like a funnel, wide at the top and narrowing to a point. To learn more about this region, complete the following activities.

Study the map
How many countries are there in Central America? What bodies of water do they border?

Consider the geography
Mexico is a large country, while the countries of Central America are small. How do you think geography helped divide Central America into small countries?

Resource Directory

Media and Technology

Case Study: Cleaning up the Air in Mexico City, from the World Video Explorer, enhances students' understanding of one of the major consequences of urbanization and what Mexico City is doing to meet this challenge.

Chapter 6

Mexico

ONE FAMILY'S MOVE TO THE CITY

BEFORE YOU READ

Reach Into Your Background

Have you ever moved from one house to another or from one city to another? Did you have to change schools? Think about what the move was like and make a few notes about how you felt at the time.

Questions to Explore

1. Why have many Mexicans been moving from the countryside to the city?

2. What challenges do Mexicans from the country face when they build new lives in the city?

Key Terms
squatter
plaza
migrant farmworker

Key Places
Mexico City

R amiro Avila (rah MEE roh ah VEE lah) is one of seven children. He grew up in the state of Guanajuato (gwah nuh HWAH toh), in central Mexico. In his small village, Ramiro knew everyone and everyone knew him.

Ramiro's family were campesinos who owned no land. Even as a young child, Ramiro had to work to help support the family. He and his father had jobs as farm laborers. They worked on someone else's farm. They made less than a dollar a day.

The Move to Mexico City

Ramiro's village is located in the southern part of the Mexican Plateau. This area has Mexico's best farmland. It also is home to more than half of the country's people. Not surprisingly, it is the location of Mexico's largest city—Mexico City. Find Mexico City on the map on the previous page.

When Ramiro was 13, his parents decided to move the family to Mexico City. They hoped to find better work. The city was far away and their lives would be completely different. But moving offered them a chance to make a decent living.

Mexico's Population

Chart Study What pattern of population movement does this chart show?

	Total Population	Urban (%)	Rural (%)
1995	93,986,000	71.0	29.0
2000*	102,912,000	77.7	22.3
2010*	120,115,000	81.6	18.4

*Projected population

Teaching Resources

📁 **Reproducible Lesson Plan** in the Chapter and Section Resources booklet, p. 54, provides a summary of the section lesson.

📁 **Guided Reading and Review** in the Chapter and Section Resources booklet, p. 55, provides a structure for mastering key concepts and reviewing key terms in the section. Available in Spanish in the Spanish Chapter and Section Resources booklet, p. 34.

Program Resources

Material in the *Primary Sources and Literature Readings* booklet extends content with a selection from the region under study.

Outline Maps Mexico political map

Lesson Objectives

1 Explain reasons for the migration of rural Mexicans to urban centers.

2 Describe challenges faced by poor people who move to Mexico City.

3 Summarize the problems of growing cities in Mexico.

Lesson Plan

1 Engage

Warm-Up Activity

Ask students whether they have ever worked and been paid for their work. Write responses on the board. Ask them to name some of the things they bought with their earnings. Point out that in some families, the money children earn is used to buy food and clothing for the family. Help students distinguish between working by cleaning the garage, baby-sitting, or helping an uncle at a restaurant and working at a regular job.

Activating Prior Knowledge

Have students read Reach Into Your Background in the Before You Read box. Ask students who have moved to tell how they felt about changing schools and moving to a new neighborhood.

Answers to...

CHART STUDY

• People are moving to cities from rural areas.

SECTION 1 83

2 Explore

Have students read the section. Then discuss with them life in rural Mexico, identifying characteristics of that life that lead people to move to cities. Point out that new problems arose when Ramiro's family moved. Ask students to list things Ramiro might like about living in the country and things he might like about living in the city.

3 Teach

Have students create a cause-effect tree based on information in the section. Direct students to list causes such as the following: family cannot earn enough in the country; family could not afford house in the city; Mexico's population rising dramatically; Mexico's cities growing quickly. For each cause, ask students to write at least one effect. Use their completed charts as a springboard for a discussion of possible solutions to the problems of Mexico's cities. This activity should take about 20 minutes.

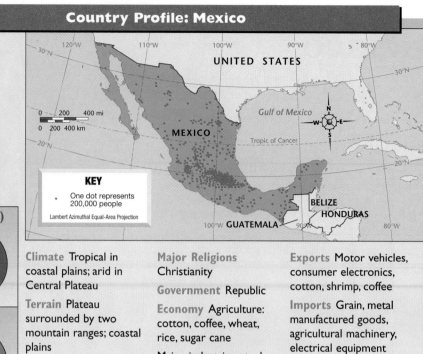

Country Profile: Mexico

Location Southern North America

UNITED STATES

Gulf of Mexico

MEXICO

Tropic of Cancer

BELIZE
HONDURAS

GUATEMALA

KEY

• One dot represents 200,000 people

Lambert Azimuthal Equal-Area Projection

Age Structure (in years)

- Under 15
- 15–64
- 65 and over

4
36
60

Ethnic Groups

- Mestizo
- Native American
- European
- Other

60
30
9
1

Climate Tropical in coastal plains; arid in Central Plateau

Terrain Plateau surrounded by two mountain ranges; coastal plains

Population 94 million

Major Religions Christianity

Government Republic

Economy Agriculture: cotton, coffee, wheat, rice, sugar cane

Major industries: steel, chemicals, electronic goods, textiles

Exports Motor vehicles, consumer electronics, cotton, shrimp, coffee

Imports Grain, metal manufactured goods, agricultural machinery, electrical equipment

Map Study The map above shows Mexico's population distribution. Some parts of Mexico are sparsely populated, while others are very crowded.

Location Where do most of Mexico's people live? Why do you think that they live in that area and not elsewhere?

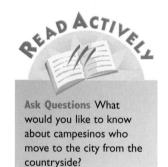

Ask Questions What would you like to know about campesinos who move to the city from the countryside?

Housing in the City Like thousands of other campesino families coming to the city, Ramiro's family did not have much money. When they arrived in Mexico City, they could not afford a house. They went to live in Colonia Zapata, which is one of many neighborhoods where poor people become **squatters.** That means they settle on someone else's land without permission. Many small houses of squatters cling to the sides of a steep hill in the Colonia. The older houses near the bottom of the hill are built of concrete. However, most people cannot afford to make sturdy houses when they first arrive. Therefore, many of the newer houses higher up the hill are constructed of scrap metal.

Ramiro's family made a rough, one-room house of rock. Ramiro felt that his new house was ugly. He and his family hoped that soon they would be able to buy land from the government. Then they could build a real house with a garden and a patio.

Answers to...
MAP STUDY

- in and around Mexico City; to be near job opportunities

Work and School Ramiro went to school in Mexico City, but he also worked as a cook in a tiny restaurant. He started work at 7 A.M. and worked until 2 P.M., preparing scrambled eggs and sausage. For these seven hours of work he earned about $3. His mother and some of his brothers and sisters worked, too. Ramiro went to a school that held night classes, attending classes until 9:30 at night.

Ramiro's father could not get a job in Mexico City. He decided to go to Texas in the United States. He found work as a farm laborer there. He sent money home every month. The move to Mexico City brought a lot of responsibilities for Ramiro. It became his job to look after his younger brothers and sisters while his father was gone. Ramiro's life was very different from how it had been in his village.

Life in Rural Mexico

Before Ramiro's family moved, they lived in a village where life has changed little over the years. Every village has a church and a market. At the center of most villages is a public square called a **plaza.** Farm families grow their own food. If they have extra food, they sell it at the market. Rural people buy nearly everything they need—clothing, food, toys, housewares—at the market rather than in stores.

Markets of Rural Mexico

This photograph shows a market in Oaxaca, Mexico. People in rural Mexico buy many of their groceries and housewares from markets like these. **Critical Thinking** What details in this photograph show similarities between rural markets and urban supermarkets? What details show differences?

SKILLS MINI LESSON

Using Distribution Maps

To **introduce** the skill, point out to students that if they walk two miles through a crowded city, they are likely to see more people than if they walk two miles through farmland. Tell students that a distribution map is a special-purpose map that presents this kind of information.

Direct students' attention to the population distribution map in the Country Profile. Help students **practice** the skill by asking them to describe the dot pattern they see on the map. Have them discuss how the dot pattern helps them visualize how many more people live in central Mexico than live farther south. Ask students to explain how they could use the map to locate Mexico City.

Farm Work Most farm families in Mexico and Central America are poor. Many campesinos work their own small farms. They often plow the land and harvest their crops by hand because they cannot afford expensive equipment. **Migrant farmworkers** do not own land. Like Ramiro and his father, they work on large farms owned by rich landowners. Migrants travel from one area to another, picking the crops that are in season.

Lack of Jobs Mexico's population has risen dramatically over the last 20 years. The country's population is growing at a rate of more than two percent each year—one of the highest rates in the world. There is not enough farm work for so many people. A large family cannot support itself on a small farm. And there are not enough jobs for all the migrant workers. Many people move to the cities because they cannot find work in the countryside.

About 70 percent of Mexico's people now live in cities and large towns. Many of them live in Mexico City. If you count the people in all the outlying areas, Mexico City has over 23 million people. Only Tokyo, Japan, has more people than Mexico City.

Mexico City: A Megacity

Mexico City is huge. Its population sprawls over a large area. It is a megacity, an urban center where many of Mexico's people live. Unlike most big cities, Mexico City does not have many skyscrapers and major streets. Two- and three-story buildings still form its downtown. Only a

Predict What problems might occur as more people move into a city?

Mexico: Volcanoes and Earthquake Faults

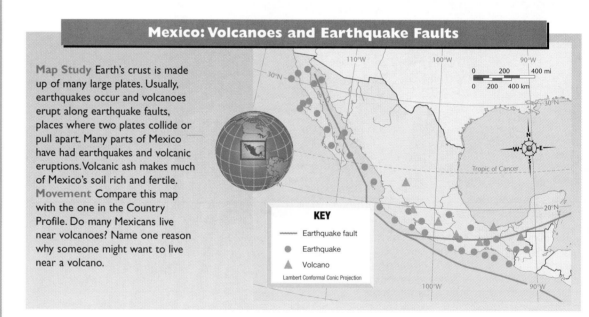

Map Study Earth's crust is made up of many large plates. Usually, earthquakes occur and volcanoes erupt along earthquake faults, places where two plates collide or pull apart. Many parts of Mexico have had earthquakes and volcanic eruptions. Volcanic ash makes much of Mexico's soil rich and fertile. **Movement** Compare this map with the one in the Country Profile. Do many Mexicans live near volcanoes? Name one reason why someone might want to live near a volcano.

KEY

———— Earthquake fault

● Earthquake

▲ Volcano

Lambert Conformal Conic Projection

The Growth of Mexico City

Map Study Mexico City covers more than twice the land that it did in 1945. **Interaction** How do you think the challenges of living in a city might be different from the challenges of living in a rural area?

KEY

City limits, 1945

City limits, 1995

Lambert Azimuthal Equal-Area Projection

Lake Zumpango

Lake Texcoco (dry)

0   5   10 mi
0   5   10 km

Activity

Skills

Recognizing Cause and Effect *Suitable as a whole class activity.* Discuss with students the causes of air pollution in Mexico City and the geographic features that contribute to it. Have students create a diagram that shows the process. Diagrams should start with causes and show how they lead to effects. Diagrams should also show how effects can then become causes. *Visual*

few streets are wide enough for the city's traffic. The subway, the underground railroad system, carries thousands of people each day.

Small neighborhoods of very wealthy people are tucked away from the rest. But most of Mexico City's residents are not wealthy. They live in all areas of the city. The poorest, like Ramiro and his family, live on the outskirts. Some must travel several hours a day to get to their jobs and back.

Pollution and Geography   Because the cities have grown so large, Mexico's capital and other large cities in the region are facing problems of pollution and traffic jams. Four million cars and trucks jam Mexico City's narrow streets. They compete with taxis, trolleys, and buses. Mexico City's location traps pollution close to the city. The city spreads across a bowl-shaped valley. The mountains surrounding the valley stop winds from carrying away factory smoke, automobile exhaust fumes, and other pollution. The pollution creates smog. It hangs over the city like a black cloud.

Making a Living   Large cities offer many ways to make a living. Factories and offices employ millions of people. Thousands more sell goods from stalls in the street. Ramiro's sister, Carmela, is a street vendor. She sells juice at a stand in the bus station near their neighborhood.

LINKS ACROSS TIME

Tenochtitlán—A Clean City Tenochtitlán, the Aztec capital, did not have a pollution problem. In fact, the first Europeans to visit Tenochtitlán were amazed at how clean the city was. At least 1,000 workers cleaned and swept the city's streets. Clean water was piped in from springs. At the time, European cities did not have fresh, clean water.

SKILLS MINI LESSON

Writing for a Purpose To **introduce** this skill, point out to students that we use different kinds of writing for different purposes. Indicate that songs and poems are ideal for expressing feelings. Encourage students to **practice** the skill by writing a poem or song lyrics that explain how Ramiro might have felt about moving to Mexico City. Encourage students to rely on facts from the text to support the imagined feelings. Invite volunteers to read their poems or lyrics to the class.

Answers to...

MAP STUDY

- Accept any reasonable answer. Students should support their answer with evidence given in the photograph.

1. (a) people who settle on someone else's land without permission (b) a public square in the center of a Mexican village (c) farm-workers who travel with the seasons and the crops to work on large farms

2. megacity in Mexico, where more than 23 million people live.

3. to find jobs

4. Answers may vary. Possible answers: People have to find or create housing when they move to the city. They may live without running water or electricity. Some children work part of the day. It may take hours to get to and from jobs.

5. Answers may vary. Possible answer: The lives of rural Mexicans improve because they may find some work and can support themselves and their families. Their lives are difficult in that they must work very hard. They live in poor housing and spend many hours a day getting to and from work.

6. Students' journal entries will vary but should contrast their own lives with that of Ramiro.

Answers to...

SMOG OVER MEXICO CITY

- Pollutants from traffic and industry are part of smog. These pollutants are trapped by the air inversion caused by the city's valley location. Accept any reasonable discussion of how smog might affect how people live.

Smog Over Mexico City

Even on a sunny day, buildings a few blocks away appear dim and blurry in Mexico City because of smog. **Interaction** Why do you think Mexico City has so much smog? How do you think the smog affects the way people in Mexico City live?

Every morning, she gets up at 5:30 to make juice from oranges and carrots. People on their way to work buy her juice for their long trip into the city.

Mexico City is not the only city that is growing. All of Mexico's major cities are becoming more crowded. City life is not easy for most Mexicans. Hard work and hope are what keep people going.

SECTION 1 REVIEW

1. Define (a) squatter, (b) plaza, (c) migrant farmworker.

2. Identify Mexico City.

3. What is the main reason that rural people from all over Mexico have been moving to the cities?

4. What difficulties do rural people face when they move to Mexico City?

Critical Thinking

5. Expressing Problems Clearly How do the lives of rural Mexicans improve when they move to the city? How do their lives continue to be difficult?

Activity

6. Writing to Learn Write an entry in your journal comparing and contrasting Ramiro's life with your own. How are your lives different? What similarities do you notice?

Resource Directory

Teaching Resources

Section Quiz in the Chapter and Section Resources booklet, p. 56, covers the main ideas and key terms in the section. Available in Spanish in the Spanish Chapter and Section Resources booklet, p. 35.

Guatemala

DESCENDANTS OF AN ANCIENT PEOPLE

BEFORE YOU READ

Reach Into Your Background

Each year the Nobel Peace Prize is awarded to someone who has worked for peace in the world. What qualities do you think a person should have in order to receive such a prize?

Questions to Explore

1. How are the indigenous people of Guatemala a unique culture?

2. What are the main issues that indigenous people face?

3. How did Rigoberta Menchú become a leader of her people?

Key Terms

ladino
ethnic group
strike

Key People and Places

Rigoberta Menchú
Guatemala

"**W**here I live is practically a paradise, the country is so beautiful. There are no big roads and no cars. Only people can reach it." These are the words of a Guatemalan woman named Rigoberta Menchú (ree goh BEHR tah men CHOO). Menchú is a Mayan woman. She was born in 1959. She speaks a language called Quiché (kee CHAY). In 1984, Menchú wrote a book about her life in Guatemala.

The mountains where Menchú was born are beautiful. But Menchú's family was very poor. They farmed their land, but the soil was not good. "Where we live in the mountains," Menchú wrote, "you can barely grow maize and beans. The land isn't fertile enough for anything else."

The Struggle for Land

Menchú's mountain home is in the country of Guatemala. This southern neighbor of Mexico is "first" in Central America in many categories. For example, it has the largest population among Central American countries. To learn more about Guatemala, study the Country Profile on the next page.

▼ Most Mayas who live in the highlands of Guatemala have only small plots of land to farm.

Teaching Resources

📁 **Reproducible Lesson Plan** in the Chapter and Section Resources booklet, p. 57, provides a summary of the section lesson.

📁 **Guided Reading and Review** in the Chapter and Section Resources booklet, p. 58, provides a structure for mastering key concepts and reviewing key terms in the section. Available in Spanish in the Spanish Chapter and Section Resources booklet, p. 36.

Media and Technology

💿📼 **Making a Living: Farming in Central America,** from the World Video Explorer, enhances understanding of how the region's physical geography combines with unique farming methods to contribute to the success of farming.

Chapter 7

Section

Lesson Objectives

❶ Describe the indigenous people of Guatemala.

❷ Discuss how Guatemala's indigenous people have been mistreated.

❸ Explain how Rigoberta Menchú became the leader of a political movement.

Lesson Plan

1 Engage

Warm-Up Activity

Ask students to imagine that one day soldiers come to all the houses in their neighborhood and order the people to leave. Prompt the discussion by asking, *How would you feel? What would you do?* Have students try to imagine what life is like in a country where such actions really happen.

Activating Prior Knowledge

Have students read Reach Into Your Background in the Before You Read box. Students are likely to list several qualities, including kindness, courage, and a sense of fairness.

2 Explore

Direct students to read the section. Next, ask them to explain who the indigenous people of Guatemala are and what happened to them. Review how Rigoberta became involved in fighting for campesinos' rights. Why is she important to her people? Conclude the discussion by reviewing students' lists of qualities for Nobel Peace Prize winners. Have students identify how Rigoberta Menchú exemplifies the qualities on their lists.

3 Teach

Have students create posters showing who the indigenous people of Guatemala are and how Rigoberta Menchú helped them. Remind students to use facts from the section to support their work. Use completed posters as the basis for a discussion on the future of Guatemala. This activity should take about 20 minutes.

Answers to ...
MAP STUDY

- Mexico, Belize, Honduras, and El Salvador; responses may vary. Possible answer: Ladinos have historically been more involved in government.

Country Profile: Guatemala

Location Northernmost country in Central America

Climate Highlands; tropical along the coasts

Terrain Central plateau and mountain areas bordered by Pacific coast; plains and valleys along the Caribbean Sea; many volcanoes in the south

Population 11 million

Age Structure (in years)
- Under 15
- 15–64
- 65 and over

52
45
3

Ethnic Groups
- Native American
- Ladino
- Other

55
44
1

Major Religions Christianity

Government Republic

Economy Agriculture: coffee, sugar, bananas, cotton, corn

Major industries: furniture, tires, textiles

Exports Coffee, sugar, bananas, beef

Imports Fuel and petroleum products, machinery, grain, fertilizers, motor vehicles

KEY
— National boundary
⊛ National capital
• Other city
Mercator Projection

0   50   100 mi
0   50   100 km

Map Study This map shows the country of Guatemala. **Location** What four countries border Guatemala? **Chart Study** The chart on the bottom left shows the percentages of ethnic groups in Guatemala. Most Mayas live in rural communities, speak a Mayan language, and follow Mayan customs. Ladinos speak Spanish, have adopted Spanish customs, and often live in towns or cities. **Critical Thinking** Which ethnic group do you think has been more involved in Guatemala's government? Why?

Menchú's parents lived in the mountains because it was the only land available to Native Americans. Most land in Guatemala belongs to a few rich families. The rich landowners of Guatemala are **ladinos** (luh DEE nohs), mestizos who are descended from Native Americans and Spaniards. Native Americans who follow European ways are also considered to be ladinos.

Menchú's parents worked hard to make their land produce crops. "You had to pay a fee so that you could clear the land," she wrote. "Of course, it's not very easy to make things grow on land that's just been cleared. You don't get a good yield for at least eight or nine years."

Resource Directory

Media and Technology

Planet Earth CD-ROM includes an interactive political map of Guatemala, as well as the other countries of Latin America.

Material World CD-ROM includes a portrait of a Guatemalan family plus geographic data on Guatemala.

Teaching Resources

Reading a Circle Graph in the *Social Studies and Geography Skills* booklet, p. 55, provides additional skill practice.

Losing a Home During most of Menchú's childhood, there was a civil war going on in Guatemala. The Mayas were caught in the middle. Indigenous people do not always think of themselves as citizens of the country in which they live. A Mayan woman is more likely to think of herself as a Maya than as a Guatemalan.

Also, most Native Americans in Guatemala cannot read or write. Most Mayas have not filed any papers with the government showing that they own land. The Mayas often have no way to prove that their land belongs to them. The people of Menchú's village worked hard for many years, and soon the land began to produce crops. But then the civil war and landowners caught up with Menchú's village.

Menchú wrote that when she was twelve years old, the landowners came with soldiers. They disagreed with the village's claim to the land. Now that it was cleared and producing crops, they wanted it. They forced Menchú's family and their neighbors to leave.

"First they went into our houses without permission and got all the people out," Menchú remembered. Then, the soldiers were ordered to throw away each family's belongings. The soldiers took all the corn the people had stored. The villagers had nowhere to go but out into the rain.

A Guatemalan Market

Mayas in rural Guatemala do much of their shopping at open-air markets like this one. **Movement** What types of goods are being traded or sold at this market?

Program Resources

Outline Maps Central America and the Caribbean political map

Biography

Another Guatemalan Hero
Justo Rufino Barrios (1835–1885) served as president of Guatemala from 1873 to 1885. Barrios strengthened local government. Under his administration, education improved, roads were built, and employment figures rose. Barrios hoped that someday the countries of Central America would unite to form a strong political force.

Activity

Cooperative Learning

Scenes From a Life of Purpose Have the class select five events in the life of Rigoberta Menchú. Direct students to work in five groups—each creating a skit to illustrate one of the events. One or two students can write the dialogue, one can be responsible for props, and all students can act out the scene. Have groups perform their skits in chronological order. Afterwards, discuss Menchú's contribution to her people and to humanity.
Kinesthetic, Auditory

Answers to ...
COLORFUL CLOTHING

- Accept any reasonable answers such as attention to detail, manual dexterity, patience.

CITIZEN HEROES

Overcoming Obstacles
Justina Tzoc travels through rural Guatemala, teaching Quiché Maya women about their rights and teaching them to read. Her work is dangerous, because she sometimes travels through areas that are torn by civil war. But Tzoc is determined to help every woman she can reach.

Colorful Clothing

Mayan communities each have their own hand-woven style of clothing. **Critical Thinking** What skills do you think are needed to weave cloth into a certain pattern?

A 500-Year-Old Struggle Menchú's story is a common on The indigenous people of Guatemala have fought against injustice f 500 years. They started when the Spanish first arrived.

The Spanish conquered Native Americans by force. Many we killed. Others died of hunger or the hardships of slavery. Still othe died from European diseases. In many Latin American countries, the are few indigenous people left.

But in Guatemala, Native Americans are the majority of the popu tion. They form 23 ethnic groups. An **ethnic group** is a group of peop who share language, religion, and cultural traditions. The indigeno groups of Guatemala are related to each other. However, each group different. Each has its own language and customs. Rigoberta Mench comes from the largest group, the Quiché Maya.

Rigoberta Menchú Takes a Stand

Rigoberta Menchú began working with campesinos all over th country. She learned several other indigenous languages. She al learned Spanish. She wanted to be able to work with ladinos wh supported Native American land rights. Menchú became part of nationwide political movement, which is a large group of people who work together to defend their rights or to change the leaders in power. This political movement was to defend campesino rights. Menchú helped villages plan ways to protect themselves. She taught people how to read. She also taught people about the history of their land. Menchú helped the movement organize meetings, protests, and **strikes,** or work stoppages. She was determined to defend Native American land rights.

Menchú's mother, father, and brother were killed fighting against the landowners. But Menchú continued to fight for the rights of her people. Her life, too, was in danger. For her own safety, Menchú had to leave the country. She went to live in Mexico.

Peace in Guatemala   In 1992, Rigoberta Menchú was awarded the Nobel Peace Prize. She was the first indigenous person in the world ever to win the prize. Since 1992, Menchú has continued to work for justice in Guatemala. Her efforts have brought important changes. Recently, Guatemala's government appointed 21 Mayan priests to advise officials about Mayan culture. New Mayan organizations are being formed every day. In addition, Mayan languages are being used in books, newspapers, and radio programs. Government officials and Mayan leaders hope these changes will bring peace to Guatemala.

Rigoberta Menchú

Rigoberta Menchú never went to school. Instead, she worked on farms and as a maid. Later, she taught herself to speak and read several languages. She knew that command of these languages would help her get her message to all Guatemalans.

Ask Questions What questions would you like to ask Rigoberta Menchú about her activities?

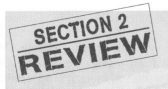

SECTION 2 REVIEW

1. **Define**   (a) ladino, (b) ethnic group, (c) strike.

2. **Identify**   (a) Rigoberta Menchú, (b) Guatemala.

3. How does Rigoberta Menchú describe the land where she was born?

4. How do most indigenous people in Guatemala make a living? What difficulties do they face?

Critical Thinking

5. **Identifying Cause and Effect**   Explain the main reason that Guatemala's indigenous people and other farmers have formed a political movement.

Activity

6. **Writing to Learn**   Write a short essay explaining what you would have done if you were in Rigoberta Menchú's position. Then, explain what you would do if you were the president of Guatemala.

Resource Directory

Teaching Resources

📁 **Section Quiz** in the Chapter and Section Resources booklet, p. 59, covers the main ideas and key terms in the section. Available in Spanish in the Spanish Chapter and Section Resources booklet, p. 37.

📁 **Critical Thinking Activity** in the Chapter and Section Resources booklet, p. 67, helps students apply the skill of identifying central issues.

Background

Global Perspectives

Women Champions of Peace   In addition to Rigoberta Menchú, eight other women have won the Nobel Peace Prize. Perhaps the best known is Mother Teresa, a nun in Calcutta, India, who founded the Missionaries of Charity to care for the poor, sick, and dying. She received the Nobel Peace Prize in 1979. The 1991 recipient of the prize, Aung San Suu Kyi, has led the struggle for democracy in Myanmar, formerly Burma.

Section 2 Review

1. (a) rich landowners of Guatemala and Native Americans who follow European ways (b) group of people who share language, religion, or cultural traditions (c) work stoppages

2. (a) a Mayan woman who led indigenous people in a fight to keep their land and other rights (b) Central American country just south of Mexico

3. She calls it a paradise without roads or cars.

4. Answers may vary. Sample answer: Most indigenous people in Guatemala farm for a living. The soil is poor and does not yield much.

5. They formed a political movement to defend campesino rights.

6. Students' essays should reflect actions appropriate to Menchú's position. Essays describing the president's actions should indicate causes as well as their effects.

Previewing a Reading Selection

Lesson Objectives

❶ Explain the process of previewing.

❷ Apply previewing to a reading selection.

Lesson Plan

1 Engage

Warm-Up Activity

To **introduce** the skill, write the word *preview* on the chalkboard. Ask students to name the prefix and the word that form the word *preview.* (pre-, view) Have a volunteer suggest a meaning for the word based on the root word.

Activating Prior Knowledge

Ask students how they decide which television program to watch, which CD to buy, or what to order at a restaurant. Have them discuss how previewing might help them make a decision.

Sean asked his mom if he could go for a bike ride before it got dark. His mom said, "Sure, if you finish your homework first." Sean didn't have much homework. "If I can finish it in an hour," Sean thought to himself, "I'll have a whole hour for a killer mountain bike adventure."

He settled down to study. His assignment was to answer ten questions about the Panama Canal using two books he had checked out from the school library. He read the first question: "What are three obstacles workers faced when building the Panama Canal?" He picked up the first book and began reading on page 1. Five pages and 10 minutes later he didn't have his answer. He tried the other book. Ten pages and 20 minutes later he still hadn't found what he was looking for. "Half an hour gone and not one question answered!" he thought, disgustedly. "No bike ride tonight!"

Sean missed out on his bike ride because he forgot to apply an important skill: previewing. Previewing means looking over a book or chapter before you read it or try to find information in it. Previewing is a valuable study skill that will help you read more efficiently.

Get Ready

How do you preview? You might be surprised to learn that this is one skill you already know! If you've ever seen a preview for a movie, you've "previewed" that movie. You have a gen-

1 Read the title of the book.

2 Read the table of contents at the front of the book.

eral idea what the movie is about. If you've ever looked over a menu, you've "previewed" your meal. You have a general idea of what the food will be like.

Of course, previewing a reading selection is a little different from previewing a movie or meal. Previewing means looking over something you are about to read in a general way to become familiar with it. The idea is to get a "sense" of the material. To get a sense of what a book is about, you can use five things: the title, the table of contents, the illustrations, the index, and sample paragraphs. To do this with a chapter, you can use titles, subtitles, illustrations, and captions.

Resource Directory

Teaching Resources

Social Studies and Geography Skills
Previewing the Headings and the Pictures, p. 68

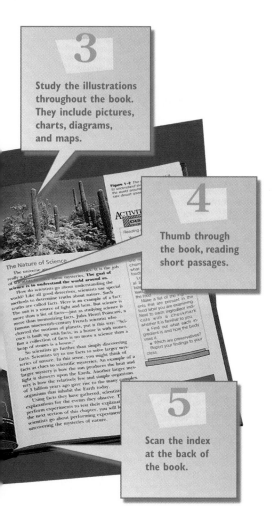

3 Study the illustrations throughout the book. They include pictures, charts, diagrams, and maps.

4 Thumb through the book, reading short passages.

5 Scan the index at the back of the book.

Try It Out

You can practice previewing a book in a fun and easy way by playing a "What Does It Tell Us?" game with a group of six students. Choose your group members, and choose a book. Then sit down and preview it together. Your group will follow the script to the right. After each person reads his or her part to the group, the other group members should work together to answer the question. Group Member 6 is the group secretary, who writes the answers down.

Group Member 1: "The title indicates the main subject of the book. Many books have a subtitle that gives even more information. What does the title of our book tell us?"

Group Member 2: "The table of contents is like a menu at a restaurant. It tells us what general topics are available in the book. What does the table of contents tell us?"

Group Member 3: "The illustrations in a book provide clues to the subjects discussed in the book. What do the illustrations tell us about the book?"

Group Member 4: "The index lists the specific topics in a book and the pages where they are discussed. What does the index tell us about the content of our book?"

Group Member 5: "By thumbing through a book and reading a few paragraphs here and there, you can get an idea of how a book is written. You can see if there are special headings in the book. What does a little reading tell us about our book?"

When you've completed this process, use the secretary's notes to find specific information in the book. If you are going to read the whole book, this process can help you get the most out of your reading.

Apply the Skill

Now that you know how to preview, practice by previewing Chapter 4. What do the titles and subtitles tell you about the chapter? How about the illustrations and captions? Take notes as you preview the chapter. Then, use your notes to write a short description of the chapter. Finally, as you read through the chapter, see how it matches your description.

2 Explore

Direct students to read the text under the heading Get Ready. Then have them read the rest of the skills activity. Ask each of five volunteers to list one part of a book they can use for previewing. (title, table of contents, illustrations, index, and sample paragraphs)

3 Teach

Organize students into groups of six. Have students **practice** the skill by directing groups to play the game What Does It Tell Us? as described in Try It Out. Suggest that student groups pool their answers and then create a class list of them.

4 Assess

Have students **apply** the skill by previewing Chapter 4. Have students use their notes to write no more than three sentences that they think describe the chapter. To **assess,** evaluate students' sentences, as well as their notes indicating what the titles, subtitles, illustrations, and captions reveal about Chapter 4.

Section 3

Panama

WHERE TWO OCEANS MEET

Lesson Objectives

1 Explain why Panama is a good site for a canal.

2 Summarize how the Panama Canal was built.

3 Describe how Panama gained control of the canal.

Lesson Plan

1 Engage

Warm-Up Activity

Use a cardboard box or a three-dimensional drawing on the board to estimate the size of a cubic yard. Ask students to estimate how many such boxes could fit in their classroom or in their school. Have students judge how many of the boxes could fit in a football field or local stadium.

Then tell students that to build the Panama Canal, workers scooped out and removed 211 million cubic yards of earth and rock. Explain that the Panama Canal is considered one of the great engineering feats of all time. In this section, students will read why this is so.

Activating Prior Knowledge

Have students read Reach Into Your Background in the Before You Read box. Students' responses will vary. Allow students to pose solutions without judgment.

BEFORE YOU READ

Reach Into Your Background

Have you ever agreed to a deal or given away something and then wondered if you made the best choice? Think about how you felt. Write down some ways you might try to undo the deal.

Questions to Explore

1. What geographic and political factors made Panama a good site for a canal?
2. How was the Panama Canal built?
3. How did Panama gain control of the Panama Canal?

Key Term

lock

Key Places

Panama Canal
Canal Zone

The Panama Canal is the shortcut of the Western Hemisphere. It's the only way to get from the Pacific Ocean to the Atlantic by ship without going all the way around South America. That's a savings of 7,800 miles (12,553 km).

But be prepared to wait. Traffic jams can leave you bobbing in the ocean for up to 20 hours. Then the trip through the 40-mile (64.4-km) canal takes another eight hours. That's about walking speed. Then there is the toll: as much as $34,000.

Going Through the Canal

Cruising through the Pacific Ocean, a tanker approaches the city of Balboa, in the country of Panama. It is heading for the Panama Canal. The ship is loaded with petroleum. Other ships sailing toward the canal carry lumber, metal ores, and other cargo. Ships pass through the Panama Canal 24 hours a day, 365 days a year. The canal is crowded. The tanker must get in line.

The tanker enters the canal at sea level. But parts of the canal go through mountains and are not at sea level. The tanker will need to be raised and lowered several times as it travels toward the Atlantic Ocean.

Miraflores Lock The ship sails north to Miraflores (mee ruh FLOR uhs) Lock. A **lock** is a section of waterway in which ships are raised or lowered by adjusting the water level. The tanker passes through a set of gates into a lock chamber. The water in the chamber is still at sea level. Then, more water comes pouring into the chamber.

Resource Directory

Teaching Resources

📁 **Reproducible Lesson Plan** in the Chapter and Section Resources booklet, p. 60, provides a summary of the section lesson.

📁 **Guided Reading and Review** in the Chapter and Section Resources booklet, p. 61, provides a structure for mastering key concepts and reviewing key terms in the section. Available in Spanish in the Spanish Chapter and Section Resources booklet, p. 38.

Media and Technology

💿 **Planet Earth** CD-ROM includes an interactive political map of Panama, as well as the other countries of Latin America.

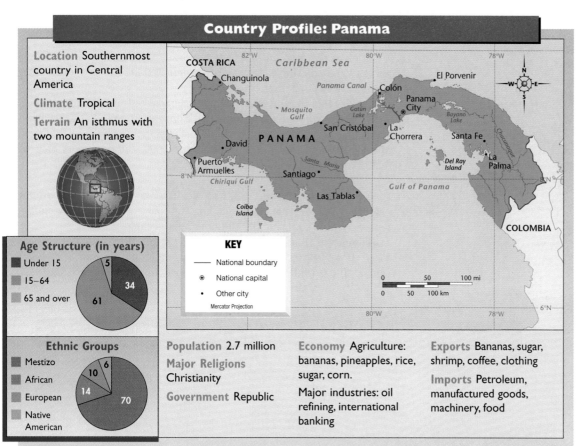

Country Profile: Panama

Location Southernmost country in Central America

Climate Tropical

Terrain An isthmus with two mountain ranges

Age Structure (in years)
- Under 15
- 15–64
- 65 and over

5, 34, 61

Ethnic Groups
- Mestizo
- African
- European
- Native American

6, 10, 14, 70

KEY

— National boundary

⊛ National capital

• Other city

Mercator Projection

0   50   100 mi
0   50   100 km

Population 2.7 million

Major Religions Christianity

Government Republic

Economy Agriculture: bananas, pineapples, rice, sugar, corn.

Major industries: oil refining, international banking

Exports Bananas, sugar, shrimp, coffee, clothing

Imports Petroleum, manufactured goods, machinery, food

Map Study This map shows the country of Panama and the location of the Panama Canal. Find the Panama Canal on the map.

Movement How do you think the new shipping route created by the canal affected the economy of the city of Colón? Explain your answer.

through valves. The tanker rises like a toy boat in a bathtub filling with water. When the water rises high enough, the ship passes through a second set of gates and enters a small lake. It proceeds to the next lock, and the water level is raised again.

Galliard Cut During the voyage, the tanker will pass through two more sets of locks. It will zigzag through the eight-mile (13-km) Galliard (GAL yurd) Cut. The Galliard Cut was blasted through the hard rock of Panama's mountains. The tanker will sail through a huge artificial lake and past an island that is home to a wild game preserve. Finally, eight hours after entering the canal, the tanker exits at Limón (lih MOHN) Bay in the city of Colón (kuh LOHN). It has traveled only 40 miles (64 km), but it is now in the Atlantic Ocean.

Program Resources

Outline Maps Central America and the Caribbean political map

2 Explore

Have students read the section. Discuss traveling through the Panama Canal. Ask students to describe what this experience might be like. Have students consider how the United States gained the right to build the canal and what its construction was like. Finally, discuss how its ownership has changed since 1979. Have students list some reasons why the United States transferred ownership.

3 Teach

Organize students into three groups, telling them that they are journalists assigned to cover the Panama Canal. The assignment for students in the first group is to write brief news reports about traveling through the canal. Direct students in the second group to write a news report about the U.S. role in the canal. Have students in the third group write about the decision to return the canal to Panama. Then have students form new groups of three in which each student has prepared a different report. Have them read their reports to one another. This activity should take about 20 minutes.

Answers to . . .
MAP STUDY

- Responses should indicate that Colón probably had an economic boom because it is located at one end of the canal.

See answers to the Section Review. You may also use students' news reports as an assessment.

Acceptable reports include suitable facts from the text.

Commendable reports may include appropriate opinions, supported by facts.

Outstanding reports draw reasonable conclusions about the topic.

Background

Global Perspectives

Canals Change the World Other canals have significantly changed countries and world travel. For example, the Erie Canal, completed in 1825, changed American history. The canal linked Chicago, Detroit, and Buffalo to the Atlantic Ocean. The resulting industry made the Midwest a magnet for settlement by immigrants. In the Middle East, the Suez Canal—connecting the Mediterranean Sea to the Red Sea and the Indian Ocean—opened in 1869. The canal greatly shortens the distance between Europe and Asia.

Answers to ...
MAP STUDY

- Responses may vary but should indicate that both countries wanted to profit from control of the Canal Zone and the United States wanted a faster route for its ships.

The Idea for a Canal Takes Hold

Look at the map on this page and trace the route the canal follows across Panama. This waterway has dominated life in Panama for much of the twentieth century.

Sailors had dreamed of a canal through Central America since the 1500s. A canal could shorten the trip from the Atlantic to the Pacific by thousands of miles. It would cut the cost of shipping goods by thousands of dollars for each ship. But not until the 1900s did engineers have the technology to make such a canal.

A Struggle Over Rights to Build The first real attempt came in 1881. At that time, Panama was part of Colombia. Colombia gave a French company the rights to build a canal.

Digging through Panama posed several problems for the builders. First, they struggled with mud slides as they dug. Second, a mountain range, the Cordillera de San Blas (kord ul YEHR uh day san blas),

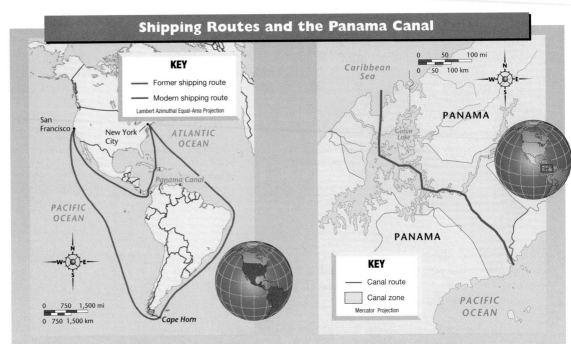

Shipping Routes and the Panama Canal

KEY
— Former shipping route
— Modern shipping route
Lambert Azimuthal Equal-Area Projection

San Francisco
New York City
ATLANTIC OCEAN
Panama Canal
PACIFIC OCEAN
Cape Horn
0   750   1,500 mi
0   750   1,500 km

Caribbean Sea
PANAMA
Gatún Lake
PANAMA
PACIFIC OCEAN
KEY
— Canal route
☐ Canal zone
Mercator Projection
0   50   100 mi
0   50   100 km

Map Study The map on the left shows shipping routes from New York to San Francisco before and after construction of the Panama Canal. The map on the right is a close up of the Panama Canal route. Before the Panama Canal was built, ships had to travel more than 13,000 miles (20,900 km) around South America. After the Canal was built, ships only had to travel 5,200 miles (8,370 km). **Movement** Why do you think that Panama and the United States both wanted to control the Canal Zone?

Panama's Tropical Rain Forest

Panama's Barro Colorado rain forest is inside the Canal Zone. **Critical Thinking** This photograph shows a trail through the rain forest. Where is it? Based on this photograph, think of some difficulties that might have faced the Panama Canal workers.

blocked the way. Disease was also a problem. Much of Panama is covered with dense tropical forest. Tropical diseases such as malaria and yellow fever killed many workers. After several years of digging and blasting, the French company went bankrupt. Work on the canal stopped.

In 1902, the United States government bought what was left of the French company. Then, the United States began talks with Colombia about getting the rights to continue building a canal.

Colombia refused to grant the United States rights to build the canal. The businesspeople of Panama were disappointed. They knew that a canal would bring business to Panama. They wanted the canal to be built as soon as possible. Also, many Panamanians wanted to be free of Colombia's rule. They saw the canal as a chance to win independence.

In November 1903, the United States helped Panama revolt against Colombia. Two weeks after Panama declared its independence, the United States received the rights needed to build the canal.

LINKS ACROSS THE WORLD

Not Made in Panama You would assume the "Panama hat," a hand-woven straw hat, is made in Panama. However, you would be wrong—the hats were originally made in Ecuador. They were named for Panama because it was a shipping center for hats in the 1800s. Ecuadorans still make the Panama hat. But today, many hats are made even farther from Panama—in Asia.

The cut through Panama's soft earth hills was the hardest part of the canal to build. Earth still slides into the canal there today. **Movement** Based on the picture on the left, how were workers and supplies moved to and from the canal?

Activity

Interdisciplinary Connections

Math Have students use their knowledge of math applications to answer the following questions.

1. If it takes 8 hours for a ship to pass through the canal, how many miles per hour does a ship average? (40 miles in 8 hours = 5 miles per hour)

2. What fraction of the total time it took to build the canal was spent in controlling the mosquito problem? Make a circle graph to show the fraction. (1/8)

Building the Canal The builders of the canal faced numerous problems. They had to scoop out and remove mountains of earth and rock. The hills were made of soft earth. Whenever the diggers carved out a hole, more earth would slide into its place. The project called for a dam to be built to form a lake. There were locks to design and build.

While the work was difficult and slow, by far the biggest problem facing the project was disease. Some 25,000 workers had died of malaria and yellow fever while the French worked on the canal. Scientists did not know what caused these diseases, so they could do little to prevent them.

In the early 1900s, doctors discovered that malaria and yellow fever were both carried by mosquitoes. The mosquitoes bred in swamps and also in people's drinking water. In 1904, the Panama Canal Company hired a doctor and a large crew to deal with the mosquito problem. It took one year, 1,000 tons (907 metric tons) of timber, 200 tons (181 metric tons) of wire mesh, and 4,500 workers to do the job. Workers burned sulfur in every house to kill mosquitoes. They covered

Predict How do you think workers overcame problems to build the Panama Canal?

Resource Directory

Teaching Resources

📁 **Chapter Summary** in the Chapter and Section Resources booklet, p. 63, provides a summary of chapter content. Available in Spanish in the Spanish Chapter and Section Resources booklet, p. 40.

📁 **Cooperative Learning Activity** in the Activities and Projects booklet, pp. 32–35, provides two student handouts, one page of teacher's directions, and a scoring rubric for a cooperative learning activity on simulation: who should build the Panama Canal.

Media and Technology

🎧 Guided Reading Audiotapes (English and Spanish)

Answers to ...

LIKE DIGGING THROUGH SAND

• railroad

every water vessel with mesh so mosquitoes could not get in. They filled in swampy breeding grounds with dirt. Without this effort, the Panama Canal probably could not have been built.

Modern medicine and machinery were important to the project. So was good planning. Still, it took eight years and the sweat of 45,000 workers, mostly Caribbean islanders, to make the waterway. The Panama Canal remains one of the greatest engineering feats of modern times.

Control of the Canal

When the United States gained rights to build a canal, it signed a treaty with Panama. The treaty gave the United States the right to build the Panama Canal, and to control it forever.

The Canal Zone The United States also controlled an area called the Canal Zone. The Canal Zone included the land on either side of the canal, the ports, the port cities, and the railroad. The treaty allowed the United States to run the Zone according to its laws, and gave the United States the right to invade Panama to protect the canal.

Many Panamanians felt this was too high a price to pay for the privilege of having the canal in their country. The canal gave the United States a great deal of power in Panama. The United States built 14 military bases in the Canal Zone and stationed thousands of soldiers there.

For years, Panama talked with the United States about regaining control of the canal. In the 1960s and 1970s, many Panamanians grew angry. They rioted to protest U.S. control.

A Change of Ownership In 1978, after years of talks, U.S. President Jimmy Carter signed two new treaties with Panama's government. The Panama Canal Neutrality Treaty and the Panama Canal Treaty gave Panama more control over the canal. In 1999, the Panama Canal will belong to Panama for the first time.

Ask Questions What would you like to know about life near the Canal Zone?

SECTION 3 REVIEW

1. **Define** lock.

2. **Identify** (a) Panama Canal, (b) Canal Zone.

3. How did a canal come to be built in Panama?

4. What difficulties did the builders of the canal face?

5. How did the United States gain control of rights to build the canal?

6. Two sets of treaties have determined the control of the Panama Canal, the original treaty of 1903 and two in 1978. Describe the terms of these treaties.

Critical Thinking

7. **Identifying Central Issues** It has been very important to Panamanians to regain control of the canal. Explain why, in both political and economic terms.

Activity

8. **Writing to Learn** Imagine that you are a newspaper editor in 1900. Decide whether you think Panama or Nicaragua is a better choice for the location of the canal, and write a short editorial defending your position.

SKILLS MINI LESSON

Expressing Problems Clearly

To **introduce** the skill, tell students that expressing a problem clearly can help them find possible solutions to the problem. Help students **practice** the skill by having small groups choose the point of view of either the United States or Panama. Work with them to express clearly what the problems were. Have them list positive and negative effects of relinquishing control of the canal. You may want to have groups debate the issue.

Section 3 Review

1. a double pair of steel gates, which allows ships to change water levels when moving through a canal

2. (a) constructed waterway in Panama that links the Atlantic and Pacific Oceans (b) land on either side of the canal, ports, port cities, and railroad

3. Sailors had dreamed of a canal through Central America since the 1500s. In 1881, a French company gained the rights to build a canal.

4. Workers had to cut through the Cordillera de San Blas. They struggled with mudslides as they dug. They had to build a dam and design and build locks. They had to control yellow fever and malaria.

5. Answers may vary. Sample answer: The United States helped Panama gain independence from Colombia. In return, Panama gave the United States the right to build and control the canal.

6. Answers may vary. Sample answer: The original treaty gave the United States the right to build the canal and to control it forever. The new treaties gave Panama more control over the canal until 1999, at which time it will belong to Panama.

7. Student responses may vary, but should include the following points: It seems right to Panamanians to have control over their own country. It will be a boon to Panama, since the owner of the canal charges fees for passing through it.

8. Answers may vary. However, most students will likely defend Panama as the better location of the canal. Panama is a narrower piece of land than Nicaragua.

Review and Activities

Reviewing Main Ideas

1. Many Mexicans move from one rural area to another and from rural to urban areas in search of work, so they can earn money to support their families.

2. Many people live in makeshift houses made out of scrap metal or even rock. Transportation and air pollution are major problems, too.

3. The indigenous cultures consist of Native Americans, who try to maintain their traditional ways. Ladinos, many of whom are rich landowners, follow European ways.

4. Indigenous Guatemalans are struggling to hold on to their land and to assure that equal rights are guaranteed in their country.

5. The United States supported and aided the Panamanian revolt against Colombia. The Panamanians signed a treaty with the United States, giving it the right to build and control the canal.

6. (a) important to United States for economic and defense reasons; important to Panamanians to have control in their own country and gain economic benefits (b) Panama is gaining control of the canal and will own it in 1999.

Reviewing Key Terms

1. c	3. a	5. b
2. f	4. e	6. d

Critical Thinking

1. Answers may vary. Sample answer: Rigoberta Menchú and others want to force the government and landowners to change. Menchú wants indigenous people to own land and live there peacefully. She wants equal rights for all and an end to racism against indigenous people.

2. Answers may vary. Sample answer: The Panama Canal shows that the United States had nearly unlimited power in Central America; the United States helped Panama become chdependent, then took part of the country under its own control. The United States seems to be relinquishing its influence in the area, as evidenced by letting go of control of the canal.

Reviewing Main Ideas

1. Describe the movement of Mexicans from one area to another—rural to rural, rural to urban. Why do many people make these moves?

2. What problems has Mexico City experienced as a result of its rapid population growth?

3. How are the indigenous cultures of Guatemala distinct from the ladino culture?

4. What are the main challenges that indigenous Guatemalans face?

5. How did the United States gain the rights to build a canal in Panama?

6. (a) Why was the canal important to the United States and Panama?
   (b) How is control of the canal currently changing?

Reviewing Key Terms

Match the definitions in Column I with the key terms in Column II.

Column I

1. a landless person who travels from one area to another working other people's land
2. a section of a waterway in which ships are raised or lowered by adjusting the water level
3. a person who settles on someone else's land without permission
4. a work stoppage
5. a public square
6. people who share race, language, religion, and cultural traditions

Column II

a. squatter
b. plaza
c. migrant farmworker
d. ethnic group
e. strike
f. lock

Critical Thinking

1. **Identifying Central Issues** What are the main demands that Rigoberta Menchú and others like her have made of the government and landowners? How has the government responded?

2. **Drawing Conclusions** Over the years, the United States has exercised a great deal of economic and political influence in Central America. How does the Panama Canal demonstrate U.S. influence in the region? What do you think the changes taking place over the control of the canal say about U.S. influence in the region today?

Graphic Organizer

Copy the tree map onto a piece of paper. In the first set of boxes, note the three kinds of population movement. In the second set, note details about these movements.

Population Movements in Mexico

Graphic Organizer

Population Movements in Mexico

Poor people move from rural to urban areas.	Some Mexicans move to the United States.	Population movement to cities is increasing.
They make more money but live in substandard housing. Children work to earn money for family. Workers spend hours traveling to and from work.	They work as migrant laborers. They send money home to families.	There is not enough housing. Air pollution is a problem because of cars and factories. Cities are spread out, and transportation can be a problem.

Map Activity

For each place listed below, write the letter from the map that shows its location.

1. Guatemala
2. Colón, Panama
3. Panama
4. Mexico City

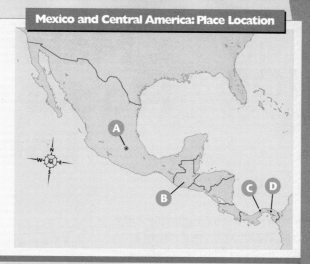

Mexico and Central America: Place Location

Writing Activity

Writing News Stories
Imagine you are a writer for a radio news program. Write brief news stories on population movements in Mexico, the work of Rigoberta Menchú, and the history of the Panama Canal. Be sure that each of your stories can be read in two to three minutes.

Internet Activity
Use a search engine to find the site **Ancient Guatemala**. Read **Our Mayan Legacy**. Then, click on **Guatemalan Home Page**. Click on the links **Modern Guatemala and Our People**. Make a chart comparing the architecture, language, people, and culture of ancient and modern Guatemala.

Skills Review

Turn to the Skill Activity.
Review the steps for previewing. Then use these steps to preview Chapter 5. Based on your preview, write a brief paragraph describing what you expect to read in the chapter.

How Am I Doing?

Answer these questions to help you check your progress.

1. Can I explain why a Mexican family might decide to leave the countryside for the city?
2. Do I understand the major challenges that face the indigenous peoples of Guatemala?
3. Can I describe the building of the Panama Canal and its impact on the Panamanian people?
4. What information from this chapter can I use in my book project?

Map Activity

1. B   3. D
2. C   4. A

Skills Review

Students' paragraphs will vary. Sample response: The chapter will tell about life in the Caribbean countries of Cuba, Haiti, and Puerto Rico. The chapter will describe communism in Cuba and the people who live there. The country of Haiti has struggled to be a democracy. Puerto Rico, a commonwealth of the United States, has ties to the U.S. mainland and to the Caribbean.

Writing Activity

Students' news stories will vary, but should contain the main ideas of each section.

Internet Link

If students are having difficulty finding this site, you may wish to have them use the following URLs, which were accurate at the time this textbook was published:

> http://www.ualr.edu/
> ~degonzal ez/guhtml/
> antgua.html

> http://www.ualr.edu/
> ~degonzal ez/guatemala.html

You might also guide students to a search engine. Four of the most useful are AltaVista, Lycos, Infoseek, and Yahoo. For additional suggestions on using the Internet, refer to the Prentice Hall Social Studies'

Educator's Handbook "Using the Internet," in the *Prentice Hall World Explorer Program Resources.*

For additional links to world geography and culture topics, visit the Prentice Hall Home Page at http://www.phschool.com.

How Am I Doing?

Point out to students that this checklist is just a quick reminder for them of what they learned in the chapter. If their answer to any of the questions is *no* or if they are unsure, they may need to review the topic.

LAB ACTIVITY SHOP

Making a Model Canal Lock

Lesson Objectives

❶ Describe the purpose of canal locks.

❷ Illustrate how canal locks operate to raise and lower ships.

Lesson Plan

1 Engage

Warm-Up Activity

To illustrate the value of the Panama Canal, ask for two volunteer travelers. Tell the volunteers that they will start in London by ship; they want to reach San Francisco. The first of the two to reach San Francisco will claim a large fortune. Allow the volunteer with the birthday closest to January 1 to use the Panama Canal. Then ask the volunteers to trace their routes for the class on a large map or on a map displayed on an overhead projector.

Activating Prior Knowledge

Read Step One of the Activity Lab to the class. Ask students to write a paragraph explaining how a ship can be raised or lowered 85 feet (25.9 m) in a canal lock. Tell students to keep their papers until they have completed the lab.

The Panama Canal cuts a stunning 7,800 miles (12,553 km) off the distance a ship would have to travel from New York to San Francisco.

The canal could not work without locks. Canal locks are huge chambers filled with water that raise and lower ships.

The Panama Canal needs locks because the sea level at the Atlantic and the Pacific entrances to the canal is not the same. Also, the path of the canal is not level—it goes up one slope to the continental divide and down the other.

Purpose

The best way to understand how canal locks work is to build a model of one. As you complete this activity, you will understand how a real ship travels through a real canal.

Materials

- two half-gallon cardboard juice or milk cartons
- modelling wax
- scissors
- duct tape
- a ballpoint pen
- a cork
- a paper clip
- a pitcher of water

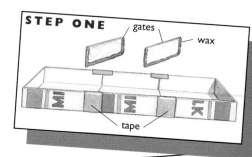

STEP ONE — gates, wax, tape

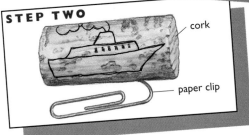

STEP TWO — cork, paper clip

Procedure

STEP ONE

Construct a model canal and lock. Follow the illustrations. Cut the cartons in half lengthwise. Line up three of the four halves lengthwise and connect them on the outside with duct tape. Then carefully cut out the walls of cardboard that separate the boxes and divide your canal. Line three edges of each cut-out wall with modelling wax. Then replace the walls. Use

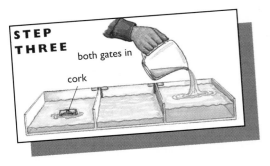

STEP THREE

both gates in

cork

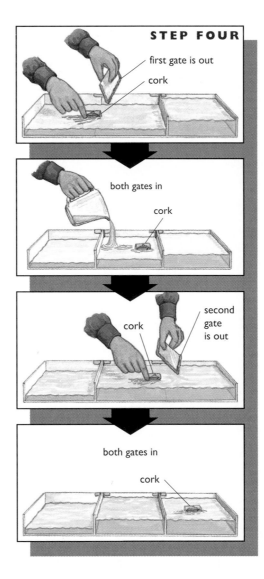

STEP FOUR

first gate is out

cork

both gates in

cork

cork

second gate is out

both gates in

cork

enough wax to make a watertight seal. These are the gates in the canal lock.

STEP TWO

Use the pen, cork, and paper clip to make a model ship. Look at the picture for an example. Stick the paper clip into the bottom of the ship to make it float upright.

STEP THREE

Fill your canal with water. Fill one end and the middle of the carton with water about one inch deep. Fill the other end with water almost to the top. Float your boat in the end of the canal with the lower water level.

STEP FOUR

Operate the canal lock to raise your ship to the higher water level. Remove the gate that separates your ship from the middle chamber. Sail your ship into the middle chamber and close the gate behind it by carefully replacing it. To raise your ship to the next level, slowly pour water into the middle chamber until the water level matches the level in the last chamber. Remove the second gate, sail your ship into the last chamber, and replace the gate. You have successfully navigated a canal!

Observations

1 How did you raise your ship from one level to a higher level?

2 Why does the canal lock need gates to work?

ANALYSIS AND CONCLUSION

1. How do you think the water level is raised in a real lock?

2. Repeat the activity in reverse. How will you lower your ship?

2 Explore

Have students read through the Activity Shop before they begin to follow its directions. Tell students that many of today's ships are too large to pass through the locks of the Panama Canal. At least one company has investigated the possibility of building a new canal through Nicaragua. Ask students to look at the Latin America political map in the Activity Atlas and speculate on the route of such a canal. Ask students to list some of the problems involved in building such a canal.

3 Teach

You might build and display the model as a class project. Organize the class into groups. Assign one group to collect the materials for the cork boat and to construct it. Tell another group to collect the milk cartons, cut and connect them. A third group can line the cartons with wax and make the gates. Choose students to fill the canal with water and to operate the gates.

Before students fill the model canal, cover the surface and floor with newspaper in case of spills. If there is a leak, ask students what would happen if an actual canal lock sprung a leak.

4 Assess

Ask students to revise their paragraphs explaining how a canal lock operates. Invite several students to read their revisions to the class.

Answers to...

OBSERVATIONS

1. raised the water level
2. to separate different levels of water

ANALYSIS AND CONCLUSION

1. The water is pumped in.
2. Take water out of the lock.

Exploring the Caribbean

To help you plan instruction, the chart below shows how teaching resources correspond to chapter content. Use the resources to vary instruction, add activities, or plan block schedules. Where appropriate, resources have **suggested time allotments** for students. Time allotments are approximate.

Managing Time and Instruction

		Latin America Teaching Resources Binder		World Explorer Program Resources Binder	
		Resource	**mins.**	**Resource**	**mins.**
1	**SECTION 1** Cuba Clinging to Communism	**Chapter and Section Support** Reproducible Lesson Plan, p. 69 ⓢ Guided Reading and Review, p. 70 ⓢ Section Quiz, p. 71	20 25	**Outline Maps** Central America and the Caribbean political map **Nystrom Desk Atlas** Ⓣ Primary Sources and Literature Readings	20 40
	SKILL ACTIVITY Locating Information	**Social Studies and Geography Skills,** Using your Textbooks, p. 94 Using the Library, p. 95	30 30		
2	**SECTION 2** Haiti The Road to Democracy	**Chapter and Section Support** Reproducible Lesson Plan, p. 72 ⓢ Guided Reading and Review, p. 73 ⓢ Section Quiz, p. 74	20 25	**Outline Maps** Central America and the Caribbean political map	20
3	**SECTION 3** Puerto Rico Cultural Identity of a People	**Chapter and Section Support** Reproducible Lesson Plan, p. 75 ⓢ Guided Reading and Review, p. 76 ⓢ Section Quiz, p. 77 Critical Thinking Activity, p. 82 ⓢ Vocabulary, p. 79 Reteaching, p. 80 Enrichment, p. 81 ⓢ Chapter Summary, p. 78 **Tests** Forms A and B Chapter Tests, pp. 26–31	20 25 30 20 25 25 15 40	**Outline Maps** Central America and the Caribbean political map **Writing Process Handbook** Proofreading, p. 37	20 20

Assessment Opportunities

Block Scheduling Folder
PROGRAM TEACHING RESOURCES

Activities and Projects

Block Scheduling Program Support

Interdisciplinary Links

Resource Pro™ CD-ROM

Media and Technology

From Guiding Questions to Assessment A series of Guiding Questions serves as an organizing framework for this book. The Guiding Question that relates to this chapter is listed below. Section Reviews and Section Quizzes provide opportunities for assessing students' insights into this Guiding Question. Additional assessments are listed below.

Media and Technology

Resource	mins.
⬛ ✎ Ⓢ World Video Explorer	20
✎ Planet Earth CD-ROM	20
✎ Material World CD-ROM	20
▫ Color Transparency 66	20
✎ Planet Earth CD-ROM	20
▫ Color Transparency 66	20
🎧 Ⓢ Guided Reading Audiotapes	20
▫ Color Transparency 174 (Graphic organizer table template)	20
✎ The Writer's Solution CD-ROM	30
🖫 Computer Test Bank	30

T Teaming Opportunity
This resource is especially well-suited for teaching teams.

Ⓢ Spanish
This resource is also in Spanish Support.

✎ CD-ROM
✎ Laserdisc
▫ Transparency
🖫 Software
⬛ Videotape
🎧 Audiotape

GUIDING QUESTION

- *What is the relationship of the nations of Latin America with the United States and the world?*

ASSESSMENTS

Section 1

Students should be able to write a paragraph describing what life in Cuba is like today.

▶ **RUBRIC** See the Assessment booklet for a rubric on assessing a writing assignment.

Section 2

Students should be able to describe how Haiti's struggle for democracy affected people's lives.

▶ **RUBRIC** See the Assessment booklet for a rubric on assessing cause-and-effect statements.

Section 3

Students should be able to create a concept web of the factors that have influenced Puerto Rican culture.

▶ **RUBRIC** See the Assessment booklet for a rubric on assessing graphic organizers.

Activities and Projects

Mental Mapping

Sea Cruise Ask students to imagine that they are planning a cruise through the Caribbean. Have them suggest islands they would like to visit.

Then ask students to pair up. One student in each pair will locate islands they would like to visit and work out an itinerary for the order in which they would visit the islands. Then ask them to provide the compass directions for getting from one island to the other.

The other student in each pair will use the directions provided by the first student to navigate through an unlabeled outline map of the Caribbean. Using the itinerary and directions provided by the first student, the second student will label islands on the map. Students may then reverse roles.

At the end of the activity, both students will check their own map against a published map to evaluate the accuracy of the directions and their ability to follow them.

Links to Current Events

Foreign Policies Tell students that although Cuba, Haiti, and Puerto Rico are in the same region and fairly close to each other, the United States has very different relationships with each one.

Divide the class into three large groups. Assign one of the three countries to each group. Have each student in each group use the library to look for some event in the history of the relationship between the United States and their country. They should work together to avoid duplicating the same events.

Each student should write the date and a description of the event on an index card. The groups can then arrange their index cards along a time line.

Hands-On Activities

Sorting Help students distinguish among islands, countries, cities, and continents by writing those categories on the chalkboard.

Invite students to take turns walking to the front of the room to read a label from a wall map. Another student will decide in which category the label belongs.

Every student should have the chance to suggest a name and choose a category. This activity should be performed briskly, with some of the quality of a relay race. You may want to provide time limits for placing names into categories. Emphasis should be placed on cooperative efforts and the performance of the class as a whole, however, rather than on the ability of individual students.

Once everyone has had a chance at each type of action, have students work together to determine whether the names were properly categorized.

Compare and Contrast Have students visit a travel agency or look at travel magazines for information and descriptions of a Caribbean country. Have them list descriptions used in travel literature. Then ask them to compare and contrast those descriptions with information they find in a nonfiction book that describes the geography, history, economy, and culture of the same country. Encourage students to discuss the reasons for the differences and similarities they find. *Average*

Get to Know Someone Ask students to write a letter that could be sent to a potential pen pal in Cuba, Haiti, or Puerto Rico. As they work on their letters,

suggest they think about what they would want to tell a student in one of these countries about themselves. Urge them to list several questions they might have about their pen pal, and the pen pal's country as well. *Basic*

A Nation of Immigrants Tell students that there are communities of immigrants from Cuba, Haiti, and Puerto Rico in different parts of the United States. Ask them to research one of these immigrant groups to answer questions such as: What led (or leads) people to come to the United States from this country? What problems do they encounter in getting here? What problems do they have settling

here? What parts of the country are they most likely to live in? What festivals and customs do they bring with them when they come to the United States? *Challenging*

Make a Collage Have students make a picture collage poster of images they associate with one of the countries in this chapter. Encourage students to include pictures that illustrate the geography, history, culture, and economy of the country they are depicting. Students may clip pictures from old magazines or brochures or create the pictures themselves. *English Language Learners*

F.Y.I.

This page can help you extend your own and students' understanding of the concepts in this chapter. You may want to browse through some of the suggestions in the **Bibliography**. **Interdisciplinary Links** can connect social studies understandings to areas elsewhere in the curriculum through the use of other Prentice Hall products. **National Geography Standards** reflected specifically in this chapter are listed for your convenience. Some hints about appropriate **Internet Access** are also provided. **School to Careers** provides insights into the practical uses of some of the concepts in this chapter as they might pertain to various careers.

BIBLIOGRAPHY

FOR THE TEACHER

Ada, Alma Flor. *Where the Flame Trees Bloom.* Atheneum, 1994.

Aliotta, Jerome J. *The Puerto Ricans.* Chelsea, 1995. (Immigrant Experience series)

Sheehan, Sean. *Jamaica.* Cavendish, 1993.

FOR THE STUDENT

Easy
Dorros, Arthur. *Isla.* Dutton, 1995

Average
Hoobler, Thomas. *Toussaint L'Ouverture.* Chelsea, 1990.

Challenging
Hauptly, Dennis J. *Puerto Rico: An Unfinished Story.* Atheneum, 1991.

Temple, Frances. *Taste of Salt: A Story of Modern Haiti.* Orchard, 1992.

Temple, Frances. *Tonight, By Sea.* Orchard, 1995.

LITERATURE CONNECTION

Mohr, Nicholasa. *Going Home.* Dial, 1986.

Taylor, Theodore. *The Cay.* Doubleday, 1969.

INTERDISCIPLINARY LINKS

Subject	Theme: Identity
MATH	Middle Grades Math: Tools for Success *Course 1,* Lesson 2–8, **Congruent and Similar Figures** *Course 3,* Lesson 7–9, **Math and Science: Scientific Notation**
SCIENCE	Prentice Hall Science *Matter: Building Block of the Universe,* Lesson 5–1, **Arranging the Elements** *Electricity and Magnetism,* Lesson 2–1, **The Nature of Magnets**
LANGUAGE ARTS	Choices in Literature *The Adventure of Me,* **Eleven** *The Adventure of Me,* **Mummy No. 1770** Prentice Hall Literature *Bronze,* **I Am a Native of North America**

NATIONAL GEOGRAPHY STANDARDS

Students explore the 18 National Geography Standards throughout Latin America. Chapter 5, however, concentrates on investigating the following: standards 1, 3, 5, 6, 9, 10, 11, 12, 13, 17, 18. For a complete list of the standards, see the *Teacher's Flexible Planning Guide.*

SCHOOL TO CAREERS

In Chapter 5: Exploring the Caribbean, students learn about the different political systems of Cuba, Haiti, and Puerto Rico. Additionally, they address the skill of locating information. Understanding different political systems can help students prepare for careers in politics, economics, business, sociology, and so on. Information locating skills are particularly useful for writers, researchers, real estate agents, employment counselors, teachers, and others. The curriculum presented in this book, as in all eight titles of Prentice Hall's *World Explorer* program, is designed to prepare students not only for careers but also for good citizenship—of the world as well as of this country.

INTERNET ACCESS

Many social studies teachers and students use Internet browsers, or search engines, to investigate particular topics. For the best results, use narrow rather than broad topics. Try these for Chapter 5: Jean-Bertrand Aristide, Cuban exiles, Port-au-Prince, condado. Finding age-appropriate sites is an important consideration when using the Internet. For links to age-appropriate sites in world studies and geography, visit the Prentice Hall Home Page at: http://www.phschool.com

Exploring the Caribbean

Connecting to the Guiding Questions

In this chapter, students will read about life in present-day Cuba, Haiti, and Puerto Rico; identify the reasons behind current changes in economic and political life; and examine the relationships of these places to the United States. Content in this chapter thus corresponds to the Guiding Question:

● What is the relationship of the nations of Latin America with the United States and the world?

Using the Map Activities

Draw students' attention to the map. Lead a class discussion about how Caribbean nations might get the goods and services their people need.

- Answers should indicate that fishing and shipping would be important.

- Answers should include that islanders traded among themselves, but they did not have boats that could take them to either North or South America.

Heterogeneous Groups

The following Teacher's Edition strategies are suitable for heterogeneous groups.

Cooperative Learning
Create a Play   p. 114
Critical Thinking
Drawing Conclusions   p. 116
Interdisciplinary Connections
Science   p. 115
Language Arts   p. 124

SECTION 1
Cuba
CLINGING TO COMMUNISM

SECTION 2
Haiti
THE ROAD TO DEMOCRACY

SECTION 3
Puerto Rico
CULTURAL IDENTITY OF A PEOPLE

The islands of the Caribbean stretch about 1,500 miles (2,414 km) across blue-green waters. Each island has its own traditions and cultures. To learn more about the Caribbean, complete the following activities.

Understanding geography
How do you think the sea may have affected the economies of the Caribbean islands?

Study the map
Before the Europeans arrived in the region, how do you think the sea may have served as both a highway and a barrier to contact with other people?

Resource Directory

Media and Technology

Spotlight on: Music of the Caribbean, from the World Video Explorer, enhances students' understanding of how the blending of Indian, European, and African influences have resulted in a unique Caribbean culture.

Chapter 8

Cuba

CLINGING TO COMMUNISM

BEFORE YOU READ

Reach Into Your Background

Suppose that you had to move tomorrow and you could pack exactly one suitcase. You could never come back for the things you left behind. What would you pack?

Questions to Explore

1. What is life in Cuba like today?
2. What ties do Cuban Americans have to Cuba?

Key Terms

dictator
communist
exile
illiterate

Key People and Places

Fidel Castro
Fulgencio Batista
Miami

Twelve-year-old Venesa Alonso (vuh NEH suh uh LAHN zoh) lives in Miami, Florida. Her home is just a few miles away from the ocean. Venesa hardly ever goes to the beach, however. The blue waves and roaring surf remind her of her trip from Cuba to the United States. The memory still gives her nightmares.

Venesa and her family left Cuba in the summer of 1994. They built a rickety raft and carried it to the ocean. They were among the 35,000 Cubans who took to the sea that summer. They sailed on anything that would float—rubber tires, old boats, and home-made rafts. One hope kept them going. It was the thought of making it to the United States. They planned to apply to enter the United States as immigrants.

Venesa's family and thousands of others left Cuba for two main reasons. The first reason was that Cuba's economy was in bad shape. People often did not have enough food to eat. Clothing, medicine, and other basic necessities were hard to get. A desire for freedom was the second reason why many people left. Cuba's leader, Fidel Castro (fee DEL KAS troh), does not allow Cubans to speak out against government policies they disagree with.

▼ Cubans trying to reach the United States in 1995 took to the sea in boats like this one.

Teaching Resources

📁 **Reproducible Lesson Plan** in the Chapter and Section Resources booklet, p. 69, provides a summary of the section lesson.

📁 **Guided Reading and Review** in the Chapter and Section Resources booklet, p. 70, provides a structure for mastering key concepts and reviewing key terms in the section. Available in Spanish in the Spanish Chapter and Section Resources booklet, p. 43.

Program Resources

Material in the *Primary Resources and Literature Readings* booklet extends content with a selection from the region under study.

Outline Maps Central American and the Caribbean political map

---

Lesson Objectives

1. Describe current life in Cuba and relate it to the history of Cuba's governments.

2. Analyze ties of Cuban-Americans to Cuba.

Lesson Plan

1 Engage

Warm-Up Activity

Invite students to imagine that they must leave America and move to another country. Inform them that the new country will have a very different way of life, climate, landscape, language, and set of customs. Direct students to do a quick-write, listing the people and things they would miss most. Have volunteers share their lists. Discuss how they might feel about such changes.

Activating Prior Knowledge

Have students read Reach Into Your Background in the Before You Read box. Students' lists will vary. Record responses on the chalkboard and use them as a springboard for a discussion of feelings about what students would have to leave behind.

Ask students what they know of immigration from their own family histories or from books, movies, or television. Discuss feelings immigrants retain for their place of origin.

2 Explore

Have students read the section. Encourage them to find answers to the following questions as they read: Why did some Cubans leave their country? What ties do they still have to Cuba? Why has it been difficult for them to go back? Direct students to work with partners and draw three waves labeled *1994, 1970,* and *1960.* Inside each wave, have them list the reasons Cubans left their homeland during that time.

3 Teach

Have students create a chart about Cuba with the following column headings: *Before Castro, Under Castro Until 1991,* and *Recent Changes.* Have students fill in the chart with facts from the section. Students may include opinions, but the opinions must be backed by facts. Invite students to use the completed charts as the basis for predictions about the future of Cuba. This activity should take about 20 minutes.

Answers to ...
MAP STUDY

- Havana; along the coast

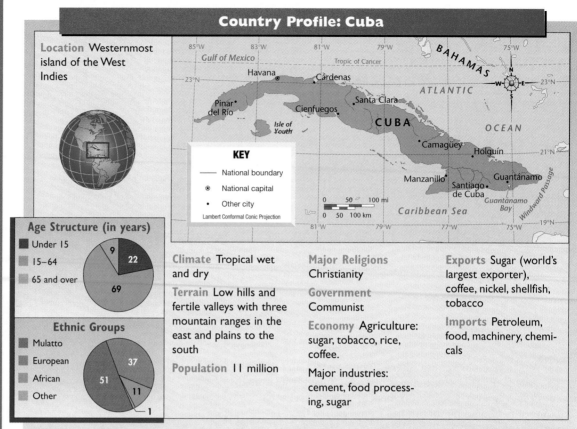

Country Profile: Cuba

Location Westernmost island of the West Indies

Age Structure (in years)
- Under 15
- 15–64
- 65 and over

9, 22, 69

Ethnic Groups
- Mulatto
- European
- African
- Other

37, 51, 11, 1

Climate Tropical wet and dry

Terrain Low hills and fertile valleys with three mountain ranges in the east and plains to the south

Population 11 million

Major Religions Christianity

Government Communist

Economy Agriculture: sugar, tobacco, rice, coffee.

Major industries: cement, food processing, sugar

Exports Sugar (world's largest exporter), coffee, nickel, shellfish, tobacco

Imports Petroleum, food, machinery, chemicals

KEY
— National boundary
⊛ National capital
• Other city
Lambert Conformal Conic Projection

Map Study Hundreds of thousands of Cubans have left Cuba in recent years. Many Cubans traveled on small boats and on rafts made of plywood and inner tubes. They were trying to cross 90 miles (145 km) of ocean to reach Florida. **Location** What is the capital of Cuba? Where are Cuba's capital and most of its major cities located?

Cuba's History

Cuba is a small country. It is about the size of the state of Pennsylvania. Cuba's farmland is fertile, and Cuba is the third largest sugar producer in the world. Look at the political map in the Activity Atlas in the front of your book. Cuba is located between the two entrances to the Gulf of Mexico. It also has excellent harbors. This makes it a good place to trade with the United States and other parts of the Caribbean. But Cuba's relationship with the United States and many of its neighbors has not been friendly since the 1960s.

Cuban Independence Cuba's government and economy were not always like they are now. Cuba was a Spanish colony. In 1898, the United States defeated Spain in the Spanish-American War, and Cuba won its independence. In the years that followed, Cuba became the richest country in the Caribbean. Sugar planters made money

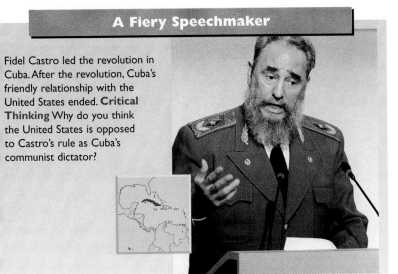

Fidel Castro led the revolution in Cuba. After the revolution, Cuba's friendly relationship with the United States ended. **Critical Thinking** Why do you think the United States is opposed to Castro's rule as Cuba's communist dictator?

READ ACTIVELY

Ask Questions If you could interview Fidel Castro, what questions would you ask him?

4 Assess

See answers to the Section Review. You may also use students' completed charts as assessment.

Acceptable charts include at least four factually correct entries in each column.

Commendable charts show changes in the economy, government, and U.S.-Cuba relations.

Outstanding charts explore the causes for changes in the economy and government.

selling to people in the United States. Hotels were built, and tourists came to Cuba to enjoy its beautiful beaches and great climate. Many Cubans became businesspeople, teachers, doctors, and lawyers.

Not all Cubans shared the country's wealth, however. Most farm and factory workers earned low wages. Cuba also had many harsh leaders who ruled as dictators. A **dictator** is a ruler who has complete power. In the 1950s, Fulgencio Batista (fool HEN see yoh bah TEE stah) was Cuba's leader. During his rule, some people formed rebel groups to remove Batista and change the country.

Communism in Cuba A young lawyer named Fidel Castro led one of these small rebel groups. He tried three times to overthrow the government during the 1950s. By his third attempt, he had gained many supporters. Finally, Batista gave up and left the country in 1959.

When Batista left, Fidel Castro took control of Cuba. He still holds power today. Castro's government is **communist.** In a communist country, the government owns all large businesses and most of the country's land. Under Castro, the Cuban government took over private businesses and land. Further, Castro said that newspapers and books could print only information supporting his government. Anyone who disagreed with government policy was put in jail. Huge numbers of Cubans fled the island. Many settled in Miami, Florida.

Cuba became a communist country in the early 1960s. At the same time, it became friendly with the Soviet Union. The Soviet Union was then the most powerful communist nation in the world. It sent money and supplies to Cuba. The United States and the Soviet Union, however, were not friendly. As a result, Cuba's relationship with the United States became tense. Relations grew worse when the United States openly welcomed the people who fled from Cuba.

CITIZEN HEROES

To Be a Leader When José Martí grew up in Cuba in the 1800s, it was still a colony of Spain. At age 16, he started a newspaper dedicated to Cuban independence. Martí later became famous for his poems and essays. In 1895, he led the revolution that eventually liberated Cuba. By the time independence was achieved, however, Martí had died in a battle with the Spanish.

Background

Biography

Fidel Castro (1926–) As a young lawyer in the 1950s, Castro gathered supporters who wanted to end the rule of dictator Fulgencio (Juan) Batista. On July 26, 1953, Castro led a small group in an attack on the Moncada Army barracks in the city of Santiago de Cuba. Castro was captured and spent two years in prison, followed by exile to Mexico. There he organized a small group of revolutionaries who invaded Cuba in 1956. When Batista fled on January 1, 1959, Castro became the head of the new government.

SKILLS MINI LESSON

Reading Tables and Analyzing Statistics As a way to **introduce** the skill, tell students that many important facts about a country can be presented in table form. Help students **practice** the skill by assisting them in finding the following information from the Country Profile of Cuba: Cuba's main agricultural product (sugar); most common ethnic group (mulatto); most common age group (15–64). Have students **apply** the skill by forming questions whose answers can be found in the table. Direct students to share and answer one another's questions.

Answers to ...
A FIERY SPEECHMAKER

- Accept any reasonable answer, for example, a Communist dictatorship is not democratic.

Journal Writing

Discuss with students how young refugees probably felt as they fled to the United States. What hopes for the future might they have had? Challenge students to write in their journals as if they were one of these young people. If students are keeping an Explorer's Journal as described in the Book Opener, you may wish to do this writing activity as part of that journal.

There is a large Cuban American community in Miami, Florida. These men are playing dominoes in a Miami park. Behind them is a mural showing the presidents of many countries in the Western Hemisphere.

Cubans Leaving Cuba

Lydia Martin left Cuba in 1970. She was only six years old. Her mother had grown tired of the limits on freedom and lack of opportunity in communist Cuba. She wanted to take Lydia to the United States with her. Lydia's father begged her to stay.

"For years [my mother] had been anxious to leave Cuba . . . to take me to a place where I could learn about freedom. Her exit papers had finally arrived, but my father wouldn't let me go. . . . There was no talking sense into a man who feared losing his little girl forever. . . . While my mother was away at the church, I called him.

"I'm leaving with my mother," I told him with all the bravery a six-year-old could muster. . . .

"Have you stopped to think you may never see me again?" my father asked. . . ."

Cuban Exiles Many Cuban exiles tell stories like Lydia's. An exile is a person who leaves his or her homeland for another country because of political problems. From the 1960s onwards, large numbers of people left Cuba. Many families were torn apart.

Dreams of Returning to Cuba Some Cubans never got over the loss of their home. In the 1970s, relations between the United States and Cuba grew worse. Even if she wanted to, Lydia Martin could not write to her father. The government might punish him if he got a letter from the United States. Still, Lydia hoped to reunite with him one day. Lydia's mother now spoke of Cuba with longing. She said that in Cuba, the sky was bluer, the sand whiter, and the palm trees greener.

In 1991, the government of the Soviet Union collapsed and could no longer help Cuba. Food, medicine, tools, and other necessities became more scarce. Lydia began worrying about her father and her other relatives. In 1995, she flew back to the island for the first time. Visitors from the United States are not always welcome in Cuba, especially if they once fled the island. Lydia was nervous.

Cuba: Today and Tomorrow

When Lydia stood on the beach in Cuba, she thought of her mother. Her mother had been right. The sky did seem bluer here, the sand whiter, and the palm trees greener.

Lydia had heard about the food shortages in Cuba, but she had not known how bad they were. Her father's new family sometimes had little more than rice to eat. When Lydia unpacked the shoes, soap, powdered milk, and underwear she had brought, her father and his new family took them with joy. They cooked her a delicious meal of lobster and rice on her first night. They had been saving money for it for months.

LINKS ACROSS THE WORLD

Livan Hernandez At 21 years old, Livan Hernandez was close to becoming a star pitcher in the Cuban Baseball League. He left Cuba for a chance to make millions of dollars pitching for a major league team in the United States. If that decision sounds easy, consider that Hernandez left behind everyone who is dear to him in Cuba. Hernandez hopes his family can one day enjoy the same freedom he has found.

◀ After Lydia Martin (left) departed from Cuba, she did not see or talk to her father (right) again for 25 years.

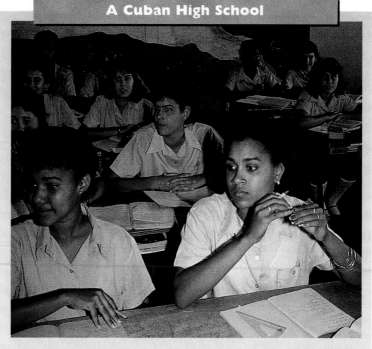

A Cuban High School

At many of Cuba's rural schools, students spend four hours in the classroom and four hours doing manual labor. **Critical Thinking** How is this school similar to yours? How is it different?

One thing that Cubans do not need to save money for is education. In the 1960s and 1970s, Castro overhauled Cuba's schools. At the time, many Cubans were **illiterate,** or unable to read and write. Castro sent students and teachers into the countryside to teach. Soon, more Cubans could read and write than ever before. Today, about 95 percent of Cubans can read and write.

Schools in Cuba may have helped many Cubans to learn how to read. However, they teach only communist ideas. But because Cuba is close to the United States, Cubans can tune in to American radio stations. Cuban teenagers listen to popular American dance music. They wear jeans from the United States whenever they can get them. Castro has allowed some businesses to be privately owned. The tourist industry is growing.

No one knows what Cuba's future will bring. Many think the time is near when those who left Cuba will be able to return home to visit or live there in freedom.

SECTION 1 REVIEW

1. **Define** (a) dictator, (b) communist, (c) exile, (d) illiterate.

2. **Identify** (a) Fidel Castro, (b) Fulgencio Batista, (c) Miami.

3. How did the collapse of the Soviet Union affect Cuba's economy?

4. What problems did communism bring to Cuba?

Critical Thinking

5. **Drawing Conclusions** Do you think that Cubans born in the United States feel as strongly about Cuba as their Cuban-born parents do? Why or why not?

Activity

6. **Writing to Learn** Work with a partner. One of you will write a letter to a relative in Cuba from the point of view of a Cuban exile in the United States. The other will write a response from the point of view of a Cuban who has never left Cuba.

Haiti

THE ROAD TO DEMOCRACY

Reach Into Your Background

Is there something in your life that you have had to try many times to achieve? What strate-gies did you use to try to get what you wanted? Did they work? Why or why not?

Questions to Explore

1. How did Haiti's struggle for democracy affect people's lives?

2. How does the history of Haiti affect the culture of its people?

Key Terms

Creole
dialect

Key People and Places

Jean-Bertrand Aristide
Toussaint L'Ouverture
François Duvalier
Jean-Claude Duvalier
Port-au-Prince

The plane dipped toward Port-au-Prince (port oh PRINS), the capital of Haiti. It flew over a spreading slum. The slum was a neighborhood of crumbling cardboard huts with tin roofs. In the streets, people were jammed into a solid mass. All heads turned up toward the sky.

As if in one voice, a cheer of joy rose from the crowd. In the plane, Haiti's president, Jean-Bertrand Aristide (zhan behr TRAHND uh ris TEED), was returning to his country after a three-year exile. He had been elected by the people, but Haiti's military had forced him to leave. Then, a group of generals had taken over the country. The United States and other nations had pressured the military to give power back to Aristide. Many hoped that Aristide's return would also bring back democracy.

▼ After his exile, Haitian President Jean-Bertrand Aristide returned to Haiti amid cheers of support.

Haiti's Struggle for Democracy

Aristide was the first president to be elected democratically in many years. This does not mean that most Haitians did not want democracy. Their country was born out of a desperate struggle for freedom. Haiti is the only nation in the Americas formed from a successful revolt of enslaved Africans.

Teaching Resources

📁 **Reproducible Lesson Plan** in the Chapter and Section Resources book-let, p. 72, provides a summary of the section lesson.

📁 **Guided Reading and Review** in the Chapter and Section Resources book-let, p. 73, provides a structure for mastering key concepts and reviewing key terms in the section. Available in Spanish in the Spanish Chapter and Section Resources booklet, p. 45.

Program Resources

Outline Maps Central America and the Caribbean political map

Section 2

Lesson Objectives

❶ Summarize the Haitian struggle for freedom and describe the effects of this struggle on the Haitian people.

❷ Examine the influence of Haiti's history on its culture.

Lesson Plan

1 Engage

Warm-Up Activity

Have students try to imagine what it must be like to be poor and live in a country where there is no chance for a better life. Then have them imagine that there is an election. A president is elected who promises better living condi-tions, improved education, and more freedom. Finally, tell stu-dents to consider how they might feel if suddenly the army took over, removing the president from power. Discuss with students how would they feel about their hopes and dreams. Have them describe what they and their families might do.

Activating Prior Knowledge

Have students read Reach Into Your Background in the Before You Read box. Stu-dents' description of their attempts to achieve a goal may vary. Listen to their descriptions without judg-ment. Ask students to recall what they learned about dicta-torships from the previous section on Cuba. Prompt stu-dents with questions such as *What freedoms are absent in a dictatorship?* (freedom of speech, freedom to dissent, sometimes freedom of religion)

2 Explore

Have students read the section. Indicate that as they read, they will find answers to questions like these: Why have Haitians had to fight over and over again for freedom? Why are most Haitians poor? What is Haitian rural life like? Haitian city life? Why did so many Haitians flee after the military took over? Discuss these questions after students have finished reading.

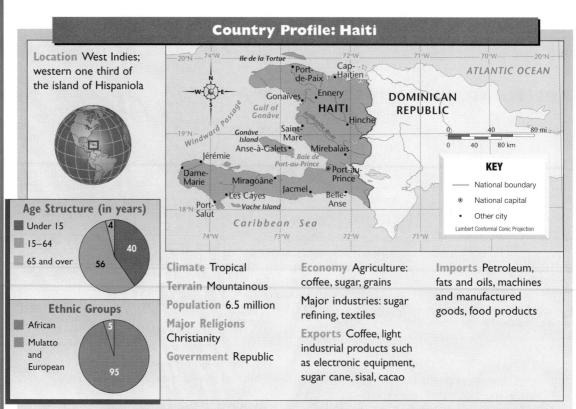

Country Profile: Haiti

Location West Indies; western one third of the island of Hispaniola

Age Structure (in years)
- Under 15
- 15–64
- 65 and over

4, 40, 56

Ethnic Groups
- African
- Mulatto and European

5, 95

Climate Tropical

Terrain Mountainous

Population 6.5 million

Major Religions Christianity

Government Republic

Economy Agriculture: coffee, sugar, grains

Major industries: sugar refining, textiles

Exports Coffee, light industrial products such as electronic equipment, sugar cane, sisal, cacao

Imports Petroleum, fats and oils, machines and manufactured goods, food products

Map and Chart Study This map shows the country of Haiti. Haiti is on the island of Hispaniola. **Region** What other country is on the island? Find the city of Cap-Haïtien. This is near the spot where Columbus landed in 1492. **Location** On what side of the island is Cap-Haïtien? In 1492, the Arawaks lived on Hispaniola. Look at the chart of ethnic groups. Do the Arawaks, a Native American group, still live in Haiti? What group makes up the largest part of the population?

The Birth of Haiti As you can see on the Country Profile above, Haiti lies on the western third of the island of Hispaniola. Haiti was once a colony of France. Europeans brought enslaved Africans to Haiti to work on sugar cane and coffee plantations. In the 1790s, slave revolts began. A Haitian leader named Toussaint L'Ouverture helped banish slavery from Haiti in 1801. He also offered Haitians a new way of life, based on the idea that all people could live as equals.

Troubled Years In the years that followed, Toussaint L'Ouverture's goal of freedom and equality was never fully realized. Most of Haiti's presidents became dictators once they got into power. One of the worst was François Duvalier (frahn SWAH doo VAHL yay), who took power in 1957. Because Duvalier had been a country doctor, Haitians called him "Papa Doc."

Papa Doc died in 1971. He was followed by his son, Jean-Claude Duvalier (zhan KLAHD doo VAHL yay), or "Baby Doc." Both Papa Doc and Baby Doc were cruel leaders. They stole government funds and used violence to keep power. During their rule, Haiti became the poorest country in the Western Hemisphere.

In 1986, rebels forced Baby Doc to leave the country. Many Haitians thought a period of freedom and prosperity was about to begin. But this was not to be. Haiti was ruled by one military leader after another. And most Haitians still made a living trying to farm small plots of land.

Life on a Farm   When farmer Pierre Joseph stands at the top of his land, he can see the calm waters of the Caribbean. When he looks down, he sees the dry, cracked earth of his one acre.

About two thirds of the people in Haiti make their living by farming. The land has been overused. Most trees have been cut. Rains wash the topsoil into the sea. Joseph is thin because he rarely gets enough to eat. "The land just doesn't yield enough," he says. He points to the few rows of corn and beans that he can grow on his one acre.

Farmers like Pierre Joseph can barely make a living, but many feel they are rich in other ways. Haitian culture blends African, French, and West Indian tradition. The blend of traditions gives Haiti a Creole culture. **Creole** is a word referring to people of mixed ancestry.

Creole also refers to the dialect spoken in Haiti. A **dialect** is the different version of a language that is spoken in a particular region. The Creole dialect is based on both French and African languages.

Papa Doc and Baby Doc

François (left) and Jean-Claude Duvalier (right) often used violence to rule Haiti. The country also became much poorer during their rule. By the time Baby Doc was forced from power, the average Haitian earned only about $300 a year.

READ ACTIVELY

Connect How do most people in the United States make a living?

3 Teach

Organize students into four groups of reporters. Each group should cover one of the following topics: (1) what life was like under military rule, (2) reasons why people fled Haiti for the United States, (3) Aristide's plans for a better Haiti. Students should use the information in the text to collaborate on a short report on their topic. This activity should take about 20 minutes.

Activity

Interdisciplinary Connections

Science Have students work in groups to research how land such as Pierre Joseph's can yield larger crops. Have students choose from the following topics: 1) tree-planting to stop erosion, 2) methods of irrigation, 3) improving soil through fertilizers, and 4) help available for farmers from agencies such as the United Nation's UNESCO. Each group should prepare and present a short report. Encourage students to use pictures as well as text to show how farming can be improved.

4 Assess

See the answers to the Section Review. Assess each group's understanding of the information they presented by the content and clarity of their reports.

Acceptable work covers the main ideas presented in the text.

Commendable work includes further research.

Outstanding work includes some analysis of the causes and effects of events. Save the reports for a "Television News Special."

Activity

Critical Thinking

Drawing Conclusions
Suitable as a whole class activity. Tell students that knowing how to draw conclusions about what they read helps them better understand the text. Explain that to draw a conclusion they must use evidence in the text plus what they already know. Pose the following question: *Why do you think some Haitians tried to come to the United States?* Ask students to draw conclusions about what Haitians hoped to find once they reached the United States. Record their answers on the chalkboard. Then, have them find evidence to support their conclusions in the paragraphs that describe the military takeover.

Answers to . . .
A RURAL VILLAGE IN HAITI

• There are only a few houses, but much grass, trees, and dirt roads. Responses should include clues such as palm trees.

Life in the City   Haiti's capital, Port-au-Prince, is a blend not only of cultures, but also of rich and poor. The wealthy live in spacious wooden houses on the hills overlooking the city. There is a small middle class of doctors, lawyers, teachers, and owners of small businesses, that also live fairly well. Many poor people from the country live in tiny homes of crumbling concrete.

Hopes for the Future

In December 1990, Jean-Bertrand Aristide was elected president. Haitians held high hopes for the future. Aristide was a Catholic priest who had long defended the rights of the poor. He took office in February 1991.

A Military Takeover   Aristide served as president for seven months. Then Haiti's military forced him to leave the country. The military also attacked his supporters. "We have been in hiding since police shot up our house in October," an Aristide supporter told reporters in 1991. "We got away because people warned us they were coming."

The year after the election, thousands of Aristide supporters fled the capital. They feared for their lives. They squeezed into trucks by the dozen and went to hide in the hills. Others tore their homes apart to make rafts. Then they took to the sea. Many headed for the United States. Some were sent back.

READ ACTIVELY

Predict Why do you think that Haitians were so glad to see Jean-Bertrand Aristide?

Cange Walthe
age 12
Haiti

This student drawing of rural Haiti contrasts with the urban scene on the next page. **Critical Thinking** What clues does this student provide to show that this village is in a rural area? What clues show that the village is in a place that has a tropical climate?

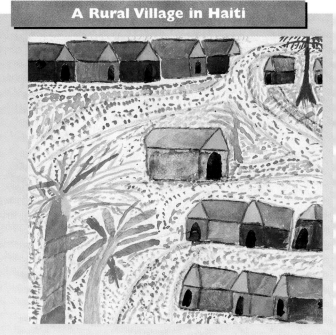

A Rural Village in Haiti

Dancing in the Streets

Haiti's people danced in the streets of Port-au-Prince when they heard that Aristide was returning to the country. They hoped that peace would return to Haiti along with Aristide.

Hundreds of children also left Haiti on rafts. Fifteen-year-old Fresenel Pierre (frehz uh NEL pea EHR) was one. He had an older brother waiting for him in Miami, where there is a large Haitian community. The children Fresenel sailed with were the children of Aristide supporters. Many were coming to the United States with no one to take them in.

Returning to Roots In 1995, Aristide came back to Haiti. Since his return, a new spirit seems to be everywhere in Haiti. It has led to a movement to return to Haiti's Creole roots. For many Haitians, the idea of Creole has become an idea of equality. It suggests that people of different races and cultures must all work together to give Haiti its special identity.

SECTION 2 REVIEW

1. **Define** (a) Creole, (b) dialect.

2. **Identify** (a) Jean-Bertrand Aristide, (b) Toussaint L'Ouverture, (c) François Duvalier, (d) Jean-Claude Duvalier, (e) Port-au-Prince.

3. How did Haiti win its independence?

4. What obstacles to making a living do farmers like Pierre Joseph face?

Critical Thinking

5. **Making Comparisons** Give an example of how Haitian culture blends African and European traditions.

Activity

6. **Writing to Learn** Write a diary entry from the point of view of Pierre Joseph about how economic and political conditions in Haiti affect his life.

Resource Directory

Teaching Resources

Section Quiz in the Chapter and Section Resources booklet, p. 74, covers the main ideas and key terms in the section. Available in Spanish in the Spanish Chapter and Section Resources booklet, p. 46.

Section Review

1. (a) a person of mixed ancestry (b) different version of a language spoken in a particular region

2. (a) current president of a democratic Haiti (b) leader who helped banish slavery from Haiti in 1801 (c) and (d) dictators of Haiti (e) capital of Haiti

3. Through a slave revolt in 1790 led by L'Ouverture.

4. Students' responses should identify obstacles such as poor soil, insufficient land, lack of modern machinery, and poverty.

5. Creole, a mix of French and African languages.

6. The diary entry should reflect the point of view of a poor farmer. Students should mention that poverty keeps Joseph from bettering his condition, and previous dictatorships kept him from voting for change. Now, under Aristide's democracy, he has hope of government help and greater economic opportunity.

SKILLS ACTIVITY

Locating Information

Lesson Objectives

Lesson Objectives

❶ Identify important ways to locate information.

❷ Use the skill to seek specific information.

Lesson Plan

1 Engage

To **introduce** the skill, invite a volunteer to read aloud the opening scenario. Ask students what advice they would give Marisol to help her focus and begin her search. Record students' ideas on the board.

Activating Prior Knowledge

Ask each student to write on a sheet of paper a place or resource they have used to successfully find a piece of information. Invite students to share their responses with the class. Use students' responses to compile a class information resource bank.

2 Explore

With students, read the material under the heading Get Ready. Ask students to name some situations in which they have used the skill of locating information. Encourage them to describe both frustrating and rewarding aspects of their search. Then have students read the rest of the skills activity.

Marisol felt like a sailor lost at sea.

She was surrounded by an ocean of information. Shelves overflowing with books towered above her. Beyond the bookshelves, more shelves loomed, filled with magazines. Past the magazines were computer terminals. Enough information to fill millions of pages could be accessed through them. Although she was in her community library, Marisol felt just as lost as if she were adrift in a lifeboat.

Marisol had gone to the library to find information about Toussaint L'Ouverture. Marisol had read in her textbook how L'Ouverture had led the Haitian people to freedom more than 200 years ago. Marisol's assignment was to write a one-page biography, or life story, about L'Ouverture. One question loomed in her mind: Where should she begin?

Get Ready

Locating information is an essential skill. Throughout your school career, you will need to locate information to complete homework assignments and class projects. As an adult, you will need to locate information to help you decide many things such as where to live, what job to do, and how to do it.

The first rule about locating information is *Don't panic!* Marisol felt lost in the library. But libraries and other sources of information are carefully designed to make your search for information as easy as possible. Just like a sailor at sea, it's a matter of choosing your destination, planning your route, and finally sailing to the one little island where the information you need is located.

Try It Out

Locating the information you need can be an exciting adventure. When you locate the information you've been searching for, you will feel

Resource Directory

Teaching Resources

Social Studies and Geography Skills
Using Your Textbooks, p. 94

Using the Library, p.95

the satisfaction and excitement of an explorer who finds the right island. Work with a partner to plan a voyage out into the Sea of Information:

A. Choose your destination. Your destination is the information you need. You and your partner should pick one now, and write it down. It might look like this: *"Destination: Information about how many Cubans live in the United States."*

B. Determine the best way to get there. Just as there are many ways to travel, there are many ways to locate information. Five important routes to information are listed in the box to the right. Discuss each source of information with your partner. Choose the source most likely to have the information you seek.

C. Prepare for your journey. You're about to depart, so pack your bags! You'll need a notebook and a pencil to jot down information. You might need a few coins for the copy machine.

D. Use signposts. Just as signposts can help you find your way on a real journey, different "signposts" can help you on your journey to find information. Read about these "signposts" in the box.

Five Important Routes To Information

Libraries Most of the world's information is stored in libraries. *Signposts:* the card catalog and librarians.

Books There are books about nearly every subject. *Signposts:* book titles and tables of contents.

Periodicals Magazines and newspapers can provide up-to-date information on a huge range of topics. *Signposts:* magazine indexes and newspaper indexes found in libraries.

The Internet The Internet is a worldwide network of computers containing information. *Signposts:* special electronic search indexes on the Internet.

People By interviewing experts, you can learn what they know about their specialties. *Signposts:* the telephone directory to locate appropriate people to interview.

Apply the Skill

Now that you've made an information-seeking journey with a partner, it's time to do it alone. Choose one of the following destinations:

- Destination: Information that identifies the chief agricultural product grown in Cuba.

- Destination: Information that identifies the President of Haiti.

- Destination: Information that identifies three historic sites you could visit in Puerto Rico.

  Once you have reached your destination by locating the information, draw a map to show how you found it.

Puerto Rico

CULTURAL IDENTITY OF A PEOPLE

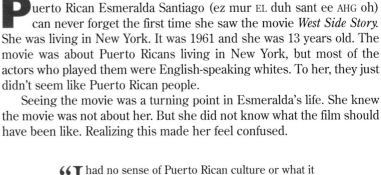

BEFORE YOU READ

Reach Into Your Background
Do you ever feel that you have "two selves"? One that acts a certain way with some people? And another that comes out when you are with other people? Are both of them the real you?

Questions to Explore
1. What factors influenced Puerto Rican culture?
2. What is Puerto Rico's relationship with the United States?

Key Terms
citizen
commonwealth
constitution

Key Places
San Juan
Condado

Puerto Rican Esmeralda Santiago (ez mur EL duh sant ee AHG oh) can never forget the first time she saw the movie *West Side Story*. She was living in New York. It was 1961 and she was 13 years old. The movie was about Puerto Ricans living in New York, but most of the actors who played them were English-speaking whites. To her, they just didn't seem like Puerto Rican people.

Seeing the movie was a turning point in Esmeralda's life. She knew the movie was not about her. But she did not know what the film should have been like. Realizing this made her feel confused.

▼ Esmeralda Santiago moved from Puerto Rico to New York City when she was 13 years old.

> **"I** had no sense of Puerto Rican culture or what it was to me. Where did I come from? Who is this person who calls herself a Puerto Rican and what does that mean? . . . [W]hen I think Puerto Rican, there's this big void, this empty space where my history should be.**"**

Puerto Rican and American

Even though Esmeralda felt confused about who she was, she remembered her early days in Puerto Rico vividly. When Esmeralda's mother brought her to New York City, everything changed.

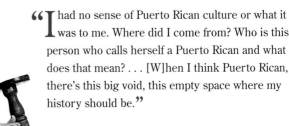

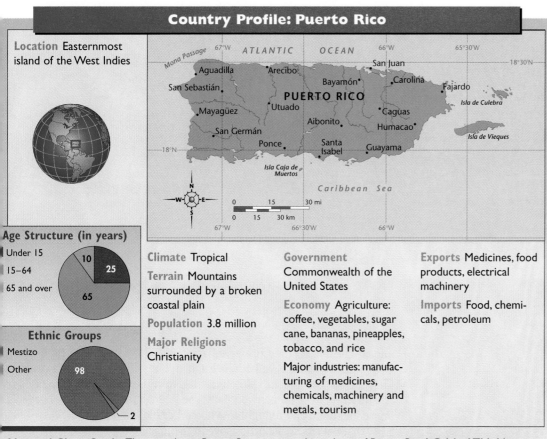

Country Profile: Puerto Rico

Location Easternmost island of the West Indies

Age Structure (in years)

- Under 15
- 15–64
- 65 and over

10
25
65

Ethnic Groups

- Mestizo
- Other

98
2

Climate Tropical

Terrain Mountains surrounded by a broken coastal plain

Population 3.8 million

Major Religions Christianity

Government Commonwealth of the United States

Economy Agriculture: coffee, vegetables, sugar cane, bananas, pineapples, tobacco, and rice

Major industries: manufacturing of medicines, chemicals, machinery and metals, tourism

Exports Medicines, food products, electrical machinery

Imports Food, chemicals, petroleum

Map and Chart Study This map shows Puerto Rico. **Location** Read the description of Puerto Rico's terrain. Where are Puerto Rico's mountains located? How do you know? **Movement** How do you think most exports are shipped out of Puerto Rico? **Critical Thinking** Look at the chart that shows age structure. Would you say that Puerto Rico's population is old, young, or evenly balanced? Why?

It was not that Esmeralda was completely separated from her people. Puerto Ricans are U.S. citizens. **Citizens** are individuals with certain rights and responsibilities under a particular government. However, Puerto Ricans cannot vote in U. S. presidential elections. They do not pay U.S. taxes. And they have only a non-voting representative in the U.S. Congress. Puerto Rico is a commonwealth of the United States. A **commonwealth** is a place that has its own government but also has strong ties to another country. Esmeralda had the right to return to Puerto Rico whenever she chose.

Esmeralda found life on the mainland strange and confusing. One problem was that to succeed in school, she had to improve her English. Esmeralda was also confused by her new group of friends. She found that Puerto Ricans living on the mainland were different from her friends on the island of Puerto Rico. Instead of the salsa and merengue

Program Resources

Outline Maps Central America and the Caribbean political map

2 Explore

Have students read the section. Tell them that after they read, they should be able to describe (a) the differences between life on the island and life on the mainland; (b) the ties mainland Puerto Ricans have to the island; and (c) how island life is influenced by both American and Caribbean cultures.

3 Teach

To explore the issue of Puerto Rico's status, ask students to make a chart with three column headings like the following:

Statehood	
Pro	Con

Commonwealth	
Pro	Con

Nationhood	
Pro	Con

Have students fill in the pro and con columns with arguments from the section. Students' opinions must be backed by facts. (You may want to save students' charts for use in a later activity in this section.) This activity should take about 20 minutes.

Answers to ...

MAP AND CHART STUDY

- In the middle of the island because the land is described as having mountains surrounded by a broken coastal plain; by ship; evenly balanced because the greatest age range contains the highest percent of the population.

4 Assess

See the answers to the Section Review. You may also use students' completed charts as assessment.

Acceptable charts include arguments from the text.

Commendable charts reflect students' thoughts on these issues.

Outstanding charts contain relevant, well-thought-out, original arguments backed by facts.

Background

Daily Life

Baseball Many Caribbean people share America's passion for baseball. In Puerto Rico, *beisbol* has produced such stars as Roberto Clemente and Ruben Sierra. Puerto Rico has a league of six teams that play all over the island. Cubans also enjoy baseball. In America Latina stadium in Havana, crowds cheer their teams energetically, and even dance in the aisles to the sound of bongo drums to celebrate an exceptionally good play.

Answers to ...

CHART STUDY

- northeastern United States; accept any reasonable answer such as family already living there or job availability.

Puerto Ricans in the Mainland United States

Chart Study Many Puerto Ricans have moved to the mainland United States. **Critical Thinking** Which region of the mainland has the most Puerto Ricans? What do you think draws Puerto Ricans to a particular area?

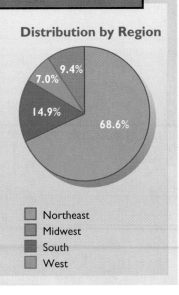

Population	
Total	2,728,000
Northeast	1,872,000
Midwest	258,000
South	406,000
West	192,000

Distribution by Region

9.4%
7.0%
14.9%
68.6%

- Northeast
- Midwest
- South
- West

Connect What kind of music do you listen to? Does the music you listen to reflect your feelings about your life and your community? Why or why not?

music she loved, they preferred rock music. Most of the time they spoke neither pure Spanish nor English, but a mixture of the two that they called "Spanglish." Although they were Puerto Rican, Esmeralda felt different from them. Eventually, she learned their ways. She became more like them and thought less about her old life on the island.

Most Puerto Ricans who move to the mainland keep connections to Puerto Rico. As people travel back and forth between the mainland and Puerto Rico, they bring customs and products with them. If you visited Puerto Rico, you would see many influences from the U.S. mainland. You would also see that in Puerto Rico, there is a strong cultural connection to the Caribbean. Most people are a mix of Spanish and African ancestry. Some Puerto Ricans like to look even further back into their history by calling themselves "Boricuas" (bohr ee KOO uhs). The name comes from the Boriqueno (bohr ee KAY noh), an indigenous farming people who lived on the island before the Spanish arrived.

More Than the Four Walls

The land of Puerto Rico is a memory no Puerto Rican forgets. Some, like Esmeralda Santiago, never go back to it. But others return, longing for the familiar ways they left behind. Julia de Jesus Chaparro (HOO lee a day HAY soos sha PAHR ro) moved back to a small mountain village in Puerto Rico after more than 14 years in Boston. She is fond of saying that where she lives now there are "more than the four walls of the city." To prove what she means, she takes visitors to her back porch. Outside it, one can see a row of steep mountains. Peeking between them is the bright blue of the Caribbean Sea. The mountain slopes steeply

Resource Directory

Media and Technology

Planet Earth CD-ROM includes an interactive political map of Puerto Rico, as well as the other countries of Latin America.

down from her back porch, but she has managed to clear some land. Her garden of mangoes, coconuts, grapefruit, and lemons thrives in the sun. Behind a nearby tree, a hen and six chickens are pecking in the dirt.

On other parts of the island, farmers ride horses through fields of tall sugar cane. Higher in the hills, Puerto Rican cowhands, called *jíbaros* (HEE bahr ohs), hunt, fish, and raise chickens, pigs, and cattle. To the southwest, where the land gets lower, fishing villages dot the coast.

Puerto Rico is an island of cities as well as countryside. Puerto Rican cities show influences of Spanish, Caribbean, and U.S. mainland cultures. About 70 percent of Puerto Ricans live in cities. Many city people work in factories. Others work in the hotels and restaurants that draw many tourists. Puerto Rico's capital, San Juan (san HWAHN), has a large waterfront area known as the Condado (kohn DAH do). It is packed with luxury hotels. Not far away, modern skyscrapers pierce the brilliant sky. In the old section of San Juan, Spanish-style buildings are everywhere. A 450-year-old Catholic church built by the Spanish has been carefully restored. Not far from it sit ancient houses graced with iron balconies in lacy Spanish style.

A Commonwealth in Question

In 1951, Puerto Ricans voted to adopt their own constitution. A **constitution** is a statement of a country's basic laws and values. This gave Puerto Rico its own group of lawmakers. But it was still connected

READ ACTIVELY

Visualize What might you see if you looked out the back door of an apartment in the city? What might you see if you looked out the back door of a house in the countryside?

Background

Global Perspectives

Commonwealths The Commonwealth of Nations, an association of over 40 independent countries, is composed of Great Britain and countries once under its rule. Commonwealth nations include Canada; Australia; New Zealand; Bangladesh and India in Asia; Kenya, Ghana, and Tanzania in Africa; Fiji in the South Pacific; and many Caribbean islands, such as Jamaica, Barbados, Trinidad, and Tobago. Commonwealth members meet regularly to set goals and provide one another with economic aid and technical help. They cooperate in matters of health care, education, and scientific research.

New York City's Spanish Harlem

Puerto Ricans are the largest ethnic group in New York City's Lower East Side, and they make up about 12 percent of the city's total population.

SKILLS MINI LESSON

Identifying Central Issues

To **introduce** the skill, indicate to students that the information in this section has been organized around a central issue, which is a question or problem that Puerto Ricans face. Help students **practice** the skill by asking them to identify this issue. Record their responses on the chalkboard. If students need help; suggest that they review the headings and subheadings of the section for clues. Have students **apply** the skill by finding evidence in the text that supports their answer.

Interdisciplinary Connections

Language Arts Have students use the charts they made for the Teach activity to produce a debate on the central issue of Puerto Rico's future status. Organize students into three groups, directing each group to present arguments for and against one of the three status options. Invite groups to choose spokespersons to present their arguments in a debate. After all arguments have been presented, hold a secret ballot to determine which solution students think should be adopted. *English Language Learners, Auditory*

READ ACTIVELY

Connect Would people in your area want to become part of another state? Why or why not?

to the United States. Puerto Rico is bound by many United States laws Puerto Ricans have many questions about this. Is it good for Puert Rico? Should Puerto Rico become independent? Or should it become state of the United States?

What Direction to Take? Puerto Ricans have man disagreements over the answers to these questions. Many feel tha having "one foot" in Puerto Rico and "one foot" in the United States ca lead to problems. Others point out how the relationship with the Unite States has helped Puerto Rico. U.S. businesses on the island have raise the standard of living. Each year, the U.S. government sends millions o dollars to the island to help people in need.

Some people still feel that Puerto Rico has a disadvantage becaus people there cannot vote in U.S. elections. They say Puerto Rico shoul try to become a state. But if it does, it will become the poorest state i the union. Puerto Ricans earn more money than people in othe Caribbean countries. However, they earn less than people on the U.S mainland. Also, if Puerto Rico becomes a state, Puerto Ricans will hav

San Juan: Old and New

San Juan, Puerto Rico's oldest city, is famous for historic forts and the wrought iron balconies of its oldest neighborhoods. But San Juan is also a vacation spot for tourists, with modern hotels lining its sandy beaches.

Resource Directory

Teaching Resources

Section Quiz in the Chapter and Section Resources booklet, p. 77, covers the main ideas and key terms in the section. Available in Spanish in the Spanish Chapter and Section Resources booklet, p. 48.

Vocabulary in the Chapter and Section Resources booklet, p. 79, provides a review of key terms in the chapter. Available in Spanish in the Spanish Chapter and Section Resources booklet, p. 50.

Reteaching in the Chapter and Section Resources booklet, p. 80, provides a structure for students who may need additional help in mastering chapter content.

Enrichment in the Chapter and Section Resources booklet, p. 81, extends chapter content and enriches students' understanding.

Spanish Glossary in the Spanish Chapter and Section Resources, pp. 62–65, provides key terms translated from English to Spanish as well as

► These women are celebrating Puerto Rico's Spanish heritage. Puerto Ricans celebrate many holidays with traditional music and dancing.

to pay U.S. taxes. This could lower the earnings of many who have little to spare. For these reasons, in 1993, Puerto Ricans voted not to become the 51st state of the United States.

The Question of Independence   Some people who voted against statehood have even bigger dreams for the country. They want Puerto Rico to become a separate nation. If not, they fear that Puerto Ricans will become confused about their identity, just as Esmeralda Santiago became confused about hers. They stress Puerto Rico's connection to other Caribbean nations. They want to make sure that Puerto Ricans always identify with the Spanish language and Spanish culture. But for now, Puerto Rico will keep its links to the mainland. Many Puerto Ricans hope that their relationship with the United States will lead to a profitable and peaceful future.

SECTION 3 REVIEW

1. **Define**   (a) citizen, (b) commonwealth, (c) constitution.

2. **Identify**   (a) San Juan, (b) Condado.

3. What is the political connection between Puerto Rico and the United States?

4. Compare life in the mainland United States with life in Puerto Rico.

Critical Thinking

5. **Identifying Central Issues**   What are the three options Puerto Ricans consider in terms of their relationship with the United States? What are the benefits and drawbacks of each?

Activity

6. **Writing to Learn**   Try to put yourself in Esmeralda Santiago's place. Write a paragraph telling what it was like to move to New York from Puerto Rico.

Reviewing Main Ideas

1. Cuba lost economic aid and trade with the Soviet Union. The result was economic decline and shortages of food and other necessities.

2. Lydia Martin noticed food and clothing shortages.

3. Haiti is the only nation in the Americas formed from a successful revolt of enslaved Africans.

4. Democracy ended, and Aristide's followers were persecuted by the military government.

5. Among the examples students might cite are the Spanish language, customs, and architecture; American baseball, English language, popular music and culture, and American form of government.

6. Students might mention stronger ties to American culture and weaker identity as Puerto Ricans. They might also state that large numbers have moved permanently to the mainland.

Reviewing Key Terms

Sentences should show the correct meaning of the term through context.

Critical Thinking

1. Answers may vary. Students might cite these similarities: Both groups had to learn English and new ways of life. Both groups include those who wish to return to their homeland and others, especially those born here, who are adopting American culture and language. Differences include: Some Cubans cannot, or do not want to, return while Castro is in power. On the other hand, Puerto Ricans are American citizens and can travel freely between the island and the mainland.

2. Student answers should show understanding of how the slave revolt against the colonial French inspires Haitians with their heritage of victory over oppression.

CHAPTER 5 Review and Activities

Reviewing Main Ideas

1. What happened to Cuba when the communist regime in the Soviet Union fell?

2. What changes did Lydia Martin notice when she visited Cuba in 1995?

3. How is Haiti's history unique?

4. What were two results of Jean-Bertrand Aristide's forced exile from Haiti?

5. How do the cultures of Spain and the United States influence Puerto Rico? Give one example of how each has influenced Puerto Rico.

6. How have frequent trips to the U.S. mainland affected some Puerto Rican families?

Reviewing Key Terms

Use each key term below in a sentence that shows the meaning of the term.

1. communist
2. dictator
3. exile
4. illiterate
5. Creole
6. dialect
7. commonwealth
8. citizen
9. constitution

Critical Thinking

1. Making Comparisons Both Cubans and Puerto Ricans have settled in the United States. How has the experience been similar for both? How has it been different?

2. Drawing Conclusions How do you think Toussaint L'Ouverture's fight for independence inspires Haitians to fight for democracy?

Graphic Organizer

Copy the chart to the right onto a piece of paper, then fill in the empty boxes to complete the chart.

	Cuba	Haiti	Puerto Rico
Form of government			
United States Influence			

Graphic Organizer

	Cuba	Haiti	Puerto Rico
Form of Government	communist	republic	commonwealth of United States
United States Influence	radio, music, clothing styles	United States is helping to restore democracy	bound by U.S. laws, confused cultural identity

Map Activity

For each place listed below, write the letter from the map that shows its location.

The Caribbean: Place Location

1. Port-au-Prince
2. San Juan
3. Havana
4. Miami
5. Gulf of Mexico
6. Guantánamo Bay
7. Dominican Republic

Writing Activity

Writing a Poem
Write a poem describing the culture in your region. Does your region have a blend of cultures, like Haiti?

Why or why not? How does the culture in your region affect the way you feel about yourself?

Skills Review

Turn to the Skill Activity. Review the steps for locating information. Then write a one page biography of Fidel Castro. Make a list of four routes you could take to find information.

Internet Activity

Use a search engine to find the site **Nueva Vista: Latino/Puerto Rican Home Page.** Click on **Viewpoint.** Then, click on **The 51st State: the State of Confusion** and read one person's view on Puerto Rico's status as a U.S. commonwealth. Use this information to debate the issue with your classmates.

How Am I Doing?

Answer these questions to help you check your progress.

1. Do I understand why many Cubans have emigrated to the United States?

2. Can I explain how Haiti's people have struggled for democracy?

3. Do I understand Puerto Rico's relationship with the United States?

4. Can I describe what factors have affected culture in the Caribbean islands?

5. What information from this chapter can I use in my book project?

Internet Link

If students are having difficulty finding this site, you may wish to have them use the following URL, which was accurate at the time this textbook was published:

http://www2.epix.net/ ~escobar/Vista.html

http://www.latinolink.com/ opinion/hi01212e.html

You might also guide students to a search engine. Four of the most useful are AltaVista, Lycos, Infoseek, and Yahoo. For additional suggestions on using the Internet, refer to the Prentice Hall Social Studies' Educator's Handbook "Using

the Internet," in the *Prentice Hall World Explorer Program Resources.*

For additional links to world geography and culture topics, visit the Prentice Hall Home Page at:

http://www.phschool.com.

How Am I Doing?

Point out to students that this checklist is just a quick reminder for them of what they learned in the chapter. If their answer to any of the questions is *no* or if they are unsure, they may need to review the topic.

Map Activity

1. E	4. B	6. D
2. G	5. A	7. F
3. C		

Skills Review

Students' routes will vary. Sample resources: library, almanac, encyclopedia, newspaper articles on Cuba and Castro, books on Castro.

Writing Activity

Students' poems will vary, but should reflect their views of the local culture.

Resource Directory

Teaching Resources

Chapter Tests Forms A and B are in the Tests booklet, pp. 26–31.

Program Resources

Writing Process Handbook includes Proofreading, p. 37, to help students with the Writing Activity.

Media and Technology

Color Transparencies
Color Transparency 174
(Graphic organizer table template)

Prentice Hall Writer's Solution
Writing Lab CD-ROM

Computer Test Bank Resource Pro™ CD-ROM

Exploring South America

To help you plan instruction, the chart below shows how teaching resources correspond to chapter content. Use the resources to vary instruction, add activities, or plan block schedules. Where appropriate, resources have **suggested time allotments** for students. Time allotments are approximate.

Managing Time and Instruction

	Latin America Teaching Resources Binder		World Explorer Program Resources Binder	
	Resource	**mins.**	**Resource**	**mins.**
1 SECTION 1 **Brazil** **Resources of the** **Rain Forest**	**Chapter and Section Support** Reproducible Lesson Plan, p. 84 Ⓢ Guided Reading and Review, p. 85 Ⓢ Section Quiz, p. 86 Critical Thinking Activity, p. 100	20 25 30	**Outline Maps** Brazil political map **Interdisciplinary Explorations** Ⓣ *Fate of the Rain Forest* **Nystrom Desk Atlas** Ⓣ**Primary Sources and Literature Readings** **Environmental and Global Issues** Topic: Environmental Damage	20 20 40 40
SKILL ACTIVITY **Using Isolines to** **Show Elevation**	**Social Studies and Geography Skills,** Understanding Isolines, p. 29 Reading a Contour Map, p. 30			
2 SECTION 2 **Peru** **Life in the Altiplano**	**Chapter and Section Support** Reproducible Lesson Plan, p. 87 Ⓢ Guided Reading and Review, p. 88 Ⓢ Section Quiz, p. 89	20 25	**Outline Maps** South America political map	20
3 SECTION 3 **Chile** **A Growing Economy** **Based on Agriculture**	**Chapter and Section Support** Reproducible Lesson Plan, p. 90 Ⓢ Guided Reading and Review, p. 91 Ⓢ Section Quiz, p. 92	20 25	**Outline Maps** South America political map	20
4 SECTION 4 **Venezuela** **Oil Powers the** **Economy**	**Chapter and Section Support** Reproducible Lesson Plan, p. 93 Ⓢ Guided Reading and Review, p. 94 Ⓢ Section Quiz, p. 95 Ⓢ Vocabulary, p. 97 Reteaching, p. 98 Enrichment, p. 99 Ⓢ Chapter Summary, p. 96 **Tests** Forms A and B Chapter Tests, pp. 32–37	20 25 20 25 25 15 40	**Outline Maps** South America political map **Writing Process Handbook** Locating Information, pp. 17–18	20 25
ACTIVITY SHOP **Interdisciplinary** **Rain Forest** **Resources**	**Activities and Projects** Ⓣ Activity Shop: Interdisciplinary, p. 7	30		
LITERATURE *Question Book* **by Pablo Neruda**				

Block Scheduling Folder
PROGRAM TEACHING RESOURCES

Activities and Projects

Block Scheduling Program Support

Interdisciplinary Links

Resource Pro™ CD-ROM

Media and Technology

Assessment Opportunities

From Guiding Questions to Assessment A series of Guiding Questions serves as an organizing framework for this book. The Guiding Questions that relate to this chapter are listed below. Section Reviews and Section Quizzes provide opportunities for assessing students' insights into these Guiding Questions. Additional assessments are listed below.

Media and Technology

Resource	mins.
🔘 🖉 Ⓢ World Video Explorer	20
🖉 Planet Earth CD-ROM	20
🖉 Material World CD-ROM	20
🖵 Color Transparencies 36, 37, 64	20
🖉 Planet Earth CD-ROM	20
🖵 Color Transparencies 19, 69	20
🖉 Planet Earth CD-ROM	20
🖵 Color Transparencies 34, 35, 64	20
🖉 Planet Earth CD-ROM	20
🖵 Color Transparency 69	20
🎧 Ⓢ Guided Reading Audiotapes	20
🖵 Color Transparency 174	20
(Graphic organizer table template)	
🖉 The Writer's Solution CD-ROM	30
🖫 Computer Test Bank	30

T **Teaming Opportunity**
This resource is especially well-suited for teaching teams.

Ⓢ **Spanish**
This resource is also in Spanish Support.

🖉 **CD-ROM**

🖉 **Laserdisc**

🖵 **Transparency**

🖫 **Software**

🔘 **Videotape**

🎧 **Audiotape**

GUIDING QUESTIONS

- *Why have many Latin Americans been moving to cities in recent years?*

- *How has geography influenced the ways in which Latin Americans make a living?*

ASSESSMENTS

Section 1

Students should be able to write a letter to the editor detailing the rain forest's effect on Brazil's economy.

▶ **RUBRIC** See the Assessment booklet for a rubric on assessing a letter to the editor.

Section 2

Students should be able to write a poem that expresses what life is like for the Aymara people on the straw islands of Lake Titicaca.

▶ **RUBRIC** See the Assessment booklet for a rubric on assessing a student poem.

Section 3

Students should be able to describe how Chile's location affects the crops it grows.

▶ **RUBRIC** See the Assessment booklet for a rubric on assessing cause-and-effect statements.

Section 4

Students should be able to give an oral presentation describing Venezuela's economy and its possible future.

▶ **RUBRIC** See the Assessment booklet for a rubric on assessing an oral presentation.

Activities and Projects

Mental Mapping

Southern Lands Tell students that South America has many notable natural features, including the Amazon River, the Amazon rain forest, Lake Titicaca (the world's highest navigable lake), Angel Falls (the world's highest waterfall), and the Andes Mountains. The South American continent also includes landforms and vegetation areas such as desert, mountains, and grasslands.

Give students outline maps of South America. Ask them to locate and label some of these physical features on the map. Give them just a few minutes to do this. Then have students compare their sense of where these features are with the information on a published map.

Links to Current Events

Fact Cards Have students work in groups of four to create sets of fact cards about each of the four countries covered in this chapter. One member of each group should concentrate on one country.

Using almanacs, an encyclopedia, and other reference sources, students can collect information about the current form of government, political leaders and parties, major products, natural resources, type of currency used, language, religion, and other facts that can give them a picture of the country. Students should put one fact or piece of information on each index card.

After each student has created five to ten cards about his or her country, the members of each group can exchange cards to compare and contrast four countries.

Hands-On Activities

Are We There Yet? The Pan-American Highway is a network of roads connecting North America and South America. The system covers about 30,000 miles of roads. Although parts of the highway have yet to be completed, most of it is finished. The highway has been under construction since 1936.

Display a map of the Americas with countries and their capitals labeled. Suggest to students that the highway might link all these countries. Invite students to take turns coming up to the map to trace routes the Pan-American Highway might take. You may wish to give students push pins and yarn to mark their proposed routes. You may want to challenge students to find possible routes that would connect the capitals of all the countries in North America, Central America, and South America.

Challenge Preconceptions Ask students to brainstorm their associations with South America. Then have each student write down several of their associations on a piece of paper. As students work through this chapter, encourage them to look for information that supports their previously held ideas and information that challenges or disproves their previously held ideas about South America. Have students set up their preconceptions and information that confirms or challenges their preconceptions in chart form. *Average*

Resourceful Reinforce understanding of the economies of some countries of South America by having students make a simple chart with three columns: Rain Forest, Oil, and Agriculture. Under each column, have students list words that illustrate how the resource is used or why it is important. Under Rain Forest, students might list different products as well as the importance of the rain forest to the world's ecology. Under Oil, they may write words that describe how oil is used. Under Agriculture, they may list various agricultural products. Students may use pictures rather than words to illustrate the uses or importance of these resources. *English Language Learners*

Different Countries Help students see that the countries of South America have distinct identities by asking a group of students to put on a skit about an interaction among citizens of three or more South American countries. These people might be portrayed as encountering each other in a major airport, at the United Nations, at a major international conference, or at a tourist attraction in another country such as Disney World or the Eiffel Tower. Encourage students to develop a scenario that emphasizes some of the differences among people from different cultures and countries of South America as well as some of the similarities. *Challenging*

F.Y.I.

This page can help you extend your own and students' understanding of the concepts in this chapter. You may want to browse through some of the suggestions in the **Bibliography. Interdisciplinary Links** can connect social studies understandings to areas elsewhere in the curriculum through the use of other Prentice Hall products. **National Geography Standards** reflected specifically in this chapter are listed for your convenience. Some hints about appropriate **Internet Access** are also provided. **School to Careers** provides insights into the practical uses of some of the concepts in this chapter as they might pertain to various careers.

BIBLIOGRAPHY

FOR THE TEACHER

Ashford, Moyra. *Brazil.* Steck-Vaughn, 1991.

Beani, Laura, Francesco Dessi, and Massimo Pandolfi. *The Pampas, Andes, and Galapagos.* Steck-Vaughn, 1992.

The Cousteau Society. *An Adventure in the Amazon.* Simon, 1992.

Fox, Geoffrey. *The Land and People of Venezuela.* HarperCollins, 1991.

FOR THE STUDENT

Easy
Peru—In Pictures. Lerner, 1994.

Lewington, Anna, adapter. *Antonio's Rain Forest.* Carolrhoda, 1993.

Average
Schwartz, David. *Yanomami: People of the Amazon.* Lothrop, 1995.

Challenging
Fernandez, Jose B. *José de San Martin: Latin America's Quiet Hero.* Millbrook, 1994.

Roman, Joseph. *Pablo Neruda.* Chelsea, 1992.

LITERATURE CONNECTION

Cohen, Miriam. *Born to Dance Samba.* Harper, 1984.

Kendall, Sarita. *Ransom for a River Dolphin.* Lerner, 1993.

INTERDISCIPLINARY LINKS

Subject	Theme: Interdependence
MATH	Middle Grades Math: Tools for Success *Course 2*, Lesson 11–4, **Math and Money: Using Linear Equations** *Course 3*, Lesson 8–8, **Math and Physics: Direct and Inverse Variation**
SCIENCE	Prentice Hall Science *Ecology: Earth's Natural Resources*, Lesson 4–1, **Fossil Fuels and Minerals** *Chemistry of Matter*, Lesson 2–1, **Nature of Chemical Reactions**
LANGUAGE ARTS	Choices in Literature *Joining Hands*, **The Friends of Kwan Ming** and **A Story of How a Wall Stands** *You Are the Solution*, **Saving the Wetlands**

NATIONAL GEOGRAPHY STANDARDS

Students explore the 18 National Geography Standards throughout Latin America. Chapter 6, however, concentrates on investigating the following: standards 1, 3, 4, 6, 8, 9, 10, 11, 12, 13, 14, 15, 16, 17, 18. For a complete list of the standards, see the *Teacher's Flexible Planning Guide.*

SCHOOL TO CAREERS

In Chapter 6: Exploring South America, students learn about the economies and natural resources of Brazil, Peru, Chile, and Venezuela. Additionally, they address the skill of using isolines. Understanding the balance of economic and environmental issues can help students prepare for careers in economics, science, conservation, business, and geology. Using isolines is useful for civil engineers, forest and park rangers, surveyors, and geologists. The curriculum presented in this book, as in all eight titles of Prentice Hall's *World Explorer* program, is designed to prepare students not only for careers but also for good citizenship—of the world as well as of this country.

INTERNET ACCESS

Many social studies teachers and students use Internet browsers, or search engines, to investigate particular topics. For the best results, use narrow rather than broad topics. Try these for Chapter 6: Yanomamo, Brazilian rain forest, altiplano, Cuzco. Finding age-appropriate sites is an important consideration when using the Internet. For links to age-appropriate sites in world studies and geography, visit the Prentice Hall Home Page at: http://www.phschool.com

Exploring South America

SECTION 1
Brazil
RESOURCES OF THE RAIN FOREST

SECTION 2
Peru
LIFE IN THE ALTIPLANO

SECTION 3
Chile
A GROWING ECONOMY BASED ON AGRICULTURE

SECTION 4
Venezuela
OIL POWERS THE ECONOMY

KEY
— National boundary
⊛ National capital
• Other city
Lambert Azimuthal Equal Area Projection

MAP ACTIVITIES

South America is more than two times as large as the mainland United States. Because it is so large, its geography and cultures are diverse. To learn more about South America, complete the following activities.

Understanding geography
Much of South America is located south of the Equator. If you were to start at the Equator and travel south, how do you think the climate would change? Why?

Study the map
How do you think the Andes Mountains may have affected political boundaries in South America?

Chapter 9

Brazil
RESOURCES OF THE RAIN FOREST

BEFORE YOU READ

Reach Into Your Background
In this section, you will learn about the rain forests in Brazil.

List three things you already know or can guess about the rain forests.

Questions to Explore
1. Why are the rain forests in Brazil a global issue?
2. How does what happens to the rain forests affect Brazil's economy?

Key Terms
canopy
photosynthesis

Key People and Places
Rio de Janeiro
Salvador
Yanomamo
Brasília

D eep in the rain forest in Brazil, the light barely penetrates. At the top of the trees, the leaves form a dense mass called a **canopy.** Sun and rain beat down upon the canopy. But on the ground, the air feels almost chilly. The only sounds are the calls of birds, monkeys, and insects.

▼ The canopy of Brazil's rain forest parts only where rivers slice through it.

Brazil and Its Rain Forests

Brazil, the largest country in South America, is nearly as large as the United States. It is also one of the richest countries in the world in land and resources. Until recently, its immense rain forests remained undisturbed. Only the few Native American groups that had lived in them for centuries ever explored them.

Brazil's Geography Brazil's rain forests take up about one half of the country. Look at the map in the Country Profile. In the southeast, the forests give way to a large plateau divided by mountain ranges and river valleys. The plateau reaches Brazil's long coast. Many harbors lie along the coast. Large cities, such as Rio de Janeiro (ree oh day zhuh NER oh), grew up around harbors. Most of Brazil's people live near the coast, far from the rain forests.

Teaching Resources

📁 **Reproducible Lesson Plan** in the Chapter and Section Resources booklet, p. 84, provides a summary of the section lesson.

📁 **Guided Reading and Review** in the Chapter and Section Resources booklet, p. 84, provides a structure for mastering key concepts and reviewing key terms in the section. Available in Spanish in the Spanish Chapter and Section Resources booklet, p. 85.

Program Resources

Material in the *Primary Sources and Literature Readings* booklet extends content with a selection from the region under study.
Outline Maps Brazil political map

Lesson Objectives

1 Explain the importance of the rain forest to Brazil's economy.

2 Explore the consequences to the world of rain forest destruction.

3 Evaluate possible solutions to the conflict over rain forest use.

Lesson Plan

1 Engage
Warm-Up Activity

Invite students to think about what it might be like to share a pet dog with a friend. Have them discuss with a partner how they might divide fairly the time, chores, and costs associated with pet care. Encourage volunteers to share with the class how they compromised to make a plan. What problems did they have in reaching an agreement? What solutions did they find?

Activating Prior Knowledge

Have students read Reach Into Your Background in the Before You Read box. On the chalkboard, create a chart like the one below. Record what students already know about the rain forests of Brazil and their importance to the environment. Suggest that students copy the chart and add information to it as they read the section.

What We Already Know About Brazil	What We Learned From The Preview

2 Explore

Have students read the section. Tell them that as they read, they should look for answers to the following questions: Which groups in Brazil use the rain forests for their livelihood? Why are Brazil's rain forests important to the world? What solutions have been found to the conflict over the use of the rain forest?

3 Teach

Suggest that students work in groups of four to list the rain forest problems and solutions described in this section. Then have them discuss whether or not they feel the solutions are fair. Ask a member of the group to share with the class how the group judged the fairness of the solutions. This activity should take 15 minutes.

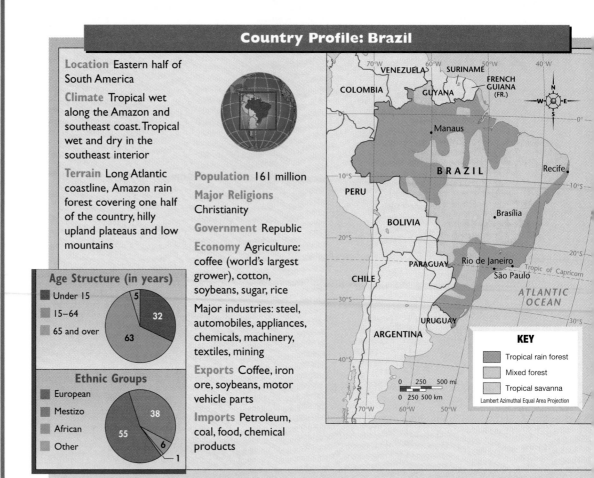

Country Profile: Brazil

Location Eastern half of South America

Climate Tropical wet along the Amazon and southeast coast. Tropical wet and dry in the southeast interior

Terrain Long Atlantic coastline, Amazon rain forest covering one half of the country, hilly upland plateaus and low mountains

Population 161 million

Major Religions Christianity

Government Republic

Economy Agriculture: coffee (world's largest grower), cotton, soybeans, sugar, rice

Major industries: steel, automobiles, appliances, chemicals, machinery, textiles, mining

Exports Coffee, iron ore, soybeans, motor vehicle parts

Imports Petroleum, coal, food, chemical products

Age Structure (in years)
- Under 15 — 5
- 15–64 — 32
- 65 and over — 63

Ethnic Groups
- European — 38
- Mestizo — 55
- African — 6
- Other — 1

Map Study This map shows the vegetation regions of Brazil. Brazil contains over 1 million square miles (2,589,900 sq km) of rain forest. Northern Brazil contains part of the largest rain forest in the world, the Amazonian rain forest. Alaska could fit inside Brazil's Amazonian rain forest twice. Texas could fit inside it five times. **Location** What four Brazilian cities are located in the rain forest?

The People of Brazil

The Native Americans living in the rain forest were some of the first people to live in Brazil. Today, most Brazilians are a mix of Native American, African, and European heritages.

Many parts of African culture still flourish in Brazil. The most African of Brazilian cities, Salvador, lies on the coastal plains. Visitors are surprised by how much Salvador is like a town in Africa. Most of the people who live here descend from the millions of Africans brought to Brazil as slaves.

Working on Farms and in Factories Many Africans in Brazil were forced to work the coffee plantations. Brazil used their labor

Answers to . . .
MAP STUDY

- Manaus, Recife, Rio de Janeiro, São Paulo

to become the world's largest coffee grower. When the slaves were freed in the late 1800s, they became paid but cheap labor.

Coffee prices dropped in the first few years of the 1900s. Brazilians realized that they could not depend on one or two crops to survive. In the 1930s, the government discouraged coffee production and tried to diversify the economy by building more factories. Today, Brazil produces many goods, including iron and steel, cars, and electrical equipment. Since 1960, about 30 million people have left farms and plantations to get jobs in these new industries. They moved into the cities.

A Brazilian City Brazilian cities are home to the rich and the very poor. Rio de Janeiro is a good example of these contrasts. It lies on the coast, surrounded by huge mountains that dip to the sea. If you climbed to the top of one, you could see the whole city. To the south, you would see expensive hotels and shops for tourists. In the downtown area, you would see old palaces and government buildings.

But to the north, you would see clusters of small houses where factory workers live. Below this neighborhood is an even poorer one, crowded with homes that have no electricity or running water. About a quarter of Rio's 12 million people live in these neighborhoods known as *favelas* (fuh VEH lus). However, most of Rio's people live in well-built houses with electricity and running water.

READ ACTIVELY

Connect How is the history of Africans in Brazil like the history of Africans brought to the United States?

Brazil's African Heritage

In Salvador, Brazil, people cook food similar to the food eaten in West Africa. Food in both places is seasoned with coconut milk, pepper, and palm oil, and cooked in earthenware pots. The women of Salvador wear lacy dresses and turbans, like many of the women of West Africa.

4 Assess

See the Answers to the Section Review. You may also use the student discussion for assessment.

Acceptable responses include several problems, solutions, and evaluations.

Commendable responses include more and show an understanding of why solutions are fair or unfair.

Outstanding responses include student suggestions of original, practical, and equitable solutions.

Background

Daily Life

Capoeira Capoeira, a Brazilian combination of dance and martial arts, developed in the northeastern part of the country. The dance form was created by enslaved Africans. Forbidden to fight each other, the slaves developed a form of fighting to music that looked like dancing. Music was played on drums and on a *berimbau* made from a bow and a gourd. Today, young men, boys, and some girls study capoeira, just as American young people study karate, judo, and other martial arts.

Global Perspectives

Global Warming The gases in our planet's atmosphere act like the glass in a greenhouse, letting sunlight in to provide warmth, then keeping the heat from escaping. Changing the mix of gases in the atmosphere may change the warmth inside the Earth's "greenhouse." For example, burning fuels such as coal, oil, and natural gas has increased the amount of carbon dioxide in the atmosphere. Trees remove carbon dioxide from the atmosphere, replacing it with oxygen. But as industry spreads, more carbon dioxide is sent into the atmosphere. At the same time, fewer trees are available to remove this gas from the air. As a result, the increased carbon dioxide traps more heat, leading to warmer climates and possibly disastrous results. For instance, if climates warm sufficiently, polar ice caps will melt and ocean levels will rise. Coastal ocean areas, on which large populations now live, will flood.

Visualize What do you think you would see if you climbed to the top of a tree in the rain forest?

Using the Rain Forest's Resources

On a sunny January in 1994, two boys who lived in the rain forest scrambled up the trees. The boys were Yanomamos. The Yanomamo are a Native American group that lives in the rain forests. The boys pointed to a plane soaring close to the treetops. The plane dipped down and landed on a dirt strip. "Foreign visitors!" the boys called excitedly.

Brazil's New Capital: Brasília The visitors were from Brasília (bruh ZIL yuh), the capital city of Brazil. Brasília is closer to the rain forest than the coastal cities are. On the vast interior plain where Brasília now stands, there used to be nothing but a savanna called the Cerrado (suh RAH doh). The Cerrado was a region 10 times larger than the state of Kansas. The government thought that moving the capital there would attract some people from the coastal areas.

The government wanted to develop Brazil's interior region using the resources of the rain forest. The rain forests are important to Brazil's economy because people cut timber, mine for gold, and farm there. Now, the government hoped to develop industry using the resources of the rain forest.

Worldwide Impact of the Rain Forest The rain forest where the Yanomamo live is very important to life all around the Earth. Scientists estimate that rain forests produce about one third of the world's oxygen. Green plants and trees produce their own food using

▼ São Paulo is the largest city in Brazil. It contains more than 20,000 factories, which provide jobs for 600,000 workers.

Resource Directory

Teaching Resources

Critical Thinking Activity in the Chapter and Section Resources booklet, p. 100, helps students apply the skill of assessing your understanding.

Two Cities, Two Climates

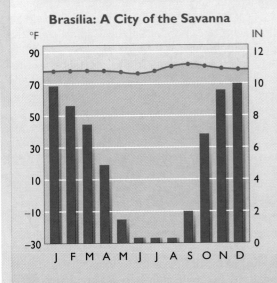

Brasília: A City of the Savanna

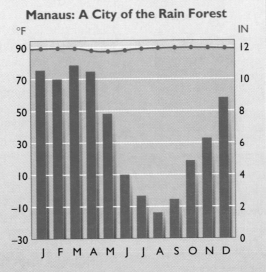

Manaus: A City of the Rain Forest

Curved lines show temperatures in Fahrenheit degrees. **Bars** show rainfall in inches.

Chart Study A climate graph shows rainfall and temperature in the same space. The bars show rainfall, while the curved lines show temperature. **Critical Thinking** How are the seasons in Brasília and Manaus different from each other?

water, carbon dioxide, and sunlight. This process is called **photosynthesis** (foht oh SIN thuh sis). In the process of photosynthesis, oxygen is given off. All people and animals need oxygen to breathe.

The rain forest also holds about one fifth of the world's fresh water. Many scientists think that when people come to the rain forest, they may upset the delicate balance of nature.

Protecting the Rain Forest Brazil's government is taking care to use the rain forest's resources without upsetting this balance. The government has started using satellites to keep an eye on the rain forest. That way, the government can respond fast to protect the rain forest from the following dangers.

First, if too much timber is cut down, there will not be enough trees to absorb the carbon dioxide in the atmosphere. The carbon dioxide layer may trap heat near the Earth, changing the world's climate. When part of the forest is destroyed, the animals and plants that live there may not survive. When plant life is destroyed, less oxygen is produced.

HEROES

A Voice of Protest Friar Hector Turrini moved from Italy to Brazil more than 45 years ago. At that time, there were so few roads that Turrini had to learn to fly a plane to get around his parish. He dedicated himself to protecting the Native Americans and rubber tappers who depend on the rain forest. Now Turrini is working to protect the rain forest.

Understanding Special Geography Graphs
To **introduce** the skill, point out that climate graphs can help students decide what kinds of clothes and gear to take on an expedition to a particular place. Direct students' attention to the climate graph of Brasília. Point out the abbreviations for the months at the base of the graph, the temperature scale at the left of the graph, and the rainfall scale at the right of the graph. Ask these questions to help students **practice** the skill: *Which are Brasília's hottest months? How much rain does Brasília usually receive in January? In July?* (August and September; about 10 inches; about less than one inch) Encourage students to **apply** the skill by writing three questions that can be answered by using the climate graph of Manaus. Have students share and answer one another's questions.

Activity

Critical Thinking

Identifying Central Issues *Suitable for an individual or whole-class activity.* Encourage students to discuss what they think are the most important issues surrounding Brazil's rain forests. Then have students prepare a one-minute news bulletin presenting the issues they feel are most important to the protection of the rain forests. Encourage volunteers to present their bulletins to the class. Ask the class to evaluate the news bulletins, choosing three they feel accurately identify the central issues. *Auditory*

Answers to ...

CHART STUDY

• Brasília has both rainy and dry seasons, Manaus is rainy nearly all year.

LINKS TO SCIENCE

Amazon Fruit What is green and bumpy, round like a softball, and looks like the sole of a shoe? It is a conde (KON day). Scientists in Brazil have discovered more than 40 types of fruits growing in the Amazon rain forest. Besides being high in vitamins and protein, these fruits taste good. Scientists hope to persuade Amazon farmers to stop clearing rain forest land and begin planting these fruits instead.

Second, there is the problem of smuggling. Each year, Brazil loses about 12 million animals to smugglers. Many of these animals are endangered. Smugglers look for monkeys, parrots, and other animals. One parrot can be sold for $10,000. One woolly monkey can be sold for as much as $50,000. It is illegal to capture or kill these animals, but the smugglers often get away with it.

Third, development can cause pollution. In the late 1980s, the discovery of gold attracted many miners to the rain forest. Mining gold involves mixing the gold with mercury. The mercury polluted streams in the forest. It made people in several Yanomamo villages sick.

The gold mining in the rain forest attracted the attention of the world. The government of Brazil passed strict laws about mining in the rain forest. Sometimes the government insisted that the miners leave. At times, military police had to be called in to make sure they did.

Giving Land to the Poor One of the main reasons that people come to the rain forest is the lack of land to farm. This may seem strange when one considers Brazil's large size. However, most of Brazil's land is owned by a few people who may choose not to farm their land. About one third of Brazil's farmland is unused. This represents about 300 million acres (122 million hectares) of crop and ranch land.

In 1995, Brazil's president gave some of this unused land to poor farmers. The goal is to resettle more than 3,600 poor families who want a new place to live and who want to return to farming. The process is a slow one. However, life for some resettled Brazilians is improving.

People are starting small farms just north of Rio de Janeiro. The farms help people make a living for themselves. On a balmy July day in 1995, farmer Joe Brum showed a reporter his farm. Brum had received the 17-acre plot from the government. Now his tin-roofed house was shaded by the coconut and banana trees he had planted. He had a couple of pigs and had earned enough money to buy a satellite dish and a television.

Brum's eyes gleamed as he pointed to the rows of vegetables. "What I have here," he explained to the reporter, "I made myself."

SECTION 1 REVIEW

1. Define (a) canopy, (b) photosynthesis.

2. Identify (a) Rio de Janeiro, (b) Salvador, (c) Yanomamo, (d) Brasília.

3. Why are Brazil's rain forests important to the whole world?

4. In what ways does Brazil depend on its rain forest?

Critical Thinking

5. Expressing Problems Clearly Some people want Brazil to stop using rain forests completely. Is this reasonable? What do you think it would do to Brazil's economy?

Activity

6. Writing a Journal Entry Use what you know about the rain forest to write a journal entry about a visit to it.

Peru

LIFE IN THE ALTIPLANO

Reach Into Your Background

Did you choose your clothing according to the weather report this morning? The decision you make is affected by climate. Think of other ways that climate affects your life.

Questions to Explore

1. How has geography affected the lifestyle of Native Americans of the altiplano?
2. How do people on the altiplano survive?

Key Terms

altiplano
sierra
montaña
tundra

Key People and Places

Lake Titicaca
Aymara
Quechua
Cuzco

W hen people on Tribuna, an island in Lake Titicaca, play soccer, they must be careful. That's because the island is made of straw. The ground is uneven, and when they walk on it they can feel the water shifting below. "It seems crazy to play soccer on water," says Luis Colo, who lives on Tribuna. "We don't jump on each other after a goal, or we'd probably fall through the field."

Tribuna is one of about 70 islands made by the Aymara (eye muh RAH). The Aymara have adapted to the geography of Lake Titicaca. The Aymara make their islands out of tortora reeds. They join the floating roots of tortora reeds together and then lay cut reeds on top. This process creates an island that is firm enough to support small communities of people with huts and livestock. When the Aymara need more land, they build another island.

▲ When the wind comes up, the Aymara must anchor their islands to keep them from being swept away.

Peru's Three Geographic Regions

The Aymara live on Lake Titicaca. Find Lake Titicaca on the map in the Country Profile. Lake Titicaca lies high in Peru's **altiplano** (al tih PLAH noh), a high plateau region in the Andes. The altiplano is about 12,000 feet (3,658 m) above sea level. It lies in the southern part of Peru near the Bolivian border.

Teaching Resources

📁 **Reproducible Lesson Plan** in the Chapter and Section Resources booklet, p. 87, provides a summary of the section lesson.

📁 **Guided Reading and Review** in the Chapter and Section Resources booklet, p. 88, provides a structure for mastering key concepts and reviewing key terms in the section. Available in Spanish in the Spanish Chapter and Section Resources booklet, p. 54.

Program Resources

Outline Maps South America political map

Lesson Objectives

1 Identify the three main geographical regions of Peru.

2 Analyze how geography affects people's way of life in the altiplano.

3 Explain why the traditional way of life of the Native Americans of Peru is changing.

Lesson Plan

1 Engage

Warm-Up Activity

Ask volunteers who have camped outdoors to describe how they lived with only fire for heat. How did they keep warm? How did they cook their food? Involve other students by asking them to imagine what it would be like to have only fire for heating and cooking and no electricity for light or for such appliances as a refrigerator.

Activating Prior Knowledge

Have students read Reach Into Your Background in the Before You Read box. Encourage students to supply other examples of how climate affects their lives.

2 Explore

Have students read the section. Direct them to keep in mind the following questions as they read. What are the three main regions of Peru like? How do people live in Peru's cities? How do the climate and geography of the altiplano affect the lives of people living there? You may wish to write these questions on the chalkboard.

3 Teach

Have partner pairs make Venn diagrams to compare the similarities and differences between life in a Quechua village and life on an island in Lake Titicaca. Have them draw two overlapping circles, one labeled *A Quechua Village,* the other labeled *Lake Titicaca.* Tell them to include details about food, housing, and livelihood. Then have them use the information in the diagram as a basis for a paragraph describing how the climate and natural resources of the altiplano and lake affect people's lives. This activity should take about 15 minutes.

Background

Links Across Time

Incas The present-day Quechuas are the descendants of the Incas. The Incas ruled the region in the 1400s and 1500s.

Answers to . . .

MAP STUDY

- over 13,000 ft (over 3,960 m); northeast; One end of the river is in the mountains where the elevation is high. It flows to the northeast where the elevation is lower.

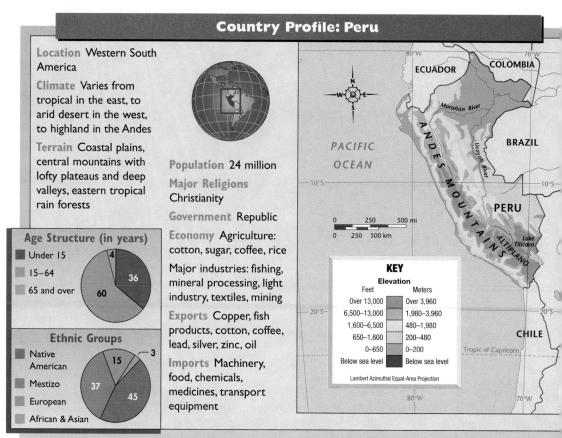

Country Profile: Peru

Location Western South America

Climate Varies from tropical in the east, to arid desert in the west, to highland in the Andes

Terrain Coastal plains, central mountains with lofty plateaus and deep valleys, eastern tropical rain forests

Population 24 million

Major Religions Christianity

Government Republic

Economy Agriculture: cotton, sugar, coffee, rice

Major industries: fishing, mineral processing, light industry, textiles, mining

Exports Copper, fish products, cotton, coffee, lead, silver, zinc, oil

Imports Machinery, food, chemicals, medicines, transport equipment

Age Structure (in years)
- Under 15 — 4
- 15–64 — 36, 60
- 65 and over

Ethnic Groups
- Native American — 15, 3
- Mestizo — 37, 45
- European
- African & Asian

KEY

Elevation

Feet	Meters
Over 13,000	Over 3,960
6,500–13,000	1,980–3,960
1,600–6,500	480–1,980
650–1,600	200–480
0–650	0–200
Below sea level	Below sea level

Lambert Azimuthal Equal-Area Projection

Map Study This map shows the elevation of land in Peru. The higher you climb in the mountains, the colder the climate gets. In the Andes Mountains, trees will not grow above 10,000 feet (3,048 m) because it is too cold. But east of the Andes, the elevation is lower. Much of the eastern lowlands is covered with a dense tropical rain forest. **Location** How high in the mountains is Lake Titicaca? What direction do the rivers on this map flow? How can you tell?

Peru's mountains divide the country into three geographic regions. The altiplano and Peru's highest mountains are in the **sierra,** the mountains that run from northwest to southeast Peru. The mountains are so high that the temperature can drop as low as 20°F (–7°C). People who live in this region must sleep under many blankets. They sometimes wear sweaters to bed.

Their life is far different from the lives of those who live on the coastal plain, which is Peru's second geographical region. This dry region is warmed by the sun and cooled by sea breezes. Several cities including Trujillo (troo HEE yoh), Chimbote (chim BOH tay), and Lima (LEE muh), dot the coast.

The third region is called the **montaña.** The montaña is made of large stretches of tropical forests on the lower slopes of mountains in northeast Peru. Here the weather is warm and humid all year round.

Resource Directory

Media and Technology

Planet Earth CD-ROM includes an interactive political map of Peru, as well as the other countries of Latin America.

Peru's People

Native Americans make up almost half of Peru's population. Most Native Americans living in Peru are Quechua. About 15 percent of Peruvians are of European descent. Another 37 percent are mestizo. The remaining Peruvians are of African and Asian descent.

Peru's Cities The altiplano contains cities and isolated towns. City life is very different from village life. Most city dwellers have electricity. The streets are paved, and there are telephones. But in Peru's cities, the old mixes with the new.

One Peruvian city, Cuzco, is the site of the ancient Incan capital. Parts of the old Incan wall that once surrounded the city are still standing. Today's modern houses are made of adobe, with red tile roofs. But their foundations are the remains of Incan stonework. There are buildings from the time of the Spanish colonists as well.

Spanish conquistador Francisco Pizarro founded Peru's largest city and capital, Lima, in 1535. Lima lies on the coastal plain. Like Cuzco, Lima is a mix of old and new. Historic Spanish cathedrals and government buildings from the 1600s and 1700s stand next to modern skyscrapers.

Bridging Canyons The Incas invented the technology for building suspension bridges. First, they built stone towers on each side of a canyon. They suspended cables woven from plants from the stone towers. Then, they laid wooden slats across the cables to make a bridge. They used smaller cables for railings. People still use Incan bridges today. Modern suspension bridges have steel cables and are reinforced with iron beams.

◄ Lima is the busiest and most modern of Peru's cities. What details in the photo are modern? What details are more traditional?

Background

Links Across Time

Quechuas When Spain con-quered the Incas, the Que-chua were forced to work on large farms for Spanish land-lords. The Quechua people were treated poorly and bare-ly survived; the Quechua cul-ture was mostly destroyed. Even so, the Quechua are now Peru's largest ethnic group. Quechua and Spanish are the two official languages of Peru.

Background

Daily Life

High-Altitude Living The Quechua have been the sub-jects of medical studies to understand how they thrive at such high altitudes. It was found that their bodies have adapted to the thin air with larger-than-average lungs and hearts.

Life in Rural Areas In the isolated towns of the altiplano, life is very different from life in the city. There are no telephones to ring. Few buses drive through the villages. Most people are Quechua or Aymara.

A Day in a Quechua Village Modesto Mamani (moh DES toh muh MAN ee) is a 13-year-old Quechua boy. He wakes before dawn to the freezing mountain air. He eats breakfast as soon as the sun comes up. Breakfast is always the same: a couple of rolls, coffee with sugar, and whole wheat kernels that can be eaten like popcorn. The only other meal may be lunch. It is usually potato and barley soup with chunos—freeze-dried potato skins.

For much of the day, Modesto works in the field with his father and brothers. On other days, he looks after the sheep or goes with his mother to the market. Despite all of these chores, Modesto finds time to play soccer on the tundra in back of his house. A **tundra** is an area where no trees grow because the soil is always cold.

Predict How do you think the Quechuas of the altiplano make a living?

Modesto Mamani at School and at Work

Modesto's life mixes the modern and the traditional. He wants to study to become an engineer so that he can bring technology to the altiplano. But even when he is studying, Modesto is never far from his soccer ball. He also spends a lot of time tending sheep and knitting wool sweaters. Sometimes he even knits when he is playing soccer!

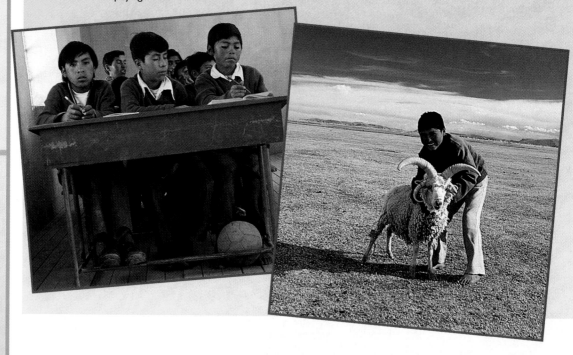

The Straw People Modesto's village is not far from the Aymara islands on Lake Titicaca. The people there live on one of the 70 tortora reed islands that float on the lake. The islanders use tortora reeds for many other purposes besides building islands. They weave it to make boats. They use it as fuel for cooking. They eat the soft inside of the reeds. Most important, though, they use the reeds to repair the islands. Tortora reeds last only a few months before they start to rot. A person who slipped through them could die in the lake's icy waters.

On the straw islands, women wake at dawn to get water from the lake for cooking and washing. They spend the rest of the day washing clothes, untangling fishing nets, and making new homes out of reeds. Once or twice a week they go to market to trade fish for rice, potatoes, and sugar. Meanwhile, the men fish and help to repair the straw islands.

A Modern Future Quechuas and other Native Americans living on the altiplano follow traditions that are hundreds of years old. Their communities, however, are slowly changing. Thousands of Native Americans have left for jobs in the city. Life is changing even for those who stay in the village. The future holds a promising mix of old and new ways.

Quechua Market Day

On market days, Quechua from several communities gather together to buy and sell goods. What kinds of goods are being sold at this market?

SECTION 2 REVIEW

1. Define (a) altiplano, (b) sierra, (c) montaña, (d) tundra.

2. Identify (a) Lake Titicaca, (b) Aymara, (c) Quechua, (d) Cuzco.

3. How is the daily life of the Quechua affected by the high altitude of the altiplano?

4. Describe people's lives on the straw islands of Lake Titicaca.

Critical Thinking

5. Recognizing Bias Do you think the Quechua see their way of life as outsiders see it? Explain.

Activity

6. Writing to Learn Compare life in a Peruvian city with life in a rural Quechua or Aymara community.

Resource Directory

Teaching Resources

Section Quiz in the Chapter and Section Resources booklet, p. 89, covers the main ideas and key terms in the section. Available in Spanish in the Spanish Chapter and Section Resources booklet, p. 55.

Using Isolines to Show Elevation

Lesson Objectives

❶ Demonstrate how isolines show elevation.

❷ Describe how to interpret an isoline map.

Lesson Plan

1 Engage

Warm-Up Activity

To **introduce** the skill, ask volunteers to role-play the scenario in the opening paragraphs. You might point out to students that hikers are not the only people who use maps that show elevation. Engineers also use such maps to figure out the best places to build highways, tunnels, and dams.

Activating Prior Knowledge

Encourage students to think of some of the other advantages of Melissa and José's map. Ask: *How could such a map save time? How would it help them estimate how long their hike would take? How could they use the map to avoid danger?*

2 Explore

Read the paragraphs under the heading Get Ready with students. Review with students what the terms *isoline* and *contour* mean. Assemble materials and organize students into small groups. Then have them read the rest of the skills activity.

Climb straight up, hike over the side, or walk all the way around? That was the question Melissa and José faced.

They stared up at the huge hill in front of them. According to the map, the campsite they were hiking to was exactly on the opposite side of the hill. What was the best route to take?

Melissa spread the map out on a fallen log. "Look," she said, pointing at the map. "This hill is steep on this side, but we can climb it." She traced the route on the map. "But look what we'd run into on the other side!"

"A cliff!" José responded. "We'd never be able to get down. It's way too steep. I guess we'll have to walk around the hill."

"Not so fast. If we head to our left, we can climb up a gentle slope and work our way past the cliff down the hill on the other side. It's kind of steep, but at least we'll be going downhill!"

Get Ready

How could Melissa tell from the map how steep different parts of the hill were? The answer is that the map showed isolines. The word *isolines* comes from the Greek word *iso,* which means "equal," and our word *lines.* Isolines link together equal parts of a map. On the map Melissa and José used, every part of the hill that was the same elevation was linked by an isoline. By studying the pattern of the isolines, Melissa could figure out the best route to take.

Isolines that show elevation are also called contour lines, because their pattern shows the contour, or shape, of the land.

You can make your own contour map. To do this, you will need:

- an irregularly shaped rock, about the size of a cantaloupe
- a pan of water big enough and deep enough to submerge the rock
- a crayon or waterproof marker
- a sheet of blank paper and a pencil

Resource Directory

Teaching Resources

Social Studies and Geography Skills
Understanding Isolines, p. 29
Reading a Contour Map, p.30

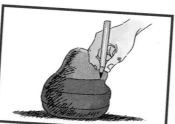
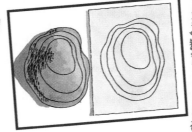

Try It Out

A. Fill the pan with water deep enough to cover the rock.

B. Holding the top of the rock, dip the bottom of it evenly about one inch into the water. Don't drop it! Remove the rock. Use the crayon or marker to trace the waterline all the way around the rock.

C. Dip the rock again, about one inch deeper. The waterline will now be about one inch higher up on the rock. Trace the new waterline with the crayon or marker, all the way around the rock.

D. Continue this process, dipping the rock about one inch deeper each time. Do this until you can go no farther.

E. Now, put the rock on the floor, and look at it from above. Can you see how each crayon or marker line connects the parts of the rock that are the same height? These are isolines. Using a pencil, copy the pattern you see looking down on the rock onto to your piece of paper. Next, label each of your isolines from the outside in. The outside line should be marked "1 inch," the next line "2 inches," and so on.

You have just drawn a map of the top of the rock using isolines.

Apply the Skill

The map on this page shows isolines of a region around the city of Lima, Peru. Use the map to visualize the shape of the land.

❶ Remember that isolines connect places of equal elevation. Just like the isolines you made on the rock, the isolines on this map connect places of equal elevation. The lines are numbered to show their elevation. What is the lowest elevation shown on the map? What is the highest elevation?

❷ Use the isolines to get useful information from the map. Remember that where the land is steep, isolines are close together. Where the land is flatter, isolines are farther apart. As you head east from Lima, does the elevation increase or decrease? Now sketch a side view of the map. What is the highest point? What is the lowest? How can you tell?

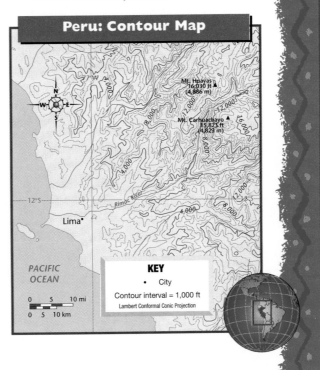

Peru: Contour Map

Mt. Huayas
16,030 ft ▲
(4,886 m)

Mt. Carhuacbayo ▲
15,823 ft
(4,823 m)

Rimac River

Lima•

PACIFIC
OCEAN

0   5   10 mi
0   5   10 km

KEY
• City
Contour interval = 1,000 ft
Lambert Conformal Conic Projection

---

3 Teach

Have students **practice** the skill by carrying out the Try It Out demonstration. You might suggest that group members take turns immersing and marking the rock. Display students' rocks and "maps" and discuss how even slight variations in size and shape between different groups' rocks correspond to differences in maps.

For additional reinforcement, students might perform the demonstration again using a much flatter rock. Students should add the pattern of the flat rock to their maps. Ask students to compare the two isoline patterns and explain what the lines reveal about the differences between the two rocks.

4 Assess

Have students **apply** the skill by completing the final part of the activity. To **assess,** evaluate the accuracy of students' answers to the questions and their side-view sketches of the topography shown on the map.

Answers to...
APPLY THE SKILL

1. 4,000 ft.; 16,030 ft.
2. East of Lima, the elevation increases. Students' sketches should show relatively low land in the western portion, with much higher elevations in the eastern portion. The elevation of Mt. Huayas is labeled, and it is higher than any other point on the map. The lowest point is probably in the area surrounding Lima.

Chile

A GROWING ECONOMY BASED ON AGRICULTURE

BEFORE YOU READ

Reach Into Your Background

Do you like eating fresh fruit in summer? What if you could have fresh, juicy strawberries and peaches in the middle of winter? Think of ways to make this possible.

Questions to Explore

1. How does Chile's location affect the crops it grows?
2. How does producing more crops help Chile?

Key Terms

pesticide

Key Places

Santiago
Andes
Atacama Desert

It was a fairly quiet day at the airport of Santiago (san tee AH goh), the capital of Chile. Two passengers from Venezuela stepped off a plane. They had their carry-on luggage and a couple of maracas. A maraca is a musical instrument that sounds like a rattle. It is made from a hollow gourd filled with dried-out seeds or pebbles.

▼ Maracas are normally used to play music.

There is nothing very surprising about seeing maracas in South America. They are used in many orchestras and bands to play Latin music. So why was the customs officer staring at them suspiciously? Before the travelers had time to pass through customs, the officer grabbed the maracas and X-rayed them. Then he broke them open. Just as he thought, they did not contain dried-up seeds or pebbles. They were full of new seeds that were good for planting.

Life in Chile

Chile may be the only country in the world that inspects maracas brought into its borders. In recent years, Chile's agriculture has been booming. Chile makes millions of dollars a year by exporting peaches, grapes, cherries, and other

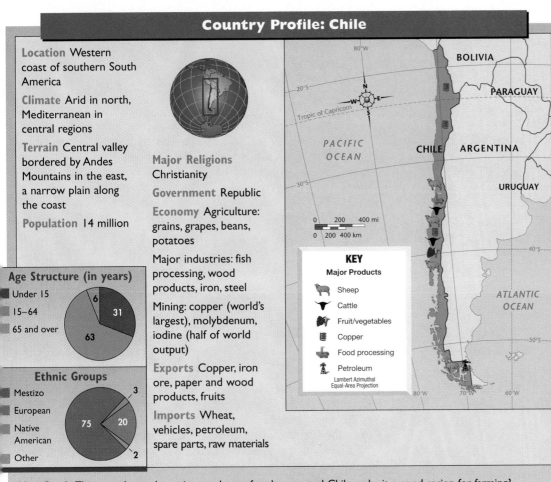

Country Profile: Chile

Location Western coast of southern South America

Climate Arid in north, Mediterranean in central regions

Terrain Central valley bordered by Andes Mountains in the east, a narrow plain along the coast

Population 14 million

Age Structure (in years)
- Under 15
- 15–64
- 65 and over

6
31
63

Ethnic Groups
- Mestizo
- European
- Native American
- Other

3
75
20
2

Major Religions Christianity

Government Republic

Economy Agriculture: grains, grapes, beans, potatoes

Major industries: fish processing, wood products, iron, steel

Mining: copper (world's largest), molybdenum, iodine (half of world output)

Exports Copper, iron ore, paper and wood products, fruits

Imports Wheat, vehicles, petroleum, spare parts, raw materials

KEY
Major Products
- Sheep
- Cattle
- Fruit/vegetables
- Copper
- Food processing
- Petroleum

Lambert Azimuthal Equal-Area Projection

Map Study This map shows the major products of each region in Chile. Most of Chile's people live in its central valley. Read the description of the climate and terrain in central Chile. **Place** How do the climate and terrain of central Chile make it a good region for farming? **Movement** The Andes Mountains run down the whole length of Chile. What do you think would be the easiest way to ship Chile's products out of the country?

fruits and vegetables. Their country is protected by the Andes mountains, so some of the insect pests and animal diseases that plague other countries never reach Chile. That is why the government is so concerned about what enters now. Protecting Chile's crops is very important. No plant or animal matter from foreign places is allowed because it might bring disease to the crops.

The Geography of Chile Look at the physical map of Latin America in the Activity Atlas at the front of your book. Find the Andes Mountains. They run down the whole length of this long country like a giant spine. Chile is narrow. On average, it is about 100 miles (161 km) wide. If Chile were flat, it would take less than two hours to drive

The Atacama Desert looks barren and empty compared to Cerro Santa Lucia, a park in Santiago. But they are both in Chile. **Critical Thinking** What factors do you think make it possible for one country to have such different climates?

LINKS TO LANGUAGE ARTS

What Makes a Poem? What do you think is a proper topic for a poem? Chilean poet Pablo Neruda was willing to write a poem about anything. He wrote many poems about everyday subjects, like dusty wheels, sweat, and his socks. He even wrote a poem about a person wearing out a pair of shoes. He called it "You Flame Foot!"

across it. However, because of the mountains, it takes much longe Chile may not be very wide, but it is extremely long. It runs 2,650 mile (4,265 km) down the Pacific Coast. Chile reaches all the way to the ti of South America. It is the longest, narrowest country in the world.

Chile contains an amazing variety of lands and climates. In the nort is the Atacama Desert, one of the driest regions in the world. The lor central valley near the coast has rolling hills, high grasses, and dens forests. This is the region where most of the people live.

The People of Chile Chile's early Spanish settlers marrie Native Americans already living there. Today, mestizos make up abou 75 percent of the population. Only 3 percent of Chileans are Nativ Americans.

The lifestyles of Chileans vary from region to region. In the fa south, sheep herders in heavy wool sweaters brave the strong wind Farther north in the central valley, farmers grow wheat, potatoes, suga beets, corn, tomatoes, and many fruits. In the cities, people in busines suits hurry in and out of tall skyscrapers. Few people live in the Atacam Desert of the far north. Not many plants or animals can survive he either. But the desert is rich in copper, so the region is dotted wit mines. Chile exports more copper than any country in the world.

A Chilean City A visit to Santiago is unforgettable. Old Spanis buildings stand near gleaming skyscrapers. The city is in the valley the central plain, so the altitude is low enough to produce mild weathe

The sea makes the air humid. Palm trees grow in the public parks. The snowcapped Andes lie to the east.

The beautiful sights of Santiago are sometimes blocked by a thick layer of smog. Pollution has become so bad that it makes many small children and old people sick. The signs of pollution are everywhere. On a bad day, people wear surgical masks in order to breathe, or they press scarves to their faces. Few mothers bring their babies out on a day like this. If they do, the babies may have to be rushed to the hospital to receive oxygen.

The Problems of Industry   How did pollution get to be so bad in Santiago? One cause is the city's location. It is surrounded by the Andes on three sides. The mountains trap the exhaust from vehicles and smoke from factories in the valley. This is especially true during the winter, when there is not much wind.

Another reason for the increase in pollution is the economy. Before the 1980s, Chile's economy depended mostly on its copper exports. Part of the copper industry was owned by the government. The profits went into projects that were supposed to help everyone in the country.

READ ACTIVELY

Connect What cities in the United States have problems with pollution? Which of these cities, like Santiago, are surrounded by mountains?

▼ German architecture can be found in many parts of southern Chile. German immigrants arrived here more than 100 years ago.

Activity

Interdisciplinary Connections

Science   Remind students that smog is a major problem in many cities and industrial areas worldwide. Direct students to work in groups of four to research these questions: What is smog? How is it produced? What harm can it do? How can we prevent smog? One member of each group can present a short oral report to the class. *Kinesthetic*

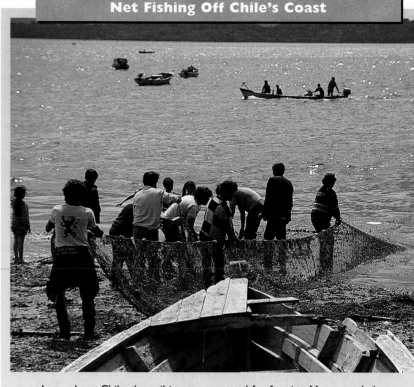

Net Fishing Off Chile's Coast

In northern Chile, the soil is not very good for farming. Many people here fish for a living. Chile's fishing industry is one of the largest in the world.
Critical Thinking What difference do you see between people who fish for a living and those who fish for fun?

ACROSS THE WORLD

Falling Copper Prices Other countries besides Chile suffered when copper prices dropped in the 1980s. Zaire, in Central Africa, paid all its trade bills in 1980, mostly from the money it earned selling copper. By 1990, however, Zaire was heavily in debt because of the fall in copper prices.

In the early 1980s, world copper prices began to drop. The govern ment tried to solve the problem by encouraging industry. The govern ment relaxed the laws that protected the environment from pollution Government leaders thought that if the laws were too strict, some pri vate industries would not survive. Encouraging private industry di save Chile's economy. It was easier to mine and process copper. Tons steel, cement, glass, and electronic equipment were made and sold.

The standard of living rose. But so did pollution levels. Also, mor people moved to the cities to get jobs in the new industries. More tha 80 percent of Chile's people now live in cities.

During the 1990s, Chile's government took action to reduce th problems of pollution in the city. On days when the wind does not blo industries are shut down. And only a limited number of cars may ente the city. Further, the government may also require new cars to have spe cial exhaust systems that do not produce much pollution. No one know how well these solutions will work. But most Chileans are hoping for cleaner and healthier future.

Chile's Agricultural Revolution

The drop in copper prices in the early 1980s made it clear that Chile could not depend on copper to survive. Chile decided that one way to improve the economy was to sell more crops.

Pest-Free Produce   Chile's fruits and vegetables are free of many common plant pests. As a result, these products are welcome in many other countries. To supply the demands of these countries, about 15 percent of Chile's people farm. Chilean workers are also employed at packing plants for fruits and vegetables. Modern farming methods help grow even more crops.

By the late 1980s, agriculture was especially important for Chile. It had become a billion dollar industry, providing jobs for about 900,000 Chileans. Chile shipped wheat, potatoes, sugar beets, corn, grapes, melons, apples, peaches, apricots, cherries, and other fruits and vegetables around the world.

The United States, Japan, and Europe are an especially good market for Chilean produce from October through May. These months are winter in the Northern Hemisphere, but summer in the Southern Hemisphere. This means that Chile can provide fruits and vegetables to the United States, for example, during the months when American farmers cannot.

Although the Andes mountains protect Chile from many common plant pests and diseases, Chile has some pests of its own. To prevent them from destroying the fruits and vegetables, Chilean farmers use different kinds of pesticides. A **pesticide** (PES tuh syd) is a chemical used to kill insects and stop diseases that can hurt crops. Pesticides have helped farmers to increase crop production. But some people think that the pesticides may have caused certain kinds of illness in young children. As a result, Chilean scientists and farmers are trying to find ways to control pests without using chemicals. They want to make sure that Chilean fruits and vegetables are the tastiest and healthiest that people can buy.

SECTION 3 REVIEW

1. **Define** pesticide.

2. **Identify** (a) Santiago, (b) Andes, (c) Atacama Desert.

3. What aspect of Chile's location gives it an advantage in agriculture?

4. How has the growth of agriculture helped Chileans?

Critical Thinking

5. **Expressing Problems Clearly** Industries can cause pollution, but when industries close down, people lose their jobs. If you were the mayor of an industrial city with a pollution problem, what would you do?

Activity

6. **Writing to Learn** Like many places around the world, Chile is a popular tourist destination. Think about the reasons why a tourist might like to visit Chile. Describe the country's most interesting features. Present these paragraphs in the form of a tourist brochure.

Resource Directory

Teaching Resources

📁 **Section Quiz** in the Chapter and Section Resources booklet, p. 92, covers the main ideas and key terms in the section. Available in Spanish in the Spanish Chapter and Section Resources booklet, p. 57.

Section 3 Review

1. a chemical used to kill insects and stop diseases that can hurt crops

2. (a) the capital city of Chile (b) mountains that run along the length of Chile (c) desert in northern Chile that is one of the driest regions in the world

3. Because Chile is protected by the high Andes, some of the agricultural pests and diseases are naturally kept out of the country. This allows Chile to be highly productive in growing fruits and vegetables.

4. The growth of agriculture saved the Chilean economy after the price of its chief export, copper, fell in the 1980s.

5. Answers may vary. Student responses should propose a balance between expansion of jobs and industry, a strong concern for health, and industry responsibility for a livable environment.

6. Students' brochures may vary, but should highlight several of the country's interesting features, such as the Andes, the Atacama Desert, and the beautiful sights of Santiago.

SECTION
4

Venezuela

OIL POWERS THE ECONOMY

BEFORE YOU READ

Reach Into Your Background

There are some things in life that people can control and others that they cannot. Think of at least one thing in your life that you can control. Think of another thing that is beyond your control.

Questions to Explore

1. How was Venezuela affected by the oil boom?

2. How is Venezuela trying to change its economy for the future?

Key Terms
boom
privatization

Key Places
Caracas
Lake Maracaibo

Welcome to Caracas (kuh RAHK us), population about 3.3 million. The view from a high-rise apartment can be breathtaking. At night, thousands of lights dot the surrounding hills. Below, on the street, fashionable-looking people walk by on their way to dinner or a movie.

Outside, the air is balmy. You won't find much pollution in the air, either. The city is in a valley that runs from east to west. Winds blow through it. They sweep the exhaust of the many cars out of the city.

Why not visit one of the cafes? Or if you're lucky, you might find a party for teenagers going on right in the street. They may be listening to American-style rap music. But the words will be in Spanish. If you have the time, take the Caracas subway. It cost the government millions to build, more than any other subway in the world. You can get almost anywhere in the city on it, and the fare is only about 25 cents.

▼ Many of Venezuela's largest petroleum deposits lie beneath the floor of Lake Maracaibo.

A Land Made Wealthy by Oil

Venezuela's government could pay for the subways because of money it made from the sale of oil. Venezuela has vast supplies of oil. The Country Profile map shows where Venezuela's oil is located. Venezuela's oil has earned millions of dollars on the world market. People migrated from the countryside to work for the oil companies.

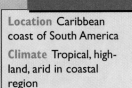

Country Profile: Venezuela

Location Caribbean coast of South America

Climate Tropical, highland, arid in coastal region

Terrain Flat coastal plain bordered by mountains and hills

Population 21 million

Major Religions Christianity

Government Republic

Economy Agriculture: coffee, rice, corn

Major industries: steel, oil products, textiles

Exports Petroleum, bauxite, aluminum, steel, chemicals

Imports Industrial machinery and equipment, manufactured goods, chemicals, food

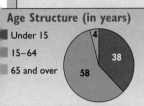

Age Structure (in years)
- Under 15
- 15–64
- 65 and over

4 / 38 / 58

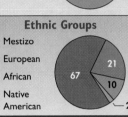

Ethnic Groups
- Mestizo
- European
- African
- Native American

21 / 10 / 67 / 2

KEY

Major Products
- Petroleum
- Steel
- Gold
- Cocoa
- Coffee
- Fruit

Lambert Azimuthal Equal-Area Projection

0   250   300 mi
0   250   300 km

Map Study This map shows the natural resources of Venezuela. Venezuela is famous for its deposits of petroleum. However, Venezuela also has many other resources, including soil that is good for farming and raising livestock. **Interaction** What part of Venezuela has the most natural resources? What area do you think has the most cities?

2 Explore

Have students read the section. Indicate that they should read to find answers to questions such as: How did the oil boom change Venezuela? What happened to Venezuela when the price of oil fell? How is the government of Venezuela dealing with its economic problems? Once students have read the section, discuss the answers to these questions.

3 Teach

Work with the class to create a time line showing the changes in Venezuela's economy. The time line should include the 1920s: Oil Is Discovered; the 1970s: Oil Prices Go Up; the mid-1980s: Oil Prices Fall; and the late 1980s and 1990s: Government Privatizes Its Industries and Encourages New Industries. Have students work in pairs to supply an *effect* for each *cause* listed on the time line. Have them place the effects in the correct time sequence. Encourage them to add more of the effects that they learned from the text. This activity should take about 20 minutes.

They helped maintain the giant oil rigs in Lake Maracaibo. They also worked in oil refineries.

Both the government and individuals own oil companies in Venezuela. They have grown rich mining, processing, and selling oil. By the early 1980s, Venezuela was the richest country in Latin America. Much of the money has gone to Caracas, where most Venezuelans live.

Ups and Downs of Oil Prices Venezuela's oil was discovered about 75 years ago. Since then, Venezuela has pumped about 67 billion barrels of oil. There seemed to be no end to the money that could be made in the oil industry. Except for the Persian Gulf region, Venezuela has the biggest oil reserves in the world.

During the 1970s, the price of oil went up. An oil boom began. A **boom** is a period of increased prosperity during which more of a product is produced and sold. The standard of living of many Venezuelans went up, too. That is when the government started spending huge sums

SKILLS MINI LESSON

Interpreting Graphs: Circle Graphs
To **introduce** the skill, tell students that many important facts can be shown in a graph. Help students **practice** the skill by asking them to find the following information in the Venezuela Country Profile: the most common ethnic group (mestizo); the most common age group (15–64). Ask them to predict, then find, the sum of the percents shown in the Age Structure graph. Have students explain why the sum is 100 percent. Have students **apply** the skill by forming questions using the circle graphs in the Country Profile. Direct students to share and answer one another's questions.

Answers to ...
MAP STUDY

- north; north

4 Assess

See the answers to the Section Review. You may also use students' time lines as assessment.

Acceptable time lines show one effect for each cause.

Commendable time lines include more than one effect for each cause and show understanding of how the causes and effects are linked.

Outstanding time lines exhibit greater detail and depth of understanding regarding how causes and effects are linked.

Background

Global Perspectives

Oil Cartel Venezuela was a founding member of the Organization of Petroleum Exporting Countries (OPEC). The organization was formed in 1960 so that oil-producing countries could control the price of oil throughout the world. Other members of OPEC include Ecuador in South America; Iran, Iraq, Kuwait, Saudi Arabia, Qatar, Libya, and the United Arab Emirates in the Middle East; Algeria, Nigeria, and Gabon in Africa; and Indonesia in Asia. In late 1973, OPEC raised the price of oil by 200 percent, which greatly affected life in the industrial countries of the world. The costs of heating homes, running factories, and fueling motor vehicles skyrocketed.

READ ACTIVELY

Predict Do you think that one resource, such as oil, can support a country forever? Why or why not?

of money. Many people were hired to run government agencies and government-owned businesses. The government built expensive subway and high-quality roads. The government began to borrow money so that it could spend even more.

In the mid-1980s, too much oil was produced in the world. The price of oil started to fall, but millions of people were still employed by the government. They ran the many government offices. Or they worked in government industries. Finally, the government was spending much more than it could earn. As the price of oil continued to drop, many people lost their jobs.

The New Poverty Poor people from the country were hit the hardest by the drop in oil sales. They had come to Caracas and other cities to work in the growing industries. When the oil industries cut back, many of these people were left without jobs.

Venezuelan Culture

During the oil boom, Venezuela changed from a traditional culture based on agriculture to a modern urban country. Now about 80 percent of the population lives in cities.

A Venezuelan Life Juan Varderi (hwahn var DEHR ee) is about 28 years old. He is a good example of the new Venezuelan. Juan grew up in a densely populated coastal area north of Caracas.

▼ Caracas is the largest city in Venezuela. It is also the country's capital.

Resource Directory

Media and Technology

Planet Earth CD-ROM includes an interactive political map of Venezuela, as well as the other countries of Latin America.

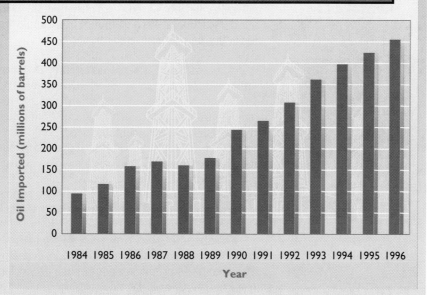

Chart Study The United States has several major petroleum deposits, but still uses more petroleum than it produces. The United States imports petroleum from Canada, Mexico, Nigeria, Saudi Arabia, and Venezuela. **Critical Thinking** When did the United States import the least amount of petroleum from Venezuela? When did it import the most?

Activity

Journal Writing

Pen Pal Ask students to choose the country of Brazil, Peru, Chile, or Venezuela and consider what it would be like to have a pen pal there. Have students make a list of the things they would like to know about the country they chose. Then direct them to write a letter to their pen pal, introducing themselves, telling about their lives, and asking questions.

Juan's grandfather raised sheep on a ranch east of Lake Maracaibo. He made a fairly good living selling wool and meat to people in Caracas. He fully expected that his son, Juan's father, would work with him, so he never encouraged him to go to school. But in the 1970s, Juan's father was lured by the oil industry, which was beginning to boom.

Varderi's father left the ranch at age 16. He went to work on an oil rig that was owned by the government. By the time Juan was born, the family was living in Caracas in a small apartment. They had a radio but no telephone. Juan Varderi grew up playing baseball on the streets of Caracas. Baseball is very popular in Venezuela.

By the early 1980s, Juan's father was making more money. The family bought a television. Televisions had become popular. Varderi remembers those years as the most exciting time of his life.

> "There were American programs you could watch on television, dubbed into Spanish. My friends and I paid attention to the clothes that the Americans wore. We tried to dress like them. We thought their music was the coolest in the world. We used to watch rock videos and try to learn the words of songs. In the early 1980s, we thought we could live just like rich Americans seemed to live. We didn't understand it was only taking place on TV. We didn't know what was going to happen to us in just a few years."

LINKS ACROSS THE WORLD

Germany in Venezuela In 1843, the Venezuelan government recruited almost 400 Germans to live in the mountains west of Caracas. For over 100 years their colony, Colonia Tovar, was isolated. The people spoke German, ate German food, and married only Germans. The town is still so different from the rest of the country that it deserves its nickname, "Germany in Venezuela."

Teaching Resources

📁 **Section Quiz** in the Chapter and Section Resources booklet, p. 95, covers the main ideas and key terms in the section. Available in Spanish in the Spanish Chapter and Section Resources booklet, p. 59.

📁 **Vocabulary** in the Chapter and Section Resources booklet, p. 97, provides a review of key terms in the chapter. Available in Spanish in the Spanish Chapter and Section Resources booklet, p. 61.

📁 **Reteaching** in the Chapter and Section Resources booklet, p. 98, provides a structure for students who may need additional help in mastering chapter content.

📁 **Enrichment** in the Chapter and Section Resources booklet, p. 99, extends chapter content and enriches students' understanding.

📁 **Spanish Glossary** in the Spanish Chapter and Section Resources, pp. 62–65, provides key terms translated from English to Spanish as well as definitions in Spanish.

Answers to . . .

CHART STUDY°

• 1984, 1996

Links Across Time

Venezuelan Farming
Traditionally, agriculture has played a small role in Venezuela's economy. Less than 5 percent of Venezuelan land is used for farming. During the oil-boom years, there was little interest in developing farmland. The country had enough money to import even basic agricultural goods. Currently, large modernized farms produce sugar cane, cotton, and rice. Smaller, family-run farms produce corn and beans for local markets and coffee and cacao for urban and export markets.

READ ACTIVELY

Ask Questions If you had a chance to meet Juan Varderi, what questions would you ask? What questions do you think that Juan would ask you?

A few years later, when Juan Varderi turned 15, oil prices fell. His father lost his job. Three years after that, the family was in danger of losing its apartment. Varderi thought his family would have to move. But his father found another solution.

Government Businesses Go Public The solution Juan's father found lay in a new government policy of privatization. **Privatization** (pry vuh tih ZAY shun) occurs when the government sells its industries to individuals or private companies. In the late 1980s and the 1990s, the government decided to sell some of its businesses to private corporations. It hoped that the corporations would make big profits. The profits would help workers. When the government turned over an oil refinery to a private company, Varderi's father applied for a job there. He was hired. The salary was less than he had earned working for the government, but it was enough to keep his family in their apartment.

Finding Other Ways to Make Money Venezuela started new industries in an attempt to make its economy less dependent on oil. The country is producing goods such as steel, gold, cocoa, coffee, and tropical fruits. Varderi's oldest brother, Julio, received money from the government to start a small fruit orchard. This year he made enough money to support his family and help pay for a ticket for Juan to visit New York City. It was a trip Juan had always dreamed of.

Planting Corn in Venezuela

The Piaroa, one of Venezuela's Native American groups, farm on land they have cleared in Amazonas Territory. **Critical Thinking** What details from this photograph provide clues that these men are planting?

Resource Directory

Teaching Resources

📁 **Chapter Summary** in the Chapter and Section Resources booklet, p. 96, provides a summary of chapter content. Available in Spanish in the Spanish Chapter and Section Resources booklet, p. 60.

📁 **Cooperative Learning Activity** in the Activities and Projects booklet, pp. 40–43, provides two student handouts, one page of teacher's directions, and a scoring rubric for a cooperative learning activity on making a mural.

Media and Technology

🎧 **Guided Reading Audiotapes** (English and Spanish)

Many Venezuelans like to wear fashions from the United States, especially jeans. They also like to meet each other in plazas, or public squares. In fact, addresses in Caracas are given by plazas and corners, not streets.

A Changed Venezuela Whatever Venezuela's economic fortune is, one thing is certain. The oil boom brought Venezuela into the modern world. When televisions, cellular phones, and other conveniences came into Venezuelan homes, life changed permanently. Juan Varderi dreams of having these things again in the future. And he is willing to work as hard as necessary to get them.

SECTION 4 REVIEW

1. **Define** (a) boom, (b) privatization.

2. **Identify** (a) Caracas, (b) Lake Maracaibo.

3. (a) What happened to many Venezuelans during the oil boom? (b) What happened to them after?

4. Explain how Venezuela is trying to improve its economy.

Critical Thinking

5. **Drawing Conclusions** (a) Why did the drop in oil prices affect Venezuela so much? (b) What do you think Venezuela should do to avoid economic problems in the future?

Activity

6. **Writing Activity** Juan Varderi learned about United States culture from television programs. Describe America as shown on television.

SKILLS MINI LESSON

Organizing Your Time
Suitable as a whole-class activity. To **introduce** the skill, indicate to students that often the best way to tackle a large task is to divide it into small steps and to set a time to complete each step. Have students **practice** the skill by assigning groups of four a South American country not covered in this chapter. Groups can then write profiles that follow the Country Profile format used in the student text. Remind students that the information they need is in recent almanacs, atlases, and encyclopedias. Encourage each group to keep track of the time it spends researching and composing the Country Profile. Discuss students' findings as a class.

Section 4 Review

1. (a) a period of increased prosperity during which more of a product is produced and sold (b) the process of a government's selling its industries to individuals and private companies

2. (a) city in Venezuela with a population of about 3.3 million people (b) site of giant oil rigs

3. (a) Many Venezuelans moved from farms to the cities to work in the oil industry and for government agencies and industries. Their standard of living improved. (b) When oil prices fell, many government and oil company workers lost their jobs.

4. Answers may vary. Sample answer: Venezuela's government has privatized some of its industries. It has also encouraged the development of industries other than oil and has made loans to farmers.

5. Students' answers will vary. (a) Students should indicate that the country was too dependent on income from oil, and that when oil prices dropped, the government should have cut its spending. (b) Suggestions for the future might include working within a budget and keeping debt at a minimum.

6. Students' answers should show that they understand that the parts of American culture shown on TV do not reflect the lives of all Americans. Accept reasonable examples of typical TV sitcoms, dramas, music, and sports that show some aspects of our culture. Students might mention how American TV ads might give a false picture of Americans.

Review and Activities

Reviewing Main Ideas

1. Through a process called photosynthesis, the trees and plants of the rain forest convert the waste gas carbon dioxide into oxygen that people and animals need to breathe.

2. Timber and gold are natural resources from the rain forest that provide income for the country. Hunters, working illegally, capture exotic animals for pets, food, or for their skins, selling them for personal gain. Farmers clear land for farming. Native American groups depend on the rain forest for their livelihood.

3. (a) The climate of the altiplano is cold, with freezing nights. There is little rain for farming. (b) The Quechua sleep with many sweaters and blankets and are accustomed to the cold climate. Because there is little rain, they plant hardy crops like rice and potatoes.

4. They are moving to the cities for jobs in industry.

5. Chile wants to keep out agricultural products that might contain insect pests that eat crops and spread diseases among Chilean animals.

6. (a) The mountains surrounding Santiago, Chile's capital city, trap the pollution from automobile exhaust and industry smoke. (b) The mountains also keep out insect pests that transmit diseases to plants and animals.

7. Many moved from farms to the cities to take jobs in government, oil, and other industries.

8. Relying on one resource, such as oil, makes a country too dependent on and sensitive to changes in the income from that resource.

Reviewing Key Terms

Sentences should show the correct meaning of a word through context.

Reviewing Main Ideas

1. Why are the rain forests so important for the environment?
2. In what ways does the Brazilian economy depend upon the rain forest?
3. (a) What challenges does life on the altiplano present?
   (b) How do the people who live there overcome these challenges?
4. Why are many Quechua and Aymara moving to the cities of Peru?
5. Why does Chile have such strict customs laws?
6. (a) How does geography contribute to Chile's pollution problem?
   (b) How does it contribute to its agricultural boom?
7. What type of lifestyle changes did many Venezuelans make during the oil boom of the 1970s?
8. Why is it important for Venezuela to develop new ways to boost its economy?

Reviewing Key Terms

Use each key term below in a sentence that shows the meaning of the term.

1. canopy
2. photosynthesis
3. altiplano
4. sierra
5. montaña
6. tundra
7. pesticide
8. boom
9. privatization

Critical Thinking

1. **Making Comparisons** In what ways have Chile's and Venezuela's economic histories been similar? How have they differed?

2. **Recognizing Cause and Effect** How do you think the coming of modern conveniences like electricity will change life for the Quechua?

Graphic Organizer

Copy the chart onto a piece of paper. Then fill in the empty boxes to complete the chart.

	Brazil	Peru	Chile	Venezuela
Important exports				
Major cities				

Graphic Organizer

	Brazil	Peru	Chile	Venezuela
Important exports	coffee	copper	copper, fruits	oil
Major cities	Rio de Janeiro, Brasília	Cuzco	Santiago	Caracas

Map Activity

For each place listed below, write the letter from the map that shows its location.

1. Amazon River
2. Rio de Janeiro
3. Brasília
4. Cuzco
5. Lake Titicaca
6. Santiago
7. Andes
8. Caracas
9. Orinoco River

South America: Place Location

Writing Activity

Writing a Test
Write your own test about the economies of Chile and Venezuela. You may include multiple choice, true/false, fill in the blank, and essay questions on your test. Ask questions about how natural resources are important in each country's economy. Ask about benefits and problems that have affected each economy. Write an answer key to go with your test. Then trade tests with a partner. Take each other's tests. How did you do?

Internet Activity

Use a search engine to find the site **Rainforest Action Network.** Click on **Kid's Corner.** Here you can learn about life in the rain forest, issues of concern, and action that you can take. After exploring, click the BACK button on your browser. Click on **Rainforest Information**. Then click on **Take a Rainforest Quiz** to take a fun, on-line quiz.

Skills Review

Turn to the Skill Activity. Review the steps for making a contour map. Then answer the following: (a) What are isolines? (b) Explain in your own words how you can use isolines to get useful information from a map.

How Am I Doing?

Answer these questions to help you check your progress.

1. Can I explain how changes in Brazil's rain forests affect the rest of the world?
2. Do I understand how geography has affected the lifestyles of Native Americans in Peru?
3. Can I explain why agriculture is important to Chile's economy?
4. Do I understand how the oil boom affected Venezuela's economy?
5. What information from this chapter can I use in my book project?

Internet Link

If students are having difficulty finding this site, you may wish to have them use the following URL, which was accurate at the time this textbook was published:

http://www.ran.org/

You might also guide students to a search engine. Four of the most useful are AltaVista, Lycos, Infoseek, and Yahoo. For additional suggestions on using the Internet, refer to the Prentice Hall Social Studies' Educator's Handbook "Using the Internet," in the *Prentice Hall World Explorer Program Resources.*

For additional links to world geography and culture topics, visit the Prentice Hall Home Page at:

http://www.phschool.com.

How Am I Doing?

Point out to students that this checklist is just a quick reminder for them of what they learned in the chapter. If their answer to any of the questions is *no* or if they are unsure, they may need to review the topic.

Critical Thinking

1. Both countries depended too much on one industry—Chile on copper and Venezuela on oil. When prices dropped for these products, the economies of both countries suffered. Chile returned to an emphasis on agriculture, which has been very successful. Venezuela has emphasized industry and is still working to recover.

2. Electricity may make their lives easier because of better heating and lighting. It will also connect them to the outside world through radio, TV, and the telephone.

Map Activity

1. D		4. E		7. C	
2. H		5. F		8. A	
3. G		6. I		9. B	

Skills Review

(a) On a contour map, isolines are lines that connect places of equal elevation. (b) If the isolines are close together on a map the land is steep. Where the isolines are far apart, the land is nearly flat.

Writing Activity

Students' tests will vary, but all should cover the main ideas presented about the economies of Chile and Venezuela.

Resource Directory

Teaching Resources
Chapter Tests Forms A and B are in the Tests booklet, pp. 32–37.
Final Exam Form A and B are in the Tests booklet, pp. 38–43.

Media and Technology
Computer Test Bank
Resource Pro™ CD-ROM

Rain Forest Resources

Lesson Objectives

1. Identify and describe some of the renewable rain forest resources.

2. Design a product that might be made from renewable rain forest resources.

3. Use interdisciplinary skills to create packaging, advertising, and pricing for the product.

Lesson Plan

1 Engage

Warm-Up Activity

Ask students to write a two- or three-line description of their favorite television commercials. Discuss with the class the qualities that make these commercials effective. Make a class list of the features of effective commercials and advertising.

Activating Prior Knowledge

Talk with students about products made from the rain forest. Ask them whether they have seen any consumer products labeled as coming from the rain forest.

The tropical rain forests of South America are in danger. Lumbering, mining, ranching, and farming are destroying the trees and plants of the rain forests. As you know, some people are trying to save the rain forests by using the renewable, or replaceable, parts of the trees and plants in products for sale. For example, cashews and brazil nuts from rain forest trees can be harvested without harming the trees themselves. Oils from rain forest plants and nuts can be used in lotions and shampoos. If people can make money from a rain forest without cutting or burning it, people will have reasons to preserve the forests.

Purpose

In this activity, you will invent a new rain forest product. As you work on this activity, you will discover how rain forest products can be used without destroying rain forest resources.

Invent a Product

Think of a product that can be made with a renewable rain forest resource. Rain forest nuts are used in candy, ice cream, and cookies. Natural rubber from rubber trees is used to make bath toys. Use encyclopedias and other references to find out about the fruits of the assai tree, the oil of the babacu tree, and the resin of the copaiba tree. Think of something from the rain forest that many people need. Once you decide on your product, give it a name that people will remember.

Resource Directory

Teaching Resources

Activity Shop: Interdisciplinary in the Activities and Projects booklet, p. 7, provides a structure that helps students complete the interdisciplinary activity.

Design a Package

When you have a product in mind, decide how it should look in a store. Should it come in a bag, a box, a can, or a bottle? Design the package, including art work and a product description.

Set a Price

Do some research to find out what products like yours cost. Visit or call a store. Then decide on the price for your product that is in the range of similar products. Put the price on your package.

Figure Your Costs

Now figure out how much money is needed to make your product. Assume that your costs are half of the selling price. For example, if your selling price is $6.50, then your manufacturing cost is $3.25. Divide your total manufacturing cost into the categories listed below.

- 50 percent for labor
- 25 percent for materials
- 10 percent for transportation
- 10 percent for advertising
- 5 percent for taxes

Then make a circle graph showing the percentage and dollar amount for each type of expense.

Make a Poster

Make a poster showing the layers of rain forest life: herb layer, shrub layer, understory, canopy, and emergent layer. Use encyclopedias and reference books such as *Usborne Science and Experiments: Ecology* (Usborne Publishing, 1988). Show the different kinds of creatures that live at each level and explain how they survive.

Links to Other Subjects

Designing a package for a new product	**Art**
Making a circle graph	**Math**
Doing research on the layers of the rain forest	**Science**
Writing a script	**Language Arts**
Writing a song	**Music**

Create a Commercial

You can make a commercial to advertise your rain forest product. Use the poster you made as a prop for your commercial. Write a short script that explains why it is important to protect rain forests and how your product helps in that effort. Write and perform an original jingle or music for the commercial. You can produce your commercial on computer or shoot it with a video camera. Or, you can perform your commercial for the rest of the class. Remember that your commercial should make people want to buy your product.

ANALYSIS AND CONCLUSION

Write a summary that describes the process you used to create your product. Be sure to answer the following questions in your summary.

1. What did you learn about using rain forest resources?

2. How can rain forest resources be used without destroying them?

3. Do you think it is possible for people to protect rain forests by using their renewable resources?

2 Explore

Have students read the Activity Shop completely. Then ask students to give an example of a renewable resource from the rain forest. (The fruits and nuts of the trees are renewable.)

3 Teach

You might wish to organize the class into groups to work as "companies" for these activities. Within each company, students may serve as researchers, artists, copywriters, cost analyzers, television producers, writers, actors, and so on. Students may serve in more than one role. Groups should prepare a written list of their members and their assignments.

4 Assess

Students or groups may create a display of their package and product description, circle graph, and poster. Students may have a video of their commercial or be ready to perform it. They may include an audiotape of their jingle. Evaluate the circle graph for accuracy and clarity of presentation. Evaluate the other materials for the quality of research about rain forest materials, creativity, attractiveness, and originality.

Question Book

BY PABLO NERUDA

BEFORE YOU READ

Reach Into Your Background

Do you pay close attention to the world around you? Describe a plant, a building, or a person that you saw on your way to school today. Remember as many details as you can. If you saw a tree, try to remember the shape of its leaves and whether its roots were visible above the ground. If you saw a person, try to remember what the person was wearing and how old the person seemed to be.

Many of Pablo Neruda's poems help readers pay more attention to the world around them. Neruda, who lived in Chile, often wrote about subjects that people take for granted. The following poem is from a book of Neruda's poetry called *Question Book.*

Questions to Explore

1. How does this poem help you look more closely at the changes of the seasons?

2. Because Chile is in the Southern Hemisphere, its seasons are the reverse of the seasons in the United States. Does knowing this change your understanding of the poem? Why or why not?

Ask Questions If you were going to write a poem of questions, what questions would you ask?

LXXII

Si todos los ríos son dulces
de dónde saca sal el mar?

Cómo saben las estaciones
que deben cambiar de camisa?

Por qué tan lentas en invierno
y tan palpitantes después?

Y cómo saben las raíces
que deben subir a la luz?

Y luego saludar al aire
con tantas flores y colores?

Siempre es la misma
      primavera
la que repite su papel?

If all rivers are sweet
where does the sea get its salt?

How do the seasons discover
it's time to change shirts?

Why are winters so slow
and the aftermaths, volatile?

How do the roots know
they must climb toward the light?

And then greet the air
with such colors and flowers?

Is it always the same spring,
repeating the same role?

aftermath (AF ter math) *n.:* the period that comes after an event
volatile (VOL a til) *adj.:* explosive
role (roll) *n.:* a part played by an actor

◄ ▲ These photos show winter and summer in Chile's Patagonian Andes. How can you tell which season is which?

READ ACTIVELY

Visualize What does a root look like as it pushes away from a seed and up toward the sky?

EXPLORING YOUR READING

Look Back

1. What do all the questions in this poem have in common?

Think It Over

2. Seasons don't wear shirts. What does Neruda mean when he refers to the seasons changing their shirts?

3. How is spring like an actor playing a role in a play?

4. Based on this poem, does Neruda seem to think that nature is friendly or unfriendly? Explain your answer.

Go Beyond

5. How can paying attention to details around you help you appreciate nature?

Ideas for Writing: Answer Poem

6. The questions that Neruda asks all have scientific explanations. Find out the scientific answer to Neruda's questions. Then, write an answer poem in response to Neruda's.

Background

About the Author

Pablo Neruda was born in Parral, Chile, in 1904. Neruda, whose original name was Neftalí Ricardo Reyes Basoalto, began writing poetry when he was 10. By the age of 20, Neruda was already one of Chile's best-known poets. His interest in political affairs led to his appointment as Chilean representative to several different countries. Neruda won the Nobel Prize for Literature in 1971. He died in 1973.

About the Selection

"Book of Poems" appears in a volume of Pablo Neruda's work titled *Late and Posthumous Poems, 1968–1974,* published by Grove Press, 1988.

Lesson Objectives

1 Display knowledge of Latin America in dioramas, bulletin boards, presentations, dictionaries, or other projects.

2 Apply information from the text to create presentations.

Lesson Plan

1 Engage

Warm-Up Activity

Review the Guiding Questions by reading the beginning of the page with students. Then read the paragraph under the heading Project Menu to them. Explain that students will choose one of these projects to work on as they read this book.

Activating Prior Knowledge

Ask students to describe projects they have completed in other classes. Invite them to share some of their experiences. For example, did students encounter unexpected difficulties in finding materials or transporting their projects to school?

LATIN AMERICA
PROJECT POSSIBILITIES

As you study Latin America, you will be reading and thinking about these important questions.

☛ **What are the main physical features of Latin America?**

☛ **What factors have affected cultures in Latin America?**

☛ **Why have many Latin Americans been moving to cities in recent years?**

☛ **What is the relationship of the nations of Latin America with the United States and the world?**

☛ **How has geography influenced the ways in which Latin Americans make a living?**

Doing a project shows what you know! Are you doing this project? Muy bueno!

GEO LEO

Project Menu

The chapters in this book have some answers to these questions. Now it's time for you to find your own answers by doing projects on your own or with a group. Here are some ways to make your own discoveries about Latin America.

A Latin American Concert As you study Latin America, find out about the music of each region. Find out what kinds of instruments people play and what the instruments are made of. Then try to find examples of each kind of music. You might find some in public libraries, which usually have a music collection. Play the music for your class. You might explain how history and geography had an effect on the development of each kind of music. For example, in the Andes, people make a kind of rattle out of llamas' hooves. Talk about the roles of different types of music. For example, merengue is dance music, and reggae often serves as political protest.

Resource Directory

Teaching Resources

Book Projects in the Activities and Projects booklet, pp. 8–19, provide a guide to completing the projects described on these two pages. Each project is supported by three pages of structured guidance.

From Questions to Careers

INTERPRETER

When people who speak different languages need to talk to each other, they often need an interpreter. An interpreter is someone who speaks both languages and can translate for both people as they talk.

In the United States, most interpreters work for the government. They translate during meetings between U.S. officials and visitors from other countries. Interpreters are especial-ly important when there is an emergency. For example, when a major earthquake struck San Francisco in 1989, interpreters helped Spanish speakers get medical attention and talk to telephone operators.

Interpreters also work for companies doing business in other countries. Large corporations often have a whole team of interpreters.

Many interpreters have a degree in their second language and additional training in interpreting. However, some bilingual people are able to become interpreters for small companies or agencies without training.

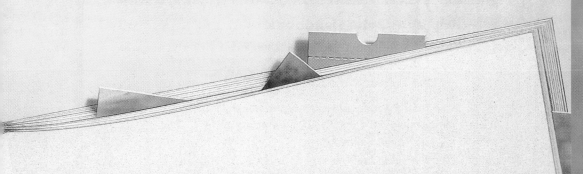

Visions of Latin America
Create a diorama showing the effect of geography on the way people live in Latin America. Your diorama can be realistic or it can show a symbol. Work in groups of three or four.

After you finish your diorama, write a short report to explain how the subject of your diorama affects the people of Latin America today. Display the whole set of dioramas with the reports. Invite other students to look at them. You might also display them at parents' night.

Latin America in the News
As you read about Latin America, keep a bulletin board display called *Latin America in the News*. Look in magazines and newspapers for articles that describe life in Latin America. For example, when you study Mexico, you can collect articles about Mexican culture, politics, or economics.

When you have finished your study of Latin America, choose the articles that you want to keep. Make a scrapbook to contain the articles. Display the scrapbook in the school library or resource center.

Explorer's Dictionary
Many languages are spoken in Latin America. As you work on this book, create a dictionary of important terms. Use a foreign-language dictionary to translate your terms into Spanish or another Latin American language.

Illustrate your dictionary with drawings or pictures cut out from magazines or travel brochures. Bind the pages together with yarn or staples. Display your dictionary so other students can use it.

Other Resources
Prentice Hall Science

---

2 Explore

Have students read the two pages. Talk with them about the careers of interpreters. Invite bilingual students to offer their expertise in translating from one language to another. Then allow students to work in groups interested in one of the project possibilities. Ask the groups to list the steps needed to complete the project.

3 Teach

Ask each student to select a project from those listed or to design a project of his or her own. As an alternative, you might wish to assign projects to students. Work with students to create a project description and a schedule. You may wish to have all students working on a similar project follow the same schedule. Some projects can be carried out by cooperative groups. *Latin America in the News* is a good possibility. Post project schedules in the classroom and monitor student progress by asking for progress reports.

4 Assess

Display projects or allow students to make their presentations.

Acceptable projects provide basic, accurate information about the topic and follow the guidelines in the project description.

Commendable projects show evidence of detailed research and understanding of the geography of Latin America.

Outstanding projects show evidence of detailed research, are of high interest and creativity, and demonstrate a clear understanding of the guiding questions about Latin America.

Reference

TABLE OF CONTENTS

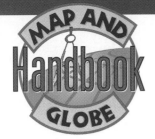

MAP AND GLOBE Handbook GLOBE

This Map and Globe Handbook is designed to help you develop some of the skills you need to be a world explorer. These can help you whether you explore from the top of an elephant in India or from a computer at school.

You can use the information in this handbook to improve your map and globe skills. But the best way to sharpen your skills is to practice. The more you practice, the better you'll get.

GEO CLEO and GEO LEO

Table of Contents

You may choose to present the Map and Globe Handbook as a special unit of study at the beginning of the year or at another point in the school year. As an alternative, you might prefer to choose among the activities in the Map and Globe Handbook to meet the specific needs of your class or of individual students.

Point out to students that they already know a great deal about maps. Ask them to sketch a quick map of the route from their house to school. Discuss the map elements that students include on their maps.

Read through the page with students.

Lesson Objective

Identify and define the five themes of geography.

Lesson Plan

1 Engage

Warm-Up Activity

Work with students to define the word *theme*. (An underlying idea built into or expanded upon in a work of art or study.)

Activating Prior Knowledge

Have students work in small groups for five minutes to write a definition of *geography*. Discuss their definitions. Then write the five themes on the chalkboard and ask students to break up their definitions, putting phrases under the proper headings. For example, if students wrote "studying where other countries are," that would fall under the theme of location. Add to students' definitions as needed.

2 Explore

Read the first verse of the poem "Midwest Town" by Ruth De Long Peterson to the class:

Farther east it wouldn't be on
  the map—
Too small—but here it rates a
  dot and a name.
In Europe it would wear a
  castle cap
Or have a cathedral rising like
  a flame.

Ask students to identify the geography themes in the verse (location and place).

Five Themes of Geography

Studying the geography of the entire world can be a huge task. You can make that task easier by using the five themes of geography: location, place, human-environment interaction, movement, and regions. The themes are tools you can use to organize information and to answer the where, why, and how of geography.

1 **Location** answers the question, "Where is it?" You can think of the location of a continent or a country as its address. You might give an absolute location such as "22 South Lake Street" or "40°N and 80°W." You might also use a relative address, telling where one place is by referring to another place. "Between school and the mall" and "eight miles east of Pleasant City" are examples of relative locations.

2 **Place** identifies the natural and human features that make one place different from every other place. You can identify a specific place by its landforms, climate, plants, animals, people, or cultures. You might even think of place as a geographic signature. Use the signature to help you understand the natural and human features that make one place different from every other place.

1. Location
Chicago, Illinois, occupies one location on the Earth. No other place has exactly the same absolute location.

2. Place
Ancient cultures in Egypt built distinctive pyramids. Use the theme of place to help you remember features that exist only in Egypt.

3 **Human-Environment Interaction** focuses on the relationship between people and the environment. As people live in an area, they often begin to make changes to it, usually to make their lives easier. For example, they might build a dam to control flooding during rainy seasons. Also, the environment can affect how people live, work, dress, travel, and communicate.

4 **Movement** answers the question "How do people, goods, and ideas move from place to place?" Remember that, often, what happens in one place can affect what happens in another. Use the theme of movement to help you trace the spread of goods, people, and ideas from one location to the next.

5 **Region** is the last geographic theme. A region is a group of places that share common features. Geographers divide the world into many types of regions. For example, countries, states, and cities are political regions. The people in these places live under the same type of government. Other features can be used to define regions. Places that have the same climate belong to a particular climate region. Places that share the same culture belong to a cultural region. The same place can be found in more than one region. The state of Hawaii is in the political region of the United States. Because it has a tropical climate, Hawaii is also part of a tropical climate region.

3. Human-Environment Interaction
Peruvians have changed steep mountain slopes into terraces suitable for farming. Think how this environment looked before people made changes.

PRACTICE YOUR WORLD EXPLORER SKILLS

1. What is the absolute location of your school? What is one way to describe its relative location?

2. What might be a "geographic signature" of the town or city you live in?

3. Give an example of human-environment interaction where you live.

4. Name at least one thing that comes into your town or city and one that goes out. How is each moved? Where does it come from? Where does it go?

5. What are several regions you think your town or city belongs in?

4. Movement
Arab traders brought not only goods to Kuala Lumpur, Malaysia, but also Arab building styles and the Islamic religion.

5. Regions
Wheat farming is an important activity in Kansas. This means that Kansas is part of a farming region.

Planet Earth is part of our solar system. The Earth revolves around the sun in a nearly circular path called an orbit. A revolution, or one complete orbit around the sun, takes 365 1/4 days, or a year. As the Earth revolves around the sun, it is also spinning around in space. This movement is called a rotation. The Earth rotates on its axis—an invisible line through the center of the Earth from the North Pole to the South Pole. The Earth makes one full rotation about every 24 hours. As the Earth rotates, it is daytime on the side facing the sun. It is night on the side away from the sun.

The Earth's axis is tilted at an angle. Because of this tilt, sunlight strikes different parts of the Earth at certain points in the year, creating different seasons.

Earth's Revolution and the Seasons

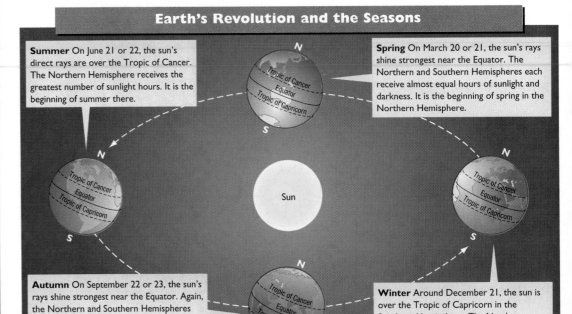

Summer On June 21 or 22, the sun's direct rays are over the Tropic of Cancer. The Northern Hemisphere receives the greatest number of sunlight hours. It is the beginning of summer there.

Spring On March 20 or 21, the sun's rays shine strongest near the Equator. The Northern and Southern Hemispheres each receive almost equal hours of sunlight and darkness. It is the beginning of spring in the Northern Hemisphere.

Autumn On September 22 or 23, the sun's rays shine strongest near the Equator. Again, the Northern and Southern Hemispheres each receive almost equal hours of sunlight and darkness. It is the beginning of fall in the Northern Hemisphere.

Winter Around December 21, the sun is over the Tropic of Capricorn in the Southern Hemisphere. The Northern Hemisphere is tilted away from the sun and it is the beginning of winter there.

▲ **Location** This diagram shows how the Earth's tilt and orbit around the sun combine to create the seasons. Remember, in the Southern Hemisphere the seasons are reversed.

PRACTICE YOUR WORLD EXPLORER SKILLS

 What causes the seasons in the Northern Hemisphere to be the opposite of those in the Southern Hemisphere?

❷ During which two months of the year do the Northern and Southern Hemispheres have about equal hours of daylight and darkness?

Maps and Globes Represent the Earth

Globes

A globe is a scale model of the Earth. It shows the actual shapes, sizes, and locations of all the Earth's landmasses and bodies of water. Features on the surface of the Earth are drawn to scale on a globe. This means a smaller unit of measure on the globe stands for a larger unit of measure on the Earth.

Because a globe is made in the true shape of the Earth, it offers these advantages for studying the Earth.

- The shape of all land and water bodies are accurate.
- Compass directions from one point to any other point are correct.
- The distance from one location to another is always accurately represented.

However, a globe presents some disadvantages for studying the Earth. Because a globe shows the entire Earth, it cannot show small areas in great detail. Also, a globe is not easily folded and carried from one place to another. For these reasons, geographers often use maps to learn about the Earth.

Maps

A map is a drawing or representation, on a flat surface, of a region. A map can show details too small to be seen on a globe. Floor plans, mall directories, and road maps are among the maps we use most often.

While maps solve some of the problems posed by globes, they have some disadvantages of their own. Maps flatten the real round world. Mapmakers cut, stretch, push, and pull some parts of the Earth to get it all flat on paper. As a result, some locations may be distorted. That is, their size, shape, and relative location may not be accurate. For example, on most maps of the entire world, the size and shape of the Antarctic and Arctic regions are not accurate.

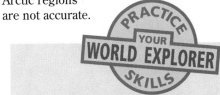

1. What is the main difference between a globe and a map?

2. What is one advantage of using a globe instead of a map?

Global Gores

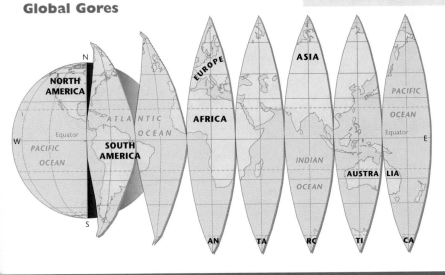

◀ **Location**
When mapmakers flatten the surface of the Earth, curves become straight lines. As a result, size, shape, and distance are distorted.

Teaching Resources

📁 **Comparing Globes and Maps,** in the Social Studies and Geography Skills booklet, p. 12, helps students understand and apply the skill of understanding differences between maps and globes.

The Hemispheres

Another name for a round ball like a globe is a sphere. The Equator, an imaginary line halfway between the North and South Poles, divides the globe into two hemispheres. (The prefix *hemi* means "half.") Land and water south of the Equator are in the Southern Hemisphere. Land and water north of the Equator are in the Northern Hemisphere.

Mapmakers sometimes divide the globe along an imaginary line that runs from North Pole to South Pole. This line, called the Prime Meridian, divides the globe into the Eastern and Western Hemispheres.

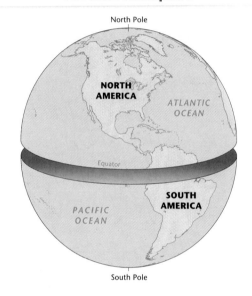

Northern Hemisphere

North Pole

NORTH AMERICA

ATLANTIC OCEAN

Equator

SOUTH AMERICA

PACIFIC OCEAN

South Pole

Southern Hemisphere

▲ The Equator divides the Northern Hemisphere from the Southern Hemisphere.

ATLANTIC OCEAN

Prime Meridian

EUROPE

AFRICA

Western Hemisphere   Eastern Hemisphere

▲ The Prime Meridian divides the Eastern Hemisphere from the Western Hemisphere.

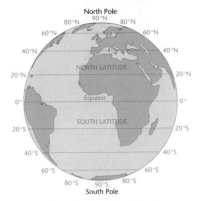

Parallels of Latitude

The Equator, at 0° latitude, is the starting place for measuring latitude or distances north and south. Most globes do not show every parallel of latitude. They may show every 10, 20, or even 30 degrees.

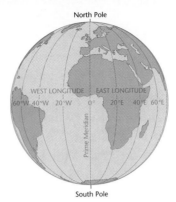

Meridians of Longitude

The Prime Meridian, at 0° longitude, runs from pole to pole through Greenwich, England. It is the starting place for measuring longitude or distances east and west. Each meridian of longitude meets its opposite longitude at the North and South Poles.

The Global Grid

Two sets of lines cover most globes. One set of lines runs parallel to the Equator. These lines, including the Equator, are called *parallels of latitude*. They are measured in degrees (°). One degree of latitude represents a distance of about 70 miles (112 km). The Equator has a location of 0°. The other parallels of latitude tell the direction and distance from the Equator to another location.

The second set of lines runs north and south. These lines are called *meridians of longitude*. Meridians show the degrees of longitude east or west of the Prime Meridian, which is located at 0°. A meridian of longitude tells the direction and distance from the Prime Meridian to another location. Unlike parallels, meridians are not the same distance apart everywhere on the globe.

Together the pattern of parallels of latitude and meridians of longitude is called the global grid. Using the lines of latitude and longitude, you can locate any place on Earth. For example, the location of 30° north latitude and 90° west longitude is usually written as 30°N, 90°W. Only one place on Earth has these coordinates—the city of New Orleans, in the state of Louisiana.

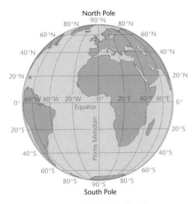

The Global Grid

By using lines of latitude and longitude, you can give the absolute location of any place on the Earth.

PRACTICE YOUR WORLD EXPLORER SKILLS

1. Which continents lie completely in the Northern Hemisphere? The Western Hemisphere?

2. Is there land or water at 20°S latitude and the Prime Meridian? At the Equator and 60°W longitude?

2 Explore

Read through these two pages with students. Using a large map, have students begin at the Prime Meridian and put their fingers on each of the meridians of longitude as they move east and then west. Do the same with the parallels of latitude, moving from the Equator to the North Pole and then to the South Pole. Some students may need help in understanding the definition of *parallel.* (Parallel lines are lines that never meet.)

3 Teach

Ask a volunteer to work with a large map or globe. Have other students name cities around the world. The volunteer must locate them and state their coordinates.

4 Assess

To assess students' understanding, give students coordinates that you have found in an atlas and ask them to locate the city. Have students discuss the process. Use students' discussion to assess their understanding of how to locate places on maps and globes.

Teaching Resources

📁 **Understanding Latitude and Longitude** and **Using Latitude and Longitude,** in the Social Studies and Geography Skills booklet, pp. 10–11, help students understand and apply the skill of reading latitude and longitude lines.

Media and Technology

🖥 **Color Transparency** 99

Answers to . . .

PRACTICE YOUR WORLD EXPLORER SKILLS

1. Asia, North America, Europe; North America, South America
2. water, land

Lesson Objectives

❶ Compare maps of different projections.

❷ Describe distortions in map projections.

Lesson Plan

1 Engage

Warm-Up Activity

Ask students to look at the maps on these two pages. To introduce the skill of understanding map distortions, ask them to find as many differences as they can between the maps.

Activating Prior Knowledge

Ask students whether a person traveling in space could ever see the entire Earth at one time. Ask them why people want or need to use maps that show the entire world.

Map Projections

*I*magine trying to flatten out a complete orange peel. The peel would split. The shape would change. You would have to cut the peel to get it to lie flat. In much the same way, maps cannot show the correct size and shape of every landmass or body of water on the Earth's curved surface. Maps shrink some places and stretch others. This shrinking and stretching is called* distortion—a change made to a shape.

To make up for this disadvantage, mapmakers use different map projections. Each map projection is a way of showing the round Earth on flat paper. Each type of projection has some distortion. No one projection can accurately show the correct area, shape, distance, and direction for the Earth's surface. Mapmakers use the projection that has the least distortion for the information they are studying.

Same-Shape Maps

Some map projections can accurately show the shapes of landmasses. However, these projections often greatly distort the size of landmasses as well as the distance between them.

One of the most common same-shape maps is a Mercator projection, named for the mapmaker who invented it. The Mercator projection accurately shows shape and direction, but it distorts distance and size. In this projection, the northern and southern areas of the globe appear stretched more than areas near the Equator. Because the projection shows true directions, ships' navigators use it to chart a straight line course between two ports.

Mercator Projection

Resource Directory

Teaching Resources

📁 **Understanding Projection,** in the Social Studies and Geography skills booklet, p. 13, helps students understand and apply the concept of map projection. You may also wish to use the following:

Maps With Accurate Shapes:
  Conformal Maps on p. 15,
Maps With Accurate Areas:
  Equal-Area Maps on p. 16, and
Maps With Accurate Directions:
  Azimuthal Maps on p. 18

Equal-Area Maps

Some map projections can show the correct size of landmasses. Maps that use these projections are called equal-area maps. In order to show the correct size of landmasses, these maps usually distort shapes. The distortion is usually greater at the edges of the map and less at the center.

Robinson Maps

Many of the maps in this book use the Robinson projection. This is a compromise between the Mercator and equal-area projections. It gives a useful overall picture of the world. The Robinson projection keeps the size and shape relationships of most continents and oceans but does distort size of the polar regions.

Azimuthal Maps

Another kind of projection shows true compass direction. Maps that use this projection are called azimuthal maps. Such maps are easy to recognize—they are usually circular. Azimuthal maps are often used to show the areas of the North and South Poles. However, azimuthal maps distort scale, area, and shape.

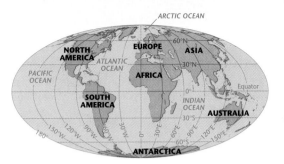

Equal-Area Projection

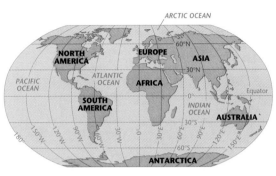

Robinson Projection

Azimuthal Projection

PRACTICE YOUR WORLD EXPLORER SKILLS

1. What feature is distorted on an equal-area map?

2. Would you use a Mercator projection to find the exact distance between two locations? Tell why or why not.

3. Which would be a better choice for studying the Antarctic—an azimuthal projection or a Robinson projection? Explain.

Media and Technology

 Color Transparency 100

Lesson Objective

Identify and use the parts of a map.

Lesson Plan

1 Engage

Warm-Up Activity

If possible, show students several maps, such as subway or bus route maps and road maps. To introduce the skill, ask students to describe several parts that all of the maps seem to have in common (probably titles, keys, scales, and compasses).

Activating Prior Knowledge

Ask students why they should pay attention to different parts of a map. (They help the user locate places on it.)

2 Explore

Read the page with students. Help them identify the title, compass, scale, and key on several different maps.

3 Teach

Show students several maps, including those in the Atlas of this book. Students can practice and apply using the parts of a map by asking each other questions such as What is this map about? Which city is north of the river? How far apart are these two cities?

4 Assess

Assess students' understanding by the accuracy of their answers.

Answers to ...

PRACTICE YOUR WORLD EXPLORER SKILLS

1. the title
2. key
3. scale

Mapmakers provide several clues to help you understand the information on a map. As an explorer, it is your job to read and interpret these clues.

Compass
Many maps show north at the top of the map. One way to show direction on a map is to use an arrow that points north. There may be an N shown with the arrow. Many maps give more information about direction by displaying a compass showing the directions, north, east, south, and west. The letters N, E, S, and W are placed to indicate these directions.

Title
The title of a map is the most basic clue. It signals what kinds of information you are likely to find on the map. A map titled *West Africa: Population Density* will be most useful for locating information about where people live in West Africa.

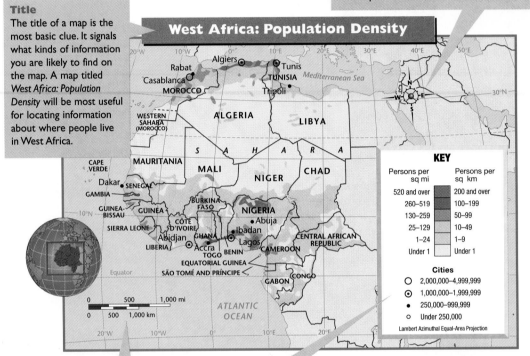

West Africa: Population Density

KEY

Persons per sq mi	Persons per sq km
520 and over	200 and over
260–519	100–199
130–259	50–99
25–129	10–49
1–24	1–9
Under 1	Under 1

Cities
- ○ 2,000,000–4,999,999
- ◉ 1,000,000–1,999,999
- ● 250,000–999,999
- ○ Under 250,000

Lambert Azimuthal Equal-Area Projection

Scale
A map scale helps you find the actual distances between points shown on the map. You can measure the distance between any two points on the map, compare them to the scale, and find out the actual distance between the points. Most map scales show distances in both miles and kilometers.

Key
Often a map has a key, or legend, that shows the symbols used on the map and what each one means. On some maps, color is used as a symbol. On those maps, the key also tells the meaning of each color.

PRACTICE YOUR WORLD EXPLORER SKILLS

1. What part of a map tells you what the map is about?

2. Where on the map should you look to find out the meaning of this symbol? ●

3. What part of the map can you use to find the distance between two cities?

Resource Directory

Teaching Resources

Using the Map Key, in the Social Studies and Geography Skills booklet, p. 3, helps students understand and apply the skill of using parts of a map. You may also wish to use the following:
Using the Compass Rose on p. 4 and
Using the Map Scale on p. 5.

Comparing Maps of Different Scale

Here are three maps drawn to three different scales. The first map shows Moscow's location in the northeastern portion of Russia. This map shows the greatest area—a large section of northern Europe. It has the smallest scale (1 inch = about 900 miles) and shows the fewest details. This map can tell you what direction to travel to reach Moscow from Finland.

Find the red box on Map 1. It shows the whole area covered by Map 2. Study Map 2. It gives a closer look at the city of Moscow. It shows the features around the city, the city's boundary, and the general shape of the city. This map can help you find your way from the airport to the center of town.

Now find the red box on Map 2. This box shows the area shown on Map 3. This map moves you closer into the city. Like the zoom on a computer or camera, Map 3 shows the smallest area but has the greatest detail. This map has the largest scale (1 inch = about 0.8 miles). This is the map to use to explore downtown Moscow.

Map 1

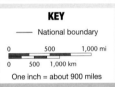

KEY
— National boundary

0   500   1,000 mi

0   500   1,000 km

One inch = about 900 miles

Map 2

KEY
▨ Built-up area
--- Road or street

0   5   10 mi

0   5   10 km

One inch = about 12.5 miles

Map 3

KEY
— Road or street
■ Point of interest

0   .5   1 mi

0   .5   1 km

One inch = about 0.8 miles

PRACTICE YOUR WORLD EXPLORER SKILLS

1 Which map would be best for finding the location of Red Square? Why?

2 Which map best shows Moscow's location relative to Poland? Explain.

3 Which map best shows the area immediately surrounding the city?

Teaching Resources

📁 **Comparing Maps of Different Scale,** in the Social Studies and Geography Skills booklet, p. 6, helps students understand and use maps of different scale.

Lesson Objective
Compare maps with different scales.

Lesson Plan

1 Engage
Warm-Up Activity
To introduce the skill, ask students why they cannot find the exact location of their school on a world map. Ask them what kind of map would show the exact location of their school.

Activating Prior Knowledge
Ask students what the zoom on a video camera does. Tell students that changing a map scale can help them "zoom in" on a small area.

2 Explore
Have students read the page and study the maps. How are the maps alike? How are they different?

3 Teach
To practice and apply the skill, work with students to identify the steps in drawing a map of their classroom to the scale of 1 inch = 1 foot. Ask students how the map would be different if the scale were 1 inch = 3 feet.

4 Assess
Have students complete the Practice Your World Explorer Skills. Assess their understanding by the accuracy of their answers.

Answers to...
PRACTICE YOUR WORLD EXPLORER SKILLS

1. map 3 2. map 1 3. map 2

Lesson Objective

Use political maps.

Lesson Plan

1 Engage

Warm-Up Activity

To introduce the skill, tell students that American writer Mark Twain once wrote about people in a hot-air balloon who were confused because the ground below them was not colored like maps.

Activating Prior Knowledge

Point out that the word *political* comes from a Greek word meaning "citizen." A political map is one that emphasizes the boundaries of an area established by its citizens.

2 Explore

Read through the page with students. Make sure they realize that a political map mainly shows how people have divided and named the land.

3 Teach

Ask students to practice using a political map by locating a boundary between countries, the capital of Russia, and a river that is also a boundary.

4 Assess

Have students complete the Practice Your World Explorer Skills. Assess their understanding by the accuracy of their answers.

Answers to ...

PRACTICE YOUR WORLD EXPLORER SKILLS

1. red line **2.** star in a circle; solid circle **3.** none

---

Mapmakers create maps to show all kinds of information. The kind of information presented affects the way a map looks. One type of map is called a political map. Its main purpose is to show continents, countries, and divisions within countries such as states or provinces. Usually different colors are used to show different countries or divisions within a country. The colors do not have any special meaning. They are used only to make the map easier to read.

Political maps also show where people have built towns and cities. Symbols can help you tell capital cities from other cities and towns. Even though political maps do not give information that shows what the land looks like, they often include some physical features such as oceans, lakes, and rivers.

Political maps usually have many labels. They give country names, and the names of capital and major cities. Bodies of water such as lakes, rivers, oceans, seas, gulfs, and bays are also labeled.

1. What symbol shows the continental boundary?

2. What symbol is used to indicate a capital city? A major city?

3. What kinds of landforms are shown on this map?

Russia: Political

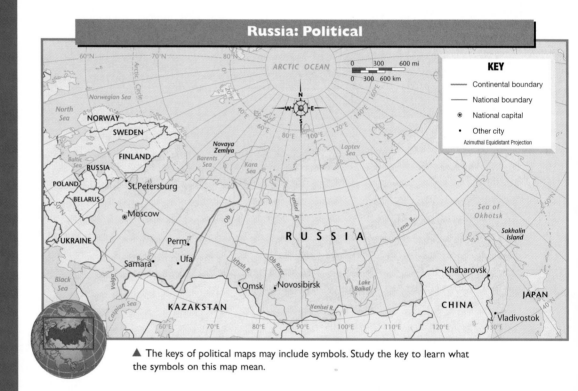

▲ The keys of political maps may include symbols. Study the key to learn what the symbols on this map mean.

Resource Directory

Reading a Political Map, in the Social Studies and Geography Skills booklet, p. 19, helps students practice using political maps.

Physical Maps

Like political maps, physical maps show country labels and labels for capital cities. However, physical maps also show what the land of a region looks like by showing the major physical features such as plains, hills, plateaus, or mountains. Labels give the names of features such as mountain peaks, mountains, plateaus, and river basins.

In order to tell one landform from another, physical maps often show elevation and relief.

Elevation is the height of the land above sea level. Physical maps in this book use color to show elevation. Browns and oranges show higher lands while blues and greens show lands that are at or below sea level.

Relief shows how quickly the land rises or falls. Hills, mountains, and plateaus are shown on relief maps using shades of gray. Level or nearly level land is shown without shading. Darkly shaded areas indicate steeper lands.

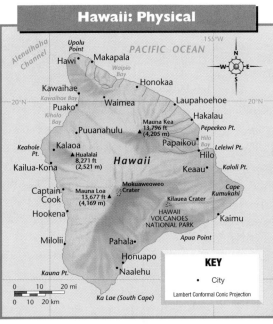

Hawaii: Physical

PRACTICE YOUR WORLD EXPLORER SKILLS

1. How is relief shown on the map to the left?

2. How can you use relief to decide which areas will be the most difficult to climb?

3. What information is given with the name of a mountain peak?

▲ On a physical map, shading is sometimes used to show relief. Use the shading to locate the moutains in Hawaii.

▼ Mauna Kea, an extinct volcano, is the highest peak in the state of Hawaii. Find Mauna Kea on the map.

Teaching Resources

📁 **Elevation on a Map,** in the Social Studies and Geography Skills booklet, p. 20, helps students understand and read physical maps that show elevation of land.

As you explore the world, you will encounter many different kinds of special purpose maps. For example, a road map is a special purpose map. The title of each special purpose map tells the purpose and content of the map. Usually a special purpose map highlights only one kind of information. Examples of special purpose maps include land use, population distribution, recreation, transportation, natural resources, or weather.

The key on a special purpose map is very important. Even though a special purpose map shows only one kind of information, it may present many different pieces of data. This data can be shown in symbols, colors, or arrows. In this way, the key acts like a dictionary for the map.

Reading a special purpose map is a skill in itself. Look at the map below. First, try to get an overall sense of what it shows. Then, study the map to identify its main ideas. For example, one main idea of this map is that much of the petroleum production in the region takes place around the Persian Gulf.

1. What part of a special purpose map tells what information is contained on the map?

2. What part of a special purpose map acts like a dictionary for the map?

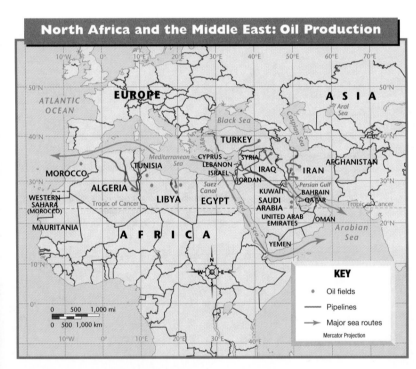

North Africa and the Middle East: Oil Production

◀ The title on a special purpose map indicates what information can be found on the map. The symbols used on the map are explained in the map's key.

KEY
- Oil fields
- Pipelines
- Major sea routes

Mercator Projection

Landforms, Climate Regions, and Natural Vegetation Regions

Maps that show landforms, climate, and vegetation regions are special purpose maps. Unlike the boundary lines on a political map, the boundary lines on these maps do not separate the land into exact divisions. A tropical wet climate gradually changes to a tropical wet and dry climate. A tundra gradually changes to an ice cap. Even though the boundaries between regions may not be exact, the information on these maps can help you understand the region and the lives of people in it.

Landforms

Understanding how people use the land requires an understanding of the shape of the land itself. The four most important landforms are mountains, hills, plateaus, and plains. Human activity in every region in the world is influenced by these landforms.

- **Mountains** are high and steep. Most are wide at the bottom and rise to a narrow peak or ridge. Most geographers classify a mountain as land that rises at least 2,000 feet (610 m) above sea level. A series of mountains is called a mountain range.

- **Hills** rise above surrounding land and have rounded tops. Hills are lower and usually less steep than mountains. The elevation of surrounding land determines whether a landform is called a mountain or a hill.
- A **plateau** is a large, mostly flat area of land that rises above the surrounding land. At least one side of a plateau has a steep slope.
- **Plains** are large areas of flat or gently rolling land. Plains have few changes in elevation. Many plains areas are located along coasts. Others are located in the interior regions of some continents.

▶ A satellite view of the Earth showing North and South America. What landforms are visible in the photograph?

Teaching Resources

📁 **Four Types of Landforms,** in the Social Studies and Geography Skills booklet, p. 21, helps students understand and read maps that show mountains, hills, plateaus, and plains.

Lesson Plan

1 Engage
Warm-Up Activity

Ask students how they would describe their community to someone moving to their area from Australia. What words would they use to describe the land, the general climate, and the kinds of trees and plants?

Activating Prior Knowledge

Invite volunteers who have moved to your area from a different region to explain how the climate and vegetation are different.

2 Explore

Write the terms *landforms, climate regions,* and *natural vegetation regions* on the chalkboard. As students read the material on this page and the following page, have them find examples for each term.

3 Teach

Divide the class into small groups. Ask each group to draw a picture of one of the following landforms: a mountain, a hill, a plateau, a plain. Then ask each group to find the landform on a map in this book or in an atlas.

Direct each student to choose one of the 12 climate types. Ask them to use the maps in this book or in an atlas to find a place in the world with that climate. Then have students use one of the natural vegetation maps in the textbook to figure out which of the 12 natural vegetation regions covers that climate location.

Climate Regions

Another important influence in the ways people live their lives is the climate of their region. Climate is the weather of a given location over a long period of time. Use the descriptions in the table below to help you visualize the climate regions shown on maps.

Climate	Temperatures	Precipitation
Tropical		
Tropical wet	Hot all year round	Heavy all year round
Tropical wet and dry	Hot all year round	Heavy when sun is overhead, dry other times
Dry		
Semiarid	Hot summers, mild to cold winters	Light
Arid	Hot days, cold nights	Very light
Mild		
Mediterranean	Hot summers, cool winters	Dry summers, wet winters
Humid subtropical	Hot summers, cool winters	Year round, heavier in summer than in winter
Marine west coast	Warm summers, cool winters	Year round, heavier in winter than in summer
Continental		
Humid continental	Hot summers, cold winters	Year round, heavier in summer than in winter
Subarctic	Cool summers, cold winters	Light
Polar		
Tundra	Cool summers, very cold winters	Light
Ice Cap	Cold all year round	Light
Highlands	Varies, depending on altitude and direction of prevailing winds	Varies, depending on altitude and direction of prevailing winds

Resource Directory

Teaching Resources

Reading a Climate Map, in the Social Studies and Geography Skills booklet, p. 26, helps students understand and read maps that show different climate regions.

Natural Vegetation Regions

Natural vegetation is the plant life that grows wild without the help of humans. A world vegetation map tells what the vegetation in a place would be if people had not cut down forests or cleared grasslands. The table below provides descriptions of natural vegetation regions shown on maps. Comparing climate and vegetation regions can help you see the close relationship between climate and vegetation.

Vegetation	Description
Tropical rain forest	Tall, close-growing trees forming a canopy over smaller trees, dense growth in general
Deciduous forest	Trees and plants that regularly lose their leaves after each growing season
Mixed forest	Both leaf-losing and cone-bearing trees, no type of tree dominant
Coniferous forest	Cone-bearing trees, evergreen trees and plants
Mediterranean vegetation	Evergreen shrubs and small plants
Tropical savanna	Tall grasses with occasional trees and shrubs
Temperate grassland	Tall grasses with occasional stands of trees
Desert scrub	Low shrubs and bushes, hardy plants
Desert	Little or no vegetation
Tundra	Low shrubs, mosses, lichens; no trees
Ice Cap	No vegetation
Highlands	Varies, depending on altitude and direction of prevailing winds

PRACTICE YOUR WORLD EXPLORER SKILLS

1 How are mountains and hills similar? How are they different?

2 What is the difference between a plateau and a plain?

Teaching Resources

Reading a Natural Vegetation Map, in the Social Studies and Geography Skills booklet, p. 25, helps students understand and read maps that show natural vegetation regions.

4 Assess

Ask students to complete the Practice Your World Explorer Skills. Assess their understanding of landforms by the accuracy of their answers.

Assess students' understanding of the effect of climate on vegetation by asking them to share the results of their work in finding places with their assigned landform, climate, and vegetation. Have students check one another's work and match appropriate climate and vegetation regions.

Answers to . . .

PRACTICE YOUR WORLD EXPLORER SKILLS

1. Mountains and hills rise above the surrounding land. Hills are usually lower and less steep than mountains.
2. Both plains and plateaus are mostly flat areas. A plateau rises above the surrounding land, and one side may have a steep slope.

Atlas

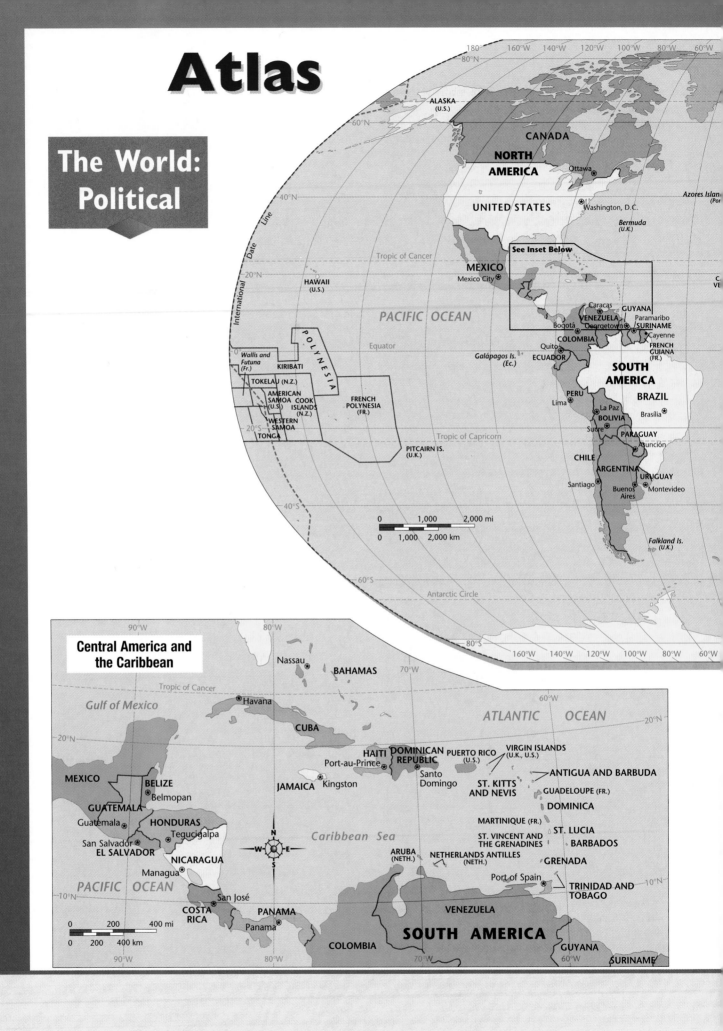

ALASKA (U.S.)

CANADA

NORTH AMERICA

Ottawa

UNITED STATES

Washington, D.C.

Azores Island (Por.

Tropic of Cancer

See Inset Below

MEXICO

Mexico City

HAWAII (U.S.)

PACIFIC OCEAN

Caracas

GUYANA

VENEZUELA   Paramaribo

Bogotá   Georgetown   SURINAME

COLOMBIA   Cayenne

FRENCH GUIANA (FR.)

Equator

Quito   ECUADOR

Galápagos Is. (Ec.)

SOUTH AMERICA

International Date Line

Wallis and Futuna (Fr.)

KIRIBATI

POLYNESIA

TOKELAU (N.Z.)

AMERICAN SAMOA (U.S.)   COOK ISLANDS (N.Z.)

FRENCH POLYNESIA (FR.)

WESTERN SAMOA

TONGA

PERU

Lima   BRAZIL

La Paz

BOLIVIA   Brasília

Sucre   PARAGUAY

Asunción

CHILE

ARGENTINA   URUGUAY

Santiago   Buenos Aires   Montevideo

PITCAIRN IS. (U.K.)

Tropic of Capricorn

0   1,000   2,000 mi

0   1,000   2,000 km

Falkland Is. (U.K.)

Antarctic Circle

Central America and the Caribbean

Nassau   BAHAMAS

Tropic of Cancer

Gulf of Mexico   Havana

CUBA

ATLANTIC OCEAN

HAITI   DOMINICAN REPUBLIC   PUERTO RICO (U.S.)   VIRGIN ISLANDS (U.K., U.S.)

Port-au-Prince   Santo Domingo   ANTIGUA AND BARBUDA

MEXICO   BELIZE   JAMAICA   Kingston   ST. KITTS AND NEVIS   GUADELOUPE (FR.)

Belmopan   DOMINICA

GUATEMALA   MARTINIQUE (FR.)   ST. LUCIA

Guatemala   HONDURAS   Caribbean Sea   ST. VINCENT AND THE GRENADINES   BARBADOS

San Salvador   Tegucigalpa   ARUBA (NETH.)   NETHERLANDS ANTILLES (NETH.)   GRENADA

EL SALVADOR   NICARAGUA

Managua   Port of Spain   TRINIDAD AND TOBAGO

PACIFIC OCEAN   San José   VENEZUELA

COSTA RICA   PANAMA

Panama   SOUTH AMERICA

0   200   400 mi

0   200   400 km   COLOMBIA   GUYANA   SURINAME

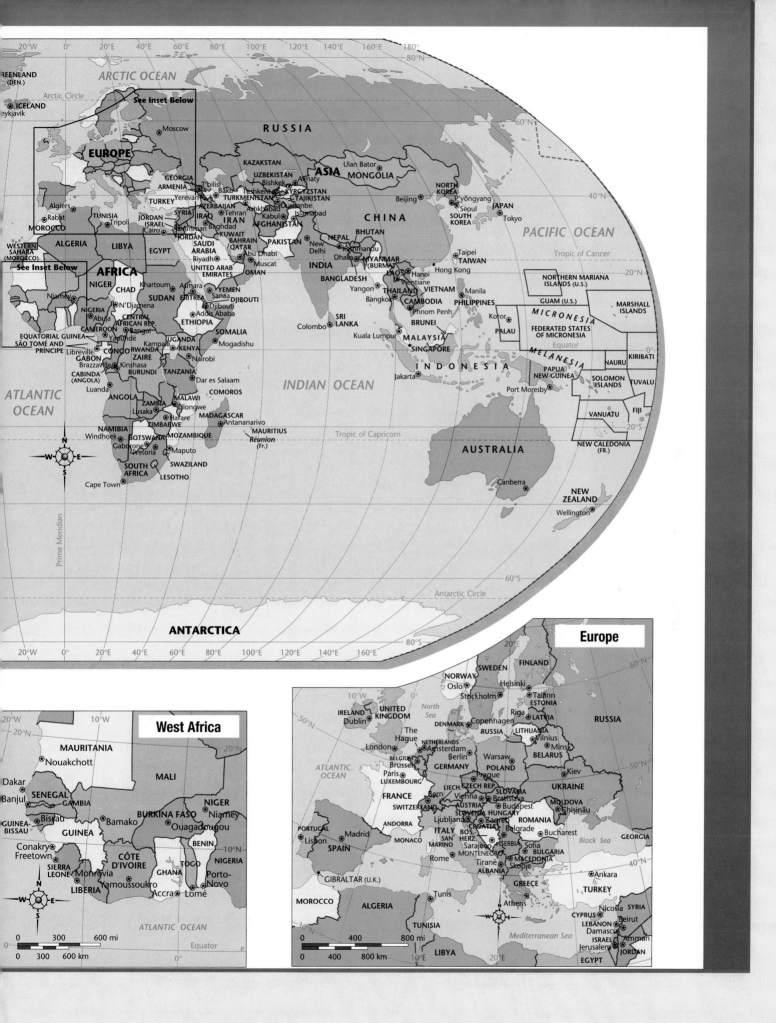

ARCTIC OCEAN

Arctic Circle

⊕ ICELAND
eykjavik

EUROPE

See Inset Below

RUSSIA

60°N

Moscow ⊕

ASIA

KAZAKSTAN

Ulan Bator ⊕

MONGOLIA

GEORGIA
ARMENIA
TURKEY
Algiers
Rabat
MOROCCO
TUNISIA
Tripoli

UZBEKISTAN
T'bilisi
Bishkek
Yerevan
Baku
Tashkent
KYRGYZSTAN
AZERBAIJAN
shkabad Dushanbe
SYRIA
IRAQ
IRAN
JORDAN
Baghdad
AFGHANISTAN
ISRAEL
Amman
Tehran
Cairo
Kabul
JORDAN
KUWAIT
Islamabad
PAKISTAN
BAHRAIN
QATAR

TAJIKISTAN

Beijing ⊕

CHINA

NORTH
KOREA
P'yŏngyang ⊕
Seoul ⊕
SOUTH
KOREA

JAPAN
Tokyo ⊕

40°N

PACIFIC OCEAN

WESTERN
SAHARA
(MOROCCO)

See Inset Below

ALGERIA
LIBYA
EGYPT

SAUDI
ARABIA
Riyadh ⊕
UNITED ARAB
EMIRATES
Abu Dhabi
Muscat
OMAN

New
Delhi
NEPAL
Kathmandu
BHUTAN
INDIA
Dhaka
BANGLADESH

Tropic of Cancer

MYANMAR
(BURMA)

Hanoi
LAOS
Vientiane

Hong Kong ⊕

Taipei ⊕
TAIWAN

20°N

NORTHERN MARIANA
ISLANDS (U.S.)

GUAM (U.S.)

AFRICA

NIGER
CHAD
SUDAN
Khartoum
NIGERIA
N'Djamena
Abuja
Asmara
ERITREA
YEMEN
Sanaa
DJIBOUTI
Djibouti
ETHIOPIA
Addis Ababa

THAILAND
Yangon
Bangkok
CAMBODIA
Phnom Penh
VIETNAM

Manila ⊕

PHILIPPINES

MARSHALL
ISLANDS

M I C R O N E S I A

Niamey ⊕

SRI
LANKA
Colombo

BRUNEI

Koror ⊕
PALAU

FEDERATED STATES
OF MICRONESIA

Equator

KIRIBATI

CENTRAL
AFRICAN REP.
CAMEROON
EQUATORIAL GUINEA
SÃO TOMÉ AND
PRINCIPE
Yaoundé
Bangui
GABON
CONGO
Libreville
UGANDA
RWANDA
KENYA
ZAIRE
Kampala
Nairobi
Brazzaville
Kinshasa
BURUNDI
TANZANIA

Kuala Lumpur ⊕
MALAYSIA
SINGAPORE

I N D O N E S I A

NAURU

MELANESIA

0°

CABINDA
(ANGOLA)
Luanda

Dar es Salaam
COMOROS

Jakarta ⊕

PAPUA
NEW GUINEA

SOLOMON
ISLANDS

TUVALU

ATLANTIC
OCEAN

ANGOLA
ZAMBIA
MALAWI
Lusaka
Lilongwe
Harare
ZIMBABWE
MADAGASCAR
Antananarivo
NAMIBIA
BOTSWANA
MOZAMBIQUE
Windhoek
Gaborone
Maputo
Pretoria
SOUTH
AFRICA
SWAZILAND
LESOTHO
Cape Town

INDIAN OCEAN

MAURITIUS
Réunion
(Fr.)

Port Moresby ⊕

FIJI

Tropic of Capricorn

20°S

VANUATU

NEW CALEDONIA
(FR.)

AUSTRALIA

Prime Meridian

Canberra ⊕

NEW
ZEALAND

Wellington ⊕

60°S

Antarctic Circle

ANTARCTICA

80°S

20°W 0° 20°E 40°E 60°E 80°E 100°E 120°E 140°E 160°E

Europe

West Africa

MAURITANIA
⊕ Nouakchott
Dakar
SENEGAL
Banjul
GAMBIA
GUINEA-
BISSAU
Bissau
GUINEA
MALI
NIGER
BURKINA FASO
Niamey ⊕
Bamako ⊕
Ouagadougou ⊕
BENIN
NIGERIA
Conakry
Freetown
SIERRA
LEONE
Monrovia
LIBERIA
CÔTE
D'IVOIRE
Yamoussoukro
GHANA
TOGO
Accra ⊕
Lomé
Porto-
Novo

0 300 600 mi
0 300 600 km

Equator

ATLANTIC OCEAN

NORWAY
Oslo
SWEDEN
FINLAND
Helsinki
Stockholm
Tallinn
ESTONIA
IRELAND
UNITED
KINGDOM
Dublin
North
Sea
DENMARK
Copenhagen
Riga
LATVIA
RUSSIA
LITHUANIA
Vilnius
Minsk
The
Hague
NETHERLANDS
Amsterdam
Berlin
Warsaw
RUSSIA
BELARUS
London
BELGIUM
Brussels
GERMANY
POLAND
Kiev
Paris
LUXEMBOURG
Prague
UKRAINE
ATLANTIC
OCEAN
FRANCE
LIECH.
CZECH REP.
SLOVAKIA
Bern
Vienna
Bratislava
MOLDOVA
Chişinău
SWITZERLAND
AUSTRIA
Budapest
ANDORRA
SLOVENIA HUNGARY
ROMANIA
PORTUGAL
Ljubljana
Zagreb
Bucharest
GEORGIA
Madrid
ITALY
CROATIA
Belgrade
Lisbon
SAN
MARINO
BOS.
HERZ.
SERBIA
Black Sea
SPAIN
MONACO
Sarajevo
Sofia
Rome
MONTENEGRO
BULGARIA
GIBRALTAR (U.K.)
Tiranë
MACEDONIA
Skopje
ALBANIA
Ankara
GREECE
TURKEY
MOROCCO
ALGERIA
Tunis
Athens
CYPRUS
Nicosia
Beirut
LEBANON
Damascus
SYRIA
TUNISIA
ISRAEL
Jerusalem
Amman
JORDAN
LIBYA
Mediterranean Sea
EGYPT

0 400 800 mi
0 400 800 km

The World: Physical

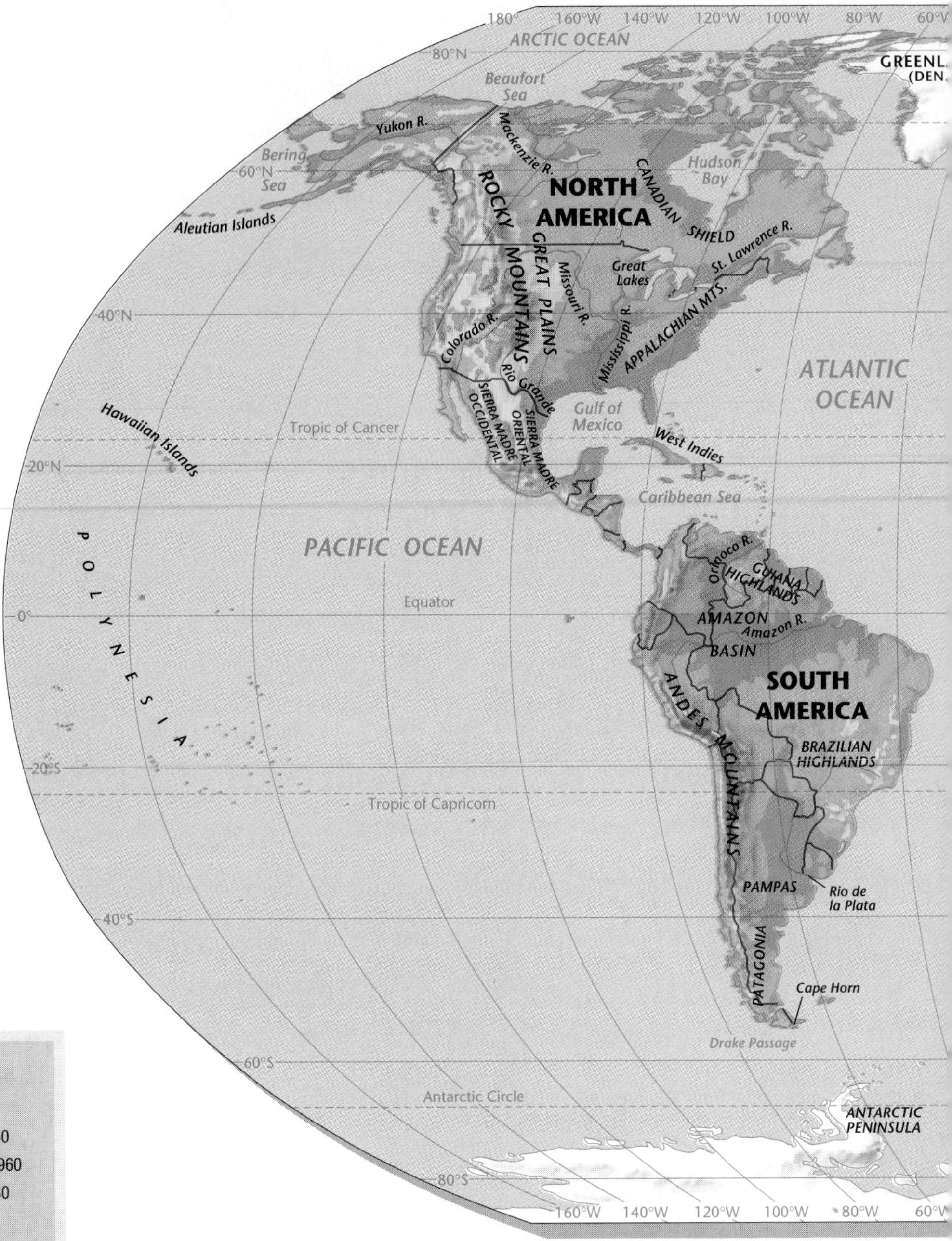

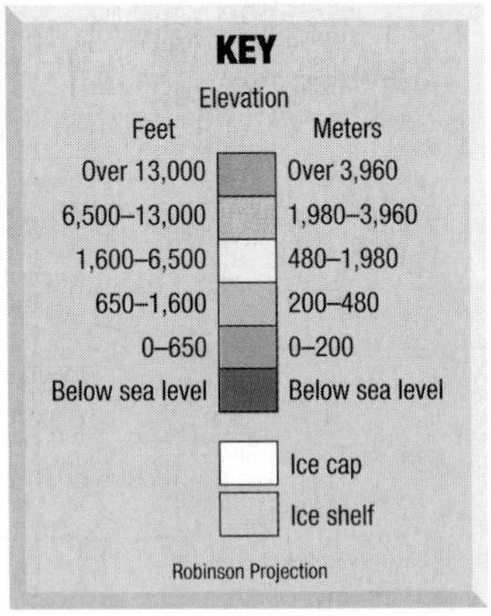

ARCTIC OCEAN
Beaufort Sea
Bering Sea
Yukon R.
Mackenzie R.
Aleutian Islands
NORTH AMERICA
ROCKY MOUNTAINS
GREAT PLAINS
CANADIAN SHIELD
Hudson Bay
GREENL (DEN
St. Lawrence R.
Great Lakes
Missouri R.
Mississippi R.
APPALACHIAN MTS.
Colorado R.
Rio Grande
SIERRA MADRE OCCIDENTAL
SIERRA MADRE ORIENTAL
Gulf of Mexico
West Indies
Caribbean Sea
ATLANTIC OCEAN
Hawaiian Islands
Tropic of Cancer
PACIFIC OCEAN
POLYNESIA
Equator
Orinoco R.
GUIANA HIGHLANDS
AMAZON BASIN
Amazon R.
SOUTH AMERICA
ANDES MOUNTAINS
BRAZILIAN HIGHLANDS
Tropic of Capricorn
PAMPAS
Rio de la Plata
PATAGONIA
Cape Horn
Drake Passage
Antarctic Circle
ANTARCTIC PENINSULA
180°
160°W
140°W
120°W
100°W
80°W
60°W
80°N
60°N
40°N
20°N
0°
20°S
40°S
60°S
80°S

KEY
Elevation
Feet
Meters
Over 13,000
Over 3,960
6,500–13,000
1,980–3,960
1,600–6,500
480–1,980
650–1,600
200–480
0–650
0–200
Below sea level
Below sea level
Ice cap
Ice shelf
Robinson Projection

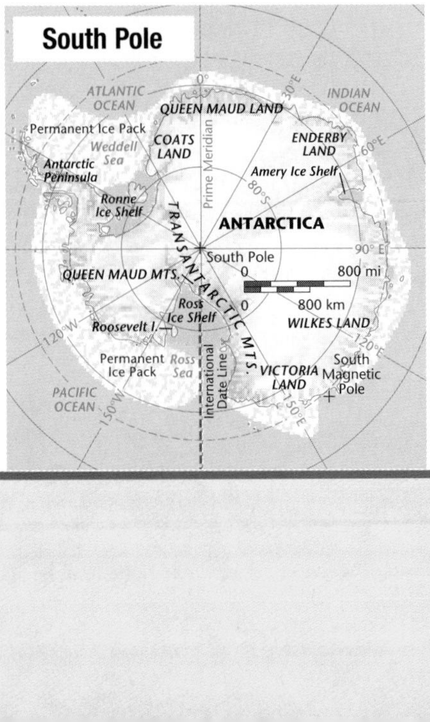

South Pole
ATLANTIC OCEAN
QUEEN MAUD LAND
INDIAN OCEAN
Permanent Ice Pack
Weddell Sea
COATS LAND
ENDERBY LAND
Antarctic Peninsula
Amery Ice Shelf
Prime Meridian
Ronne Ice Shelf
TRANSANTARCTIC MTS.
ANTARCTICA
South Pole
QUEEN MAUD MTS.
0
800 mi
800 km
Ross Ice Shelf
WILKES LAND
Roosevelt I.
Permanent Ice Pack
Ross Sea
International Date Line
VICTORIA LAND
South Magnetic Pole
PACIFIC OCEAN

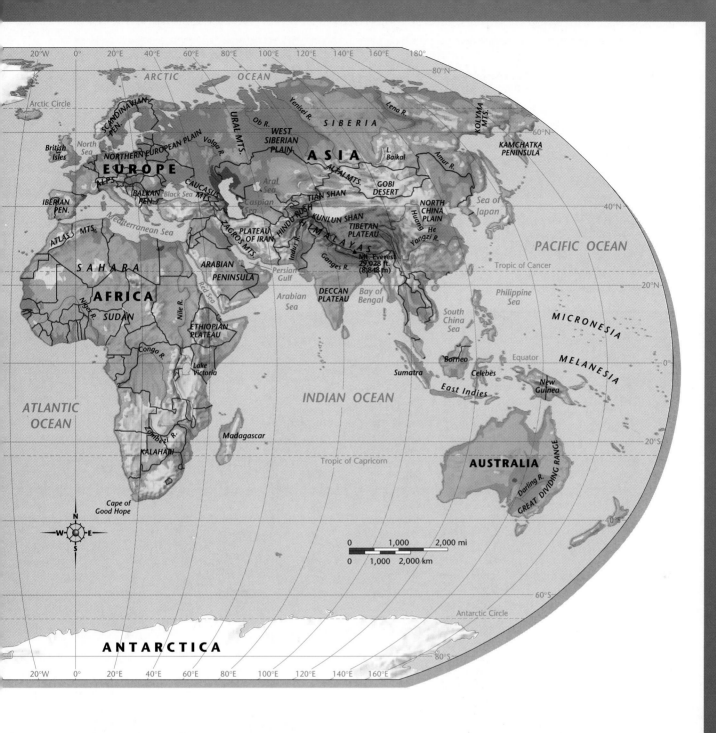

ARCTIC OCEAN

80°N

Arctic Circle

60°N

SCANDINAVIAN PEN.

SIBERIA

KOLYMA MTS.

British Isles

North Sea

NORTHERN EUROPEAN PLAIN

URAL MTS.

Ob R.

Yenisei R.

Lena R.

KAMCHATKA PENINSULA

EUROPE

Volga R.

WEST SIBERIAN PLAIN

ASIA

Amur R.

60°N

ALPS

Aral Sea

ALTAI MTS.

L. Baikal

Sea of Japan

40°N

IBERIAN PEN.

BALKAN PEN.

Black Sea

CAUCASUS MTS.

Caspian Sea

TIAN SHAN

GOBI DESERT

NORTH CHINA PLAIN

PACIFIC OCEAN

ATLAS MTS.

Mediterranean Sea

ZAGROS MTS.

PLATEAU OF IRAN

HINDU KUSH

KUNLUN SHAN

HIMALAYAS

TIBETAN PLATEAU

Huang He

Yangzi R.

SAHARA

ARABIAN PENINSULA

Indus R.

Persian Gulf

Ganges R.

Mt. Everest 29,028 ft. (8,848 m)

Tropic of Cancer

AFRICA

Red Sea

Arabian Sea

DECCAN PLATEAU

Bay of Bengal

20°N

Niger R.

SUDAN

Nile R.

Philippine Sea

MICRONESIA

ETHIOPIAN PLATEAU

South China Sea

Borneo

Equator

MELANESIA

0°

Congo R.

Lake Victoria

Sumatra

Celebes

New Guinea

East Indies

ATLANTIC OCEAN

INDIAN OCEAN

Zambezi R.

Madagascar

20°S

KALAHARI

AUSTRALIA

Tropic of Capricorn

Darling R.

GREAT DIVIDING RANGE

Cape of Good Hope

N
W   E
S

0   1,000   2,000 mi

0   1,000   2,000 km

40°S

60°S

Antarctic Circle

ANTARCTICA

80°S

20°W   0°   20°E   40°E   60°E   80°E   100°E   120°E   140°E   160°E

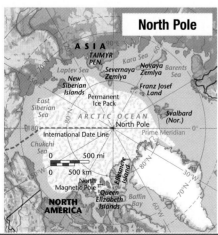

North Pole

ASIA

TAIMYR PEN.

Laptev Sea

Kara Sea

Novaya Zemlya

Barents Sea

New Siberian Islands

Severnaya Zemlya

Franz Josef Land

East Siberian Sea

Permanent Ice Pack

Svalbard (Nor.)

ARCTIC OCEAN

North Pole

Prime Meridian

International Date Line

Chukchi Sea

0   500 mi

0   500 km

North Magnetic Pole

Ellesmere Island

Baffin Bay

Queen Elizabeth Islands

NORTH AMERICA

United States: Political

RUSSIA

ALASKA

CANADA

Arctic Circle

Bering Strait

ARCTIC OCEAN

70°N

70°N

60°N

60°N

Yukon

River

Anchorage

Bering Sea

Gulf of Alaska

Juneau

0   250   500 mi
0   250   500 km

160°W   140°W

160°W   155°W

Honolulu

PACIFIC OCEAN

HAWAII

Hilo

20°N   20°N

0   50   100 mi
0   50   100 km

155°W

Seattle

Olympia

WASHINGTON

Spokane

Columbia

Portland

Salem

OREGON

IDAHO

Boise

Helena

MONTANA

Billings

Bism

Missouri   River

N

Sheridan

Rap

Klamath Falls

Snake River

Jackson

Eureka

40°N

Winnemucca

Twin Falls

WYOMING

Great Salt Lake

NEB

Carson City

Salt Lake City

Cheyenne

Sacramento

San Francisco

NEVADA

UTAH

Denver

Grand Junction

COLORADO

Pueblo

CALIFORNIA

Cedar City

Colorado   River

Las Vegas

Santa Fe

Los Angeles

Albuquerque

PACIFIC OCEAN

ARIZONA

NEW MEXICO

San Diego

Phoenix

Roswell

Rio Grande

Tucson

El Paso

MEXICO

Tropic of Cancer

120°W   110°W

50°N

120°W   110°W

CANADA

Lake Superior

0   150   300 mi
0   150   300 km

NORTH DAKOTA
Duluth
Sault Ste. Marie
MINNESOTA
MICHIGAN
Lake Huron
Minneapolis • St. Paul
WISCONSIN
Lake Michigan
SOUTH DAKOTA
Mississippi River
Milwaukee
Lansing
Madison • Detroit
Chicago
Missouri River
IOWA
Cedar Rapids
Des Moines
Lake Erie
Cleveland
PENNSYLVANIA
Omaha
ILLINOIS
INDIANA
OHIO
Harrisburg
Pittsburgh
Lincoln
Springfield
Indianapolis
Columbus
Baltimore
Topeka
Kansas City
St. Louis
Cincinnati
WEST VIRGINIA
Washington, D.C.
Annapolis
KANSAS
Louisville
Frankfort
Charleston
Richmond
Jefferson City
KENTUCKY
Ohio River
VIRGINIA
Norfolk
Wichita
MISSOURI
River
Raleigh
Tennessee River
NORTH CAROLINA
Nashville
OKLAHOMA
Tulsa
ARKANSAS
TENNESSEE
Charlotte
Oklahoma City
Memphis
Columbia
Little Rock
Atlanta
SOUTH CAROLINA
Pine Bluff
Mississippi River
Birmingham
GEORGIA
Charleston
Red River
MISSISSIPPI
ALABAMA
Dallas
Columbus
Savannah
Shreveport
Jackson
Montgomery
TEXAS
Hattiesburg
Jacksonville
Baton Rouge
Tallahassee
Austin
LOUISIANA
New Orleans
FLORIDA
San Antonio
Houston
Tampa
Lake Okeechobee
Gulf   of   Mexico
Miami

MAINE
Presque Isle
Augusta
Portland
Montpelier
NEW HAMPSHIRE
VERMONT
Concord
NEW YORK
Boston
MASSACHUSETTS
Albany
Providence
Buffalo
Hartford
RHODE ISLAND
New Haven
CONNECTICUT
New York City
Trenton
NEW JERSEY
Philadelphia
Dover
DELAWARE
MARYLAND

Lake Ontario

ATLANTIC OCEAN

Rio Grande

90°W   80°W   70°W
40°N
30°N
90°W   80°W

KEY

National boundary
State boundary
⊛ National capital
⊛ State capital
•   Other city

Transverse Mercator Projection

North and South America: Political

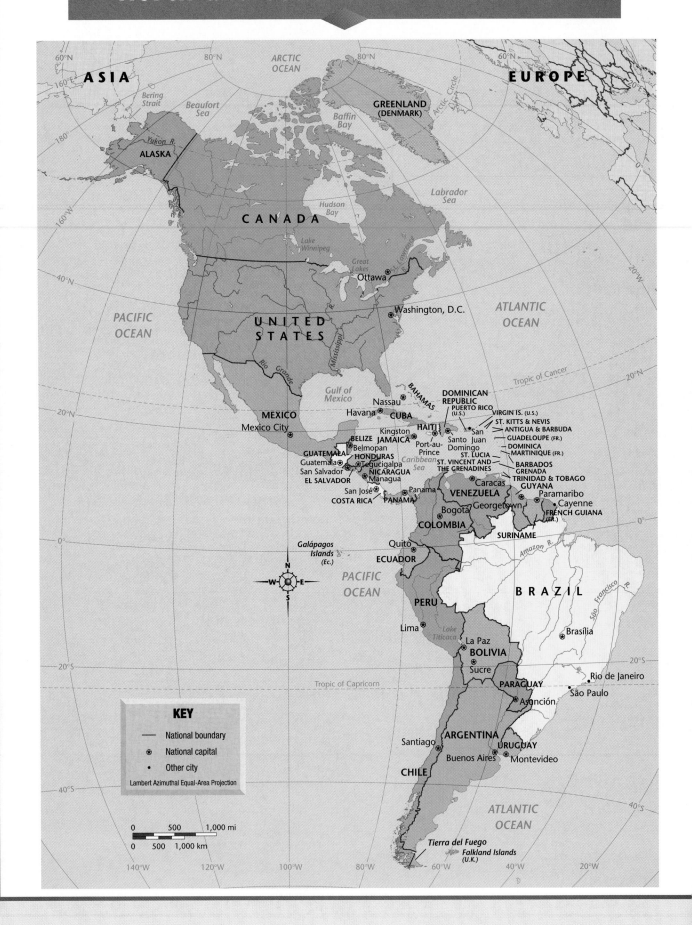

ASIA

Bering Strait

Beaufort Sea

ALASKA

Yukon R.

ARCTIC OCEAN

GREENLAND (DENMARK)

Baffin Bay

EUROPE

Arctic Circle

Labrador Sea

Hudson Bay

CANADA

Lake Winnipeg

Great Lakes

Ottawa

St. Lawrence R.

PACIFIC OCEAN

UNITED STATES

Washington, D.C.

ATLANTIC OCEAN

Rio Grande

Mississippi

Gulf of Mexico

Tropic of Cancer

MEXICO

Mexico City

Nassau

Havana

BAHAMAS

CUBA

Kingston

HAITI

BELIZE

Belmopan

JAMAICA

Port-au-Prince

DOMINICAN REPUBLIC

PUERTO RICO (U.S.)

San Juan

Santo Domingo

VIRGIN IS. (U.S.)

ST. KITTS & NEVIS

ANTIGUA & BARBUDA

GUADELOUPE (FR.)

DOMINICA

MARTINIQUE (FR.)

ST. LUCIA

BARBADOS

GRENADA

ST. VINCENT AND THE GRENADINES

GUATEMALA

Guatemala

HONDURAS

Tegucigalpa

NICARAGUA

Managua

San Salvador

EL SALVADOR

San José

COSTA RICA

Panama

PANAMA

Caribbean Sea

TRINIDAD & TOBAGO

Caracas

VENEZUELA

Bogotá

COLOMBIA

GUYANA

Georgetown

Paramaribo

SURINAME

Cayenne

FRENCH GUIANA (FR.)

Galápagos Islands (Ec.)

Quito

ECUADOR

PACIFIC OCEAN

Amazon R.

BRAZIL

São Francisco R.

PERU

Lima

Lake Titicaca

La Paz

BOLIVIA

Sucre

Brasília

Tropic of Capricorn

PARAGUAY

Asunción

Rio de Janeiro

São Paulo

Santiago

ARGENTINA

URUGUAY

Buenos Aires

Montevideo

CHILE

ATLANTIC OCEAN

Tierra del Fuego

Falkland Islands (U.K.)

KEY

— National boundary

⊛ National capital

• Other city

Lambert Azimuthal Equal-Area Projection

0   500   1,000 mi

0   500   1,000 km

North and South America: Physical

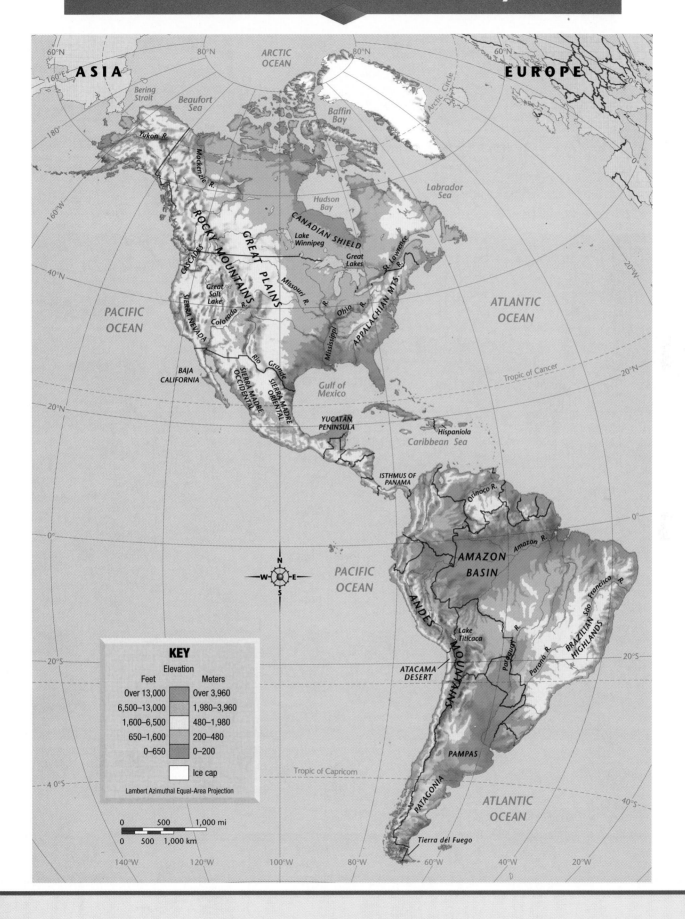

KEY

Elevation

Feet		Meters
Over 13,000		Over 3,960
6,500–13,000		1,980–3,960
1,600–6,500		480–1,980
650–1,600		200–480
0–650		0–200
	Ice cap	

Lambert Azimuthal Equal-Area Projection

0   500   1,000 mi

0   500   1,000 km

ASIA

EUROPE

ARCTIC OCEAN

Bering Strait

Beaufort Sea

Baffin Bay

Yukon R.

Mackenzie R.

Hudson Bay

Labrador Sea

Lake Winnipeg

CANADIAN SHIELD

ROCKY MOUNTAINS

GREAT MOUNTAINS

GREAT PLAINS

CASCADES

SIERRA NEVADA

Great Salt Lake

Colorado R.

Missouri R.

Great Lakes

St. Lawrence R.

Ohio R.

Mississippi R.

APPALACHIAN MTS.

ATLANTIC OCEAN

PACIFIC OCEAN

BAJA CALIFORNIA

SIERRA MADRE OCCIDENTAL

SIERRA MADRE ORIENTAL

Rio Grande

Gulf of Mexico

YUCATÁN PENINSULA

Tropic of Cancer

Hispaniola

Caribbean Sea

ISTHMUS OF PANAMA

Orinoco R.

AMAZON BASIN

Amazon R.

São Francisco R.

ANDES MOUNTAINS

Lake Titicaca

ATACAMA DESERT

Paraguay R.

Paraná R.

BRAZILIAN HIGHLANDS

PACIFIC OCEAN

PAMPAS

Tropic of Capricorn

PATAGONIA

ATLANTIC OCEAN

Tierra del Fuego

Arctic Circle

Europe: Political

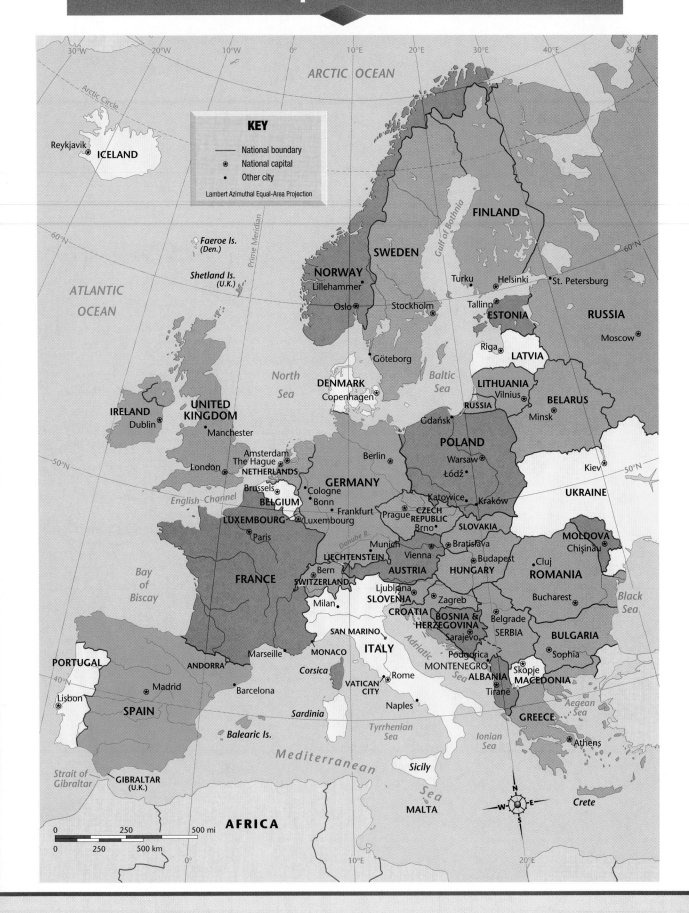

KEY

— National boundary
⊗ National capital
• Other city

Lambert Azimuthal Equal-Area Projection

ARCTIC OCEAN

Arctic Circle

Reykjavik ⊗ **ICELAND**

Faeroe Is.
(Den.)

Shetland Is.
(U.K.)

ATLANTIC
OCEAN

FINLAND

Gulf of Bothnia

SWEDEN

NORWAY
Lillehammer •

Turku • ⊗ Helsinki • St. Petersburg

Oslo ⊗ Stockholm ⊗ Tallinn ⊗ **ESTONIA** **RUSSIA**

Moscow ⊗

• Göteborg

Riga ⊗ **LATVIA**

North
Sea

Baltic
Sea

DENMARK
Copenhagen ⊗

LITHUANIA
Vilnius ⊗ **BELARUS**
RUSSIA Minsk •

IRELAND **UNITED
KINGDOM**
Dublin ⊗

Gdańsk •

Berlin ⊗ **POLAND**
Warsaw ⊗
Łódź •

Kiev ⊗

• Manchester

Amsterdam ⊗
The Hague ⊗ **NETHERLANDS**
London • ⊗ Brussels ⊗ **GERMANY**

BELGIUM • Cologne
• Bonn
English Channel **LUXEMBOURG** • Frankfurt
Luxembourg ⊗

UKRAINE

Katowice •
• Kraków
Prague ⊗ **CZECH
REPUBLIC**
Brno • **SLOVAKIA**

MOLDOVA
Chişinău ⊗

Danube R.
• Paris
Munich • • Bratislava
Vienna ⊗ • Budapest
LIECHTENSTEIN ⊗
Bern ⊗ **AUSTRIA** **HUNGARY**
SWITZERLAND

• Cluj
ROMANIA

Bay
of
Biscay

FRANCE

Ljubljana ⊗
SLOVENIA Zagreb ⊗
Milan • **CROATIA** **BOSNIA &
HERZEGOVINA** Belgrade ⊗
SERBIA

Bucharest ⊗

Black
Sea

SAN MARINO ⊗
Marseille • **MONACO** **ITALY**
ANDORRA

Sarajevo •
Podgorica •
MONTENEGRO ⊗

BULGARIA
Sophia ⊗

Skopje ⊗
ALBANIA **MACEDONIA**

PORTUGAL

Corsica • Rome ⊗
**VATICAN
CITY** ⊗

Adriatic
Sea

Tiranë ⊗

Madrid ⊗ • Barcelona

Naples •

Lisbon ⊗

SPAIN

Sardinia

Balearic Is.

Tyrrhenian
Sea

Aegean
Sea

Athens ⊗

GREECE

Ionian
Sea

Strait of
Gibraltar

GIBRALTAR
(U.K.)

Mediterranean

Sicily

N
W E
S

Crete

Sea

AFRICA

MALTA

0   250   500 mi
0   250   500 km

Europe: Physical

30°W 20°W 10°W 0° 10°E 20°E 30°E 40°E

ARCTIC OCEAN

LAPLAND

Arctic Circle

Norwegian Sea

60°N

Faeroe Is.
(Den.)

Glittertind
8,110 ft.
(2,472 m)

Lake
Ladoga

Shetland Is.
(U.K.)

ATLANTIC
OCEAN

Ben Nevis
4,406 ft
(1,343 m)

KJØLEN MTS.

SCANDINAVIAN PENINSULA

Gulf of Bothnia

Lake
Vänern

JUTLAND
PENINSULA

North
Sea

Baltic
Sea

Dnieper R.

60°N

BRITISH ISLES

50°N

Thames R.

NORTHERN EUROPEAN PLAIN

Vistula R.

English Channel

RUHR
VALLEY

Elbe River

Oder River

Dniester River

50°N

Seine River

Rhine R.

Danube River

CARPATHIAN MTS.

Loire River

Bay
of
Biscay

Mont Blanc
15,771 ft.
(4,807 m)

A L P S

Po River

TRANSYLVANIAN
ALPS

Black
Sea

MASSIF
CENTRAL

Rhône River

DINARIC ALPS

Danube River

BALKAN MTS.

Bosporus

Garonne R.

PYRENEES

A P E N N I N E S

Adriatic

BALKAN PENINSULA

ASIA

Ebro R.

Douro R.

MESETA

Corsica

ITALIAN PENINSULA

Sea

PINDUS MTS.

Dardanelles

40°N

Tagus River

IBERIAN
PENINSULA

Sardinia

Tyrrhenian
Sea

Ionian
Sea

Aegean
Sea

40°N

Balearic Is.

Sicily

PELOPONNESE

Strait of
Gibraltar

Crete

AFRICA

Mediterranean

Sea

30°N

0° 20°E 30°N

ATLAS 189

KEY

Elevation

Feet	Meters
Over 13,000	Over 3,960
6,500–13,000	1,980–3,960
1,600–6,500	480–1,980
650–1,600	200–480
0–650	0–200
Below sea level	Below sea level
	Ice cap

Lambert Azimuthal Equal-Area Projection

0 250 500 mi

0 250 500 km

Africa: Political

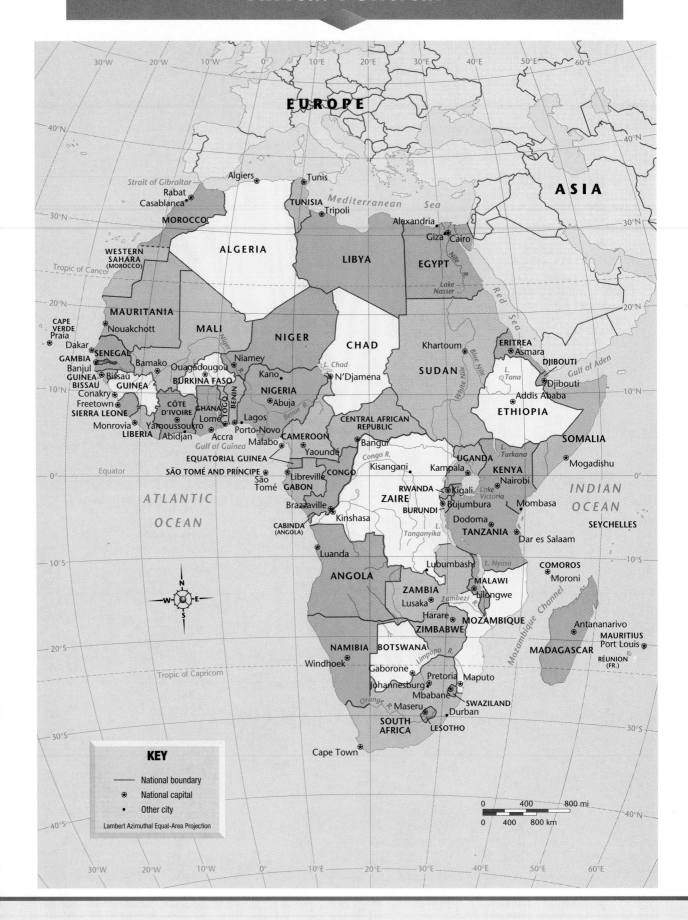

EUROPE

ASIA

Mediterranean Sea

Strait of Gibraltar
Algiers ⊛   Tunis ●
Rabat ⊛
TUNISIA
Casablanca ●   Tripoli ●
MOROCCO
                                    Alexandria ●
                                    Giza ● Cairo ⊛

**WESTERN
SAHARA
(MOROCCO)**

Tropic of Cancer

ALGERIA   **LIBYA**   **EGYPT**

Lake Nasser

MAURITANIA

**CAPE
VERDE**
Praia ⊛   Nouakchott ⊛   **MALI**   **NIGER**   **CHAD**
Dakar ●   Khartoum ⊛   **ERITREA**
GAMBIA ⊛ **SENEGAL**   Niamey ⊛   Asmara ⊛   **DJIBOUTI**
Banjul ⊛   Bamako ●   Ouagadougou ⊛   **SUDAN**   Gulf of Aden
GUINEA- Bissau ●   Kano ●   Djibouti ●
BISSAU   **GUINEA**   **BURKINA FASO**   N'Djamena ●   L. Tana   Addis Ababa ●
Conakry ⊛   **NIGERIA**
Freetown ⊛   **CÔTE**   **GHANA**   Abuja ⊛   **CENTRAL AFRICAN**   **ETHIOPIA**
SIERRA LEONE   **D'IVOIRE**   **REPUBLIC**
Monrovia ⊛ Yamoussoukro ●   Lomé ● Lagos ●   **SOMALIA**
LIBERIA   Abidjan ●   Accra ⊛ Porto-Novo ●   Bangui ⊛
               Malabo ● **CAMEROON**   **UGANDA**   L.
EQUATORIAL GUINEA   Yaoundé ●   Congo R.   Kisangani ●   Kampala ⊛ **KENYA**   Turkana   Mogadishu ●
SÃO TOMÉ AND PRÍNCIPE ⊛   Nairobi ⊛
Equator   São ● Libreville ⊛   **CONGO**   **ZAIRE**   **RWANDA** ⊛ Kigali   Lake   **INDIAN**
               Tomé **GABON**   **BURUNDI** ● Bujumbura   Victoria   Mombasa ●   **OCEAN**
ATLANTIC   Brazzaville ⊛   **ZAIRE**   Dodoma ⊛
               Kinshasa ●   L.   **TANZANIA**   **SEYCHELLES**
OCEAN   **CABINDA**   Tanganyika   Dar es Salaam ●
               (ANGOLA)
          Luanda ●   **COMOROS**
                                              Lubumbashi ●   L. Nyasa   Moroni ●
                    ANGOLA   **ZAMBIA**   **MALAWI** ⊛ Lilongwe
                                              Lusaka ⊛   Zambezi R.
                                                   Harare ⊛ **MOZAMBIQUE**   Antananarivo ●
                                              ZIMBABWE   **MAURITIUS**
                    NAMIBIA **BOTSWANA**   Limpopo R.   **MADAGASCAR**   Port Louis ⊛
                                                                                    RÉUNION
                    Windhoek ●   **(FR.)**
                         Gaborone ⊛ Pretoria ⊛ Maputo ●
                              Johannesburg ● Mbabane ⊛
                         Orange R. Maseru ⊛ **SWAZILAND**
                                        Durban ●
                              SOUTH **LESOTHO**
                              AFRICA
                    Cape Town ●

KEY

—— National boundary

⊛ National capital

● Other city

Lambert Azimuthal Equal-Area Projection

0   400   800 mi
0   400   800 km

Africa: Physical

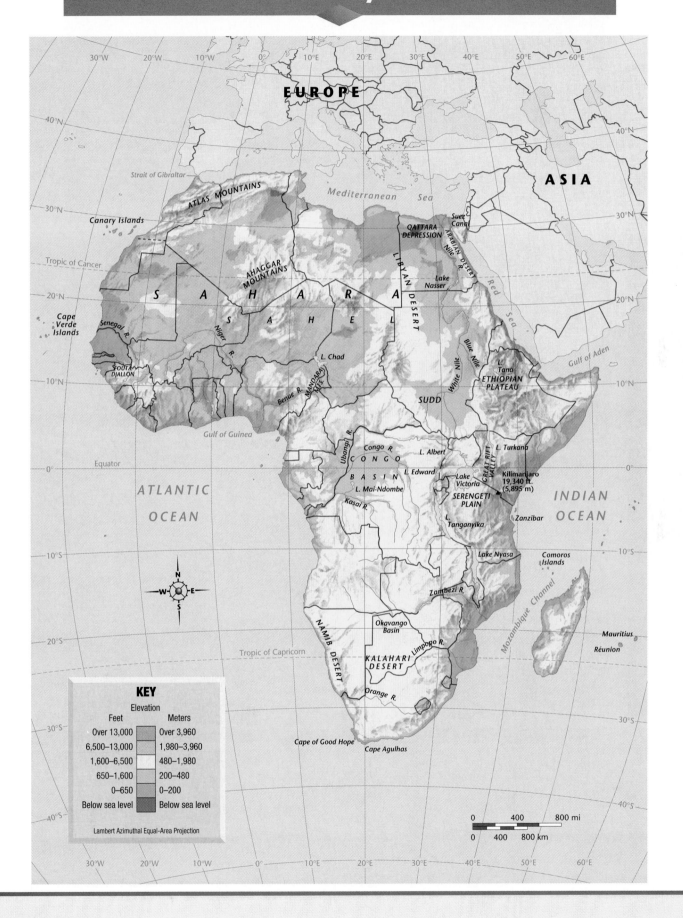

EUROPE

ASIA

Strait of Gibraltar

ATLAS MOUNTAINS

Mediterranean Sea

Canary Islands

QATTARA DEPRESSION

Suez Canal

ARABIAN DESERT

Tropic of Cancer

AHAGGAR MOUNTAINS

S A H A R A

L I B Y A N   D E S E R T

Nile R.

Lake Nasser

Red Sea

Cape Verde Islands

S A H E L

Senegal R.

Niger R.

Blue Nile

Gulf of Aden

FOUTA DJALLON

L. Chad

MANDARA MTS.

Benue R.

White Nile

L. Tana

ETHIOPIAN PLATEAU

Gulf of Guinea

SUDD

Ubangi R.

CONGO BASIN

Congo R.

L. Albert

L. Edward

L. Turkana

GREAT RIFT VALLEY

Equator

ATLANTIC OCEAN

L. Mai-Ndombe

Kasai R.

Lake Victoria

SERENGETI PLAIN

Kilimanjaro 19,340 ft. (5,895 m)

INDIAN OCEAN

L. Tanganyika

Zanzibar

N
W   E
S

Lake Nyasa

Comoros Islands

Zambezi R.

Mozambique Channel

NAMIB DESERT

Okavango Basin

Limpopo R.

Mauritius

Réunion

Tropic of Capricorn

KALAHARI DESERT

Orange R.

KEY

Elevation

Feet	Meters
Over 13,000	Over 3,960
6,500–13,000	1,980–3,960
1,600–6,500	480–1,980
650–1,600	200–480
0–650	0–200
Below sea level	Below sea level

Lambert Azimuthal Equal-Area Projection

Cape of Good Hope

Cape Agulhas

0   400   800 mi

0   400   800 km

Asia: Political

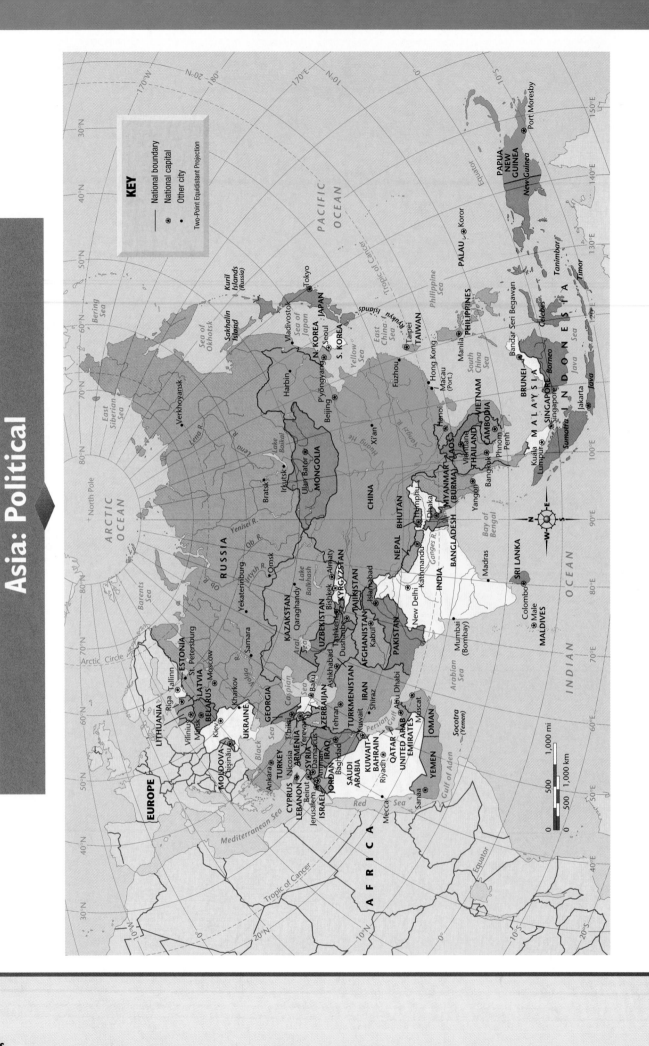

KEY

— National boundary
⊛ National capital
• Other city

Two-Point Equidistant Projection

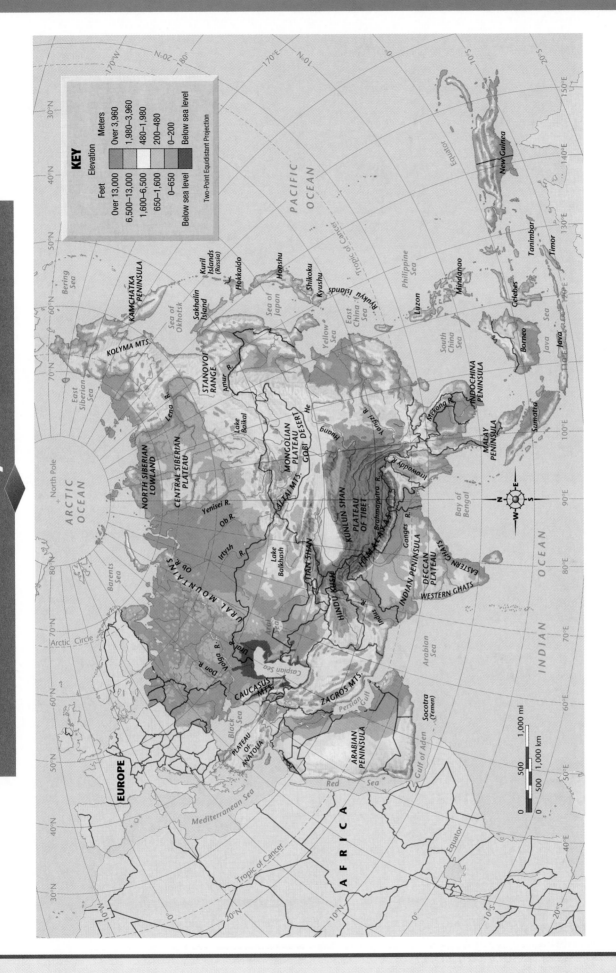

Asia: Physical

KEY

Elevation

Feet	Meters
Over 13,000	Over 3,960
6,500–13,000	1,980–3,960
1,600–6,500	480–1,980
650–1,600	200–480
0–650	0–200
Below sea level	Below sea level

Two-Point Equidistant Projection

EUROPE

AFRICA

ARCTIC OCEAN
North Pole

PACIFIC OCEAN

INDIAN OCEAN

Bering Sea

East Siberian Sea

Barents Sea

Black Sea

Mediterranean Sea

Caspian Sea

Aral Sea

Red Sea

Gulf of Aden

Arabian Sea

Bay of Bengal

Persian Gulf

Sea of Okhotsk

Sea of Japan

Yellow Sea

East China Sea

Philippine Sea

South China Sea

Java Sea

Celebes Sea

KAMCHATKA PENINSULA

KOLYMA MTS.

STANOVOI RANGE

NORTH SIBERIAN LOWLAND

CENTRAL SIBERIAN PLATEAU

URAL MOUNTAINS

CAUCASUS MTS.

PLATEAU OF ANATOLIA

ZAGROS MTS.

ARABIAN PENINSULA

Socotra (Yemen)

MONGOLIAN PLATEAU

GOBI DESERT

ALTAI MTS.

TIAN SHAN

HINDU KUSH

KUNLUN SHAN

PLATEAU OF TIBET

HIMALAYAS

INDIAN PENINSULA

DECCAN PLATEAU

WESTERN GHATS

EASTERN GHATS

INDOCHINA PENINSULA

MALAY PENINSULA

Sakhalin Island

Kuril Islands (Russia)

Hokkaido

Honshu

Shikoku

Kyushu

Ryukyu Islands

Luzon

Mindanao

Borneo

Sumatra

Celebes

Java

Timor

Tanimbar

New Guinea

Lake Baikal

Lake Balkhash

Lena R.

Amur R.

Ob R.

Yenisei R.

Irtysh R.

Volga R.

Don R.

Indus R.

Ganges R.

Brahmaputra R.

Irrawaddy R.

Mekong R.

Yangzi R.

Huang He

Equator

Tropic of Cancer

Arctic Circle

1,000 mi

1,000 km

500   1,000 km

500

0

N

S

E

W

Australia, New Zealand, and the Pacific Islands: Physical–Political

120°E
140°E
160°E
180°
160°W
140°W
20°N
0°
20°S
40°S
Tropic of Cancer
Equator
Tropic of Capricorn
International Date Line
Midway Islands (U.S.)
Hawaiian Islands (U.S.)
Wake Island (U.S.)
PACIFIC OCEAN
NORTHERN MARIANA ISLANDS (U.S.)
Philippine Sea
GUAM (U.S.)
MARSHALL ISLANDS
Palikir
CAROLINE ISLANDS
FEDERATED STATES OF MICRONESIA
Tarawa
Gilbert Islands
Line Islands
Yaren
NAURU
TUVALU
Funafuti
KIRIBATI
Honiara
SOLOMON ISLANDS
WESTERN SAMOA
Apia
AMERICAN SAMOA (U.S.)
VANUATU
New Hebrides
Port-Vila
FIJI
Suva
TONGA
Nukualofa
COOK ISLANDS (N.Z.)
Society Islands
Tahiti
FRENCH POLYNESIA (FR.)
PITCAIRN ISLAND (U.K.)
NEW CALEDONIA (FR.)
Arafura Sea
Coral Sea
Great Barrier Reef
Timor Sea
Darwin
ARNHEM LAND
CAPE YORK PENINSULA
KIMBERLY PLATEAU
BARKLY TABLELAND
QUEENSLAND
GREAT SANDY DESERT
NORTHERN TERRITORY
GREAT DIVIDING RANGE
GIBSON DESERT
SIMPSON DESERT
WESTERN AUSTRALIA
AUSTRALIA
GREAT ARTESIAN BASIN
Lake Eyre
GREAT VICTORIA DESERT
Darling R.
Brisbane
DARLING RANGE
Perth
NULLARBOR PLAIN
SOUTH AUSTRALIA
NEW SOUTH WALES
Murray R.
Sydney
Canberra
Great Australian Bight
Adelaide
VICTORIA
Melbourne
Bass Strait
TASMANIA
Hobart
INDIAN OCEAN
Tasman Sea
Auckland
Cook Strait
North Island
NEW ZEALAND
Wellington
South Island
Christchurch
Dunedin
Stewart Island
AUCKLAND ISLANDS (N.Z.)
0 500 1,000 mi
0 500 1,000 km
N
S
E
W
KEY
Elevation
Feet Meters
6,500–13,000 1,980–3,960
1,600–6,500 480–1,980
650–1,600 200–480
0–650 0–200
Below sea level Below sea level
National capital
State or territorial capital
Other city
Mercator Projection

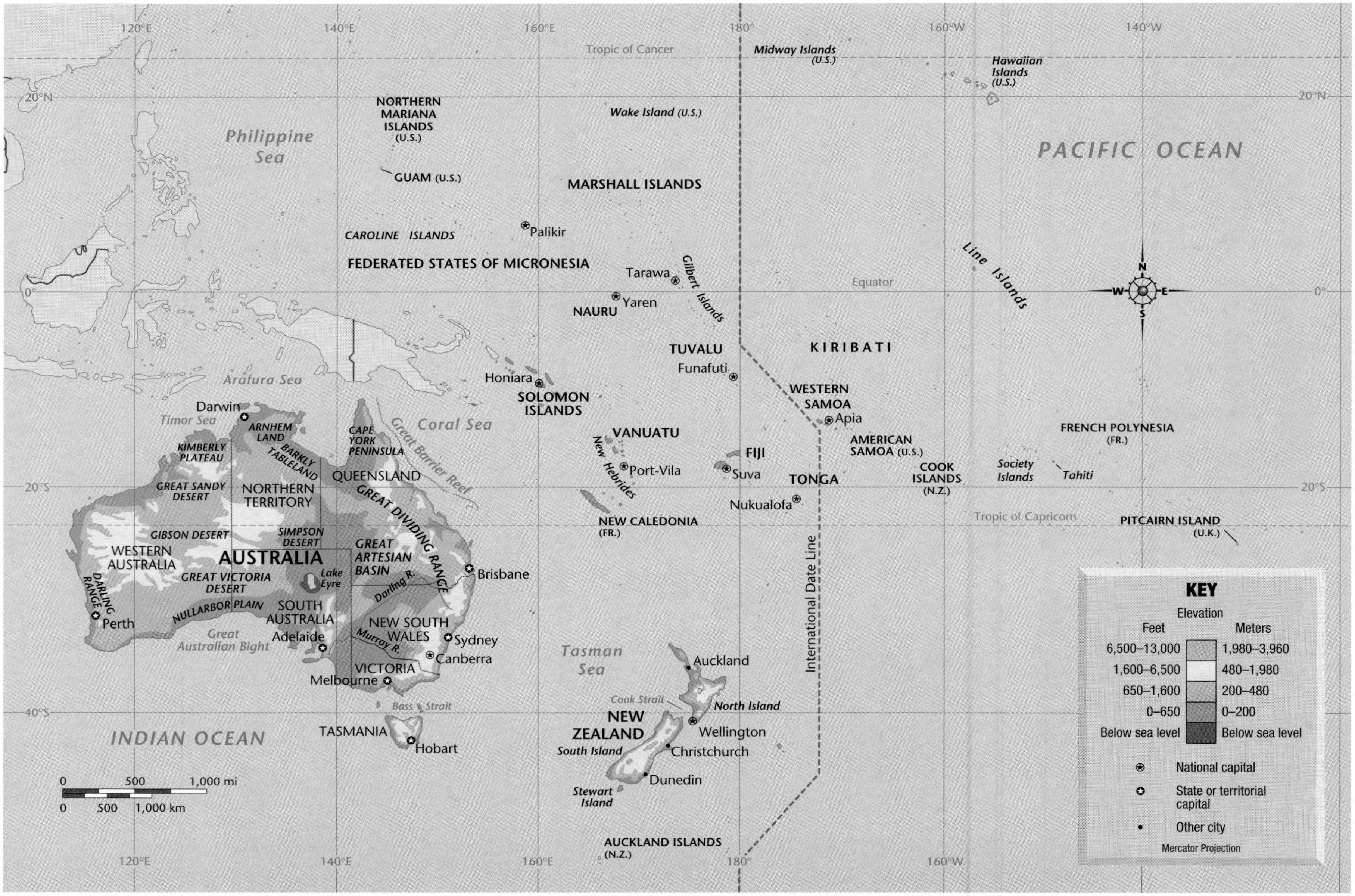

The Arctic

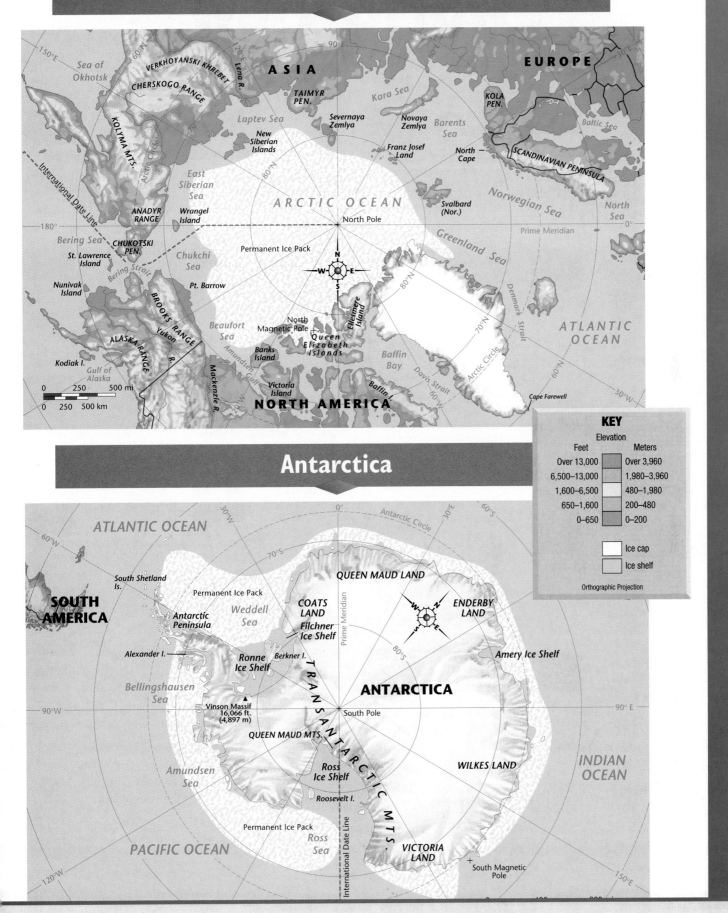

ASIA

Sea of Okhotsk
VERKHOYANSKI KHREBET
CHERSKOGO RANGE
Lena R.
TAIMYR PEN.
Kara Sea
EUROPE
KOLA PEN.
KOLYMA MTS.
Severnaya Zemlya
Novaya Zemlya
Barents Sea
Baltic Sea
Laptev Sea
New Siberian Islands
Franz Josef Land
North Cape
SCANDINAVIAN PENINSULA
International Date Line
Arctic Circle
East Siberian Sea
ARCTIC OCEAN
Svalbard (Nor.)
Norwegian Sea
North Sea
ANADYR RANGE
Wrangel Island
North Pole
Prime Meridian
180°
Bering Sea
CHUKOTSKI PEN.
Chukchi Sea
Permanent Ice Pack
Greenland Sea
Denmark Strait
St. Lawrence Island
Bering Strait
Nunivak Island
Pt. Barrow
North Magnetic Pole
Ellesmere Island
ATLANTIC OCEAN
BROOKS RANGE
Beaufort Sea
Queen Elizabeth Islands
Baffin Bay
Arctic Circle
Kodiak I.
ALASKA RANGE
Yukon R.
Banks Island
Davis Strait
Gulf of Alaska
Amundsen Gulf
Victoria Island
Baffin I.
Cape Farewell
Mackenzie R.
NORTH AMERICA

0   250   500 mi
0   250   500 km

Antarctica

KEY

Elevation

Feet	Meters
Over 13,000	Over 3,960
6,500–13,000	1,980–3,960
1,600–6,500	480–1,980
650–1,600	200–480
0–650	0–200

Ice cap
Ice shelf

Orthographic Projection

ATLANTIC OCEAN
Antarctic Circle
South Shetland Is.
Permanent Ice Pack
QUEEN MAUD LAND
ENDERBY LAND
SOUTH AMERICA
Antarctic Peninsula
Weddell Sea
COATS LAND
Filchner Ice Shelf
Amery Ice Shelf
Alexander I.
Ronne Ice Shelf
Berkner I.
TRANSANTARCTIC MTS.
Bellingshausen Sea
Vinson Massif 16,066 ft. (4,897 m)
ANTARCTICA
South Pole
Prime Meridian
90° E
90°W
QUEEN MAUD MTS.
Amundsen Sea
Ross Ice Shelf
WILKES LAND
INDIAN OCEAN
Roosevelt I.
PACIFIC OCEAN
Permanent Ice Pack
Ross Sea
International Date Line
VICTORIA LAND
South Magnetic Pole

World View

Afghanistan

CAPITAL: Kabul
POPULATION: 21,251,821
MAJOR LANGUAGES: Pashtu, Afghan Persian, Turkic, and 30 various languages
AREA: 250,010 sq mi; 647,500 sq km
LEADING EXPORTS: fruits and nuts, handwoven carpets, and wool
CONTINENT: Asia

Albania
CAPITAL: Tiranë
POPULATION: 3,413,904
MAJOR LANGUAGES: Albanian, Tosk dialect, and Greek
AREA: 11,101 sq mi; 28,750 sq km
LEADING EXPORTS: asphalt, metals and metallic ores, and electricity
CONTINENT: Europe

Algeria
CAPITAL: Algiers
POPULATION: 28,539,321
MAJOR LANGUAGES: Arabic (official), French, and Berber dialects
AREA: 919,626 sq mi; 2,381,740 sq km
LEADING EXPORTS: petroleum and natural gas
CONTINENT: Africa

Andorra
CAPITAL: Andorra La Vella
POPULATION: 65,780
MAJOR LANGUAGES: Catalan (official), French, and Castilian
AREA: 174 sq mi; 450 sq km
LEADING EXPORTS: electricity, tobacco products, and furniture
CONTINENT: Europe

Angola
CAPITAL: Luanda
POPULATION: 10,069,501
MAJOR LANGUAGES: Portuguese (official), Bantu, and various languages
AREA: 481,370 sq mi; 1,246,700 sq km
LEADING EXPORTS: oil, diamonds, and refined petroleum products
CONTINENT: Africa

Anguilla

CAPITAL: The Valley
POPULATION: 7,099
MAJOR LANGUAGE: English (official)
AREA: 35 sq mi; 91 sq km
LEADING EXPORTS: lobster and salt
LOCATION: Caribbean Sea

Antigua and Barbuda

CAPITAL: Saint John's
POPULATION: 65,176
MAJOR LANGUAGES: English (official) and various dialects
AREA: 170 sq mi; 440 sq km
LEADING EXPORTS: petroleum products and manufactures
LOCATION: Caribbean Sea

Argentina
CAPITAL: Buenos Aires
POPULATION: 34,292,742
MAJOR LANGUAGES: Spanish (official), English, Italian, German, and French
AREA: 1,068,339 sq mi; 2,766,890 sq km
LEADING EXPORTS: meat, wheat, corn, oilseed, and manufactures
CONTINENT: South America

Armenia
CAPITAL: Yerevan
POPULATION: 3,557,284
MAJOR LANGUAGES: Armenian and Russian
AREA: 11,506 sq mi; 29,800 sq km
LEADING EXPORTS: gold and jewelry, and aluminum
CONTINENT: Asia

Australia
CAPITAL: Canberra
POPULATION: 18,322,231
MAJOR LANGUAGES: English and various languages
AREA: 2,968,010 sq mi; 7,686,850 sq km
LEADING EXPORTS: coal, gold, meat, wool, and alumina
CONTINENT: Australia

Austria
CAPITAL: Vienna
POPULATION: 7,986,664
MAJOR LANGUAGE: German
AREA: 32,376 sq mi; 83,850 sq km
LEADING EXPORTS: machinery and equipment, and iron and steel
CONTINENT: Europe

Azerbaijan
CAPITAL: Baku
POPULATION: 7,789,886
MAJOR LANGUAGES: Azeri, Russian, Armenian, and various languages
AREA: 33,438 sq mi; 86,600 sq km
LEADING EXPORTS: oil and gas, chemicals, and oil field equipment
CONTINENT: Europe and Asia

Bahamas

CAPITAL: Nassau
POPULATION: 256,616
MAJOR LANGUAGES: English and Creole
AREA: 5,382 sq mi; 13,940 sq km
LEADING EXPORTS: pharmaceuticals, cement, rum, and crawfish
LOCATION: Caribbean Sea

Bahrain
CAPITAL: Manama
POPULATION: 575,925
MAJOR LANGUAGES: Arabic, English, Farsi, and Urdu
AREA: 239 sq mi; 620 sq km
LEADING EXPORTS: petroleum and petroleum products
CONTINENT: Asia

Bangladesh
CAPITAL: Dhaka
POPULATION: 128,094,948
MAJOR LANGUAGES: Bangla and English
AREA: 55,600 sq mi; 144,000 sq km
LEADING EXPORTS: garments, jute and jute goods, and leather
CONTINENT: Asia

Barbados
CAPITAL: Bridgetown
POPULATION: 256,395
MAJOR LANGUAGE: English
AREA: 166 sq mi; 430 sq km
LEADING EXPORTS: sugar and molasses, and rum
LOCATION: Caribbean Sea

Belarus

CAPITAL: Minsk
POPULATION: 10,437,418
MAJOR LANGUAGES: Byelorussian and Russian
AREA: 79,926 sq mi; 207,600 sq km
LEADING EXPORTS: machinery and transportation equipment
CONTINENT: Europe

Belgium
CAPITAL: Brussels
POPULATION: 10,081,880
MAJOR LANGUAGES: Dutch, French, and German
AREA: 11,780 sq mi; 30,510 sq km
LEADING EXPORTS: iron and steel, and transportation equipment
CONTINENT: Europe

Belize
CAPITAL: Belmopan
POPULATION: 214,061
MAJOR LANGUAGES: English (official), Spanish, Maya, and Garifuna
AREA: 8,865 sq mi; 22,960 sq km
LEADING EXPORTS: sugar, citrus fruits, bananas, and clothing
LOCATION: Caribbean Sea

Benin
CAPITAL: Porto-Novo
POPULATION: 5,522,677
MAJOR LANGUAGES: Fon, Yoruba, and at least 6 various languages
AREA: 43,484 sq mi; 112,620 sq km
LEADING EXPORTS: cotton, crude oil, palm products, and cocoa
CONTINENT: Africa

Bermuda
CAPITAL: Hamilton
POPULATION: 61,629
MAJOR LANGUAGE: English
AREA: 19.3 sq mi; 50 sq km
LEADING EXPORTS: semitropical produce and light manufactures
CONTINENT: North America

Bhutan
CAPITAL: Thimphu
POPULATION: 1,780,638
MAJOR LANGUAGES: Dzongkha (official), Tibetan dialects, and Nepalese dialects
AREA: 18,147 sq mi; 47,000 sq km
LEADING EXPORTS: cardamon, gypsum, timber, and handicrafts
CONTINENT: Asia

Bolivia
CAPITAL: La Paz
POPULATION: 7,896,254
MAJOR LANGUAGES: Spanish, Quechua, and Aymara
AREA: 424,179 sq mi; 1,098,580 sq km
LEADING EXPORTS: metals, natural gas, soybeans, jewelry, and wood
CONTINENT: South America

Bosnia and Herzegovina

CAPITAL: Sarajevo
POPULATION: 3,201,823
MAJOR LANGUAGE: Serbo-Croatian
AREA: 19,782 sq mi; 51,233 sq km
LEADING EXPORTS: none
CONTINENT: Europe

Botswana

CAPITAL: Gaborone
POPULATION: 1,392,414
MAJOR LANGUAGES: English and Setswana
AREA: 231,812 sq mi; 600,370 sq km
LEADING EXPORTS: diamonds, copper and nickel, and meat
CONTINENT: Africa

Brazil

CAPITAL: Brasília
POPULATION: 160,737,489
MAJOR LANGUAGES: Portuguese, Spanish, English, and French
AREA: 3,286,600 sq mi; 8,511,965 sq km
LEADING EXPORTS: iron ore, soybean, bran, and orange juice
CONTINENT: South America

British Virgin Islands
CAPITAL: Road Town
POPULATION: 13,027
MAJOR LANGUAGE: English
AREA: 58 sq mi; 150 sq km
LEADING EXPORTS: rum, fresh fish, gravel, sand, and fruits
LOCATION: Caribbean Sea

Brunei
CAPITAL: Bandar Seri Begawan
POPULATION: 292,266
MAJOR LANGUAGES: Malay, English, and Chinese
AREA: 2,228 sq mi; 5,770 sq km
LEADING EXPORTS: crude oil and liquefied natural gas
CONTINENT: Asia

Bulgaria
CAPITAL: Sofia
POPULATION: 8,775,198
MAJOR LANGUAGE: Bulgarian
AREA: 42,824 sq mi; 110,910 sq km
LEADING EXPORTS: machinery and agricultural products
CONTINENT: Europe

Burkina Faso
CAPITAL: Ouagadougou
POPULATION: 10,422,828
MAJOR LANGUAGES: French (official) and Sudanic languages
AREA: 105,873 sq mi; 274,200 sq km
LEADING EXPORTS: cotton, gold, and animal products
CONTINENT: Africa

Burundi
CAPITAL: Bujumbura
POPULATION: 6,262,429
MAJOR LANGUAGES: Kirundi, French, and Swahili
AREA: 10,746 sq mi; 27,830 sq km
LEADING EXPORTS: coffee, tea, cotton, and hides and skins
CONTINENT: Africa

Cambodia
CAPITAL: Phnom Penh
POPULATION: 10,561,373
MAJOR LANGUAGES: Khmer and French
AREA: 69,902 sq mi; 181,040 sq km
LEADING EXPORTS: timber, rubber, soybeans, and sesame
CONTINENT: Asia

Cameroon

CAPITAL: Yaounde
POPULATION: 13,521,000
MAJOR LANGUAGES: 24 various languages, English, and French
AREA: 183,574 sq mi; 475,440 sq km
LEADING EXPORTS: petroleum products and lumber
CONTINENT: Africa

Canada
CAPITAL: Ottawa
POPULATION: 28,434,545
MAJOR LANGUAGES: English and French
AREA: 3,851,940 sq mi; 9,976,140 sq km
LEADING EXPORTS: newsprint, wood pulp, timber, and crude petroleum
CONTINENT: North America

Cape Verde

CAPITAL: Praia
POPULATION: 435,983
MAJOR LANGUAGES: Portuguese and Crioulo
AREA: 1,556 sq mi; 4,030 sq km
LEADING EXPORTS: fish, bananas, and hides and skins
CONTINENT: Africa

Cayman Islands
CAPITAL: George Town
POPULATION: 33,192
MAJOR LANGUAGE: English
AREA: 100 sq mi; 260 sq km
LEADING EXPORTS: turtle products and manufactured goods
LOCATION: Caribbean Sea

Central African Republic
CAPITAL: Bangui
POPULATION: 3,209,759
MAJOR LANGUAGES: French, Sangho, Arabic, Hunsa, and Swahili
AREA: 240,542 sq mi; 622,980 sq km
LEADING EXPORTS: diamonds, timber, cotton, coffee, and tobacco
CONTINENT: Africa

Chad
CAPITAL: N'Djamena
POPULATION: 5,586,505
MAJOR LANGUAGES: French, Arabic, Sara, Songo, and over 100 various languages and dialects
AREA: 495,772 sq mi; 1,284,000 sq km
LEADING EXPORTS: cotton, cattle, textiles, and fish
CONTINENT: Africa

Chile

CAPITAL: Santiago
POPULATION: 14,161,216
MAJOR LANGUAGE: Spanish
AREA: 292,269 sq mi; 756,950 sq km
LEADING EXPORTS: copper and other metals and minerals
CONTINENT: South America

China

CAPITAL: Beijing
POPULATION: 1,203,097,268
MAJOR LANGUAGES: Mandarin, Putonghua, Yue, Wu, Minbei, Minnan, Xiang, and Gan and Hakka dialects
AREA: 3,705,533 sq mi; 9,596,960 sq km
LEADING EXPORTS: textiles, garments, footwear, and toys
CONTINENT: Asia

Colombia
CAPITAL: Bogota
POPULATION: 36,200,251
MAJOR LANGUAGE: Spanish
AREA: 439,751 sq mi; 1,138,910 sq km
LEADING EXPORTS: petroleum, coffee, coal, and bananas
CONTINENT: South America

Comoros

CAPITAL: Moroni
POPULATION: 549,338
MAJOR LANGUAGES: Arabic, French, and Comoran
AREA: 838 sq mi; 2,170 sq km
LEADING EXPORTS: vanilla, ylang-ylang, cloves, and perfume oil
LOCATION: Indian Ocean

Congo
CAPITAL: Brazzaville
POPULATION: 2,504,996
MAJOR LANGUAGES: French, Lingala, Kikongo, and other languages
AREA: 132,051 sq mi; 342,000 sq km
LEADING EXPORTS: crude oil, lumber, plywood, sugar, and cocoa
CONTINENT: Africa

Cook Islands

CAPITAL: Avarua
POPULATION: 19,343
MAJOR LANGUAGES: English and Maori
AREA: 95 sq mi; 240 sq km
LEADING EXPORTS: copra, fresh and canned fruit, and clothing
LOCATION: Pacific Ocean

Costa Rica

CAPITAL: San José
POPULATION: 3,419,114
MAJOR LANGUAGES: Spanish and English
AREA: 19,730 sq mi; 51,100 sq km
LEADING EXPORTS: coffee, bananas, textiles, and sugar
CONTINENT: Central America

Côte d'Ivoire

CAPITAL: Yamoussoukro
POPULATION: 14,791,257
MAJOR LANGUAGES: French, Dioula, and 59 other dialects
AREA: 124,507 sq mi; 322,460 sq km
LEADING EXPORTS: cocoa, coffee, tropical woods, and petroleum
CONTINENT: Africa

Croatia

CAPITAL: Zagreb
POPULATION: 4,665,821
MAJOR LANGUAGE: Serbo-Croatian
AREA: 21,830 sq mi; 56,538 sq km
LEADING EXPORTS: machinery and transportation equipment
CONTINENT: Europe

Cuba

CAPITAL: Havana
POPULATION: 10,937,635
MAJOR LANGUAGE: Spanish
AREA: 42,805 sq mi; 110,860 sq km
LEADING EXPORTS: sugar, nickel, shellfish, and tobacco
LOCATION: Caribbean Sea

Cyprus

CAPITAL: Nicosia
POPULATION: 736,636
MAJOR LANGUAGES: Greek, Turkish, and English
AREA: 3,572 sq mi; 9,250 sq km
LEADING EXPORTS: citrus, potatoes, grapes, wines, and cement
LOCATION: Mediterranean Sea

Czech Republic
CAPITAL: Prague
POPULATION: 10,432,774
MAJOR LANGUAGES: Czech and Slovak
AREA: 30,388 sq mi; 78,703 sq km
LEADING EXPORTS: manufactured goods
CONTINENT: Europe

Denmark
CAPITAL: Copenhagen
POPULATION: 5,199,437
MAJOR LANGUAGES: Danish, Faroese, Greenlandic, and German
AREA: 16,630 sq mi; 43,070 sq km
LEADING EXPORTS: meat and meat products, and dairy products
CONTINENT: Europe

Djibouti

CAPITAL: Djibouti
POPULATION: 421,320
MAJOR LANGUAGES: French, Arabic, Somali, and Afar
AREA: 8,495 sq mi; 22,000 sq km
LEADING EXPORTS: hides and skins, and coffee (in transit)
CONTINENT: Africa

Dominica

CAPITAL: Roseau
POPULATION: 82,608
MAJOR LANGUAGES: English and French patois
AREA: 290 sq mi; 750 sq km
LEADING EXPORTS: bananas, soap, bay oil, and vegetables
LOCATION: Caribbean Sea

Dominican Republic

CAPITAL: Santo Domingo
POPULATION: 7,511,263
MAJOR LANGUAGE: Spanish
AREA: 18,815 sq mi; 48,730 sq km
LEADING EXPORTS: ferronickel, sugar, gold, coffee, and cocoa
LOCATION: Caribbean Sea

Ecuador

CAPITAL: Quito
POPULATION: 10,890,950
MAJOR LANGUAGES: Spanish, Quechua, and various languages
AREA: 109,487 sq mi; 283,560 sq km
LEADING EXPORTS: petroleum, bananas, shrimp, and cocoa
CONTINENT: South America

Egypt

CAPITAL: Cairo
POPULATION: 62,359,623
MAJOR LANGUAGES: Arabic, English, and French
AREA: 386,675 sq mi; 1,001,450 sq km
LEADING EXPORTS: crude oil and petroleum products
CONTINENT: Africa

El Salvador

CAPITAL: San Salvador
POPULATION: 5,870,481
MAJOR LANGUAGES: Spanish and Nahua
AREA: 8,124 sq mi; 21,040 sq km
LEADING EXPORTS: coffee, sugar cane, and shrimp
CONTINENT: Central America

Equatorial Guinea

CAPITAL: Malabo
POPULATION: 420,293
MAJOR LANGUAGES: Spanish, Pidgin English, Fang, Bubi, and Ibo
AREA: 10,831 sq mi; 28,050 sq km
LEADING EXPORTS: coffee, timber, and cocoa beans
CONTINENT: Africa

Eritrea

CAPITAL: Asmara
POPULATION: 3,578,709
MAJOR LANGUAGES: Tigre, Kunama, Cushitic dialects, Nora Bana, and Arabic
AREA: 46,844 sq mi; 121,320 sq km
LEADING EXPORTS: salt, hides, cement, and gum arabic
CONTINENT: Africa

Estonia

CAPITAL: Tallinn
POPULATION: 1,625,399
MAJOR LANGUAGES: Estonian, Latvian, Lithuanian, and Russian
AREA: 17,414 sq mi; 45,100 sq km
LEADING EXPORTS: textiles, food products, vehicles, and metals
CONTINENT: Europe

Ethiopia

CAPITAL: Addis Ababa
POPULATION: 55,979,018
MAJOR LANGUAGES: Amharic, Tigrinya, Orominga, Guaraginga, Somali, Arabic, English, and various languages
AREA: 435,201 sq mi; 1,127,127 sq km
LEADING EXPORTS: coffee, leather products, and gold
CONTINENT: Africa

Fiji

CAPITAL: Suva
POPULATION: 772,891
MAJOR LANGUAGES: English, Fijian, and Hindustani
AREA: 7,054 sq mi; 18,270 sq km
LEADING EXPORTS: sugar, clothing, gold, processed fish, and lumber
LOCATION: Pacific Ocean

Finland

CAPITAL: Helsinki
POPULATION: 5,085,206
MAJOR LANGUAGES: Finnish, Swedish, Lapp, and Russian
AREA: 130,132 sq mi; 337,030 sq km
LEADING EXPORTS: paper and pulp, machinery, and chemicals
CONTINENT: Europe

France

CAPITAL: Paris
POPULATION: 58,109,160
MAJOR LANGUAGES: French and regional dialects and languages
AREA: 211,217 sq mi; 547,030 sq km
LEADING EXPORTS: machinery and transportation equipment
CONTINENT: Europe

Gabon

CAPITAL: Libreville
POPULATION: 1,185,749
MAJOR LANGUAGES: French, Fang, Myene, Bateke, Bapounou/Eschira, and Bandjabi
AREA: 103,351 sq mi; 267,670 sq km
LEADING EXPORTS: crude oil, timber, manganese, and uranium
CONTINENT: Africa

The Gambia

CAPITAL: Banjul
POPULATION: 989,273
MAJOR LANGUAGES: English, Mandinka, Wolof, Fula, and various languages
AREA: 4,363 sq mi; 11,300 sq km
LEADING EXPORTS: peanuts and peanut products, and fish
CONTINENT: Africa

Georgia

CAPITAL: T'bilisi
POPULATION: 5,725,972
MAJOR LANGUAGES: Armenian, Azeri, Georgian, Russian, and various languages
AREA: 26,912 sq mi; 69,700 sq km
LEADING EXPORTS: citrus fruits, tea, and wine
CONTINENT: Asia

Germany

CAPITAL: Berlin
POPULATION: 81,337,541
MAJOR LANGUAGE: German
AREA: 137,808 sq mi; 356,910 sq km
LEADING EXPORTS: machines and machine tools, and chemicals
CONTINENT: Europe

Ghana

CAPITAL: Accra
POPULATION: 17,763,138
MAJOR LANGUAGES: English, Akan, Moshi-Dagomba, Ewe, Ga, and various languages
AREA: 92,104 sq mi; 238,540 sq km
LEADING EXPORTS: cocoa, gold, timber, tuna, and bauxite
CONTINENT: Africa

Greece

CAPITAL: Athens
POPULATION: 10,647,511
MAJOR LANGUAGES: Greek, English, and French
AREA: 50,944 sq mi; 131,940 sq km
LEADING EXPORTS: manufactured goods, foodstuffs, and fuels
CONTINENT: Europe

Grenada

CAPITAL: Saint George's
POPULATION: 94,486
MAJOR LANGUAGES: English and French patois
AREA: 131 sq mi; 340 sq km
LEADING EXPORTS: bananas, cocoa, nutmeg, and fruits and vegetables
LOCATION: Caribbean Sea

Guatemala

CAPITAL: Guatemala
POPULATION: 10,998,602
MAJOR LANGUAGES: Spanish, Quiche, Cakchiquel, Kekchi, and various languages and dialects
AREA: 42,044 sq mi; 108,890 sq km
LEADING EXPORTS: coffee, sugar, bananas, cardamom, and beef
CONTINENT: Central America

Guinea

CAPITAL: Conakry
POPULATION: 6,549,336
MAJOR LANGUAGES: French and various languages
AREA: 94,930 sq mi; 245,860 sq km
LEADING EXPORTS: bauxite, alumina, diamonds, gold, and coffee
CONTINENT: Africa

Guinea Bissau

CAPITAL: Bissau
POPULATION: 1,124,537
MAJOR LANGUAGES: Portuguese, Criolo, and various languages
AREA: 13,946 sq mi; 36,210 sq km
LEADING EXPORTS: cashews, fish, peanuts, and palm kernels
CONTINENT: Africa

Guyana

CAPITAL: Georgetown
POPULATION: 723,774
MAJOR LANGUAGES: English and various dialects
AREA: 83,003 sq mi; 214,970 sq km
LEADING EXPORTS: sugar, bauxite/alumina, rice, and shrimp
CONTINENT: South America

Haiti

CAPITAL: Port-au-Prince
POPULATION: 6,539,983
MAJOR LANGUAGES: French and Creole
AREA: 8,784 sq mi; 22,750 sq km
LEADING EXPORTS: light manufactures and coffee
LOCATION: Caribbean Sea

Holy See (Vatican City)

CAPITAL: Vatican City
POPULATION: 830
MAJOR LANGUAGES: Italian, Latin, and various languages
AREA: 17 sq mi; 44 sq km
LEADING EXPORTS: none
CONTINENT: Europe

Honduras

CAPITAL: Tegucigalpa
POPULATION: 5,549,743
MAJOR LANGUAGES: Spanish and various dialects
AREA: 43,280 sq mi; 112,090 sq km
LEADING EXPORTS: bananas, coffee, shrimp, lobsters, and minerals
CONTINENT: Central America

Hungary

CAPITAL: Budapest
POPULATION: 10,318,838
MAJOR LANGUAGES: Hungarian and various languages
AREA: 35,920 sq mi; 93,030 sq km
LEADING EXPORTS: raw materials and semi-finished goods
CONTINENT: Europe

Iceland

CAPITAL: Reykjavik
POPULATION: 265,998
MAJOR LANGUAGE: Icelandic
AREA: 39,770 sq mi; 103,000 sq km
LEADING EXPORTS: fish and fish products, and animal products
CONTINENT: Europe

India

CAPITAL: New Delhi
POPULATION: 936,545,814
MAJOR LANGUAGES: English, Hindi, Bengali, Telugu, Marathi, Tamil, Urdu, Gujarati, Malayam, Kannada, Oriya, Punjabi, Assamese, Kashmiri, Sindhi, Sanskrit, and Hindustani (all official)
AREA: 1,269,389 sq mi; 3,287,590 sq km
LEADING EXPORTS: clothing, and gems and jewelry
CONTINENT: Asia

Indonesia

CAPITAL: Jakarta
POPULATION: 203,583,886
MAJOR LANGUAGES: Bahasa Indonesia, English, Dutch, Javanese, and various dialects
AREA: 741,052 sq mi; 1,919,251 sq km
LEADING EXPORTS: manufactures, fuels, and foodstuffs
CONTINENT: Asia

Iran

CAPITAL: Tehran
POPULATION: 64,625,455
MAJOR LANGUAGES: Farsi (official) and Turkic languages
AREA: 634,562 sq mi; 1,643,452 sq km
LEADING EXPORTS: petroleum, carpets, fruit, nuts, and hides
CONTINENT: Asia

Iraq

CAPITAL: Baghdad
POPULATION: 20,643,769
MAJOR LANGUAGES: Arabic, Kurdish, Assyrian, and Armenian
AREA: 168,760 sq mi; 437,072 sq km
LEADING EXPORTS: crude oil and refined products, and fertilizers
CONTINENT: Asia

Ireland

CAPITAL: Dublin
POPULATION: 3,550,448
MAJOR LANGUAGES: Irish Gaelic and English
AREA: 27,136 sq mi; 70,280 sq km
LEADING EXPORTS: chemicals and data processing equipment
CONTINENT: Europe

Israel

CAPITAL: Jerusalem
POPULATION: 7,566,447
MAJOR LANGUAGES: Hebrew, Arabic, and English
AREA: 10,421 sq mi; 26,990 sq km
LEADING EXPORTS: machinery and equipment, and cut diamonds
CONTINENT: Asia

Italy

CAPITAL: Rome
POPULATION: 58,261,971
MAJOR LANGUAGES: Italian, German, French, and Slovene
AREA: 116,310 sq mi; 301,230 sq km
LEADING EXPORTS: metals, and textiles and clothing
CONTINENT: Europe

Jamaica

CAPITAL: Kingston
POPULATION: 2,574,291
MAJOR LANGUAGES: English and Creole
AREA: 4,243 sq mi; 10,990 sq km
LEADING EXPORTS: alumina, bauxite, sugar, bananas, and rum
LOCATION: Caribbean Sea

Japan

CAPITAL: Tokyo
POPULATION: 125,506,492
MAJOR LANGUAGE: Japanese
AREA: 145,888 sq mi; 377,835 sq km
LEADING EXPORTS: machinery, motor vehicles, and electronics
CONTINENT: Asia

Jordan

CAPITAL: Amman
POPULATION: 4,100,709
MAJOR LANGUAGES: Arabic and English
AREA: 34,447 sq mi; 89,213 sq km
LEADING EXPORTS: phosphates, fertilizers, and potash
CONTINENT: Asia

Kazakhstan

CAPITAL: Almaty
POPULATION: 17,376,615
MAJOR LANGUAGES: Kazakh and Russian
AREA: 1,049,191 sq mi; 2,717,300 sq km
LEADING EXPORTS: oil, and ferrous and nonferrous metals
CONTINENT: Asia

Kenya

CAPITAL: Nairobi
POPULATION: 28,817,227
MAJOR LANGUAGES: English, Swahili, and various languages
AREA: 224,970 sq mi; 582,650 sq km
LEADING EXPORTS: tea, coffee, and petroleum products
CONTINENT: Africa

Kiribati

CAPITAL: Tarawa
POPULATION: 79,386
MAJOR LANGUAGES: English and Gilbertese
AREA: 277 sq mi; 717 sq km
LEADING EXPORTS: copra, seaweed, and fish
LOCATION: Pacific Ocean

Korea, North

CAPITAL: P'yongyang
POPULATION: 23,486,550
MAJOR LANGUAGE: Korean
AREA: 46,542 sq mi; 120,540 sq km
LEADING EXPORTS: minerals and metallurgical products
CONTINENT: Asia

Korea, South

CAPITAL: Seoul
POPULATION: 45,553,882
MAJOR LANGUAGES: Korean and English
AREA: 38,025 sq mi; 98,480 sq km
LEADING EXPORTS: electronic and electrical equipment
CONTINENT: Asia

Kuwait

CAPITAL: Kuwait
POPULATION: 1,817,397
MAJOR LANGUAGES: Arabic and English
AREA: 6,881 sq mi; 17,820 sq km
LEADING EXPORT: oil
CONTINENT: Asia

Kyrgyzstan

CAPITAL: Bishkek
POPULATION: 4,769,877
MAJOR LANGUAGES: Kyrgyz and Russian
AREA: 76,644 sq mi; 198,500 sq km
LEADING EXPORTS: wool, chemicals, cotton, metals, and shoes
CONTINENT: Asia

Laos

CAPITAL: Vientiane
POPULATION: 4,837,237
MAJOR LANGUAGES: Lao, French, English, and various languages
AREA: 91,432 sq mi; 236,800 sq km
LEADING EXPORTS: electricity, wood products, coffee, and tin
CONTINENT: Asia

Latvia

CAPITAL: Riga
POPULATION: 2,762,899
MAJOR LANGUAGES: Lettish, Lithuanian, Russian, and various languages
AREA: 24,750 sq mi; 64,100 sq km
LEADING EXPORTS: oil products, timber, and ferrous metals
CONTINENT: Europe

Lebanon

CAPITAL: Beirut
POPULATION: 3,695,921
MAJOR LANGUAGES: Arabic, French, Armenian, and English
AREA: 4,016 sq mi; 10,400 sq km
LEADING EXPORTS: agricultural products, chemicals, and textiles
CONTINENT: Asia

Lesotho

CAPITAL: Maseru
POPULATION: 1,992,960
MAJOR LANGUAGES: Sesotho, English, Zulu, and Xhosa
AREA: 11,719 sq mi; 30,350 sq km
LEADING EXPORTS: wool, mohair, wheat, cattle, and peas
CONTINENT: Africa

Liberia

CAPITAL: Monrovia
POPULATION: 3,073,245
MAJOR LANGUAGES: English and Niger-Congo
AREA: 43,002 sq mi; 111,370 sq km
LEADING EXPORTS: iron ore, rubber, timber, and coffee
CONTINENT: Africa

Libya
CAPITAL: Tripoli
POPULATION: 5,248,401
MAJOR LANGUAGES: Arabic, Italian, and English
AREA: 679,385 sq mi; 1,759,540 sq km
LEADING EXPORTS: crude oil and refined petroleum products
CONTINENT: Africa

Liechtenstein
CAPITAL: Vaduz
POPULATION: 30,654
MAJOR LANGUAGES: German and Alemannic
AREA: 62 sq mi; 160 sq km
LEADING EXPORTS: small specialty machinery and dental products
CONTINENT: Europe

Lithuania
CAPITAL: Vilnius
POPULATION: 3,876,396
MAJOR LANGUAGES: Lithuanian, Polish, and Russian
AREA: 25,175 sq mi; 65,200 sq km
LEADING EXPORTS: electronics, petroleum products, and food
CONTINENT: Europe

Luxembourg
CAPITAL: Luxembourg
POPULATION: 404,660
MAJOR LANGUAGES: Luxembourgisch, German, French, and English
AREA: 998 sq mi; 2,586 sq km
LEADING EXPORTS: finished steel products and chemicals
CONTINENT: Europe

Macedonia
CAPITAL: Skopje
POPULATION: 2,159,503
MAJOR LANGUAGES: Macedonian, Albanian, Turkish, Serb, Gypsy, and various languages
AREA: 9,781 sq mi; 25,333 sq km
LEADING EXPORTS: manufactured goods and machinery
CONTINENT: Europe

Madagascar
CAPITAL: Antananarivo
POPULATION: 13,862,325
MAJOR LANGUAGES: French and Malagasy
AREA: 226,665 sq mi; 587,040 sq km
LEADING EXPORTS: coffee, vanilla, cloves, shellfish, and sugar
CONTINENT: Africa

Malawi
CAPITAL: Lilongwe
POPULATION: 9,808,384
MAJOR LANGUAGES: English, Chichewa, and various languages
AREA: 45,747 sq mi; 118,480 sq km
LEADING EXPORTS: tobacco, tea, sugar, coffee, and peanuts
CONTINENT: Africa

Malaysia
CAPITAL: Kuala Lumpur
POPULATION: 19,723,587
MAJOR LANGUAGES: Malay, English, Mandarin, Tamil, Chinese dialects, and various languages and dialects
AREA: 127,322 sq mi; 329,750 sq km
LEADING EXPORTS: electronic equipment
CONTINENT: Asia

Maldives
CAPITAL: Male
POPULATION: 261,310
MAJOR LANGUAGES: Divehi dialect and English
AREA: 116 sq mi; 300 sq km
LEADING EXPORTS: fish and clothing
CONTINENT: Asia

Mali
CAPITAL: Bamako
POPULATION: 9,375,132
MAJOR LANGUAGES: French, Bambara, and various languages
AREA: 478,783 sq mi; 1,240,000 sq km
LEADING EXPORTS: cotton, livestock, and gold
CONTINENT: Africa

Malta
CAPITAL: Valletta
POPULATION: 369,609
MAJOR LANGUAGES: Maltese and English
AREA: 124 sq mi; 320 sq km
LEADING EXPORTS: machinery and transportation equipment
CONTINENT: Europe

Marshall Islands
CAPITAL: Majuro
POPULATION: 56,157
MAJOR LANGUAGES: English, Marshallese dialects, and Japanese
AREA: 70 sq mi; 181.3 sq km
LEADING EXPORTS: coconut oil, fish, live animals, and trichus shells
LOCATION: Pacific Ocean

Mauritania
CAPITAL: Nouakchott
POPULATION: 2,263,202
MAJOR LANGUAGES: Hasaniya Arabic, Wolof, Pular, and Soninke
AREA: 397,969 sq mi; 1,030,700 sq km
LEADING EXPORTS: iron ore, and fish and fish products
CONTINENT: Africa

Mauritius
CAPITAL: Port Louis
POPULATION: 1,127,068
MAJOR LANGUAGES: English (official), Creole, French, Hindi, Urdu, Hakka, and Bojpoori
AREA: 718 sq mi; 1,860 sq km
LEADING EXPORTS: textiles, sugar, and light manufactures
LOCATION: Indian Ocean

Mayotte
CAPITAL: Mamoutzou
POPULATION: 97,088
MAJOR LANGUAGES: Mahorian and French
AREA: 145 sq mi; 375 sq km
LEADING EXPORTS: ylang-ylang and vanilla
CONTINENT: Africa

Mexico
CAPITAL: Mexico City
POPULATION: 93,985,848
MAJOR LANGUAGES: Spanish and Mayan dialects
AREA: 761,632 sq mi; 1,972,550 sq km
LEADING EXPORTS: crude oil, oil products, coffee, and silver
CONTINENT: North America

Micronesia
CAPITAL: Federated states of Kolonia (on the Island of Pohnpei)
*a new capital is being built about 10 km southwest in the Palikir Valley
POPULATION: 122,950
MAJOR LANGUAGES: English, Turkese, Pohnpeian, Yapese, and Kosrean
AREA: 271 sq mi; 702 sq km
LEADING EXPORTS: fish, copra, bananas, and black pepper
LOCATION: Pacific Ocean

Moldova
CAPITAL: Chisinau
POPULATION: 4,489,657
MAJOR LANGUAGES: Moldovan (official), Russian, and Gagauz dialect
AREA: 13,012 sq mi; 33,700 sq km
LEADING EXPORTS: foodstuffs, wine, and tobacco
CONTINENT: Europe

Monaco
CAPITAL: Monaco
POPULATION: 31,515
MAJOR LANGUAGES: French (official), English, Italian, and Monegasque
AREA: .73 sq mi; 1.9 sq km
LEADING EXPORTS: exports through France
CONTINENT: Europe

Mongolia

CAPITAL: Ulaanbaatar
POPULATION: 2,493,615
MAJOR LANGUAGES: Khalkha Mongol, Turkic, Russian, and Chinese
AREA: 604,270 sq mi; 1,565,000 sq km
LEADING EXPORTS: copper, livestock, animal products, and cashmere
CONTINENT: Asia

Morocco
CAPITAL: Rabat
POPULATION: 29,168,848
MAJOR LANGUAGES: Arabic (official), Berber dialects, and French
AREA: 172,420 sq mi; 446,550 sq km
LEADING EXPORTS: food and beverages
CONTINENT: Africa

Mozambique
CAPITAL: Maputo
POPULATION: 18,115,250
MAJOR LANGUAGES: Portuguese and various dialects
AREA: 309,506 sq mi; 801,590 sq km
LEADING EXPORTS: shrimp, cashews, cotton, sugar, copra, and citrus
CONTINENT: Africa

Myanmar (Burma)
CAPITAL: Rangoon
POPULATION: 45,103,809
MAJOR LANGUAGE: Burmese
AREA: 261,979 sq mi; 678,500 sq km
LEADING EXPORTS: pulses and beans, teak, rice, and hardwood
CONTINENT: Asia

Namibia

CAPITAL: Windhoek
POPULATION: 1,651,545
MAJOR LANGUAGES: English (official), Afrikaans, German, Oshivambo, Herero, Nama, and various languages
AREA: 318,707 sq mi; 825,418 sq km
LEADING EXPORTS: diamonds, copper, gold, zinc, and lead
CONTINENT: Africa

Nauru

CAPITAL: Government offices in Yaren District
POPULATION: 10,149
MAJOR LANGUAGES: Nauruan and English
AREA: 8 sq mi; 21 sq km
LEADING EXPORTS: phosphates
LOCATION: Pacific Ocean

Nepal

CAPITAL: Kathmandu
POPULATION: 21,560,869
MAJOR LANGUAGES: Nepali (official) and 20 various languages divided into numerous dialects
AREA: 54,365 sq mi; 140,800 sq km
LEADING EXPORTS: carpets, clothing, and leather goods
CONTINENT: Asia

Netherlands

CAPITAL: Amsterdam
POPULATION: 15,452,903
MAJOR LANGUAGE: Dutch
AREA: 14,414 sq mi; 37,330 sq km
LEADING EXPORTS: metal products and chemicals
CONTINENT: Europe

New Caledonia

CAPITAL: Noumea
POPULATION: 184,552
MAJOR LANGUAGES: French and 28 Melanesian-Polynesian dialects
AREA: 7,359 sq mi; 19,060 sq km
LEADING EXPORTS: nickel metal and nickel ore
LOCATION: Pacific Ocean

New Zealand

CAPITAL: Wellington
POPULATION: 3,407,277
MAJOR LANGUAGES: English and Maori
AREA: 103,741 sq mi; 268,680 sq km
LEADING EXPORTS: wool, lamb, mutton, beef, fish, and cheese
LOCATION: Pacific Ocean

Nicaragua

CAPITAL: Managua
POPULATION: 4,206,353
MAJOR LANGUAGES: Spanish (official), English, and various languages
AREA: 50,000 sq mi; 129,494 sq km
LEADING EXPORTS: meat, coffee, cotton, sugar, seafood, and gold
LOCATION: Caribbean Sea

Niger

CAPITAL: Niamey
POPULATION: 9,280,208
MAJOR LANGUAGES: French (official), Hausa, and Djerma
AREA: 489,208 sq mi; 1,267,000 sq km
LEADING EXPORTS: uranium ore and livestock products
CONTINENT: Africa

Nigeria

CAPITAL: Abuja
POPULATION: 101,232,251
MAJOR LANGUAGES: English (official), Hausa, Yoruba, Ibo, and Fulani
AREA: 356,682 sq mi; 923,770 sq km
LEADING EXPORTS: oil, cocoa, and rubber
CONTINENT: Africa

Niue

CAPITAL: (Free association with New Zealand)
POPULATION: 1,837
MAJOR LANGUAGES: Polynesian and English
AREA: 100 sq mi; 260 sq km
LEADING EXPORTS: canned coconut cream, copra, and honey
LOCATION: Pacific Ocean

Norway

CAPITAL: Oslo
POPULATION: 4,330,951
MAJOR LANGUAGES: Norwegian (official), Lapp, and Finnish
AREA: 125,186 sq mi; 324,220 sq km
LEADING EXPORTS: petroleum and petroleum products
CONTINENT: Europe

Oman

CAPITAL: Muscat
POPULATION: 2,125,089
MAJOR LANGUAGES: Arabic (official), English, Baluchi, Urdu, and Indian dialects
AREA: 82,034 sq mi; 212,460 sq km
LEADING EXPORTS: petroleum, re-exports, and fish
CONTINENT: Asia

Pakistan

CAPITAL: Islamabad
POPULATION: 131,541,920
MAJOR LANGUAGES: Urdu (official), English (official), Punjabi, Sindhi, Pashtu, Urdu, Balochi, and other languages
AREA: 310,414 sq mi; 803,940 sq km
LEADING EXPORTS: cotton, textiles, clothing, rice, and leather
CONTINENT: Asia

Palau

CAPITAL: Koror
POPULATION: 16,661
MAJOR LANGUAGES: English (official), Sonsorolese, Angaur, Japanese, Tobi, and Palauan
AREA: 177 sq mi; 458 sq km
LEADING EXPORTS: trochus, tuna, copra, and handicrafts
LOCATION: Pacific Ocean

Panama

CAPITAL: Panama
POPULATION: 2,680,903
MAJOR LANGUAGES: Spanish (official) and English
AREA: 30,194 sq mi; 78,200 sq km
LEADING EXPORTS: bananas, shrimp, sugar, clothing, and coffee
CONTINENT: Central America

Papua New Guinea

CAPITAL: Port Moresby
POPULATION: 4,294,750
MAJOR LANGUAGES: English, pidgin English, and Motu
AREA: 178,266 sq mi; 461,690 sq km
LEADING EXPORTS: gold, copper ore, oil, logs, and palm oil
LOCATION: Pacific Ocean

Paraguay

CAPITAL: Asuncion
POPULATION: 5,358,198
MAJOR LANGUAGES: Spanish (official) and Guarani
AREA: 157,052 sq mi; 406,750 sq km
LEADING EXPORTS: cotton, soybeans, timber, and vegetable oils
CONTINENT: South America

Peru

CAPITAL: Lima
POPULATION: 24,087,372
MAJOR LANGUAGES: Spanish (official), Quechua (official), and Aymara
AREA: 496,243 sq mi; 1,285,220 sq km
LEADING EXPORTS: copper, zinc, and fish meal
CONTINENT: South America

Philippines

CAPITAL: Manila
POPULATION: 73,265,584
MAJOR LANGUAGES: Pilipino and English (official)
AREA: 115,834 sq mi; 300,000 sq km
LEADING EXPORTS: electronics, textiles, and coconut products
CONTINENT: Asia

Poland

CAPITAL: Warsaw
POPULATION: 38,792,442
MAJOR LANGUAGE: Polish
AREA: 120,731 sq mi; 312,680 sq km
LEADING EXPORTS: intermediate goods
CONTINENT: Europe

Portugal

CAPITAL: Lisbon
POPULATION: 10,562,388
MAJOR LANGUAGE: Portuguese
AREA: 35,553 sq mi; 92,080 sq km
LEADING EXPORTS: clothing and footwear, and machinery
CONTINENT: Europe

Qatar

CAPITAL: Doha
POPULATION: 533,916
MAJOR LANGUAGES: Arabic (official) and English
AREA: 4,247 sq mi; 11,000 sq km
LEADING EXPORTS: petroleum products, steel, and fertilizers
CONTINENT: Asia

Romania

CAPITAL: Bucharest
POPULATION: 23,198,330
MAJOR LANGUAGES: Romanian, Hungarian, and German
AREA: 91,702 sq mi; 237,500 sq km
LEADING EXPORTS: metals and metal products, and mineral products
CONTINENT: Europe

Russia

CAPITAL: Moscow
POPULATION: 149,909,089
MAJOR LANGUAGES: Russian and various languages
AREA: 6,952,996 sq mi; 17,075,200 sq km
LEADING EXPORTS: petroleum and petroleum products
CONTINENT: Europe and Asia

Rwanda

CAPITAL: Kigali
POPULATION: 8,605,307
MAJOR LANGUAGES: Kinyarwanda (official), French (official), and Kiswahili
AREA: 10,170 sq mi; 26,340 sq km
LEADING EXPORTS: coffee, tea, cassiterite, and wolframite
CONTINENT: Africa

Saint Kitts and Nevis

CAPITAL: Basseterre
POPULATION: 40,992
MAJOR LANGUAGE: English
AREA: 104 sq mi; 269 sq km
LEADING EXPORTS: machinery, food, and electronics
LOCATION: Caribbean Sea

Saint Lucia

CAPITAL: Castries
POPULATION: 156,050
MAJOR LANGUAGES: English and French patois
AREA: 239 sq mi; 620 sq km
LEADING EXPORTS: bananas, clothing, cocoa, and vegetables
LOCATION: Caribbean Sea

Saint Vincent and the Grenadines

CAPITAL: Kingstown
POPULATION: 117,344
MAJOR LANGUAGES: English and French patois
AREA: 131 sq mi; 340 sq km
LEADING EXPORTS: bananas, and eddoes and dasheen (taro)
LOCATION: Caribbean Sea

San Marino

CAPITAL: San Marino
POPULATION: 24,313
MAJOR LANGUAGE: Italian
AREA: 23 sq mi; 60 sq km
LEADING EXPORTS: building stone, lime, wood, and chestnuts
CONTINENT: Europe

Sao Tome and Principe

CAPITAL: Sao Tome
POPULATION: 140,423
MAJOR LANGUAGE: Portuguese (official)
AREA: 371 sq mi; 960 sq km
LEADING EXPORTS: cocoa, copra, coffee, and palm oil
CONTINENT: Africa

Saudi Arabia

CAPITAL: Riyadh
POPULATION: 18,729,576
MAJOR LANGUAGE: Arabic
AREA: 757,011 sq mi; 1,960,582 sq km
LEADING EXPORTS: petroleum and petroleum products
CONTINENT: Asia

Senegal

CAPITAL: Dakar
POPULATION: 9,007,080
MAJOR LANGUAGES: French (official), Wolof, Pulaar, Diola, and Mandingo
AREA: 75,752 sq mi; 196,190 sq km
LEADING EXPORTS: fish, ground nuts, and petroleum products
CONTINENT: Africa

Serbia and Montenegro

CAPITAL: Belgrade
POPULATION: 11,101,833
MAJOR LANGUAGES: Serbo-Croatian and Albanian
AREA: 39,436 sq mi; 102,350 sq km
LEADING EXPORTS: none
CONTINENT: Europe

Seychelles

CAPITAL: Victoria
POPULATION: 72,709
MAJOR LANGUAGES: English (official), French (official), and Creole
AREA: 176 sq mi; 455 sq km
LEADING EXPORTS: fish, cinnamon bark, and copra
CONTINENT: Africa

Sierra Leone

CAPITAL: Freetown
POPULATION: 4,753,120
MAJOR LANGUAGES: English (official), Mende, Temne, and Krio
AREA: 27,700 sq mi; 71,740 sq km
LEADING EXPORTS: rutile, bauxite, diamonds, coffee, and cocoa
CONTINENT: Africa

Singapore

CAPITAL: Singapore
POPULATION: 2,890,468
MAJOR LANGUAGES: Chinese, Malay, Tamil, and English
AREA: 244 sq mi; 633 sq km
LEADING EXPORTS: computer equipment
CONTINENT: Asia

Slovakia

CAPITAL: Bratislava
POPULATION: 5,432,383
MAJOR LANGUAGES: Slovak and Hungarian
AREA: 18,860 sq mi; 48,845 sq km
LEADING EXPORTS: machinery and transportation equipment
CONTINENT: Europe

Slovenia

CAPITAL: Ljubljana
POPULATION: 2,051,522
MAJOR LANGUAGES: Slovenian, Serbo-Croatian, and various languages
AREA: 7,837 sq mi; 20,296 sq km
LEADING EXPORTS: machinery and transportation equipment
CONTINENT: Europe

Solomon Islands

CAPITAL: Honiara
POPULATION: 399,206
MAJOR LANGUAGES: Melanesian pidgin and English
AREA: 10,985 sq mi; 28,450 sq km
LEADING EXPORTS: fish, timber, palm oil, cocoa, and copra
LOCATION: Pacific Ocean

Somalia

CAPITAL: Mogadishu
POPULATION: 7,347,554
MAJOR LANGUAGES: Somali (official), Arabic, Italian, and English
AREA: 246,210 sq mi; 637,660 sq km
LEADING EXPORTS: bananas, live animals, fish, and hides
CONTINENT: Africa

South Africa

CAPITAL: Pretoria (administrative), Cape Town (legislative), Bloemfontein (judicial)
POPULATION: 45,095,459
MAJOR LANGUAGES: Afrikaans, English, Ndebele, Pedi, Sotho, Swazi, Tsonga, Tswana, Venda, Xhosa, and Zulu (all official)
AREA: 471,027 sq mi; 1,219,912 sq km
LEADING EXPORTS: gold, other minerals and metals, and food
CONTINENT: Africa

Spain

CAPITAL: Madrid
POPULATION: 39,404,348
MAJOR LANGUAGES: Spanish, Catalan, Galician, and Basque
AREA: 194,892 sq mi; 504,750 sq km
LEADING EXPORTS: cars and trucks, and semifinished goods
CONTINENT: Europe

Sri Lanka

CAPITAL: Colombo
POPULATION: 18,342,660
MAJOR LANGUAGES: Sinhala (official) and Tamil
AREA: 25,333 sq mi; 65,610 sq km
LEADING EXPORTS: garments and textiles, teas, and diamonds
CONTINENT: Asia

Sudan

CAPITAL: Khartoum
POPULATION: 30,120,420
MAJOR LANGUAGES: Arabic (official), Nubian, Ta Bedawie, Nilotic, Nilo-Hamitic, and Sudanic dialects
AREA: 967,532 sq mi; 2,505,810 sq km
LEADING EXPORTS: gum arabic, livestock/meat, and cotton
CONTINENT: Africa

Suriname

CAPITAL: Paramaribo
POPULATION: 429,544
MAJOR LANGUAGES: Dutch (official), English, Sranang, Tongo, Hindustani, and Japanese
AREA: 63,041 sq mi; 163,270 sq km
LEADING EXPORTS: alumina, aluminum, and shrimp and fish
CONTINENT: South America

Swaziland

CAPITAL: Mbabane
POPULATION: 966,977
MAJOR LANGUAGES: English (official) and SiSwati (official)
AREA: 6,641 sq mi; 17,360 sq km
LEADING EXPORTS: sugar, edible concentrates, and wood pulp
CONTINENT: Africa

Sweden

CAPITAL: Stockholm
POPULATION: 8,821,759
MAJOR LANGUAGES: Swedish, Lapp, and Finnish
AREA: 173,738 sq mi; 449,964 sq km
LEADING EXPORTS: machinery, motor vehicles, and paper products
CONTINENT: Europe

Switzerland

CAPITAL: Bern
POPULATION: 7,084,984
MAJOR LANGUAGES: German, French, Italian, Romansch, and various languages
AREA: 15,943 sq mi; 41,290 sq km
LEADING EXPORTS: machinery and equipment
CONTINENT: Europe

Syria

CAPITAL: Damascus
POPULATION: 15,451,917
MAJOR LANGUAGES: Arabic (official), Kurdish, Armenian, Aramaic, Circassian, and French
AREA: 71,501 sq mi; 185,180 sq km
LEADING EXPORTS: petroleum, textiles, cotton, and fruits
CONTINENT: Asia

Taiwan

CAPITAL: Taipei
POPULATION: 21,500,583
MAJOR LANGUAGES: Mandarin Chinese (official), Taiwanese, and Hakka dialects
AREA: 13,892 sq mi; 35,980 sq km
LEADING EXPORTS: electrical machinery and electronics
CONTINENT: Asia

Tajikistan

CAPITAL: Dushanbe
POPULATION: 6,155,474
MAJOR LANGUAGES: Tajik (official) and Russian
AREA: 55,253 sq mi; 143,100 sq km
LEADING EXPORTS: cotton, aluminum, fruits, and vegetable oil
CONTINENT: Asia

Tanzania

CAPITAL: Dar Es Salaam
POPULATION: 28,701,077
MAJOR LANGUAGES: Swahili, English, and various languages
AREA: 364,914 sq mi; 945,090 sq km
LEADING EXPORTS: coffee, cotton, tobacco, tea, and cashew nuts
CONTINENT: Africa

Thailand

CAPITAL: Bangkok
POPULATION: 60,271,300
MAJOR LANGUAGES: Thai and English
AREA: 198,463 sq mi; 511,770 sq km
LEADING EXPORTS: machinery and manufactures
CONTINENT: Asia

Togo

CAPITAL: Lome
POPULATION: 4,410,370
MAJOR LANGUAGES: French, Ewe and Mina, Dagomba, and Kabye
AREA: 21,927 sq mi; 56,790 sq km
LEADING EXPORTS: phosphates, cotton, cocoa, and coffee
CONTINENT: Africa

Tonga

CAPITAL: Nukualofa
POPULATION: 105,600
MAJOR LANGUAGES: Tongan and English
AREA: 289 sq mi; 748 sq km
LEADING EXPORTS: squash, vanilla, fish, root crops, and coconut oil
LOCATION: Pacific Ocean

Trinidad and Tobago

CAPITAL: Port-of-Spain
POPULATION: 1,271,159
MAJOR LANGUAGES: English, Hindu, French, and Spanish
AREA: 1,981 sq mi; 5,130 sq km
LEADING EXPORTS: petroleum and petroleum products
LOCATION: Caribbean Sea

Tunisia

CAPITAL: Tunis
POPULATION: 8,879,845
MAJOR LANGUAGES: Arabic and French
AREA: 63,172 sq mi; 163,610 sq km
LEADING EXPORTS: hydrocarbons and agricultural products
CONTINENT: Africa

Turkey

CAPITAL: Ankara
POPULATION: 63,405,526
MAJOR LANGUAGES: Turkish, Kurdish, and Arabic
AREA: 301,394 sq mi; 780,580 sq km
LEADING EXPORTS: manufactured products, and foodstuffs
CONTINENT: Europe and Asia

Turkmenistan

CAPITAL: Ashgabat
POPULATION: 4,075,316
MAJOR LANGUAGES: Turkmen, Russian, Uzbek, and various languages
AREA: 188,463 sq mi; 488,100 sq km
LEADING EXPORTS: natural gas, cotton, and petroleum products
CONTINENT: Asia

Tuvalu

CAPITAL: Fongafale, on Funafuti atoll
POPULATION: 9,991
MAJOR LANGUAGES: Tuvaluan and English
AREA: 10 sq mi; 26 sq km
LEADING EXPORT: copra
LOCATION: Pacific Ocean

Uganda

CAPITAL: Kampala
POPULATION: 19,573,262
MAJOR LANGUAGES: English, Luganda, Swahili, Bantu languages, and Nilotic languages
AREA: 91,139 sq mi; 236,040 sq km
LEADING EXPORTS: coffee, cotton, and tea
CONTINENT: Africa

Ukraine

CAPITAL: Kiev
POPULATION: 51,867,828
MAJOR LANGUAGES: Ukranian, Russian, Romanian, Polish, and Hungarian
AREA: 233,098 sq mi; 603,700 sq km
LEADING EXPORTS: coal, electric power, and metals
CONTINENT: Europe

United Arab Emirates

CAPITAL: Abu Dhabi
POPULATION: 2,924,594
MAJOR LANGUAGES: Arabic, Persian, English, Hindi, and Urdu
AREA: 29,183 sq mi; 75,581 sq km
LEADING EXPORTS: crude oil, natural gas, re-exports, and dried fish
CONTINENT: Asia

United Kingdom

CAPITAL: London
POPULATION: 58,295,119
MAJOR LANGUAGES: English, Welsh, and Scottish Gaelic
AREA: 94,529 sq mi; 244,820 sq km
LEADING EXPORTS: manufactured goods, machinery, and fuels
CONTINENT: Europe

United States

CAPITAL: Washington, D.C.
POPULATION: 263,814,032
MAJOR LANGUAGES: English and Spanish
AREA: 3,618,908 sq mi; 9,372,610 sq km
LEADING EXPORTS: capital goods and automobiles
CONTINENT: North America

Uruguay

CAPITAL: Montevideo
POPULATION: 3,222,716
MAJOR LANGUAGES: Spanish and Brazilero
AREA: 68,041 sq mi; 176,220 sq km
LEADING EXPORTS: wool and textile manufactures
CONTINENT: South America

Uzbekistan

CAPITAL: Tashkent
POPULATION: 23,089,261
MAJOR LANGUAGES: Uzbek, Russian, Tajik, various languages
AREA: 172,748 sq mi; 447,400 sq km
LEADING EXPORTS: cotton, gold, natural gas, and minerals
CONTINENT: Asia

Vanuatu

CAPITAL: Port-Vila
POPULATION: 173,648
MAJOR LANGUAGES: English, French, pidgin, and Bislama
AREA: 5,699 sq mi; 14,760 sq km
LEADING EXPORTS: copra, beef, cocoa, timber, and coffee
LOCATION: Pacific Ocean

Venezuela

CAPITAL: Caracas
POPULATION: 21,004,773
MAJOR LANGUAGES: Spanish and various languages
AREA: 352,156 sq mi; 912,050 sq km
LEADING EXPORTS: petroleum, bauxite and aluminum, and steel
CONTINENT: South America

Vietnam

CAPITAL: Hanoi
POPULATION: 74,393,324
MAJOR LANGUAGES: Vietnamese, French, Chinese, English, Khmer, and various languages
AREA: 127,248 sq mi; 329,560 sq km
LEADING EXPORTS: petroleum, rice, and agricultural products
CONTINENT: Asia

Western Samoa

CAPITAL: Apia
POPULATION: 209,360
MAJOR LANGUAGES: Samoan and English
AREA: 1,104 sq mi; 2,860 sq km
LEADING EXPORTS: coconut oil and cream, taro, copra, and cocoa
LOCATION: Pacific Ocean

Yemen

CAPITAL: Sanaa
POPULATION: 14,728,474
MAJOR LANGUAGE: Arabic
AREA: 203,857 sq mi; 527,970 sq km
LEADING EXPORTS: crude oil, cotton, coffee, hides, and vegetables
CONTINENT: Asia

Zaire

CAPITAL: Kinshasa
POPULATION: 44,060,636
MAJOR LANGUAGES: French, Lingala, Swahili, Kingwana, Kikongo, and Tshiluba
AREA: 905,599 sq mi; 2,345,410 sq km
LEADING EXPORTS: copper, coffee, diamonds, cobalt, and crude oil
CONTINENT: Africa

Zambia

CAPITAL: Lusaka
POPULATION: 9,445,723
MAJOR LANGUAGES: English (official) and about 70 various languages
AREA: 290,594 sq mi; 752,610 sq km
LEADING EXPORTS: copper, zinc, cobalt, lead, and tobacco
CONTINENT: Africa

Zimbabwe

CAPITAL: Harare
POPULATION: 11,139,961
MAJOR LANGUAGES: English, Shona, and Sindebele
area: 150,809 sq mi; 390,580 sq km
LEADING EXPORTS: agricultural products and manufactures
CONTINENT: Africa

Glossary of Geographic Terms

basin
a depression in the surface of the land; some basins are filled with water

bay
a part of a sea or lake that extends into the land

butte
a small raised area of land with steep sides

▲ butte

canyon
a deep, narrow valley with steep sides; often has a stream flowing through it

cataract
a large waterfall; any strong flood or rush of water

◀ cataract

delta
a triangular-shaped plain at the mouth of a river, formed when sediment is deposited by flowing water

flood plain
a broad plain on either side of a river, formed when sediment settles on the riverbanks

glacier
a huge, slow-moving mass of snow and ice

hill
an area that rises above surrounding land and has a rounded top; lower and usually less steep than a mountain

island
an area of land completely surrounded by water

isthmus
a narrow strip of land that connects two larger areas of land

mesa
a high, flat-topped landform with cliff-like sides; larger than a butte

mountain
an area that rises steeply at least 2,000 feet (300 m) above surrounding land; usually wide at the bottom and rising to a narrow peak or ridge

▶ glacier

◀ delta

mountain pass
a gap between mountains

peninsula
an area of land almost completely surrounded by water and connected to the mainland by an isthmus

plain
a large area of flat or gently rolling land

plateau
a large, flat area that rises above the surrounding land; at least one side has a steep slope

river mouth
the point where a river enters a lake or sea

strait
a narrow stretch of water that connects two larger bodies of water

tributary
a river or stream that flows into a larger river

volcano
an opening in the Earth's surface through which molten rock, ashes, and gasses from the Earth's interior escape

▶ volcano

Gazetteer

A

Amazon Rain Forest a large tropical rain forest occupying the drainage basin of the Amazon River in northern South America and covering an area of 2,700,000 square miles, p. 19

Andes Mountains (13°S, 75°W) a mountain system extending along the western coast of South America, p. 8

Argentina (35.3°S, 67°W) a country in South America, p. 12

Atacama Desert (23.5°S, 69°W) a desert in Chile, South America; the driest place on the Earth, p. 14

B

Bolivia (17°S, 64°W) a country in South America, p. 3

Brasília (15.49°S, 47.39°W) the capital city of Brazil, p. 76

Brazil (9°S, 53°W) the largest country in South America, p. 12

C

Canal Zone a 10-mile strip of land along the Panama Canal, stretching from the Atlantic Ocean to the Pacific Ocean, p. 101

Caracas (10.3°N, 66.58°W) the capital city of Venezuela, p. 148

Caribbean (14.3°N, 75.3°W) a part of the southern Atlantic Ocean, p. 9

Central America (10.45°N, 87.15°W) the part of Latin America that includes the seven republics of Guatemala, Honduras, El Salvador, Nicaragua, Costa Rica, Panama, and Belize, p. 9

Chile (35°S, 72°W) a country in South America, p. 14

Colombia (3.3°N, 72.3°W) a country in South America, p. 25

Condado a waterfront area of San Juan, Puerto Rico, p. 123

Copán (14.5°N, 89.1°W) a ruined ancient Mayan city in western Honduras, p. 36

Cuba (22°N, 79°W) an island country, the largest of the Caribbean islands, p. 11

Cuzco (13.36°S, 71.52°W) a city in Peru; capital of the Incan empire, p. 39

G

Guatemala (15.45°N, 91.45°W) a country in Central America, p. 36

H

Haiti (19°N, 72.15°W) a country in the Caribbean Sea, on the island of Hispaniola, p. 50

Hispaniola (17.3°N, 73.15°W) an island in the Caribbean Sea, divided between Haiti in the west and the Dominican Republic in the east, p. 11

J

Jamaica (17.45°N, 78°W) an island country in the Caribbean Sea, p. 11

L

Lake Maracaibo (9.55°N, 72.13°W) a lake in northwestern Venezuela, p. 13

Lake Titicaca (16.12° S, 70.33° W) the world's largest lake, in the Andes Mountains in South America, p. 13

M

Mexico (23.45°N, 104°W) a country in North America, p. 9

Mexico City (19.28°N, 99.09°W) the capital of and largest city in Mexico; one of the largest urban areas in the world, p. 36

Miami (25.45°N, 80.11°W) a city in southeastern Florida, p. 107

P

Panama (9°N, 80°W) a country in Central America, p. 53

Panama Canal (9.2°N, 79.55°W) an important shipping canal across the Isthmus of Panama, linking the Caribbean Sea (and the Atlantic Ocean) to the Pacific Ocean, p. 96

Paraguay (24°S, 57°W) a country in South America, p. 3

Patagonia (46.45°S, 69.3°W) a desert in southern Argentina; the largest desert in the Americas, p. 17

Peru (10°S, 75°W) a country in South America, p. 13

Port-au-Prince (18.35°N, 72.2°W) the capital city and chief port of Haiti, p. 113

Puerto Rico (18.16°N, 66.5°W) an island commonwealth of the United States in the Caribbean Sea, p. 11

R

Rio de Janeiro (22.5°S, 43.2°W) a major city in Brazil, p. 129

S

Salvador (12.59°S, 38.27°W) the capital city and major port of Bahia state, in northeastern Brazil, p. 130

San Juan (18.3°N, 66.10°W) the capital and largest city in Puerto Rico, p. 123

Santiago (33.26°S, 70.4°W) the capital city of Chile, p. 142

São Paulo (23.34°S, 46.38°W) the largest city in Brazil, p. 74

South America (15°S, 60°W) the world's fourth-largest continent, bounded by the Caribbean Sea, the Atlantic Ocean, and the Pacific Ocean, and linked to North America by the Isthmus of Panama, p. 9

T

Tenochtitlán Aztec metropolis covering more than five square miles near modern Mexico City; originally located on two small islands in Lake Texcoco, it gradually grew; one of two Aztec capitals, its name means "stone rising in the water," p. 37

Tikal (17.16°N, 89.49°W) the largest Mayan city in the northern part of Guatemala, p. 36

Trinidad and Tobago (11°N, 61°W) republic of the West Indies, on the two islands called Trinidad and Tobago, p. 3

V

Valley of Mexico the area in Mexico where Lake Texcoco, Tenochtitlán, and modern Mexico City are located, p. 36

Venezuela (8°N, 65°W) a country in South America, p. 12

W

West Indies (19°N, 78°W) the islands of the Caribbean, p. 3

Glossary

A

altiplano [al tih PLAH noh] a high plateau region; a region of high plateaus in the Andes, p. 135

aqueduct a pipe or channel used to carry water from a distant source to dry areas, p. 41

B

boom a period of increased prosperity an economic activity when more of a product is produced and sold, p. 149

C

campesino [kahm pe SEE noh] a poor Latin American farmer, p. 58

canopy a dense mass of leaves forming the top layer of a forest, p.129

Carnival an annual celebration in Latin America with music, dances, and parades, p. 72

caudillo [kow DEE yoh] a military officer who rules strictly, p. 54

citizen an individual with certain rights and responsibilities under a particular government, p. 121

commonwealth a self-governing political unit with strong ties to a particular country, p. 121

communist having an economic system in which the government owns all large businesses and most of a country's land, p. 109

conquistador [kon KEES ta dor] 16th-century conquerors working for the Spanish government who were in charge of gaining land and wealth in the Americas, p. 44

constitution a statement of a country's basic laws and values, p. 123

coral a rock-like substance formed from the skeletons of tiny sea animals, p. 11

Creole a person, often of European and African descent, born in the Caribbean or other parts of the Americas, whose culture has strong French and African influence; a dialect spoken by Creoles, p. 115

criollo [kree OH yoh] a person born of Spanish parents born outside Spain; often among the best-educated and wealthiest people in the Spanish colonies, p. 50

D

dialect a version of a language that is spoken in a particular region, p. 115

dictator a ruler of a country who has complete power, p. 109

diversify to add variety; to expand, p. 27

diversity variety, p. 64

E

economy the ways that goods and services are produced and made available to people, p. 55

elevation height of land above sea level, p. 17

El Niño [el NEEN yoh] a warm ocean current that flows along the western coast of South America; this current influences global weather patterns, p. 14

emigrate move out of one country into another, p. 67

encomienda [en KOH mee en duh] a right that was granted by the Spanish government to its settlers in the Americas to demand taxes or labor from Native Americans, p. 47

ethnic group group of people who share language, religion, and cultural traditions, pp. 70, 92

exile a person who leaves or is forced to leave his or her homeland for another country because of political reasons, p. 110

H

hacienda [hah see EN duh] plantation owned by the Spanish settlers or the Catholic Church in Spanish America, p. 47

hieroglyphics [hy ur oh GLIF iks] a system of writing using signs and symbols, used by the Maya and other cultures, p. 36

hydroelectricity [hy droh ee lek TRIS ih tee] electricity produced by rushing water, p. 23

I

illiterate unable to read or write, p. 112

immigrant a person who has moved into one country from another, p. 67

import to bring products into one country from another to sell, p. 76

indigenous [in DIJ uh nus] describes people who are descendants of the people who first lived in a region, p. 64

injustice lack of fairness, p. 65

invest to spend money to earn more money, p. 55

isthmus narrow strip of land that has water on both sides and joins two larger bodies of land, p. 11

L

ladino [luh DEE noh] in Guatemala, a mestizo, p. 90

Line of Demarcation an imaginary line from the North Pole to the South Pole (at about 50° longitude) set forth in the 1494 Treaty of Tordesillas; Spain had the right to settle and trade west of the line and Portugal had the right to settle and trade east of the line, p. 44

lock a section of waterway in which ships are raised or lowered by adjusting the water level, p. 96

M

maize both the plant and the kernel of corn, p. 36

maquiladora [ma kee la DOR a] a U.S.-owned factory in Mexico that is located close to the U.S.-Mexico border, p. 66

mestizo a person of mixed Spanish and Native American ancestry, p. 46

migrant farmworker a laborer who travels from one area to another, picking crops that are in season, p. 86

montaña in northeast Peru, large stretches of tropical forests on the lower slopes of mountains, p. 136

P

pampas [PAHM puhs] flat grassland regions in the southern part of South America; a region similar to the Great Plains in the United States, p.12

pesticide [PES tuh syd] a chemical used to kill insects and diseases that can attack crops, p. 147

photosynthesis [foht oh SIN thuh sis] the process by which green plants and trees produce their own food using water, carbon dioxide, and sunlight; oxygen is released as a result of photosynthesis, p. 133

plateau [pla TOH] large raised area of mostly level land, p. 11

plaza public square at the center of a village, town, or city, p. 85

privatization [pry vuh tih ZAY shun] a policy by a government to sell its industries to individuals or private companies, p. 152

Q

quipu [KEE poo] a knotted string used by Incan government officials and traders for record keeping, p. 41

R

revolution a political movement in which people overthrow the existing government and set up another, p. 50

rural having to do with the countryside, p. 59

S

sierra a group of mountains, such as the one that runs from northwest to southeast Peru, p. 136

squatter a person who settles on someone else's land without permission, p. 84

strike work stoppage; a refusal to continue to work until certain demands of workers are met, p. 93

subsistence farming the practice of growing only as much food as a group of people needs to survive, p. 75

T

treaty an agreement in writing made between two or more countries, p. 44

Treaty of Tordesillas [tor day SEE yas] the 1494 treaty setting up the Line of Demarcation, giving Spain the right to settle and trade west of the line and Portugal the same rights east of the line, p. 44

tributary [TRIB yoo tehr ee] river or stream that flows into a main river, p. 13

tundra a cold region with little vegetation; in mountains, the area above the tree line, p. 138

U

urban having to do with cities, p. 59

Index

The *italicized* page numbers refer to illustrations. The *m, c, p,* or *t* preceding the number refers to maps *(m)*, charts *(c)*, pictures *(p)*, or tables *(t)*.

Acknowledgments

Program Development, Design, Illustration, and Production
Proof Positive/Farrowlyne Associates, Inc.

Cover Design
Olena Serbyn and Bruce Bond

Cover Photo
Jon Chomitz

Maps
GeoSystems Global Corp.

Text
30, "Where the Flame Trees Bloom," by Alma Flor Ada. Text © 1994 Alma Flor Ada. Reprinted with the permission of Atheneum Books for Young Readers, an imprint of Simon & Schuster Children's Publishing Division. 110, Excerpt from "Finding My Father," by Lydia Martin, *The Miami Herald,* June 18, 1995. Reprinted with permission of *The Miami Herald.* 158, Poem LXXII (Question Book) by Pablo Neruda. Spanish original reprinted from *Libros de las Preguntas,* by Pablo Neruda. © Pablo Neruda and Fundación Pablo Neruda, 1974. English translation from *Late and Posthumous Poems 1968–1974,* by Pablo Neruda, translated by Ben Belitt. © 1988 by Ben Belitt. Used by permission of Grove/Atlantic, Inc.

Photos
1 TL, TR, © Chip & Rosa María de la Cueva Peterson, 1B, © Mark Lewis/Tony Stone Images, 5, © Mark Thayer, Boston, 7, © Photri, 8, 11, © Chip & Rosa María de la Cueva Peterson, 12, © Bryan Parsley/Tony Stone Images, 13, © Will & Deni McIntyre/Tony Stone Images, 14, © Robert Frerck/Odyssey Productions, 15, © William J. Hebert/Tony Stone Images, 16, © Martin Rogers/Tony Stone Images, 19, © Wolfgang Kaehler/Wolfgang Kaehler Photography, 22, © Chip & Rosa María de la Cueva Peterson, 23, 25, © Robert Frerck/Odyssey Productions, 26 L, © Erik Svenson/Tony Stone Images, 26 R, © Chip & Rosa María de la Cueva Peterson, 31, © Photri, 32, 35, © Chip & Rosa María de la Cueva Peterson, 36 T, BL, BR, © Robert Frerck/Odyssey Productions, 38 L, © Chip & Rosa María de la Cueva Peterson, 38 R, © Robert Frerck/Odyssey Productions, 39, © Chip & Rosa María de la Cueva Peterson, 40, © Ed Simpson/Tony Stone Images, 41, © Robert Frerck/Odyssey Productions, 42, © Wolfgang Kaehler/Wolfgang Kaehler Photography, 43, © Daniel Aubry/Odyssey Productions, 45, © Stock Montage, 49, © David Young-Wolff/PhotoEdit, 50, © North Wind Picture Archives, 51, © Robert Frerck/Odyssey Productions, 53, © Chip & Rosa María de la Cueva Peterson, 55, © Robert Frerck/Odyssey Productions, 57, © Mark Segal/Tony Stone Images, 58, © Elizabeth Harris/Tony Stone Images, 59, © Chip & Rosa María de la Cueva Peterson, 62, © Robert Frerck/Odyssey Productions, 64, © Sheryl McNee/Tony Stone Images, 66 L, © Robert E. Daemmrich/Tony Stone Images, 66 R, © Tom Benoit/Tony Stone Images, 68, © Jason Laure'/Laure' Communications, 70, © SuperStock International, 71 L, © Corbis-Bettmann, 71 R, © Photri, 72, © Doug Armand/Tony Stone Images, 73, © Alex Irvin/Alex Irvin Photography, 74, © Ed Simpson/Tony Stone Images, 75, Untitled, by Yhaninc Puelles Enriquez, age 12, Peru. Courtesy of the International Children's Art Museum, 85, © Demetrio Carrasco/Tony Stone Images, 87, © David R. Frazier/Tony Stone Images, 88, 89, © Robert Frerck/Odyssey Productions, 91 L, © James Nelson/Tony Stone Images, 91 R, © James Strachan/Tony Stone Images, 92, © Chip & Rosa María de la Cueva Peterson, 94–95, © David Young-Wolff/PhotoEdit, 99, © Chip & Rosa María de la Cueva Peterson, 100 L, R, © Odyssey Productions, 107, © Shepard Sherbell/SABA Press Photos, 109, © Corbis-Bettmann, 110, © Alyx Kellington/D.D. Bryant Stock Photo, 111, © Miami Herald/Miami Herald Publishing Co., 112, © Mary Altier/Mary Altier Photography, 113, 115 L, R, © Corbis-Bettman, 116, Untitled, by Cange Walthe, age 12, Haiti. Courtesy of the International Children's Art Museum, 117, © Corbis-Bettman, 120, © Benno Friedman, 123, © Lawrence Migdale/Tony Stone Images, 124 L, © Robert Frerck/Odyssey Productions, 124 R, © Wolfgang Kaehler/Wolfgang Kaehler Photography, 125, © Suzanne L. Murphy/D.D. Bryant Stock Photo, 129, © Jacques Jangoux/Tony Stone Images, 131, © Sylvain Grandadam/Tony Stone Images, 132, © Ary Diesendruck/Tony Stone Images, 135, © Wolfgang Kaehler/Wolfgang Kaehler Photography, 137, © D.E. Cox/Tony Stone Images, 138 L, R, © David Mangurian/David Mangurian Photography, 139, © Robert Frerck/Odyssey Productions, 140, © David Young-Wolff/PhotoEdit, 142, © Photography by S.R.H. Spicer, Vermillion, South Dakota, U.S.A., 144 L, © Rhonda Klevansky/Tony Stone Images, 144 R, © Robert Frerck/Odyssey Productions, 145, © Chip & Rosa María de la Cueva Peterson, 146, © Charles Philip/Photri, 148, © Photri, 150, © Chip & Rosa María de la Cueva Peterson, 152, © Jacques Jangoux/Tony Stone Images, 153, © Julie Marcotte/Tony Stone Images, 156, © David Young-Wolff/PhotoEdit, 159 L, R, © Francois Gohier/Francois Gohier Pictures, 160, 163, © Mark Thayer, Boston, 164 I, © Steve Leonard/Tony Stone Images, 164 B, © Robert Frerck/Odyssey Productions, 165 T, © Wolfgang Kaehler/Wolfgang Kaehler Photography, 165 BL, © John Elk/Tony Stone Images, 165 R, © Will & Deni McIntyre/Tony Stone Images, 175, © G. Brad Lewis/Tony Stone Images, 177, © Nigel Press/Tony Stone Images, 204 T, © A & L Sinibaldi/Tony Stone Images, 204 B, © John Beatty/Tony Stone Images, 205 T, © Hans Strand/Tony Stone Images, 205 BL, © Spencer Swanger/Tom Stack & Associates, 205 BR, © Paul Chesley/Tony Stone Images.